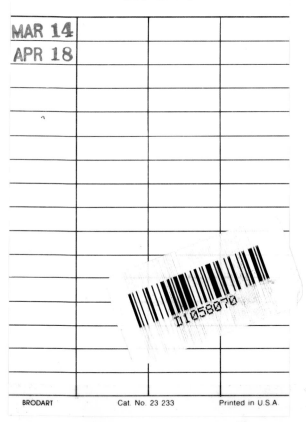

8633

Enright, Michael J.
  The Hong Kong advantage / Michael J. Enright, Edith
E. Scott, David Dodwell. --Hong Kong : Oxford
University Press, 1997.
  xvi, 369 p. : ill. ; 23 cm.

Includes bibliographical references (p. [351]-361) and
index.
853135   ISBN:0195903226

(SEE NEXT CARD)

194   98FEB03   3559/go 1-504149

THE HONG KONG ADVANTAGE

THE
HONG KONG
ADVANTAGE

Michael J. Enright
Edith E. Scott
David Dodwell

HONG KONG
OXFORD UNIVERSITY PRESS
OXFORD NEW YORK
1997

FEB 1 0 '98

Oxford University Press

Oxford New York

Athens Auckland Bangkok Bogota Bombay
Buenos Aires Calcutta Cape Town Dar es Salaam
Delhi Florence Hong Kong Istanbul Karachi
Kuala Lumpur Madras Madrid Melbourne
Mexico City Nairobi Paris Singapore
Taipei Tokyo Toronto
and associated companies in
Berlin Ibadan

Oxford is a trade mark of Oxford University Press

First published 1997

This impression (lowest digit)
3 5 7 9 10 8 6 4 2

Published in the United States
by Oxford University Press, New York

© Oxford University Press 1997

British Library Cataloguing in Publication Data
available

Library of Congress Cataloging-in-Publication Data
available

ISBN 0-19-590322-6

Printed in Hong Kong
Published by Oxford University Press (China) Ltd
18/F Warwick House, Taikoo Place, 979 King's Road,
Quarry Bay, Hong Kong

ACKNOWLEDGEMENTS

The Hong Kong Advantage project was carried out under the auspices of the Vision 2047 Foundation ('Vision 2047'), a nonprofit, nonpartisan, private organization consisting of forty volunteer members dedicated to promoting a better understanding of Hong Kong. We wish to thank the Foundation, and particularly its chairman, Sir Roger Lobo, and former Executive Director Christine Mar, for their support and encouragement. We also wish to thank our project steering committee and corporate sponsors: Mr Vincent Cheng (Hongkong and Shanghai Banking Corporation Limited), Mr Linus Cheung (Hongkong Telecommunications Limited), Dr Raymond Chien (Lam Soon Hong Kong Group), Mr Po Chung (DHL International Limited), Dr Victor Fung (Li & Fung Limited), Mr Raymond Kwok (Sun Hung Kai Properties Limited), Mr Antony Leung (Chase Manhattan Bank), Ms Barbara Meynert (Vision 2047), Mr Peter Sutch (John Swire & Sons (HK) Limited), Mr Chee-lung Tham (Harvard Business School Association of Hong Kong), Mr C. C. Tung (Orient Overseas Container Line Limited), and Mr David Wong (Dah Sing Bank Limited). Their support of this project has been only one manifestation of the commitment of these organizations and individuals to the future of Hong Kong. The steering group was a constant source of ideas, insights, and debates that helped immeasurably in our work. Dr Fung initiated the project, put together the sponsor group, and helped organize the project team. A former Harvard Business School professor himself, Dr Fung sought the counsel of his former HBS colleagues, and gave generously of his own time, original ideas, and critical insights. We wish to express our sincere gratitude for his support.

Special thanks are due to Barbara Meynert, who provided much needed logistical input throughout, and to Mary Child, Rebecca Ng, Alastair Scott, and Rebecca Lloyd of Oxford University Press (China) Ltd., who guided the book through the publication process with speed and precision. Special thanks also are due to members of our families who put up with us throughout the project. Finally, we would like to thank the hundreds of executives, managers, public officials, legislators, community activists, industry experts, and others who generously donated their time for interviews. We also are grateful to the hundreds who have attended workshops and presentations of our work in Hong Kong and elsewhere.

The views expressed in this book, of course, are those of the authors.

PREFACE

The research project on which this book is based began in the fall of 1995 when members of Hong Kong's business community approached us to help them achieve a deeper understanding of Hong Kong's economic system as well as the sources of competitive advantage and disadvantage that underlie and influence the performance of Hong Kong's industries in international markets. Their concern had been that with all the discussion of the politics of the transition from British to Chinese administration to occur on 1 July 1997, relatively little attention had been paid to the underlying competitiveness of the Hong Kong economy and its prospects through the transition. Since Hong Kong's economic future depends on the competitiveness of its industries and activities, they felt they needed such an analysis for their own planning purposes.

Michael Enright, then a professor at the Harvard Business School, had carried out similar or related work in seventeen economies on five continents, and had co-authored books on the economies of New Zealand, Switzerland, and Venezuela. Edith Scott, a consultant and attorney specializing in issues of competitiveness and international trade, had co-directed a two-year study on the competitiveness of the Venezuelan economy that resulted in a book, *Venezuela: The Challenge of Competitiveness*, co-written with Professor Enright. David Dodwell, then a director of Warren Williams International, a trade policy consultancy in Hong Kong, brought to the project an extensive knowledge of Hong Kong, mainland China, and the South-East Asian region built on many years of experience as a journalist in Asia for *The Financial Times*. He has subsequently become a director of the Jardine Fleming Group, a leading securities and fund management firm.

The approach we took looks at an economy at several levels. In our experience, one can truly understand an economy only if one addresses public policies, economic structures, the competitiveness of individual industries, and the behaviour of firms and individuals. Only by addressing all of these levels can one identify the forces that influence whether industries and firms in that economy will succeed or fail in international markets. It is an 'open system' method that approaches an economy with a set of questions, rather than a preconceived set of answers. The methodology and overall conceptual framework came out of the earlier work of Professor Enright and Ms Scott, which in turn has built upon and extended work on international competitiveness undertaken over the last ten years at the Harvard Business School.

This study of the Hong Kong economy consisted of three major components: an analysis of Hong Kong's overall economic performance; a series of studies on themes and issues that have an important impact on the performance of the Hong Kong economy in general; and a series of detailed studies of the competitiveness of specific Hong Kong industries chosen to be broadly representative of the economy as a whole. The project research carried out by the authors involved hundreds of interviews with business people, government officials, and industry experts. Field research also was conducted by Jonathan West of the Harvard Business School (technology and electronics), Winston Leong of Ermington International Limited (telecommunications), and Nicolas Bradbury of Conatus (comparative costs in the Asia–Pacific region). The results of the study were presented, concurrently with the writing of this book, in a series of seminars in Hong Kong during the summer and fall of 1996.

In the economy of every nation or territory, there are vital leverage points that contribute to or detract from the competitive strength of local firms. The 'key issues' examined by this project included the changing nature of the Hong Kong economy, Hong Kong's human resource requirements, technology development in Hong Kong industry, Hong Kong as a location for overseas firms, Hong Kong's position in the regional value-added chain, the philosophy of the Hong Kong government toward the economy, and the nature of competition in the Hong Kong economy. Comparisons of costs in Hong Kong with other centres in the region were undertaken as part of a broader study of Hong Kong's regional competitors. The goal was to understand the impact that each of these areas has had on the competitiveness of Hong Kong firms both in general and in specific industries.

The nine industries subject to study were chosen to provide a representative cross-section of the Hong Kong economy. This cross-section included two light manufacturing industries, garments and electronics; air cargo, sea cargo, and tele-communications, which all are linked to Hong Kong's role as a regional transportation and communications hub; and four service industries—export trading, fund management, civil engineering consulting services, and tourism. Together, these nine sectors and closely linked industries employ roughly 25 per cent of Hong Kong's work-force of 3.1 million and account for on the order of 40 per cent of the economy's gross domestic output. The goal was not to provide strategic plans for individual sectors nor to pick future 'winners and losers'. Rather, as nations and their firms compete in individual industries, the goal was to identify the patterns of specific advantage and disadvantage, as well as the key leverage points, in Hong Kong's economic system.

In writing any book, the difficult decisions are not what to put in, but what to leave out. Hong Kong has been the subject of many books and will be the subject of many more. In this book, we have tried to focus on issues of interest to both the local Hong Kong community and the larger international community at the expense of a detailed exposition and analysis of purely local issues or specific policy or strategy options. We hope that those interested in the latter will seek out our future works.

One question often asked of researchers is whether anyone actually does anything based on their work. In this case, we have taken matters into our own hands. Having concluded on the basis of this study that Hong Kong is perhaps the best place in the world to see the future of the global economy, Professor Enright and Ms Scott have done what Mr Dodwell did several years ago—relocate to Hong Kong, where Professor Enright is the Sun Hung Kai Properties Visiting Professor at the University of Hong Kong's School of Business Administration.

MICHAEL J. ENRIGHT
EDITH E. SCOTT
DAVID DODWELL

Hong Kong
December 1996

CONTENTS

LIST OF TABLES

CHAPTER TABLES

APPENDIX TABLES

LIST OF FIGURES

1 INTRODUCTION

Hong Kong is a place where one's preconceptions are turned upside-down on a daily basis, where skyscrapers share streets with street hawkers, and where different cultures at times interact and at times go their separate ways seeming hardly to notice each other. Hong Kong has been many things. It has been the last, shining example of a once proud, but declining empire and the last remaining symbol of another empire's defeat, shame, and re-emergence. Fundamentally, however, Hong Kong has been a utilitarian place, founded and sustained by commerce—an entrepôt, a listening post, a meeting place, and the world's quintessential business city. It has served as a window on the West for mainland China and a window into mainland China for the West.

In recent times Hong Kong has been widely discussed, but not widely understood. The transition from British rule to rule by China, to occur on 1 July 1997, has focused increasing attention on Hong Kong's future. In the West, the story has been treated almost entirely as a political story: the end of the British empire, disputes between the British and Chinese governments, the future of a 'democracy' which was recently installed and has little power, the potential human rights implications, and the politics of transition. Given Hong Kong's importance as a business and commercial centre, one would expect that Hong Kong's economic future, through '1997' and beyond, would receive particular attention. Much of the writing on the future of the Hong Kong economy, however, in the West and the East, does not say much about the territory's economic fundamentals. Instead, observers and analysts tend to focus on the political aspects of the transition and how 'the economy' (treated in aggregate) will fare under various political conditions. Relatively little detailed analysis has focused on the competitiveness of the Hong Kong economy, its sources of advantages and disadvantages, and the prospective opportunities and threats. Many have said that to miss the political story is to miss the economic story in Hong Kong, but few have recognized that, given the importance of Hong Kong's economy in shaping its relations with mainland China and the rest of the world, ignoring the economic story is to miss the political story as well.

This book attempts to relate the economic story that we see, rather than the one we often read. It is based on a year-long study by the authors and our colleagues of the competitiveness of the Hong Kong economy and its industries. The starting premise of our work is that as a small open economy, Hong Kong's economic future depends on the competitiveness of the industries that operate in the territory and the business activities performed there. Our goals were to assess the present competitiveness of the Hong Kong economy, to understand its fundamentals, to assess its future prospects, and to identify the key leverage points for the economy going forward. We tried to approach these issues without a preconceived set of answers as to what makes an economy competitive and allows it to perform well; rather, we approached them with a set of questions and flexible frameworks that let the economy and the players within it tell us what makes it succeed or fail. When one does such an analysis of the competitiveness of the Hong Kong economy and tries to project forward, one concludes that:

* Hong Kong's strong past economic performance has been due to its location, its people, and a unique economic system. This system has been characterized by balance between government and business, between local and overseas firms, between strategies of hustle

and commitment, and between management and entrepreneurship. This system has allowed Hong Kong to become not just a bridge or a gateway, but a packager and integrator of activities for the world economy.

* Over the last two decades, Hong Kong has undergone a major economic transformation. This transformation has left the economy stronger, but the rapid pace of change has created internal challenges to Hong Kong's economic competitiveness. At the same time, regional competitors are improving, trying to duplicate or surpass Hong Kong's strengths, and in some cases trying to capitalize on the uncertainties surrounding the 1997 transition. Their ability to do so has been enhanced by the fact that Hong Kong has not articulated to the local and international communities a clear and convincing vision for its economy and its future. This is due, in part, to the lack of a clear Hong Kong voice and, in part, to the intrinsic complexity of the message.

* There is substantial scope for further improvements in Hong Kong's competitiveness and economic performance. The territory is unusually well-situated to take advantage of opportunities arising from regional and global economic and business trends. Hong Kong does face uncertainties, but many of its industries are robust, even to relatively major shocks, and many of these uncertainties can be influenced or managed by Hong Kong people. This has been the case in the past and there is no reason to believe it will not be the case in the future.

* In many ways, the 1997 transition has allowed, if not forced, Hong Kong and its people to reassess the territory's strengths and weaknesses and to identify what makes Hong Kong unique. And we should be clear: Hong Kong is unique. Maintaining and developing its special attributes, its 'Hong Kong Advantage', will make its future as impressive as its past.

3

HONG KONG'S HISTORY

Hong Kong is no stranger to adversity and challenges; in fact, the last two decades of relative calm have been the exception in more than a century of upheaval on the Mainland, in the Asia–Pacific region, or both. Hong Kong's story is thus one of habitual alertness to potential adversity and of capturing virtue out of necessity. For the territory's mainly Chinese residents, Hong Kong has for most of the past century been a home by necessity rather than choice. It was a place of temporary refuge for families in flight from poverty or turmoil, many of whom planned either to return in less troubled times to ancestral villages on the Mainland, or to seek their fortunes in the United States, Canada, Australia, or South-East Asia.

The political and economic upheaval that has provided a nearly constant backdrop for Hong Kong over its 150-year colonial interlude has been the very force driving its progress toward prosperity. When Hong Kong Island was ceded to the British in perpetuity in what China has always called the 'unequal' Treaty of Nanjing of 1842, it was an inconsequential fishing community of about 15,000 people, famously dismissed by Lord Palmerston, Britain's Foreign Secretary of the day, as 'a barren rock'. The Kowloon Peninsula was ceded to Britain, also in perpetuity, in 1860. In 1898, Britain acquired, on a 99-year lease, an area of approximately 350 square miles, made up mostly of Kowloon's hinterland. The expiration of this lease is the formal reason for the handover of Hong Kong from Britain to China in 1997. The administration set up in Hong Kong mirrored that of other British colonies in which a governor appointed by London held executive power. An appointed Executive Council and an appointed Legislative Council evolved to provide a mechanism for consultation with major business and interest groups. Though the Legislative Council has become a more representative body in recent years, ultimate authority always has rested with an unelected governor.

Born in conflict, Hong Kong might still today be a second-tier entrepôt city on China's southern coast, were it not for the Sino-Japanese wars, civil war in China, the closing of China's economy for three decades from 1949, the Cold War, the disasters of the Great Leap Forward, and the excesses of the Cultural Revolution. Conflicts on the Mainland and between the Mainland and others disrupted the Chinese economy and led to the eclipse of Shanghai as Asia's most cosmopolitan city. Without such upheaval, Hong Kong might never have emerged ahead of the cities of Guangzhou, Shanghai, Ningbo, Tianjin, or Dalian.

Hong Kong's economy has survived serious challenges during this century, each time emerging stronger than before. The Japanese occupation during the Second World War reduced the territory's population from around 1.6 million in 1941 to approximately 600,000 by 1945 and largely wiped out commerce. Hong Kong's population quickly rebounded and the territory re-emerged as an entrepôt for trade between China and the world. In the year following the Red Army's defeat of the Kuomintang in 1949, more than one million refugees from the Mainland, far beyond what the city could safely accommodate, poured into Hong Kong. An international blow followed soon after, when the United Nations declared a blockade of China in 1950. The blockade cut Hong Kong off from its natural hinterland in Southern China and sapped the entrepôt trade that sustained its economy. Hong Kong's exports (approximately 90 per cent of which were Chinese goods) fell by 34 per cent from 1951 to 1952.[1] As a result, during the early 1950s, the territory's entire economic viability, strained by the influx of immigrants, was in doubt. If the barons of Shanghai's textile industries had not fled to Hong Kong at this time and received the support of British and other international bankers, Hong Kong might never have developed into a manufacturing powerhouse.[2] Because the Mainland market was closed to them, they set about building export-oriented, transnational production operations across South-East Asia, laying the roots of the dispersed manufacturing capabilities that are so distinctive in Hong Kong today.

Further turmoil in the region during the 1950s and 1960s triggered periodic surges of migration both into and out of Hong Kong. In 1962, an estimated 70,000 persons from

Guangdong Province, without opposition from the Communist border guards, streamed over the border into the New Territories in search of better living conditions, an episode that scared 'the living daylights' out of Hong Kong.[3] Riots and leftist demonstrations in Hong Kong linked with local labour unrest in 1966, and with the peak of the Cultural Revolution on the Mainland in 1967, pressed Hong Kong companies and individuals to seek safe haven elsewhere. Alongside the political adversities were economic challenges, including the introduction of a world-wide system of quotas on the export of textiles starting in 1959 and then garments in the early 1970s, which changed the rules of the game for these export-oriented sectors.

Political vulnerability has been a constant of Hong Kong's history. Since 1949, China has had the military strength to take Hong Kong.[4] Although the British stated their readiness to defend Hong Kong in the event of a Chinese invasion, a successful British defence was believed impossible. A *modus vivendi* developed early between the Chinese Communist leadership and the British colonial government based on political and economic considerations. The United Kingdom was willing to give the People's Republic of China (PRC) full diplomatic recognition in exchange for China's restraint *vis-à-vis* the territory. The PRC, in turn, valued the boost to its international standing diplomatic recognition by the United Kingdom provided and also valued a British Hong Kong as a source of foreign exchange and supplies. Hong Kong's political status since then has rested on the dynamics of reciprocal self-interest between the two powers, in Harvard sociologist Ezra Vogel's words, on 'British prudence and Chinese interests'.[5]

Migration to and from Hong Kong has received considerable attention during the countdown to 1 July 1997, but in fact Hong Kong's population has always been in flux. As early as the mid-nineteenth century, Hong Kong was one of the principal points of passage out of mainland China for masses of emigrants. The great outflows and inflows surrounding the Japanese occupation were succeeded by great waves of emigrants fleeing political and economic upheaval on the Mainland. Over the past 50 years, millions of new emigrants from the Chinese Mainland have at one time or another been counted among Hong Kong's population. Most have travelled on to make their homes in more stable parts of the world. Hong Kong's historical role as a city of departure from China has laid the foundation for a reverse flow of business investments back to and through Hong Kong in recent decades. This has helped Hong Kong become the *de facto* capital of the 50 million or more overseas Chinese who today play such an important role in the economic modernization of the Asian region and in the reconstruction of China's market economy.

Given its past, one can argue that Hong Kong has never enjoyed greater stability than since the Mainland Chinese economy began opening to the rest of the world in 1979. It is an irony, and perhaps a lucky irony for Hong Kong, that the reversion of Hong Kong to Chinese control, which has for the past decade been the focus of so much local and international anxiety, should be occurring at a time when China and the wider Asia–Pacific region are moving rapidly towards levels of prosperity that few would have imagined possible just two decades ago. Meanwhile, as 1997 has approached, Hong Kong's traditional Western export markets have grown and businesses have captured opportunities to lower costs and seek new export and investment opportunities on the Mainland. At the same time, rising living standards across Asia have provided Hong Kong Chinese businessmen with new opportunities for trade and investment in collaboration with the overseas Chinese dispersed across the region.

The negotiations between the British and Mainland Chinese governments concerning the future of Hong Kong began in earnest in 1982 and in 1984 produced 'The Joint Declaration of the Governments of the United Kingdom and Northern Ireland and the People's Republic of China on the Question of Hong Kong', an international treaty that called for the transfer of administration from the British to the Chinese on 1 July 1997. The Joint Declaration stated that Hong Kong would become a Special Administrative Region (SAR) of the People's Republic of China and that Hong Kong's capitalist system and 'way of life' would be preserved for 50 years. The 'one country–two systems' framework under which Hong Kong is to be governed was further enshrined in the 'Basic Law', the constitution for the Special Administrative Region after 1997. So began the countdown to a transition that has become the topic of countless stories and books, and upon which the hopes and fears of Hong Kong's people now rest.

HONG KONG'S ECONOMY

Any look at Hong Kong's economic future must, by necessity, start with a look at its past performance. Here Hong Kong's economy has shone. It achieved real annual growth in gross domestic product (GDP) of 6 per cent from 1965 to 1975; 8.5 per cent from 1975 to 1985; and 6.5 per cent from 1985 to 1995. Between 1975 and 1995, real GDP quadrupled to more than US$140 billion and real per capita GDP tripled to US$23,200.[6] According to the World Bank, by 1994 Hong Kong's per capita GDP was the fourth highest in the world on a purchasing-power-parity basis, behind only Luxembourg, the United States, and Switzerland (see Table 1.1). This sustained economic

Table 1.1   GDP per capita (Purchasing-power-parity Basis), Selected Economies

Country/Region	US Dollars	
	1995	1994
Luxembourg[a]	29,000	28,189
United States	26,825	26,646
Switzerland	25,070	23,484
Hong Kong	23,892	23,020
Singapore	23,565	21,518
Canada	22,220	22,316
Japan	22,200	21,616

[a] Authors' estimates for 1995.
Source: The World Bank.

Table 1.2   Hong Kong's Leading Trade Partners

	Percentage of total trade	
Country/Region	1995	1994
China	34.8	35.3
United States	14.4	14.9
Japan	10.7	10.8
Taiwan	5.8	5.6
Singapore	4.1	3.9
South Korea	3.3	3.1
Germany	3.2	3.4
United Kingdom	2.6	2.6
France	1.7	1.3
Italy	1.5	1.5

Source: Hong Kong Census and Statistics Department.

growth has been achieved with low unemployment, which peaked at around 3.5 per cent in late 1995, only to fall to less than 3 per cent in 1996. According to the Institute for Management Development's (IMD) *World Competitiveness Yearbook 1996*, Hong Kong has the world's third most competitive economy. The US-based Heritage Foundation has ranked the Hong Kong economy as the freest in the world.

Despite a population of only 6.3 million, Hong Kong is the world's eighth largest trading economy and the tenth leading exporter of commercial services. In 1995, Hong Kong's total trade in goods (US$172 billion in exports plus US$191 billion in imports) equalled US$363 billion, or 256 per cent of the territory's GDP. Including trade in services, the figure was 297 per cent, making Hong Kong the most trade dependent economy in the world.[7] (See Table 1.2 for Hong Kong's leading trade partners.) Re-exports, some 90 per cent of which were sourced from or destined for mainland China, accounted for 83 per cent of Hong Kong's total exports in 1995, while domestic exports (exports of goods produced in Hong Kong itself) accounted for 17 per cent. The leading sources of re-exports were China, Japan, and Taiwan, while the leading destinations for re-exports were China, the United States, and Japan. A significant portion of the re-exports sourced from China came from the export-processing facilities of Hong Kong firms, which also were significant destinations for China-bound, re-exported components and materials. The leading destinations for Hong Kong's domestic exports were China, the United States, and Singapore.[8] In addition to its formal trade, estimates of Hong Kong's offshore trade, or trade undertaken by Hong Kong companies but never touching Hong Kong itself, were on the order of US$84 billion in 1994 according to the Hong Kong Trade Development Council (TDC).[9]

Hong Kong's trade with Asia grew nearly sevenfold in value from 1985 to 1995, that with the United States 4.3 times, and that with the European Union six times.[10] The most important feature of Hong Kong's trade is that it has been a two-way flow and the value that stays in Hong Kong (or the value added by Hong Kong and its firms) has been, and continues to be, substantial. It is this value added—be it through logistical services, through export-processing operations, through trade finance and information, or through managing dispersed manufacturing—that has helped Hong Kong become affluent.

More surprising than the trade figures is the fact that Hong Kong has been the fourth leading source of foreign direct

Table 1.3 Outbound Foreign Direct Investment

	Billions of US Dollars		
Country/Region	1995	1994	1993
United States	95.5 (1)[a]	45.6 (1)	69.0 (1)
United Kingdom	37.8 (2)	25.3 (2)	25.7 (2)
Germany	35.3 (3)	14.7 (6)	13.2 (6)
Hong Kong	25.0 (4)	21.4 (4)	17.7 (4)
Japan	21.3 (5)	18.5 (5)	15.5 (5)
France	17.6 (6)	22.8 (3)	20.4 (3)

[a] Rank in brackets.
Source: United Nations Conference on Trade and Development (UNCTAD), *World Investment Report 1996: Investment, Trade and Industrial Policy Arrangements*, New York and Geneva: United Nations, 1996, p. 233.

investment in the world in the years 1993 to 1995 according to the UNCTAD (United Nations Conference on Trade and Development)[11] and is the leading foreign investor in China, ASEAN (Association of South-East Asian Nations), and APEC (Asia Pacific Economic Cooperation forum)[12] (see Table 1.3). Hong Kong firms, drawing upon Mainland manufacturing operations, have become the world's leading exporters of garments, imitation jewellery, travel goods, handbags, umbrellas, artificial flowers, toys, and clocks.[13] They also have leading positions in the region or the world in electronics, watches, cargo and transport, trading, financial services, media, telecommunications, and tourism, among others.

HONG KONG'S TRANSNATIONAL FIRMS

Behind the trade and investment statistics are a large number of extremely dynamic Hong Kong firms. One of the most striking features of these firms is the transnational character of even the smallest Hong Kong enterprises. For example, of the 33,000 firms that make up Hong Kong's softgoods industry (spanning clothing, textiles, and footwear), with an average work-force in Hong Kong of just eight people, at least 35 per cent employ the majority of their staff outside Hong Kong. Almost 80 per cent employ more than 20 per cent of their operatives outside Hong Kong. Today, 55 per cent of Hong Kong's clothing manufacturers have manufacturing capabilities in China. An estimated 17 per cent—almost one in five—also manufacture in other Asian countries.[14] This means that even very small Hong Kong companies are familiar with managing the logistics of operations across national borders, managing transactions in multiple currencies, conforming with the requirements of different legal systems, industrial standards, or tax regimes, and juggling the needs and sensitivities of staff from diverse cultural backgrounds—in short, operating as multinationals operate.

Unique circumstances in Hong Kong have led local companies, large and small, to develop these unusually strong transnational skills. Since the late 1970s, many Hong Kong companies have moved manufacturing operations into South China, in particular the Pearl River Delta, setting up subcontracting, joint-venture, or subsidiary arrangements to leverage low-cost land and labour. The well-chronicled migration onto the Mainland of the assembly operations of tens of thousands of Hong Kong firms, however, is only part of the story. Geographic diversification in the garment industry, for example, was driven by at least three further factors. The annual debate in the United States over renewal of China's most-favoured-nation (MFN) trading status forced US buyers to insist that their Hong Kong suppliers maintain alternative sources of supply to those in China. Second, import quotas for garments under the Multifibre Agreement (MFA) forced Hong Kong garment firms to seek sources in nations that had unexploited quotas, exemptions from quota restraints, or other preferential access to the markets of Europe and the United States. Third, as labour costs have begun to rise in mainland China and new sources of supply have come on stream, it has been cost-effective to diversify sources of production.

This idiosyncratic combination of factors has created in Hong Kong a uniquely transnational manufacturing community in light manufactured goods industries, which has been forced by necessity to hone its integrating and packaging skills across the entire region. In the garment sector, for example, the combination of global quota rules and opportunities to diversify into China has given Hong Kong manufacturers a unique opportunity to manage distributed production on a large scale. Similar practices have evolved in toys, plastic goods, and other industries. Hong Kong electronics firms have shown a similar pattern. Leading firms like Gold Peak, Johnson Electric, and VTech developed multinational operations very early in their histories. They manage dispersed networks of design, testing, production, and service personnel. Geographic diversification is also a potent source of competitive advantage for Hong Kong's export trading firms, many of which have headquarters in Hong Kong and flexible sourcing patterns focused primarily on the Asia–Pacific region.

The geographic diversification of sources of supply allows the export trading firms to exploit the comparative advantages of other locations and, in this way, permits them to do far more business than otherwise would be the case.

HONG KONG'S ECONOMIC TRANSFORMATION

Hong Kong's economy has undergone many changes throughout its history. The opening of the South China economy and the creation of special economic zones (SEZs) in 1979 triggered a new economic transformation in Hong Kong that is still in process. Although many have characterized the transformation as that from a manufacturing economy to a service economy, such characterizations are wide of the mark. Instead, the Hong Kong economy has been transformed from a 'manual economy' to a 'knowledge economy' and from an 'enclave economy' to a 'metropolitan economy'. This process has changed the territory and has added to its prosperity.

The service sector has risen dramatically in importance, accounting for 83.4 per cent of GDP in 1995. (See Table 1.4.) In that year, the leading service sectors were: wholesale, retail, import and export, restaurants, and hotels; financing, insurance, real estate, and business services; and community,

Table 1.4 Distribution of Gross Domestic Product, Hong Kong

| | Per cent | | | |
Year	Agriculture[a]	Industry	Manufacturing[b]	Services[c]
1980	0.8	31.7	23.7	67.5
1985	0.5	29.9	22.1	69.6
1990	0.3	25.3	17.6	74.5
1994	0.2	16.4	9.2	83.4

[a] 'Agriculture' includes fishing.
[b] 'Manufacturing' is a subset of 'Industry'.
[c] 'Services' includes unallocated items.
Source: Hong Kong Census and Statistics Department.

Table 1.5 Hong Kong's Leading Service Industries

By Output, 1994	
Industry	**% of 1994 GDP**
Wholesale, retail, import and export, restaurants, and hotels	27.0
Financing, insurance, real estate, and business services	26.1
Community, social, and personal services	15.6

By Employment, 1995	
Industry	**Employment**
Import/export trade	535,793
Retailing	196,072
Restaurants	182,057
Finance[a]	155,031
Business services	148,225

[a] Including financial institutions, brokers, and insurance.
Source: Hong Kong Government Information Services, *Hong Kong 1996*, Hong Kong, 1996, pp. 432, 453.

social, and personal services. In terms of employment, the leading service industries were import/export trade, retailing, restaurants, and the financial sector—including financial institutions, brokers, insurance, and business services. (See Table 1.5.)

Since 1983, Hong Kong's service economy has grown at a rate of 17 per cent per year in real terms, far faster than that of any other economy in the world. (See Table 1.6.) From 1984 to 1994, the output of Hong Kong's financing, insurance, real estate, and business services sector grew at a rate of 21 per cent annually. The output of the wholesale, retail, import/export, restaurants, and hotels sector and the transport, storage, and communications sector grew at identical 17 per cent per annum rates. Value added in these sectors increased at a rate of 17 per cent.[15] In 1995, Hong Kong's service sector was ranked by the World Economic Forum as the second most highly developed

Table 1.6 Compound Annual Growth in Services, 1983–1993, Selected Economies

Country/Region	Growth Rate %
Hong Kong	17.0
China	11.1
South Korea	8.3
Taiwan	7.9
Thailand	7.7
Singapore	7.4
Indonesia	6.9
India	6.4
Israel	6.2
Malaysia	5.5

Source: IMD International, *World Competitiveness Yearbook 1996*, Lausanne, 1996, p. 368.

service sector in the world, behind only the United States.[16] Exports of commercial services have grown an average of 23 per cent per year since 1989.[17] According to the World Trade Organization, Hong Kong was the world's tenth leading exporter of commercial services, with exports of US$28.9 billion in 1993. In that year Hong Kong's surplus in trade in services was US$12.7 billion, the third highest in the world behind the United States and France.

Hong Kong has solidified its position as a financial centre. The territory is home to 500 banks (including offices of 85 of the world's top 100 banks), the world's eighth largest and Asia's second largest stock market (with a total capitalization of US$383 billion as of 30 September 1996), the world's fifth largest foreign exchange market, and the third largest gold market. Hong Kong is a centre for fund management, equity analysis, and project finance for the entire Asian region. The city-state has emerged as the leading hub for foreign investment into and out of China and throughout the region—as a source of direct investment, as a conduit for direct investment, and through its stock market, where 22 Mainland state-owned companies and 15 or so Chinese concept companies (with a

15

market capitalization of more than US$10 billion) and other non-Hong Kong-based companies have listed.

At the heart of Hong Kong's growth as a service centre is a dramatic rise in the importance of Asia, and China in particular, as a source and destination for world trade. As a result, Hong Kong's trade in goods has expanded 44-fold and trade in services 26 times in the past two decades. This trade has created one of the world's largest communities of sourcing companies, traders, freight forwarders, and trade financiers. Burgeoning trade has made Hong Kong the world's busiest container port in terms of volume and the world's second leading handler of international air cargo (as measured by weight). It has made Hong Kong Asia's trade fair capital and host to some of the world's largest exhibitions, conferences, and trade fairs. More than 100,000 Hong Kong import and export trading companies[18] help make Hong Kong the trading hub of East Asia. Hong Kong's export traders match sources of supply of light manufactures—in Hong Kong, on the Mainland, and in South-East Asia—with demand in North America, Europe, and elsewhere. Hong Kong's import traders bring machinery and technical equipment from the rest of the world into China and the region.

Hong Kong is a leading business service centre. Many of the world's leading consulting, legal, and accounting firms use Hong Kong as a base for work throughout the region. In 1995, more than 20,000 business service firms employed nearly 150,000 persons in Hong Kong.[19] Hong Kong has nearly 8,500 professional accountants. The territory's consultants, lawyers, and accountants have deep knowledge of Mainland business and of Chinese joint venture law, including the ins and outs of drawing up trading contracts with the Mainland, and the complexities of assessing Mainland companies.

An unfettered press, freedom of information flows, and an outstanding communications infrastructure have fostered one of Asia's most dynamic media centres. According to the World Competitiveness Report, newspaper readership per capita in Hong Kong is higher than in any of the world's major nations.[20] Hong Kong is the home of 730 newspapers and magazines[21] (though this figure is inflated somewhat by a liberal definition of the term 'newspaper' which includes a wide variety of newsprint publications). In addition to being the home of local publications and regional periodicals, such as *Asiaweek* and *The Far Eastern Economic Review*, Hong Kong is an Asian printing centre for such leading publications as *The Asian Wall Street Journal, The Financial Times, The International Herald Tribune,* and *The Economist.* And these are examples only of English language publications, which make up a minority of the total. Hong Kong is home to one of the world's most successful film industries and is second only to the United States in income from film exports. Hong Kong serves as a regional base for many of the world's leading television and media groups, such as CNN, CNBC, Star TV, Turner International, Reuters TV, and ESPN. Hong Kong's all-digital telecommunications system is expected to provide the world's first large-scale, commercial multimedia services. Free flows of information provide locally based product designers, advertisers, and marketing specialists with unique knowledge of the fast-developing tastes of emerging Asian consumer markets, as well as the ability to stay on top of trends in more mature markets.

Hong Kong's own infrastructure spending (including a new airport and associated projects costing US$19 billion, another US$2.4 billion in reclamation projects,[22] and a commercial development boom that has created one of the world's most rapidly changing skylines) has nurtured one of Asia's largest communities of professional service providers—from construction and marine engineers, architects and designers, to surveyors and estate agents. Many of these professionals use Hong Kong as their base from which to pursue opportunities in mainland China and in Asia's other fast growing economies, particularly Thailand, Vietnam, Malaysia, and Indonesia.

Hong Kong is Asia's leading tourist destination, with 10.2 million arrivals in 1995. Tourism added US$9.6 billion, or 6.7 per cent of GDP, to the Hong Kong economy in 1995 and was the territory's second largest earner of foreign exchange.[23] Roughly 30 per cent of foreign arrivals were for business purposes, underlining Hong Kong's importance as a business centre. Here again, Hong Kong acts not only as a destination in its own right, but as a gateway into and out of mainland China. The tourist trade is underpinned by a dense network of commercial air service in Asia as well as numerous hotels, restaurants, cultural amenities, events, and attractions.

The strong performance of Hong Kong's service sector has been accompanied by an apparent decline in its manufacturing sector. Indeed, Hong Kong's manufacturing sector, as measured by the Hong Kong Census and Statistics Department fell from 24 per cent of GDP in 1980 to around 18 per cent in 1990, and to 9 per cent in 1994.[24] The leading manufacturing sectors have been garments, textiles, printing and publishing, machinery and equipment, and electronics. (See Table 1.7.) Manufacturing's share of employment, which fell from 42 per

Table 1.7　Hong Kong's Leading Manufacturing Industries

By Domestic Exports,[a] 1995

Industry	% of Manufacturing Domestic Exports
Clothing	31.9
Electronics	27.7
Textiles	6.1
Watches and Clocks	5.9
Chemicals	4.0
Jewellery	2.5

By Employment

Industry	1995	1993
Garments	82,432	134,841
Textiles	57,499	75,742
Printing and publishing	44,790	40,918
Other machinery and equipment	29,383	35,813

[a] Since over 80 per cent of goods manufactured in Hong Kong are exported, domestic exports (exports of goods manufactured in Hong Kong) is a good proxy for manufacturing output.
Source:　Hong Kong Government Information Services, *Hong Kong 1996*, pp. 95, 453.

cent in 1980 to 15.3 per cent in 1995 saw an even more precipitous decline.[25] The number of people employed in manufacturing in Hong Kong fell from over 900,000 in 1984 to just over 386,000 in 1995.[26]

The decline of Hong Kong manufacturing, however, is more apparent than real. Hong Kong manufacturing firms are arguably stronger today than they have ever been. Hong Kong remains a centre of high value-added manufacturing. Although manufacturing employment in Hong Kong has fallen, real value added per manufacturing employee increased by a factor of 3.3 from 1982 to 1993.[27] As a result, Hong Kong's manufacturing output rose from US$4.1 billion in 1980 to US$12.7 billion in 1992 before falling to US$11.4 billion in 1995. What these figures do not capture is that Hong Kong firms have developed dispersed production networks on a massive scale. By 1996, Hong Kong-based manufacturing firms employed an estimated 5 million workers in the Pearl River Delta and hundreds of thousands elsewhere. By tapping into the labour potential of the Mainland and South-East Asia, Hong Kong-based firms have overcome a variety of critical resource constraints and have grown far beyond the size that would have been possible in Hong Kong alone. The output of Hong Kong's manufacturing firms is several times greater than the Hong Kong-based statistics would indicate. As a result, Hong Kong firms have kept or extended their positions as world leaders in industries such as garments, certain electronic products, toys, and watches.

Surveys of representative samples of Hong Kong manufacturing and trading firms by the Hong Kong Trade Development Council tell an interesting story.[28] The surveys showed that Hong Kong and mainland China each were manufacturing locations for nearly 36 per cent of the firms' exports in 1988 with other nations, mostly in South-East Asia, accounting for 28 per cent. By 1995, Hong Kong was the source of only 11 per cent of the firms' exports, with the Mainland accounting for 59 per cent, and other nations 30 per cent (see Figure 1.1). Hong Kong was the source of 63 per cent of the jewellery exports of the surveyed companies and 15 per cent of the computers and telecommunication equipment, but only 2

Figure 1.1 Manufacturing Location of Exports of Hong Kong Firms

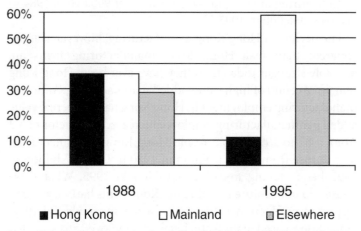

Source: Hong Kong Trade Development Council, *Hong Kong's Trade and Trade Supporting Services*, April 1996, p. 5.

per cent of the toys and less than 1 per cent of the audio-visual equipment.

But the story does not end there. While the firms may have done their manufacturing or had their manufacturing done outside Hong Kong, most of the other activities associated with manufacturing—such as headquarters operations, trade finance, transport, research and development, design, and marketing—were not only performed in Hong Kong, they were expected to stay there (see Figure 1.2). Hong Kong firms have retained the high value-added, knowledge-intensive activities associated with manufacturing in Hong Kong while decentralizing the lower value-added, labour-intensive activities to the Mainland and elsewhere. In the process, the Hong Kong firms and the host nations have benefited.

Furthermore, Hong Kong's 'loss' of manufacturing jobs has been exaggerated by the procedures used to compile the statistical data. According to standard statistical practice, if the actual production process (usually physical assembly) itself is moved out of a facility, that facility's associated workers, who

Figure 1.2 Future Location of Activities, Hong Kong
Manufacturing and Trading Firms

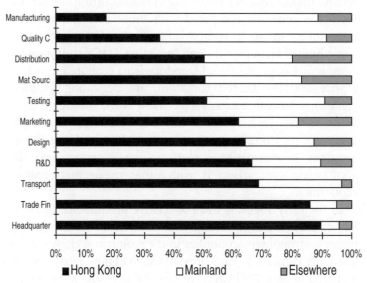

Source: Hong Kong Trade Development Council, *Hong Kong's Trade and Trade Supporting Services*,
p. 30.

were originally classified as manufacturing workers, are reclassified as service workers. In just 1992 and 1993, 6,200 Hong Kong 'manufacturers' were reclassified as service operations. At least 49,000 workers in these firms were reclassified as service workers.[29] In other words, the same workers doing the same jobs for the same companies were no longer counted as manufacturing workers. The number of workers reclassified in just 1992 and 1993 was more than 10 per cent of the total 'lost' manufacturing jobs in the 1979 to 1995 period. The reclassified establishments had sales of US$10.6 billion in 1992, or nearly as much as the total registered for all of Hong Kong's 'manufacturing industry' in 1992. Although data on reclassified workers and establishments are not available for prior years, Hong Kong statistical experts believe that the number of reclassified workers would have been 'significant' as early as 1985.[30]

21

Thus, the rise of Hong Kong's service sector has been closely linked with the strengthening of its manufacturing sector. The relative importance of Hong Kong's manufacturing and service sectors is generally compared with those of major national economies. In such comparisons Hong Kong is indeed something of an outlier, though some OECD (Organization for Economic Cooperation and Development) economies, such as France and the United Kingdom, are beginning to show somewhat similar patterns (see Table 1.8). Although these comparisons look persuasive, they are not the right comparisons. Hong Kong is not a nation. Instead, Hong Kong's economy is essentially a metropolitan economy and the appropriate comparison is with other major metropolitan economies.

In the early 1980s, it was the relative prominence of Hong Kong's manufacturing sector that made it an outlier among major metropolitan economies in the region and elsewhere, as shown by Figure 1.3. Political events, such as the United Nations embargo of mainland China imposed during the Korean War, had taken away Hong Kong's natural role as an entrepôt and cut it off from its natural economic hinterland. An influx of refugees meant that more people had to find employment. Unable to provide services to its surrounding region, as most major cities do, Hong Kong was forced to become a manufacturing enclave for labour-intensive industries, importing raw materials and machinery and exporting finished goods. Fortunately, refugees, principally from Shanghai (including leaders of the textile industry in Shanghai), helped develop a thriving textile and garment industry. Hong Kong became a leading exporter of garments and a major exporter of simple plastic products and other light manufactures.

This situation persisted until the late 1970s when the Mainland began to open its economy and set up special economic zones in the neighbouring Pearl River Delta. Deng Xiaoping's 'open door' policy, begun in 1979, heralded a new economic beginning for South China and for Hong Kong. Hong Kong began to re-establish close economic links with its surrounding region. Labour-intensive manufacturing migrated

Table 1.8 Distribution of Gross Domestic Product, Selected Countries

Per cent

Country/Region	Agriculture 1980	Agriculture 1994	Industry 1980	Industry 1994	Manufacturing[a] 1980	Manufacturing[a] 1994	Services[b] 1980	Services[b] 1994
Hong Kong[c]	1	0	32	16	24	9	68	83
United States	3	2	34	25	22	NA	64	73[d]
France	4	2	34	28	24	20	62	70
United Kingdom	2	2	43	32	27	22	55	66
Japan	4	2	42	40	29	27	54	58
Singapore	1	0	38	36	29	27	61	64
China	30	21	49	47	41	37	21	32
South Korea	15	7	40	43	29	29	45	50
Ireland	NA	8	NA	9	NA	3	NA	83
Netherlands	NA	3	NA	27	NA	18	NA	70
Australia	5	3	36	30	19	15	58	67

[a] 'Manufacturing' is a subset of 'Industry'.
[b] 'Services' includes unallocated items.
[c] Source: Hong Kong Department of Census and Statistics.
[d] Source: IMD International and World Economic Forum, *World Competitiveness Report 1995*, Lausanne, 1995, p. 368.

Source: World Bank, *From Plan to Market: World Development Report 1996*, New York: Oxford University Press, 1996, pp. 210–211.

Figure 1.3 Manufacturing Per Cent of Employment, Selected Cities, 1980–1981

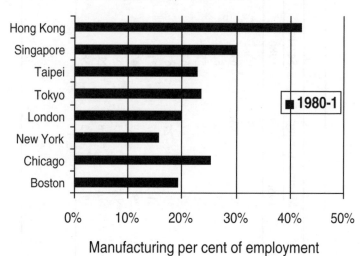

Source: National and local sources.

to the Mainland and elsewhere, while Hong Kong increased its position as a transport, logistics, financial, management, and business service centre for the Mainland and for the Asian region. By the early 1990s, the relative importance of Hong Kong's manufacturing sector was roughly comparable to that in other major metropolitan economies (which had seen their manufacturing sectors decline in relative importance as well, but not to the same extent, see Figure 1.4). Manufacturing represented a lower percentage of employment in Hong Kong than in Singapore, Taipei, Tokyo, and Los Angeles, but was comparable to Chicago and represented a greater portion of total employment than in London, Boston, and New York. It is not surprising that Singapore, which lacks a natural hinterland linked by historical and ethnic ties and has made it a national priority to maintain manufacturing employment at around 20 per cent of total employment (and manufacturing at 25 per cent of GDP), would have a higher percentage of employment in

Figure 1.4 Manufacturing Per Cent of Employment, Selected Cities, 1992–1995

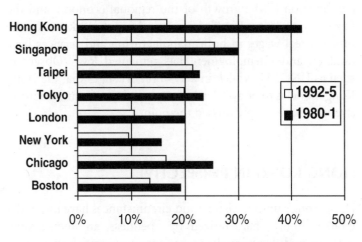

Manufacturing per cent of employment

Source: National and local sources.

manufacturing than Hong Kong. Nor is it surprising that Taipei, on an island isolated from the Mainland, also would have a higher portion of its work-force engaged in manufacturing than Hong Kong. With respect to other metropolitan areas that are closely integrated with their hinterlands, Hong Kong's mix of service and manufacturing is not surprising. This is particularly true when one realizes that the wage differential between the other leading cities and their hinterlands is often on the order of 20 per cent to 30 per cent, whereas Hong Kong's wages can be eight to ten times those of its hinterland.

When viewed in detail, it becomes clear that the economic transformation in Hong Kong, as stated above, has not been so much from a manufacturing economy to a service economy, as from a 'manual economy' to a 'knowledge economy' and from an 'enclave economy' to a 'metropolitan economy'. The change in the structure of the Hong Kong economy has been similar to that of other major metropolitan economies. The difference is that Hong Kong's transition has been much faster. Perhaps

25

the most surprising aspect of the transformation is that it has been accompanied by relatively little dislocation (due to a combination of the growth of the regional economy and the flexibility of Hong Kong's labour and input markets). In the process, real wages in both manufacturing and services have doubled and unemployment has remained low.[31] Observers such as UNCTAD, which in a 1996 report states that the Hong Kong model is to be avoided because of a loss of manufacturing strength, have simply missed the point.[32]

HONG KONG IN PERSPECTIVE

Hong Kong's unique history and circumstances have fostered a vital economy characterized by openness, an international outlook, and flexibility. Its recent economic transformation— the rise of the service economy combined with a greatly expanded manufacturing sector, strengthened by the de-centralization of lower value-added activities—has made the economy stronger. As we will see, it also has created challenges to Hong Kong's future competitiveness. Hong Kong's economic performance over the last few decades has been superb. In order to understand the reasons for such superb performance, we must delve into: the specific features of Hong Kong's economic system; the combinations of actors and forces in the economy; the roles that Hong Kong and its firms play in international business; and the other elements that contribute to Hong Kong's economic success. It is to these features we turn next.

NOTES

1 Henry Wai-chung Yeung, 'The Historical Geography of Hong Kong Investments in the Asean Region', *Singapore Journal of Tropical Geography*, 17, 1 (1996): 66–82.
2 Ezra F. Vogel, *One Step Ahead in China: Guangdong under Reform*, Cambridge, Mass.: Harvard University Press, 1989, pp. 47–8.

3   See Richard Hughes, *Borrowed Place Borrowed Time: Hong Kong and its Many Faces*, rev. 2nd edn., London: André Deutsch, 1976, p. 163; see also Jan Morris, *Hong Kong: Epilogue to an Empire*, London: Penguin Books, 1988, p. 274.

4   See Hughes, *Borrowed Place Borrowed Time*, pp. 14, 172–3.

5   Vogel, *One Step Ahead*, p. 46.

6   Hong Kong Government Information Services, *Hong Kong 1996*, Bob Howlett (ed.), 1996, p. 48; Hong Kong Government Information Services, *Hong Kong Background Facts*, August 1996, p. 3.

7   Hong Kong Government Information Services, *Hong Kong 1996*, p. 48.

8   All figures from Hong Kong Government Information Services, *Hong Kong 1996*, pp. 92–3.

9   Hong Kong Trade Development Council, *Hong Kong's Trade and Trade Supporting Services*, April 1996, p. 10.

10 Hong Kong Government Information Services, *Hong Kong Background Facts*, p. 4.

11 United Nations Conference on Trade and Development (UNCTAD), *World Investment Report 1996: Investment, Trade and International Policy Arrangements*, New York and Geneva: United Nations, 1996, Annex Table 2, 'FDI Outflows, by Home Region and Economy, 1984–1995', p. 233.

12 Japan External Trade Organization (JETRO), *JETRO White Paper on Foreign Direct Investment 1996*, Tokyo, 1996, Table 1.6, 'Matrix of Investment in APEC Region (1994)', p. 12.

13 Hong Kong Trade Development Council, 'Economic & Trade Information on Hong Kong', http://www.tdc.org.hk/main/economic.html#4, last updated 2 September 1996.

14 Kurt Salmon Associates for Hong Kong Government Industry Department, *1995 Techno-economic and Market Research Study on Hong Kong's Textiles and Clothing Industries*, Hong Kong, July 1996, pp. 14–15.

15 Hong Kong Government Information Services, *Hong Kong Report 1996*, p. 52.

16 IMD International and World Economic Forum, *World Competitiveness Report 1995*, Lausanne, 1995, p. 398. The year 1995 is the most recent year in which the IMD applied this criterion.

17 Ibid., p. 435.

18 The figure was 106,680 according to Hong Kong Government Information Services, *Hong Kong 1996*, p. 452.

19 The precise numbers were 20,482 firms and 148,225 employees. Hong Kong Government Information Services, *Hong Kong 1996*, pp. 452–3.

20 IMD International, *World Competitiveness Yearbook 1996*, Lausanne, 1996, p. 566.

21 Hong Kong Government Information Services, *Hong Kong 1996*, p. 312.

22 Hong Kong Government Information Services, *Hong Kong Background Facts*, pp. 11–13.

23 Ibid., pp. 7–8.

24   Hong Kong Government Information Services, *Hong Kong 1996*, p. 49.
25   Ibid., pp. 50, 93.
26   Hong Kong Government Information Services, *Hong Kong 1996*, p. 455; Hong Kong Government Information Services, Renu Daryanani (ed.), *Hong Kong 1995*, 1995, p. 105.
27   Hong Kong Census and Statistics Department, 'Labour Productivity in the Manufacturing Sector at Hong Kong, 1982–1993', *Hong Kong Monthly Digest of Statistics* (April 1996): FA4.
28   Hong Kong Trade Development Council, *Hong Kong's Trade and Trade Supporting Services*, p. 5.
29   Hong Kong Census and Statistics Department, 'Trading Firms with Manufacturing Related Functions', *Hong Kong Monthly Digest of Statistics* (August 1996): FA1.
30   Interviews with the Hong Kong Census and Statistics Department.
31   Hong Kong Trade Development Council, 'Economic & Trade Information on Hong Kong', http://www.tdc.org.hk/main/economic.html#4.
32   United Nations Conference on Trade and Development (UNCTAD), *1996 UNCTAD Trade and Development Report*, New York and Geneva: United Nations, 1996, pp. 121–34.

2 HONG KONG'S UNIQUE COMBINATIONS

Some of the most interesting features of the Hong Kong economy are its 'unique combinations'. The Hong Kong economy is unique in its balance between government and business, between local and overseas firms, between entrepreneurship and management, and between strategies of 'commitment' and 'hustle'. The components of each combination have mutual respect, equality of stature, and dynamic interaction. The presence of these almost counter-intuitive combinations indicates that Hong Kong is able to provide a supportive environment for many types of firms and firm strategies. The combinations, in turn, have contributed to the development of a vibrant, robust economic system.

GOVERNMENT AND BUSINESS

Hong Kong is a place where government works well, sets clear and equitable rules of the game, and leaves firms free to do business. In the absence of overriding social considerations, business decisions are generally left to the private sector, just as the allocation of economic resources is generally left to market forces. Hong Kong officials do not play any material role in business. There is no government holding company with stakes in leading firms in the economy. There are few government-owned companies and government does not engage in directing or planning the economy at the industry or firm level. The government has franchised monopolies or oligopolies for the provision of various services—like electricity, the mass transit railway system, the container port and the airport—but only in a few instances does the government have a financial interest in their performance. Instead, its predominant role is that of referee. It lays the ground rules and sets the terms of the schemes of control under which utilities operate. Private companies are left to generate electricity, operate the port, or run the ferries, trams, and buses. Many infrastructure projects are left to the private sector to develop, finance, build, and operate.

The government has largely resisted calls to pick winners, target industries, or protect or subsidize manufacturers. It shies away from micromanaging the structure of industry through regulations or tax policies. When it does regulate, it tends to do so with a comparatively light hand. The philosophy has been one that the government should set the rules, but then leave the private sector to make its own way without government inhibitions. Hong Kong also is free of serious corruption, the result of more than two decades of strong anti-corruption efforts. Government maintains an open trading environment, allows the free entry and exit of capital, and keeps the tax rate low for corporations and individuals. The result has been a system of 'positive non-intervention', in which Hong Kong companies and individuals have been free to succeed or fail based on their own skills and capabilities.

The clear separation in Hong Kong between the role of government as referee, and the role of private companies as active players in the economy, is unique in Asia, and rare world-wide. It is the anomalous by-product of British colonial arrangements which kept colonial officials aloof from commerce and firmly focused on administration and then on a gentlemanly retirement in England's home counties. Obviously, the Hong Kong Civil Service of today is quite different, largely staffed by locally born ethnic Chinese. But it has retained this distinctive separation between government and business, providing the source of a number of competitive advantages which have over time encouraged a dynamic economy, nurtured the territory's enterprise culture, and limited the scope for corrupt business activity.

This is in sharp contrast with government roles elsewhere in the Asia–Pacific region. Singapore's government directs economic development with a firm hand. Its principal holding company, Temasek, has substantial or controlling stakes in dozens of leading companies in the economy, including Singapore Airlines, Singapore Telecommunications, Keppel Shipyards, Neptune Orient Shipping, and Singapore Technologies. In Malaysia, where the ruling United Malays National Organization (UMNO) holds stakes in leading local companies, the line between government as referee and government as player in the economy is also often difficult to draw. In both economies, government officials can find themselves holding office in local enterprises. In China, the giant state trading corporations and the thousands of highly entrepreneurial 'township and village enterprises' (TVEs) that have sprung up over the past decade are commonly led by current or former government officials. The Korean government has funnelled rationed capital to the *chaebol* by state-controlled banks and has maintained protected markets to ensure their profits and domestic development. For many years in Japan, the Ministry of International Trade and Industry (MITI) developed and orchestrated market-sharing plans and the Ministry of Finance engaged in foreign exchange rationing to preferred companies and industries. It is interesting to note that in recent years there are indications that economic policy in Japan, Korea, Singapore, and other Asian nations may be moving away from selective state interventionism towards increased reliance on the market mechanism to foster economic growth, more in line with Hong Kong's traditional approach.[1]

Although government philosophy toward the economy in Hong Kong is often described by external observers as '*laissez-faire* capitalism', this characterization misses the mark. Hong Kong has evolved its own brand of government policy which is distinct from that of other economies in the region. The truth is that some significant local enterprises thrive today, as they have in the past, on the basis of protected oligopolies or monopolies. Similarly, government has intervened quite extensively in some areas of the economy, principally education, property (where government owns all land and sells leases to gain revenue), housing (half of the population lives in government housing), and medical services. The government intervenes for the social purposes of ensuring good minimum standards of service in these key areas, and ensuring that they are available to the entire relevant population. Despite the areas of intervention, the prevailing ethos can be seen in the fact that significant infrastructure projects in the territory are developed, financed, built, and operated by the private sector and by the fact that the Hong Kong government does not even issue its own currency. Instead it leaves that task to three note-issuing banks (the Hongkong and Shanghai Bank, the Standard Chartered Bank, and the Bank of China) which issue notes against reserve accounts kept with the Hong Kong Monetary Authority.

Tax policies are an important source of advantage for local and overseas firms operating in Hong Kong. Hong Kong maintains a simple tax structure with low corporate and personal rates to promote productive labour and investment. Tax policies are business-friendly to a degree matched by few other nations. According to the 1996 IMD *World Competitiveness Yearbook,* Hong Kong's fiscal policy is the most favourable to entrepreneurial activity of any fiscal policy in the world, and Hong Kong's personal taxes rank first in the world in encouraging individual work initiative.[2] The clarity of Hong Kong's tax policy translates into very substantial savings to local firms which often are able to meet tax reporting and record keeping requirements by the use of part-time bookkeepers instead of the full-time auditing staff often required elsewhere.

The result of the various policy elements is that Hong Kong's private sector has taken the leadership role in business and economic development. The territory's open economy exposes its traders and industrial producers to intense international competition, which forces Hong Kong industry to innovate and improve its products or exit. The lack of protectionist barriers in the traded sector also fosters the formation of new firms. Hong Kong's investment regime also is open and transparent, and inward and outward capital flows are free from special regulation and restriction. Hong Kong does not have a capital gains tax or an interest tax. It provides a level playing field for foreign and local investors in most sectors, encouraging entry and entrepreneurship on the part of locals and foreigners alike.

The Hong Kong system has ensured a separation of interests of public servants and business people, but a dynamic interaction in terms of communication and ongoing consultation. Traditionally, the heads of several leading firms have been members of the Executive Council, the Governor's advisory body that is Hong Kong's equivalent of Britain's Cabinet. Industry constituencies have representation in the Legislative Council (Legco), Hong Kong's legislative body. This system, in which business people can simultaneously serve as corporate managers and as legislators, and in which some specifically represent industry groups in legislative proceedings, stands in sharp contrast to the systems in place in Washington, Westminster, and elsewhere. Historically, the relationship between business and government has been close, and has been characterized by consultation rather than confrontation. In recent years, an increase in the number of Legco members elected through universal suffrage in geographic constituencies, and shifts in government priorities in the run-up to the assumption of administration by China, have somewhat reduced the influence of business interests on government decisions. Business influence remains strong, however, and business people make up a large contingent of the members of the 400 committees that advise the Hong Kong government on various issues and policies.

The unique combination of separation and interaction has fostered an environment in which businesses are free to make strategic decisions without having to take officialdom into account. It has allowed local Hong Kong Chinese to make their way in business without having to worry about the colonial administrators and it has allowed British entrepreneurs to profit handsomely alongside local businesses once they had paid their dues—in the form of fees for licenses or franchises. Separation of interests and ongoing interaction have fostered mutual respect. According to one Hong Kong executive, 'We respect government, but we do not fear it.' Where else in Asia could executives make such a statement truthfully?

LOCAL AND OVERSEAS FIRMS

While Hong Kong has a large and vibrant local business community, with over 470,000 locally registered companies, it is also home to the largest community of multinational firms in Asia. This is in part due to the territory's colonial roots, which have for the past 150 years made it the natural hub in Asia for British companies, and, in part, to its consistent and long-standing reputation for openness, simplicity of operation, and institutional familiarity. As a result, more than 2,000 multinational companies maintain regional offices or headquarters in the territory.

In addition to the hundreds of thousands of small firms, Hong Kong is the home of numerous, large local companies. (See Tables 2.1 and 2.2.), many of which are banks, conglomerates, property and development firms, and public utilities. Despite their range and depth, Hong Kong's leading banking firms are not as widely known in the West as their stature would warrant. The Hongkong and Shanghai Bank Group (HSBC Holdings plc) founded in 1865, is one of the largest banking groups in the world. HSBC controls banking groups in the United Kingdom and United States and holds a controlling interest in Hang Seng Bank, Hong Kong's second largest local bank. Hang Seng Bank has overseas offices in New York, San Francisco, Shanghai, Shenzhen, and Xiamen. The Bank of East Asia, Hong Kong's third largest listed bank, has 91 local branches, and has been the most active of the Hong Kong banks in the Mainland, with six branches, four representative offices, and four joint-venture finance companies.[3]

Several of Hong Kong's conglomerates, such as Jardine

Table 2.1 Top Twenty Hong Kong Companies by Sales, 1995

Rank	Company	Sales (Mill US$)	Profits (Mill US$)
1	Jardine Matheson	10,636	326
2	Swire Pacific	6,879	827
3	Dairy Farm	6,236	149
4	First Pacific	5,250	156
5	Hutchison Whampoa	4,491	1,130
6	Cathay Pacific Airways	3,904	382
7	Hongkong Telecommunications	3,770	1,274
8	Sun Hung Kai Properties	2,900	1,415
9	New World Development	2,238	437
10	China Light & Power	2,189	563
11	Henderson Land Development	1,958	1,072
12	Jardine Pacific	1,922	147
13	Jardine International Motors	1,867	63
14	Orient Overseas	1,672	63
15	Cheung Kong	1,554	1,426
16	Inchcape Pacific	1,400	98
17	CITIC Pacific	1,389	394
18	Li & Fung	1,181	30
19	Semi-Tech	1,103	33
20	Sime Darby HK	941	34

Source: 'The Asiaweek 1000: Top Enterprises by Country: Hong Kong', Asiaweek, 22, 47 (22 November 1996): 146.

Matheson and the Swire Group, trace their roots in the territory back to the British *hongs* of the mid-1800s. Today, Jardine Matheson has a vast and diversified presence in Hong Kong, Asia, and elsewhere. Its trading and services arm, Jardine Pacific, employs 70,000 people in 21 countries, in such lines as restaurants, engineering and construction, aviation and shipping, security and environmental services, financial services, and property. Other group companies are active in property, automobile distribution, insurance, merchant banking, food, retailing, and deluxe hotels. The Swire Group is

Table 2.2 The Twenty Largest Companies on the Hong Kong Stock Exchange by Market Capitalization

Rank	Company	Market Capitalization[a] (Billions of US Dollars)
1	HSBC Holdings	33.1
2	Sun Hung Kai Properties	25.4
3	Hutchison Whampoa	24.3
4	Hongkong Telecommunications	20.8
5	Hang Seng Bank	20.5
6	Cheung Kong Holdings	17.7
7	HSBC Holdingings-GBP Shares	16.0
8	Henderson Land Development	14.1
9	CITIC Pacific	9.7
10	Wharf Holdings	9.3
11	China Light & Power	9.3
12	New World Development	9.2
13	Swire Pacific 'A'	8.7[b]
14	Hongkong Electric Holdings	6.5
15	Cathay Pacific Airways	5.6
16	Hong Kong and China Gas	5.1
17	Whimsy Entertainment	4.5
18	Bank of East Asia	4.1
19	First Pacific	3.6
20	Hysan Development	3.2

[a] Market capitalization as of 30 September 1996.
[b] The market capitalization of Swire Pacific 'B' shares was US$1.8 billion.
Source: The Hong Kong Stock Exchange.

active in aviation (through its stake in Cathay Pacific), property, trading, marine services, air cargo services, and insurance. Swire Pacific, the group's main industrial division, has operations in beverages (Coca-Cola bottling operations in Hong Kong, mainland China, and Taiwan, as well as Carlsberg beer-bottling operations), engineering services, paints, and food production and distribution, among others.

Wheelock & Co., once a Jardine company, is one of Hong Kong's biggest conglomerates, with major business operations in real estate, retailing, travel, communications, hotels, property, and investments. Wheelock & Co. has international activities in the United States and Singapore, and is very active in China. Projects on the Mainland include container ports, cable TV networks, land transportation projects, industrial parks, power plants, and housing projects.[4] Wharf (Holdings) Ltd., a member of the Wheelock Group, is an investment company with interests in property, hotels, mass transport, container terminal operations, infrastructure, and cable television.

Cheung Kong, one of Hong Kong's most diversified companies, is the principal holding company for the interests of Li Ka-shing, one of Asia's richest men. Cheung Kong embraces property development, power generation, port development and operation, and communications, and has a controlling stake in the Hutchison Whampoa group of companies. Hutchison Whampoa is one of Hong Kong's largest property developers and investors, with projects in Hong Kong, on the Mainland, and throughout the region. Hutchison Whampoa is also active in telecommunications, retailing, utilities, and container ports. Li Ka-shing's purchase of a large share in the formerly British-owned Hutchison in 1979 was considered a milestone in the emergence of ethnic Chinese business interests in Hong Kong.[5]

Sun Hung Kai Properties is active in property and infrastructure development, counting among its recent projects: Beijing's New Town Plaza and Sun Dong An Plaza; refurbishment of Hong Kong's World Trade Centre Shopping Centre; and construction of a new highway in the New Territories (Route 3) which will improve road links with mainland China by linking existing highways that serve the metropolitan area with others that cross into the Mainland. It is also active in telecommunications, hotels, cinemas, and garment manufacturing. Sun Hung Kai Properties was voted Hong Kong's best managed company in *Asiamoney*'s 1995 survey, which noted the group's consistent strategy, prudent financial management, and focused, yet conservative management style.[6]

Henderson Land Development, majority-owned by magnate Lee Shau-kee, is active in real estate development in Hong Kong and the Mainland, including commercial and housing projects, department stores, hotels, and utilities. One of Hong Kong's largest investors in the Mainland, it is pursuing growth with a focus on mixed residential and commercial projects at prime locations in Shanghai, Beijing, and Guangzhou.

New World Development Co., Ltd., is a property company involved in large infrastructure projects and hotels in Hong Kong and on the Mainland. It is Hong Kong's single largest investor on the Mainland, with an estimated US$3.2 billion invested.[7] Its infrastructure projects on the Mainland include toll roads, bridges, and an airport in the city of Wuhan.

Hopewell Holdings is a major developer of infrastructure projects in Hong Kong, on the Mainland, and throughout the Asia–Pacific region. It is Hong Kong's second largest investor on the Mainland, where projects include the Guangzhou–Shenzhen–Zhuhai Superhighway. Other investments include power plants and transportation projects throughout the region.

Hongkong Telecommunications, Ltd., the territory's leading telecommunications group, offers a wide range of voice and data services, and operates one of the only fully digital telephone networks in the world. Once the local telephone monopoly, Hongkong Telecom still retains a monopoly on Hong Kong's international telephone gateway, and has extensive international fibre optic and satellite networks. It operates in seven countries and is actively building links in mainland China and Taiwan. Hongkong Telecom is 58 per cent controlled by Cable & Wireless of the United Kingdom and accounts for the bulk of that company's profits. A second prominent shareholder is the China International Trust and Investment Corporation (CITIC).

China Light & Power Co. has a monopoly of electricity service in Kowloon and the New Territories and is the larger of the two Hong Kong-based electricity companies. It is closely linked with the Kadoorie family, one of the territory's leading non-Chinese dynasties. China Light & Power has a stake in the Daya Bay nuclear power plant in South China, just 50 kilometres from Hong Kong, and has in recent years been an important supplier of power in the Pearl River Delta.

Hong Kong Electric Holdings, Ltd., a member of the Hutchison Whampoa Group, has the electricity monopoly on Hong Kong Island. Hong Kong Electric is currently focusing on power provision in the domestic market and is taking a cautious approach toward investing in power plants on the Mainland. Its consulting arm, Associated Technical Services Limited, has clients throughout Asia and in Saudi Arabia and Kuwait.[8]

Hong Kong also is one of the world's leading centres for overseas firms. Over 200 of the Fortune 500 companies have a presence in the territory. The American Chamber of Commerce in Hong Kong, with more than 1,100 corporate members, is the largest American Chamber outside of North America. The Japanese Chamber in Hong Kong reports that more than 2,000 Japanese companies operate from the territory. The countries with the largest number of overseas firm headquarters in Hong Kong are, in order of importance, the United States, Japan, the United Kingdom, and the People's Republic of China.[9]

The overseas firm 'sector' is so large and diverse that no one actually knows how many there are. As of May 1996, nearly 4,500 overseas companies had established a place of business in Hong Kong under Part XI of the Companies Ordinance—and these were only those that were officially registered.[10] An attempt by the Hong Kong Government Industry Department to identify all overseas companies operating in Hong Kong yielded a prospective list of 7,300 firms and 3,400 survey responses. Of the responding firms, 782 had a regional headquarters in Hong Kong and another 1,286 had a regional office as of June 1995.[11]

The presence of overseas firms in Hong Kong provides ready sources of information and access to events and markets elsewhere in the world. In addition, the fact that even very small

Hong Kong firms tend to have international operations provides a wealth of infrastructure, knowledge, and capabilities that overseas firms draw upon in managing their Asian activities from Hong Kong. Many multinationals feel 'at home' when they join such an unusually large, integrated, cosmopolitan local and expatriate business community. Bankers, accountants, lawyers, and other professionals who serve multinational firms have thrived in a community of local firms that has become increasingly transnational since the opening of the Mainland to foreign trade and investment in the late 1970s. This deep-rooted local familiarity with the needs of international business makes Hong Kong an easy place in which to find joint-venture partners, and to find expatriate professionals. Local staff can easily be recruited from local companies which have a ready familiarity with the dispersed operating needs of a multinational business.

The mixture and balance between local and overseas firms found in Hong Kong is unique within Asia if not the world. The Singaporean economy is dominated by overseas firms and state holding companies. Korea does not have a comparable contingent of overseas firms. Taiwan is perhaps closest to Hong Kong in its mix of overseas and local firms, but it still does not have the same cosmopolitan, international flavour that overseas firms bring to Hong Kong. Overseas firms do not play nearly as important a role in Japan as they do in Hong Kong. Hong Kong is unsurpassed in the extent to which it brings local and overseas firms together into a single business community. The constant interaction between thousands of overseas firms and local businesses, in a supercharged business environment, generates growth opportunities for both sides—in setting up international networks, entering new lines of business, finding new sources of supply and new markets, and linking up with business partners from Hong Kong, China, and elsewhere. As one local business executive observed: 'For multinational firms which seek out and thrive from interaction with the local environment and local firms, Hong Kong is the Asian location without par.'

ENTREPRENEURIAL AND MANAGERIAL FIRMS

Another remarkable and distinctive feature of the Hong Kong business environment is the interplay between 'entrepreneurial' and 'managerial' firms. Hong Kong is the home of almost rampant entrepreneurship. This entrepreneurship is supported by a system that encourages people to start their own companies and rewards their efforts through low taxation and other benefits. The territory boasts more than 470,000 privately owned small and medium-sized companies, most with very small staffs. The 'Hong Kong trader' mentality is one of constantly seeking out and making new deals and looking for commercial opportunity.

Some of Hong Kong's greatest fortunes have been made by individuals who started rather humble businesses and built them into vast empires over the last few decades. The stories of Li Ka-shing, who started out selling plastic flowers and now controls a multibillion-dollar industrial and property empire, or Stanley Ho, who left Hong Kong for Macau with hardly a dollar to his name in the 1940s and eventually built a multibillion-dollar entertainment group, make Horatio Alger pale in comparison. These stories, albeit extreme examples, are only two instances of a widespread phenomenon made possible by the high degree of upward social mobility in Hong Kong.

Hong Kong's entrepreneurial companies are almost invariably founded by Chinese families, and remain under the control of those same families. As such, they have distinctive characteristics: decision-making power tends to be highly concentrated at the centre of the company, often embodied in one patriarch; professional managers and technically expert staff are recruited in increasing numbers as such family companies grow, but are seldom offered—or expect to be offered—any shareholding in the company, or top executive position; and policy decisions or shifts can be taken extremely quickly, enabling the company to respond with great flexibility to shifts in market circumstances or fast-changing fashion trends.

41

It is regarded as quite normal that ambitious professional staff who are not members of the controlling family should at some point want to 'jump ship' and found their own company. Not only are such resignations commonplace, but they also rarely result in any schism between the company's owners and the resigning employee. On the contrary, once an owner learns that a member of staff plans to leave and set up his or her own company, arrangements will often be made to help the employee in the start-up of the company—either by agreeing to buy the product in which it plans to specialize, or by offering to develop the new company's product or products jointly, or to use the new company's service. It is at the same time recognized that a valued manager needs to be rewarded handsomely if he or she is to be given appropriate incentives to remain a salaried employee.

Some observers have pointed out that the owner or patriarch (as is the usual case) of a family firm in Hong Kong is in undisputed control. Even if the company has publicly traded shares, as long as the family retains a controlling block, then outside shareholders share in the good fortune of the company, but do not have much of a say in the running of the company. Other issues that can arise from unitary control are those of information flow and execution. There is a strong tendency not to wish to present the owner with bad news, which limits the information he or she has on which to base decisions. Since the owner is used to getting what he or she wants quickly, there is often a lack of detailed, long-term planning, even for deals and investments that require such planning.

Hong Kong's entrepreneurial culture has been stimulated by an ethos that values entrepreneurial success. Hong Kong's 'merchant princes' are respected and used as role models for new entrepreneurs. In addition, in Hong Kong, entrepreneurs are generally allowed second chances. One business failure does not mean the end of a career. Instead, it is a temporary set-back to be overcome the next time. Hong Kong industrialist Haking Wong, for example, started two business ventures that failed before founding W. Haking Enterprise, which became an industrial empire. This tolerance of failure is unusual for Asia, with the exception of Taiwan. In many Asian nations, individual initiative and accomplishment are subordinated to the group, and entrepreneurs who have one failure to their name often do not get a second chance. In Japan, one hears that 'the nail that stands up gets hammered down.' In Singapore, relatively few entrepreneurs of note have emerged. In Korea, a relatively small group of industrial leaders seem to have cornered much of the market for entrepreneurs. Only in the United States and Taiwan does one see similar scope for entrepreneurs, due in part to the fact that entrepreneurial success is valued and, in part, to the fact that entrepreneurs get second chances.[12]

While this entrepreneurial culture is what most outsiders associate with Hong Kong business, it would be wrong to underestimate the size and vitality of the territory's managerial-style firms. The roots of Hong Kong's managerial culture grew initially within the colonial *hongs*, and the large utilities granted monopolies or oligopolies over the provision of various key infrastructure services in the territory. Companies such as Jardine Matheson, the Swire Group, Hongkong Telecom, the Hongkong Bank, and others, are numerically a minority in Hong Kong, but in terms of their capitalization and the number of people they employ, they are important forces in the economy. They were from the outset international in their outlook, often with close links to the United Kingdom. Top executive positions were filled mainly by expatriates by a process of steady managerial promotion through a long career in the company. A substantial proportion of the benefits package of managerial staff in such companies was accounted for—and continues to be accounted for—by housing, generous pension schemes, and even memberships of clubs or the provision of annual air tickets home. Such companies today are largely staffed by Hong Kong Chinese, but their historic managerial styles have remained intact.

These firms have a style far different from the firms run by individual entrepreneurs. Many have organizations and management structures similar to those found in North America or Western Europe. Most are publicly traded or owned by publicly traded firms. They are run by professional managers who have risen through the ranks, usually within the same firm, less often through the ranks of similar firms. Decision-making tends to be more distributed in these firms than in Hong Kong's entrepreneur-run firms, with more delegation by top management. In the managerial firms, long-range planning is more the norm than in the entrepreneur-run firms. It is still less prevalent, however, than in equivalent firms in North America or Europe, where there tends to be more planning and less intuitive management.

Hong Kong's managerial firms invest in relationships just as the entrepreneurial firms do, but in many cases the relationships are of different types. Firms that operate franchises generally have good relationships with regulators that oversee the franchise and frequently are consulted on any policy initiatives that might influence the operation or value of the franchise. Historically, some local firms were able to turn such relationships into influence or other advantages in the marketplace, though in recent years this generally has been less the case.

The size of Hong Kong's community of 'managerial-style' firms has grown steadily over the past two decades, as multinational companies have settled in the territory, developing substantial local operations, and often using Hong Kong as their hub for regional business. This growth has driven strongly the demand for higher educational and professional qualifications. Firms such as Citicorp, Bank of America, and Exxon have brought in American-style professional management and management techniques, have augmented the local pool of expatriate professionals, and have added significantly to the amount of in-company training that goes on in the territory.

What has been unique about the combination of entrepreneurial and managerial firms in Hong Kong is the way they interact and influence one another. Some local entrepreneurial firms have learned from the managerial firms and have developed modern corporate practices and management systems. Many have raided the managerial firms for talented individuals and many have been founded by people who have been through the training systems of one of the larger managerial firms. Hong Kong's managerial firms, on their part, tend to be influenced by the fast-paced Hong Kong entrepreneurial style. They tend to manage in a somewhat more personal and intuitive manner than many of their Western counterparts. At the same time, the omnipresent danger that trained staff will be poached by small local companies, or leave to start up businesses of their own, has led Hong Kong's managerial firms to develop special strategies for retaining and providing incentives for valued local staff. Managerial firms find they must give managers more flexibility and responsibility than they might otherwise, and tie compensation more directly to individual performance or business unit profitability. In the process, they become more entrepreneurial themselves.

HUSTLE AND COMMITMENT STRATEGIES

Not surprisingly, the distinctive balance between small, family-controlled entrepreneurial companies and larger managerial firms has led to an unusual balance in Hong Kong between the pursuit of 'hustle' and 'commitment' strategies. 'Hustle' strategies emphasize flexibility in responding at high speed to new and emerging trends.[13] These strategies are aimed at beating competitors to the punch by recognizing new trends more quickly, and capturing a high margin of profit by being first to respond, but then moving on quickly in response to new developments, in the same or in a different industry. 'Commitment strategies', on the other hand, tend to employ large fixed investments intended over time to change the shape of competition in an industry in ways that are favourable to a company. This implies long-term strategies which aim to create and appropriate rents.[14] Neither strategy is intrinsically better or worse than the other. Each is appropriate in its own setting.

Hustle strategies are most readily seen among the territory's garments, toys, and electronics manufacturers, but are also strongly present in the many local businesses in which speed and flexibility, combined with reliable quality, delivery, and competitive pricing, are at a premium. Hong Kong manufacturers and traders have developed the agility to move from low end to higher end, from product to product, and even from one light consumer goods sector to another, sometimes at a lightning pace. In electronics, for example, Hong Kong firms started producing calculators in 1975, walkie-talkies and citizens' band radios in 1977, telephones in the early 1980s, and, in recent years, cordless telephones, video telephones, computers and related products, and printed circuit boards. In plastics and toys, Hong Kong producers started with simple toys and plastic flowers, progressed to television and hand-held games by the late 1970s, and to talking toys by 1986.[15] In watches, Hong Kong firms entered the field in the early 1950s by producing watch accessories, for example, cases, bands and dials, and then began assembling mechanical watches. In the 1970s, spurred by technological advances, they progressed from light-emitting diode (LED) display watches to liquid crystal display (LCD) watches, and in the 1980s, to quartz analogue watches, which now account for the lion's share of local production.[16]

Hong Kong firms in the light manufacturing/trading industries show a high degree of fluidity in combining light manufacturing with trading activities. The strong overlap of skills and abilities across the sectors promotes this fluidity, while the constant movement of entrepreneurs from one segment to another reinforces the skills base and influences industry strategies. For example, many of Hong Kong's watch manufacturers were originally merchants, and, according to one industry observer, as such are 'perhaps more highly motivated to respond to consumer preferences and get products into customers' hands'.[17] Hong Kong's 'merchant manufacturers' produce thousands of styles of watches and are keenly focused on changing consumer tastes. In a real sense, they have used their trader's acumen to recognize and exploit consumer demand in the international watch market.

Hong Kong companies that rely on a hustle strategy tend to invest relatively little in long-term planning, tie down comparatively little capital in technologies which need to be amortized over a long period of time, and do not spend much on research and development. They are low investors in brands, since these can also inhibit the flexibility of a company to move on to different products in response to new market trends. They tend to make extensive use of subcontracting relationships to move from product to product and sector to sector. In watches and other sectors, Hong Kong producers are expert at structuring complex subcontracting relationships to facilitate rapid and flexible manufacturing.[18] The flexibility of local garment manufacturers in responding speedily to fast-changing, fashion-driven demand is enhanced by the presence of a very large number of small and medium-sized factories organized into efficient subcontracting networks.

Commitment strategies are most evident in the activities of the territory's large infrastructure operators and utilities—such as China Light & Power, or the territory's port and air cargo operators, or Hongkong Telecommunications—or the two rail transport companies, the Kowloon–Canton Railway Corporation and the Mass Transit Railway Corporation. Commitment strategies are also evident in Hong Kong's property sector, where huge amounts of long-term capital are committed to building up a strong, sustainable business. What is interesting is that the commitment strategies found in Hong Kong are of a very particular type. Almost invariably they are found in industries in which cash flow is relatively stable and in which the commitment is made to obtain or develop a unique location or a franchise which is at least partially protected from competition. These industries include, for example, property, utilities, private infrastructure projects, port services, and airport services. As mentioned earlier, some utilities have been operated under a scheme of control that essentially guarantees a certain return on invested capital. Several private infrastructure projects have been undertaken on a BOO (build–operate–own) basis or BOT (build–operate–transfer) basis, in which the builder has the franchise to operate (and pocket the revenues from) the project indefinitely or for a specified period of time. The risks of such projects involve completing the project on time, on budget, and within specifications, as well as the risk associated with achieving forecasted demand, and the cost of failure can be substantial. But the projects have historically been packaged in a way that guarantees a good return if everything goes according to plan and a substantial return if they go better. Although the property market in Hong Kong has been volatile and is heavily influenced by government land policy, over the long term increasing incomes in a territory with limited buildable land has resulted in substantial increases in rents and property values. The operators of Hong Kong's container terminals and air cargo terminals have spent hundreds of millions, if not billions of dollars to develop their terminals and facilities, but again they have purchased franchises in industries that have seen demand continually outstrip supply.

The investments described are different from some of the commitment strategies found in other nations or regions. In Hong Kong, we see relatively little large-scale investment in research and development, relatively little large-scale development in branding, and relatively little large-scale investment in factories or 'hard assets' in terms of plant and equipment (in fact, the only fixed asset employed by many of Hong Kong's traders is a pager). There are exceptions of course, but the exceptions tend to prove rather than disprove the rule. The commitment strategies in Hong Kong tend to be in industries in which there is relatively little direct market or competitive risk. Investments in research and development, branding, and fixed assets, on the other hand, are subject to the risk that the market might not materialize or that competitors will make the investments obsolete.

There are several reasons for this phenomenon. Hong Kong does not have the cheap land required for large factories, heavy manufacturing, or some of the other industries that involve substantial investments in assets. Hong Kong's history as a transit point, rather than a home for many of its inhabitants, discouraged investments that were immobile. For others, the only immobile investments that made sense in an uncertain world were those, such as property, that tended to hold their value. Another explanation is a certain amount of impatience that pervades the Hong Kong business community. According to one manager, 'The important issue is timing. In Hong Kong, we don't want to wait for investments to pay off. It takes too long to do research and development, or to create a brand. If the technology or brands are out there, we just buy them.'

Hong Kong's hustle and commitment strategies interact in interesting ways. The commitment strategies followed by firms in some industries in Hong Kong provide a relatively stable set of support structures around which the 'hustlers' can operate. These 'hustler' firms, on the other hand, provide dynamism and a customer base that benefits the 'commiters'. The presence of hustle strategies influences the rapid pace of all Hong Kong business, a fast pace that creates a state of, at times, barely controlled frenzy. Meetings that would take two hours anywhere else in the world seem to take less than an hour in Hong Kong. People are constantly in meetings, running to meetings, or on the telephone. This style also has shaped the responses of Hong Kong firms, which often figure out how to do something only after they have committed to doing it. As one manager of a local electronics company said, 'We accept unreasonable requests, and then we deliver.' One example of this was when Gold Peak committed to supply electronic components to Sony before it even had a factory to produce the components. The factory was completed in record time and the components were delivered according to schedule. In addition, Gold Peak management claims that it was the first time a foreign supplier had passed all of Sony's quality standards on their first delivery.

Hong Kong's mix of hustle and commitment is unique in Asia. In other nations in Asia, government development strategies or dominance by multinationals tend to favour commitment strategies. The other economies in the region, with the possible exception of Taiwan, tend to lack the entrepreneurship that often goes along with a hustle strategy. Even in Taiwan, the high level of government involvement in setting industry policies has shifted the balance more to commitment than hustle strategies for major firms.

Figure 2.1 Hong Kong's Unique Combinations

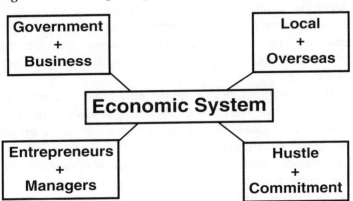

The important feature of Hong Kong's unique combinations is that Hong Kong has a balanced economy in which different types of organizations, firms, and strategies coexist, interact, and reinforce each other. Hong Kong's combinations are part of a self-consistent economic system. This system has allowed the territory to develop a balanced and robust economic system in which the combinations all contribute. (See Figure 2.1.) It has enabled Hong Kong and its firms to take on roles in the world economy far more important than its small size normally would allow. These roles are the subject of the next chapter.

NOTES

1   World Bank, *The East Asian Miracle: Economic Growth and Public Policy*, New York: Oxford University Press, 1993.

2   IMD International, *The World Competitiveness Yearbook 1996*, Lausanne, 1996, pp. 442, 436.

3   Asia Equity, Robin Hammond (analyst), 'Hong Kong Banking Sector', Hong Kong, May 1996, pp. 56–7.

4   Commonwealth of Australia, East Asia Analytical Unit, Department of Foreign Affairs and Trade, *Overseas Chinese Business Networks in Asia*, Sydney, 1995, pp. 318–19.

5   Commonwealth of Australia, *Overseas Chinese Business Networks*, p. 316.

6   Andrew Law; Kazushige Shimomura; and Heather Hutchings, 'Asia's Best

Managed Companies: Hong Kong', *Asiamoney*, VI, 6 (July/August 1995): 14.

7   Credit Lyonnais Securities, Hong Kong Research, 'China Jump II: Hong Kong's HK$140bn China Jump', Hong Kong, March 1996, p. 1.

8   Asia Equity, Osbert Tang (analyst), 'Company Update: Hong Kong Electric', 4 July 1995.

9   Germany, France, the Netherlands, Switzerland, Taiwan, Bermuda, and South Korea are also well represented. Hong Kong Government Industry Department, *Report on the 1995 Survey of Regional Representation by Overseas Companies in Hong Kong*, December 1995, pp. 5, 7.

10 Hong Kong Government Information Services, *Hong Kong Background Facts*, August 1996, p. 6.

11 Hong Kong Government Industry Department, *Report on the 1995 Survey of Regional Representation*, p. 3.

12 Many successful United States entrepreneurs have run one, two, three, or more companies into the ground before achieving their entrepreneurial success. Some venture capitalists look for people from failed start-ups when they try to match new companies and managers. They claim that one learns more from trying to prevent a start-up company from going down than one ever learns in a success story.

13 See Amar Bhide, 'Hustle as Strategy', *Harvard Business Review*, 64, Reprint No. 86503 (1 September 1986): 59–65.

14 See Pankaj Ghemawat, *Commitment: The Dynamic of Strategy*, New York: The Free Press, 1991.

15 Hong Kong Government Industry Department, 'Electronics Industry', in *1994 Hong Kong Manufacturing Industries*, 1994, p. 65.

16 Amy Glasmeier, 'Flexibility and Adjustment: The Hong Kong Watch Industry and Global Change', in *Growth and Change*, 25 (Spring 1994): 230–2.

17 Ibid., p. 228.

18 Ibid., pp. 228, 242.

3 HONG KONG'S ROLES IN THE WORLD ECONOMY

Hong Kong has emerged as an economic powerhouse with an influence in the global economy that goes far beyond what would be expected, given its tiny geographical size and its small population. By virtue of its distinctive transnational skills and its unique combinations, the territory occupies an unusual position that allows it to play many roles in the local, regional, and global economies. Hong Kong firms act as packagers and integrators of business activities for the world economy. The territory has been a major source of foreign investment, a home to one of the world's larger contingents of overseas firms, and *de facto* capital of the overseas Chinese business network. Hong Kong and its firms have been drivers of the modernization of the Mainland Chinese economy and its emergence into world markets, as well as a leading force in regional development. It is in these roles that Hong Kong has become important and has prospered.

HONG KONG AS PACKAGER AND INTEGRATOR

Hong Kong is often described as a bridge or a gateway, but such descriptions are at best incomplete. No simple bridge or gateway could have risen to such prominence. The main fault with such descriptions is that they are far too passive to describe accurately the role played by Hong Kong and its firms. Gateways get walked through and bridges get walked upon. Neither metaphor conveys the extent to which Hong Kong and its firms actively set up, direct, and manage activities for the local, regional, and global economies. Hong Kong firms are not intermediaries; they are instigators and initiators of economic activity, matching demand and supply on a local, regional, and global basis.

The role of Hong Kong firms as packagers and integrators may be seen among Hong Kong's manufacturers and export trading companies which match demand, often in North America or Europe, with sources of supply throughout Asia, and even further afield in parts of Africa and the Caribbean. A Hong Kong company, for example, might help a United States apparel company design its fall collection and then organize purchasing, manufacturing, and logistics to get the product on to retail shelves on time, meeting the right quality and product specifications, and on budget. Design and prototyping might be done in Hong Kong. Then for the long production run, fabric might be sourced in Malaysia, zippers in Japan, buttons in Taiwan, and thread in South Korea. The fabric might be cut in Hong Kong and the garment assembled on the Chinese Mainland. The customer never knows what a complex network was involved in creating the end product. In fact, the Hong Kong company managed the entire process, with a large proportion of the high value-added activities located in the territory.

Hong Kong has a particularly deep pool of talent and expertise in interpretive design that can be used across a number of light manufactured products, be they garments, watches, travel goods, jewellery, toys, or cellular phones. In each case, the Hong Kong firms are highly advanced in interpreting and anticipating consumer tastes in the world's major markets, most often by extending and developing pre-existing fashion ideas. In watches, Hong Kong producers have seized dominance in the low end of the watch market world-wide by focusing on changing consumer tastes and producing thousands of styles of watches on very rapid production and delivery cycles.[1] In export trading, the design input of Hong Kong firms is often an important added value for customers. In the words of one export trader active in garments, 'we have to lead many inexperienced buyers by the hand. We give market input on colour, styling, and texture, but we don't create a whole new line. We understand a merchandiser's niche in the market, and we offer products which we feel they can sell. What is being manufactured here is *ahead* of what is being produced in the United States and Europe.'

This is not a traditional 'middleman' function of the stereotypical trader or intermediary. It is part of a far more complex set of functions that allows the Hong Kong firms to add value—through their knowledge of source and destination markets, through their familiarity with production capabilities of literally thousands of factories scattered throughout Asia, through advanced capabilities in logistics, and through expertise in managing subcontractors. Rather than a 'middleman,' the Hong Kong firm becomes a complete business partner for the customer, coordinating and putting together, 'packaging and integrating' a range of activities often beyond the capabilities of the customer.

In many manufacturing industries, such as garments, toys, a variety of plastic products, watches, and others, Hong Kong firms have developed sources of cost-sensitive mass production and assembly activities on the Chinese Mainland and elsewhere in Asia, transforming themselves into 'trading' companies specializing in a complex of knowledge-intensive, creative activities along the length of the manufacturing value chain. They provide a complete headquarters for management, financing, technology, design, prototyping, quality control, marketing, and distribution service between dispersed assembly plants on the one hand, and retail buyers on the other. Hong Kong's companies have over the past two decades developed unparalleled reach across the entire Asia–Pacific region, as is shown by the fact that a full 30 per cent of the exports of Hong Kong manufacturers and traders are manufactured outside Hong Kong and mainland China.[2]

Hong Kong's role as a packager and integrator extends beyond manufacturing and into the service sector. As a major business service centre, Hong Kong and its firms package financial and business deals for corporate and private clients from Hong Kong, from the region, and from the rest of the world. Hong Kong is the centre where fund managers and private bankers put together Asian investment funds, portfolios, and financial vehicles. (Singapore also has emerged as a significant regional financial centre, but the absence of a local entrepreneurial community akin to that in Hong Kong means that this sector is focused less specifically on the distinctive needs of entrepreneurs, small manufacturers, and traders.) Hong Kong financiers are involved in some of the largest capital raising efforts in the region. Whether it be arranging an initial public offering (IPO) for a Mainland company on the Hong Kong Stock Exchange, structuring the financing of a joint venture for a US company in Vietnam, or raising venture capital for a new venture in the region, Hong Kong professionals are likely to be involved.

The territory also is the leading centre for packaging infrastructure projects for the region. Hong Kong firms bring together design, construction, engineering, legal, and financial expertise to build infrastructure in Hong Kong, on the Mainland, and elsewhere in South-East Asia. With its long history of private sector financed infrastructure, Hong Kong is the leading location for integrating these skills. Hong Kong virtually invented the BOT (build–operate–transfer) system in which private investors build an infrastructure project, operate it under a concession arrangement for a period of time within which they try to earn back their investment plus a return, and then transfer the project to the control of a government agency.

This packaging and integrating function allows Hong Kong firms to capture value across the region. BOT projects, and the related BOOT (build–own–operate–transfer) and BOO (build–own–operate) projects, have become increasingly important in Asia as governments have had to turn to the private sector, and to private sector finance, to build urgently needed infrastructure across the region. Hong Kong firms have structured projects to build ports, airports, tunnels, roads, power plants, mass transit systems, and low-cost housing in mainland China, the Philippines, Indonesia, Thailand, and India. Hong Kong entrepreneurs, such as Gordon Wu at Hopewell Holdings, Li Ka-shing who heads Cheung Kong and Hutchison Whampoa, Lee Shau-kee of Henderson Land, Peter Woo at Wharf Holdings, and Cheng Yu-tung of New World, have emerged as major players in the infrastructure development of the entire region. Their projects, in turn, have the potential to shape the economic development of the nations in which they operate.

The packaging and integrating role requires knowledge of demand in the developed countries, sources of supply in the developing countries, and the ability to create new combinations as demand changes and new sources of supply emerge. It requires access to information, expertise in all aspects of the business, the ability to bridge cultures, and the ability to assess new commercial opportunities quickly and accurately. These abilities and features are present to an unusual, if not unique extent in Hong Kong. They allow Hong Kong firms to capture value from diverse activities world-wide, from the sourcing of a garment manufactured on the Mainland, to the construction of a power plant in the Philippines, to an acquisition by a Thai firm financed in New York.

HONG KONG AS FOREIGN INVESTOR

One potent example of Hong Kong's globally significant role as a packager and integrator of economic activities is the territory's extraordinary emergence as one of the world's leading sources of foreign direct investment. Most economies in the region—with the exception of Japan—are preoccupied with investment inflows rather than outflows, since these have provided valuable additional impetus to their efforts to build international trading links and to attract new technology and management skills. Hong Kong, in contrast, has through the 1990s emerged to be a world leader in outward foreign direct investment. It was fourth in the world both in 1994 and in 1995—accounting for outflows of almost US$21 billion in 1994,

Table 3.1   Leading Foreign Investors into ASEAN and
APEC, 1994

Investor Country/Region	Investment Flows, Millions of US Dollars	
	Into ASEAN[a]	Into APEC[b]
World	36,258	163,063
Hong Kong	6,874	27,822[c]
United States	3,437	23,145[d]
Japan	4,894	17,132
Taiwan	4,325	8,101
Singapore	2,697	6,889

[a] 'ASEAN' includes Indonesia, Singapore, Malaysia, the Philippines, and Thailand.
[b] 'APEC' includes the United States, Canada, Mexico, Chile, Japan, South Korea, Taiwan, Hong Kong, Singapore, Thailand, Malaysia, the Philippines, Indonesia, China, and Australia.
[c] This is a larger figure than that given by UNCTAD cited earlier.
[d] Given the membership of APEC, this figure includes United States investment in Canada and Mexico, as well as in the Asian APEC economies.
Source: Japan External Trade Organization (JETRO), *Jetro White Paper on Foreign Direct Investment 1996*, Tokyo, 1996, Table 1.6, p. 12.

and US$25 billion in 1995, when only the United States (US$95.5 billion), the United Kingdom (US$38 billion), and Germany (US$35.3 billion) accounted for more substantial outflows. Hong Kong in 1995 was significantly ahead of both Japan (US$21 billion) and France (US$17.6 billion). In Asia, excluding Japan, Hong Kong accounts for more outbound foreign direct investment than all the other economies put together—seven times that of Taiwan and mainland China, eight times the foreign investment from Korea, and almost ten times that of Singapore and Malaysia.

Hong Kong's emergence as a source of foreign investment is clearly linked with the surge of investment into mainland China, but it is not exclusively so. Hong Kong has emerged as a leading foreign direct investor across Asia. In 1994, Hong Kong was the biggest foreign investor in Indonesia, the second most important investor in the Philippines, the third in Taiwan, and the fourth in Australia. In recent years, Hong Kong—not Singapore, as some might imagine—has been the leading foreign investor into the ASEAN region. Even more surprisingly, Hong Kong is the biggest foreign investor into the 18-country APEC region, which embraces the United States and Canada (most US investment continues to be targeted at the European Union rather than Asia). (See Table 3.1.)

There are many reasons why Hong Kong has emerged as the region's largest foreign investor. Paramount among them are its large and liquid capital market, the absolute freedom with which capital can enter and leave the economy, and the fact that such a large majority of the world's leading banks, whether Japanese, European, American, or Asian, coordinate regional operations from their bases in Hong Kong. Perhaps even more significant is the role played by thousands of Hong Kong companies each making relatively small investments that have dispersed their manufacturing operations both into mainland China and across Asia to capture competitive advantage wherever it can be found. The thousands of multinational and regional transnational companies which use Hong Kong as their logistical hub for Mainland Chinese and regional operations also help to perpetuate Hong Kong's outward investment position. The numerous Hong Kong softgoods manufacturers with foreign operations already have been described. Similarly, Hong Kong's electronics, watch, and other industries have moved the bulk of their production capacity to the Mainland's Pearl River Delta.

Hong Kong has been the base through which local firms, as well as firms from North America, Europe, and elsewhere have invested in mainland China. One reason has been Hong Kong's traditional role as a financial centre and as a home for Western overseas firms. Another is that the Hong Kong government accords full national treatment to any Hong Kong registered entity and makes no attempt either to distinguish or to discriminate between companies based on their ethnic or sovereign origins. Any company registered in Hong Kong is a Hong Kong company. On this basis, many of the 3,000-odd

Taiwanese companies using Hong Kong as their hub for investment in mainland China and the region are regarded as Hong Kong companies. So too are the many overseas Chinese companies based in Hong Kong. For this reason, the Hong Kong-listed company of the Thai CP Pokphand Group has become one of Hong Kong's leading outward investors, particularly on the Chinese Mainland, where it has approximately 70 ventures in operation. So too has Sime Darby (wholly Malaysian-owned) and Shangri-La Asia (controlled by Robert Kuok of Malaysia), for example.

Hong Kong's recent, rapid emergence as a key player in large infrastructure projects across the region is perhaps the most surprising contributor to the territory's role as a foreign investor. This emergence has been the result of the strength and experience of Hong Kong's large private sector property and infrastructure-building companies combined with locally based financial capabilities. As Hong Kong firms have pioneered private sector BOT and BOO projects across the region, so such large investments have amplified the value of outward foreign investment. Major projects which have boosted Hong Kong investment in the Asia–Pacific region include power projects in the Philippines and Indonesia by CEPA (formerly controlled by Gordon Wu), a number of road and mass transit projects in Thailand by Hopewell Holdings, and, recently, a light rail project in Singapore by Gammon Construction.[3]

Furthermore, Mainland Chinese companies based in Hong Kong are investing on the Mainland and elsewhere, with some even 'round-tripping' (routing funds from mainland China through Hong Kong and back into the Mainland) in order to capitalize on tax breaks offered to foreign investors. However, intensive work by the UNCTAD's Division on Transnational Corporations and Investment has concluded that even at its peak in 1992, this 'round-tripping' has not exceeded 25 per cent of all Hong Kong-based investment in mainland China.[4] Although Hong Kong is often not the original source of capital for 'round-trip' investments or investments from overseas firms, the fact that investors use Hong Kong to make their investments is testament to the strength of Hong Kong as a business and financial service centre. Hong Kong-owned companies might not be the source of some of this capital, but Hong Kong experts, firms, and financial institutions package, and profit from, the transactions.

Another striking feature of Hong Kong outward investment is that it is business-to-business, not government-to-government. Flows build up through thousands of small investments rather than a few large ones. There is little or no government intermediation. The Hong Kong government has made it a policy not to maintain data on foreign direct investment inflows and outflows. The investments succeed—or fail—by commercial criteria. It is on this basis that Hong Kong has become the world's fourth largest source of foreign direct investment—and there is no sign at present that its role as a management hub for investment across the region will subside any time soon.

HONG KONG AS A LOCATION FOR OVERSEAS FIRMS

Hong Kong has always attracted overseas firms. The British-owned, Hong Kong-based trading companies that were set up early in the territory demanded a strong legal system, sophisticated communications and transportation infrastructure, professional services, and staff proficient in English. This combination of attributes, combined with Hong Kong's role as entrepôt, the widespread use of Western business practices, and its distinctly cosmopolitan business circles, attracted firms from throughout Asia and the West. Hong Kong's international business community, originally largely British, became more diverse after the Second World War with the arrival of firms from the United States, Europe, Japan, and South-East Asia.[5] Since the late 1970s, the opening of mainland China to foreign investment and trade has strongly lured overseas firms to Hong Kong.

Because of the geographic dispersal of the activities of large multinational corporations, the question is increasingly not 'whether' to locate in any major centre of corporate activity, but which activities to locate there and in what proportion. Large multinational firms with a presence in Hong Kong tend to conduct major business activities throughout Asia, including mainland China, Taiwan, Singapore, Japan, South Korea, and Australia. Many of these firms use Hong Kong as a location for conducting marketing and sales, procurement, and logistics management operations across a broad geographic region.[6] Hong Kong's proximity to and business connections with mainland China have attracted to the territory firms from the world over. Hong Kong's business hub and its central position within the Asia–Pacific region are also strong advantages, and the regional headquarters of overseas firms in the territory on average do much more than just Hong Kong and mainland China business.[7] Over one-half of the regional headquarters of overseas firms in Hong Kong serve a geographic region that extends beyond Hong Kong and mainland China. Nearly one quarter serve South-East Asia, including mainland China; nearly one-quarter serve the entire Asia–Pacific region, including Japan, Korea, Australia, and New Zealand; and one-tenth serve East Asia, excluding Australasia. Thirty-four per cent of regional headquarters focus exclusively on Hong Kong and mainland China.[8]

Hong Kong's role as a regional hub for marketing, sales, procurement, and logistics operations is underscored by the breadth of the local operations of overseas firms in the wholesale/retail and import/export areas. Forty per cent of the regional headquarters of overseas firms are engaged in these areas as a 'major line of business'.[9] Depending on their strategies, such firms may sell to mainland China and throughout the region, buy from mainland China and throughout the region, and use Hong Kong to oversee regional operations. Hong Kong attracts wholesalers, retailers, and traders from the West and Asia. Clothes and softgoods destined for shopping malls across the United States are sourced through Hong Kong by The Limited, J. C. Penney, Sears, The Gap,

Montgomery Ward & Co., and other firms. Europe's leading merchandise distributors, from Sweden to Italy, are well-represented, including Marks & Spencer, Laura Ashley, and Colruyt (a Belgian department store group). Japan's giant traders, such as the *sogo shosha* Itochu, Mitsubishi, Mitsui, Marubeni, and Sumitomo, use Hong Kong as a logistics, procurement, sales, and finance base for their extensive business empires on the Mainland. The big Mainland Chinese trading houses, such as China Resources and Guangdong Enterprises, have regional headquarters in Hong Kong, as do trading companies from Taiwan and countries throughout the world.

Professional service operations are also a strong focus of overseas firms. Nearly 10 per cent of regional headquarters of overseas firms in Hong Kong are active in finance and banking, another 7 per cent in transportation and related services, and nearly 5 per cent in construction and architectural and civil engineering. In addition, another 17 per cent of overseas firms with regional headquarters in Hong Kong have 'other business services' as a major line of business.[10] Overseas firms active in banking and finance include: American Express, Bank of America, Chase Manhattan Bank, Citibank, Daewoo Securities (Korea), Daiwa (Japan), DBS Bank (Singapore), Deutsche Genossenschaftsbank (Germany), Equity Trust (Netherlands), Fidelity, Generale Bank (Belgium), Merrill-Lynch, Morgan Stanley, and the Swiss Bank Corporation. More Japanese banks operate in Hong Kong than in any city outside Japan. Despite uncertainties over 1997, firms such as the German insurer Allianz, and NatWest from the United Kingdom continue to set up new fund management operations. Due to Hong Kong's dense network of airline routes, foreign air carriers, such as Air France, British Airways, Lufthansa, Qantas Airways, and United Airlines, are well-represented, and their presence will grow in 1998 when operations start at Hong Kong's airport at Chek Lap Kok. The new airport also has attracted corporate jet maker Gulfstream Aerospace, which has set up in Hong Kong to promote local sales of corporate aircraft. Hong Kong's infrastructure improvements in energy, communications, and air transport are generating a large volume of business for Siemens, Bechtel, and others. Many of the world's leading civil engineering consulting firms, international corporate law firms, accounting firms, and insurance firms are present. So are the world's leading luxury hotel chains.

One in ten of the overseas firms headquartered in Hong Kong use the territory as the site for manufacturing production operations, with Japanese, United States, and Mainland Chinese firms accounting for the greatest investments.[11] In 1996, Motorola Inc. signed a cooperation agreement with Taiwan's Mosel Vitalix to fabricate T-metal oxide semiconductor (TMOS) wafers locally. Other recent manufacturing ventures by foreign firms include Eastman Chemical Company's acquisition of a local plant for manufacturing fine chemicals for the Asian market, and Matsushita's new factory for the production of power supplies and other electronic components. Ohuchi Manufacturing Co. Ltd. of Japan has set up a precision metal-stamping factory to produce parts for office automation equipment, for the Hong Kong and mainland China markets.

Hong Kong has strong advantages over competing locations as a site for certain activities of overseas firms. These advantages, which have been well-documented by business surveys, draw upon multiple features of the Hong Kong economic system. Hong Kong's superb geographic location, strong transportation and communications infrastructures, free and open trade, professional administration, fair legal system, and liberal taxation policies are among the attributes most often cited by overseas firms as advantages to locating in Hong Kong.[12] These features, combined with the free flow of people, capital, and information, and the ease of setting up business, make Hong Kong an advantageous location for foreign firms.

Overseas firms have made distinct contributions to the competitiveness of Hong Kong's economic system. They have helped upgrade the quality of human inputs through extensive human resource training, and the importation of world-class skills (particularly in professional services), and technical capabilities. Traditionally, the top-tier overseas firms in Hong Kong have taken the lead in in-house human resource training, at the executive trainee and office worker level. Companies such as Citibank and Bank of America have instituted extensive training schemes that are intrinsic elements of overall firm strategy. It is normal practice for such firms to train employees in Hong Kong and also to send trainees with high potential to overseas firm locations for further training.

Overseas firms also are an important component of Hong Kong's support service and transport/logistics clusters, and provide business and technical spillovers in many areas. They have helped to develop the integration and locational strengths of Hong Kong and helped to build up individual industries. They generate cutting-edge, sophisticated demand for support services, products, and infrastructure; they serve as world-class competitors for local firms and a source of joint-venture opportunities.

Hong Kong's strengths as a location for overseas firms are rooted in its unique combinations. Hong Kong's balance between government and business, resulting in a system of 'positive non-intervention', has produced a uniquely level playing field for firms from overseas. Hong Kong's managerial firms provide the structure that allows foreign firms to operate friction-free, while the dynamic pressures of its entrepreneurs force managerial firms, regardless of country of origin, to reward talent and keep pace with the market. Hong Kong's mix of commitment and hustle strategies provide superior business infrastructure, hard and soft, as they address myriad opportunities focused on mainland China and Asia.

HONG KONG AS THE CAPITAL OF THE OVERSEAS CHINESE

A phenomenon that has developed rapidly around Hong Kong over the past decades—and which appears likely to develop

Table 3.2   Per Cent of Stock Market
Capitalization Controlled
by Ethnic Chinese,
Selected Countries

Country	Per cent
Indonesia	73
Malaysia	61
Philippines	50–60
Singapore	81
Thailand	81

Source: Yamaguchi, Masaaki, 'The Emerging Chinese Business
Sphere', *Nomura Asian Perspectives*, 11, 2 (July 1993):
3–18.

even more strongly in the decades ahead—is the growing economic influence of the overseas Chinese. Hong Kong has emerged as the *de facto* business capital of the overseas Chinese communities spread across the Asia–Pacific region, providing a focal point for investments and expansion strategies. Overseas Chinese firms routinely use Hong Kong as a business hub, and tap its equity and bond markets for expansion into mainland China, the ASEAN region, and the West.

The overseas Chinese account for a very large share of the entrepreneurial wealth of the Asia–Pacific region. The total assets of the largest 500 public companies in Asia controlled by ethnic Chinese were estimated in 1994 to exceed US$500 billion.[13] While ethnic Chinese account for less than 10 per cent of South-East Asia's population, they control up to two-thirds of the region's retail trade, and are leading players in land and property development, banking, hotels, engineering, and construction. Ethnic Chinese-controlled firms also make up the vast majority of the market capitalization of stock markets in the region. (See Table 3.2.) They are only in a loose sense a community, dispersed as they are among geographically distant nations and fragmented into various ethnic identities.[14] Nevertheless, common loyalties to ancestral origins and roots in business and trade have created bonds that are important within and between countries across the Asia–Pacific region. For reasons of history, Hong Kong occupies a central place in this network.

The origins of the overseas Chinese lie in China's history of sporadic contact with the outside world, and political and economic upheavals. Until the early nineteenth century, most migrants were traders (a social grouping which had low social standing in dynastic China) who became stranded during the long periods in which trade and other contact between China and the outside world were banned. Most settled in Indochina and South-East Asia. From the 1840s onwards, millions of emigrants fleeing persecution or starvation passed through Hong Kong, ending up in South-East Asia or the United States.[15] Emigration to South-East Asian destinations through Hong Kong intensified between the 1880s and 1930s, making Hong Kong a common reference point for the Chinese businessmen dispersed throughout the region who were starting business concerns—some of which would become major business empires—in their adopted homes. These entrepreneurs retained strong attachments to China and their ancestral villages, which they passed on to later generations.

For overseas Chinese throughout the region, Hong Kong was the natural communications and business conduit back to Southern China. Geographically, it was perfectly positioned as an urban gateway to Guangdong. Its commercial and communications infrastructures were excellent, and there were strong ties with the population of neighbouring Guangdong Province. Two-thirds of Hong Kong's Chinese population in the 1930s had been born in mainland China, mostly in nearby parts of Guangdong. After the Second World War, Hong Kong grew in importance as an international business centre. Improving air transport and communications links with other ASEAN members brought ethnic Chinese businessmen to Hong Kong from Indonesia, Malaysia, Thailand, Singapore, and the Philippines, to do business in Hong Kong and, to the extent possible, on the Mainland.[16]

Since Beijing began opening up mainland China to trade and investment almost two decades ago, Hong Kong has become the nodal point through which these overseas Chinese have reconstructed relationships with the communities in their ancestral homes. All of the special economic zones (SEZs) set up by Beijing to attract overseas Chinese investment (focused on the ancestral communities of the Hokkien, Chiu-chow, and Cantonese) were, and remain, best accessed through Hong Kong. Investors naturally have set up companies in Hong Kong to act as vehicles for investment.

Hong Kong has been a safe place to do business for overseas Chinese facing problems at home. British rule in Hong Kong engendered political stability, efficient government, openness to people, goods, and ideas, and a strong legal system—all strong advantages over the business environments in which Chinese traders and businesses historically have operated. British neutrality within the region made Hong Kong comparatively safe as a locus of outward investment. The territory's liberal rules on the movement of capital, its excellent financial system, and its simple, light-handed tax regime, also made Hong Kong an attractive place in which to reap and keep returns on investment. While Hong Kong continues to be perceived as a 'very Chinese international city', its unique blend of Chinese culture and Western institutions proved a powerful catalyst in attracting overseas Chinese firms.[17]

These factors have combined to make Hong Kong the central nexus in the geographically dispersed activities of the overseas Chinese. Hong Kong acts as a key business hub for a large number of these firms in tandem with their domestic bases of operations elsewhere in the region. Much of this activity in Hong Kong used to be covert, since governments in the region frowned on capital leaving their countries. As sensitivities over outward investment subside across South-East Asia, however, it is increasingly open, as evidenced by some of the landmarks defining the city's skyline, such as the Lippo Centre and the Shangri-La Hotel.

The Kuok Group of Malaysia is active in Hong Kong through Shangri-La Asia, the Kerry Group (including property, trading, and financial services), the Aberdeen Marina, the Western Harbour Tunnel Consortium, TVB Ltd., South China Morning Post Publishers, and CITIC Pacific. The Lippo Group of Indonesia is present through Lippo Limited (a merchant bank), the Hong Kong Chinese Bank, Asia Securities (strategic investment), and Hong Kong China (property investment), among other firms.[18] The First Pacific Group, a member of the Salim Group of Indonesia, is active in marketing and distribution, cellular telecommunications (Pacific Link Communications), property, and banking.[19] Hong Kong-based Asia Financial, part of the Sophonpanich Group of Thailand, is active in banking, insurance, and commodity trading, with operations in Hong Kong, Taiwan, Macau, San Francisco, and mainland China.[20] The Charoen Pokphand Group of Thailand operates numerous businesses on the Mainland through its Hong Kong subsidiary, CP Pokphand. Other major South-East Asian Chinese entrepreneurs present in Hong Kong include Oei Hong Leong of Indonesia (China Strategic Holdings) and Frank Chan of the Philippines (Eton Properties).

Hong Kong has served as a cornerstone for the overseas expansion of some of the largest and most powerful of the overseas Chinese conglomerates. Typically, it is their first international location, their primary locus for tapping international capital markets, their springboard for managing investment into mainland China, and their primary base for foreign direct investment elsewhere. A common strategy for an overseas Chinese conglomerate originating elsewhere in South-East Asia has been to establish a publicly owned company or other business in Hong Kong, and then use its Hong Kong operations to facilitate its subsequent investment on the Mainland and in other ASEAN countries.[21] For example, Chairman Mochtar Riady initially expanded the Lippo Group from Indonesia to Hong Kong, and bond investors in Hong Kong were an important source of funds for the group's later expansion. The Lippo Group has since formed strategic alliances with two major PRC companies in Hong Kong— China Resources and China Travel Service—in order to enter the Mainland market.[22] Other overseas Chinese conglomerates which have used publicly listed companies or other vehicles in Hong Kong to invest in mainland China include: the Charoen Pokphand Group and Bangkok Land Group of Thailand; the Salim Group and Oei family/Sinar Mas Group of Indonesia; the Kuok Group, Hong Leong Group, and Berjaya Group of Malaysia; and the Singaporean Far East Group.[23] This, however, is only part of the picture: the sphere of overseas expansion out of Hong Kong for these business groups extends far beyond mainland China. For example, the lead company in Hong Kong of the Salim Group, First Pacific Group, has highly diversified overseas interests in 25 countries in such areas as communications, real estate, trading, pharmaceuticals, and consumer products.[24]

In addition, the Chinese business community in Hong Kong, local and overseas, serves as a hub for the overseas Chinese world-wide in providing services in such areas as finance, the media, and hotels. Lippobank (HK) has set up Lippo Finance Australia in Sydney to serve that city's Asian community in trade financing; it also has banks in Los Angeles and San Francisco targeted at those cities' ethnic Chinese communities.[25] Since 1994, the Chinese Television Network, an international 'Chinese CNN' based in Hong Kong, has covered news events for Chinese communities throughout the world.[26] Sing Tao Holdings, a major Hong Kong newspaper publisher, has Chinese-language newspapers in the United States, Canada, the United Kingdom, and Australia, and has plans for further expansion in Asia. Shangri-La Asia, based in Hong Kong, is targeting locations around the world with large ethnic Chinese communities for its upscale hotels and resorts.[27] Hong Kong has played a central role in the growth and international expansion of the overseas Chinese business network. Trend guru John Naisbitt claims that the overseas Chinese business network is one of the driving forces in the world economy today. If, as he also claims, the overseas Chinese network provides the prototype for the dominant business organizational form for the twenty-first century, then Hong Kong is well-situated indeed.[28]

HONG KONG AS A DRIVER OF THE MODERNIZATION AND INTERNATIONALIZATION OF THE MAINLAND CHINESE ECONOMY

Hong Kong is often called a gateway to and from mainland China, or the Mainland's window on the world, or its major source of foreign exchange. It has been all of these things, and a great deal more. The territory and its firms, in fact, have served as a driver of the modernization of the Mainland economy and an orchestrator of its emergence into international markets. Hong Kong has provided not just capital, logistical support, and access to world markets, but also management know-how, technology, equipment, design and research, marketing skills, procurement services, and quality assurance. As the Mainland's export economy has boomed, it has done so on the basis of Mainland labour, land, and natural resources orchestrated by management and numerous other support services from Hong Kong partners. It is this combination that has allowed China, a nation cut off from the international economy for decades, to emerge as a major trading nation in a little more than a decade.

The territory's role as China's interface with the rest of the world has expanded as mainland China has joined the world economy. Hong Kong and Hong Kong firms today handle 50 per cent of mainland China's exports—and 80 per cent of the international trade of neighbouring Guangdong Province alone. Not counting re-exports to and from mainland China, Hong Kong is mainland China's third largest trading partner.[29] More than 800 sailings, 72 flights, 20 trains, and 26,000 vehicles cross the Hong Kong–China border daily.[30] Beneath these exchanges of goods and people lie huge capital flows from Hong Kong to the Mainland which have propelled the development of mainland China's private and collective economy.

Mainland China's private and collective economy has developed rapidly over the past 17 years, today accounting for more than half of the country's industrial output, compared with just 5 per cent in the early 1980s. (See Table 3.3.) In the

Table 3.3   Mainland China, Gross Industrial Output and Employment by Type of Ownership

Ownership	Industrial Output (Billions of yuan)		
	1985	1990	1994
State-owned	630.2 (64.9%)	1,306.4 (54.6%)	2,620.1 (34.1%)
Collective-owned	311.7 (32.1)	852.3 (35.6)	2,021.3 (40.9)
Individual-owned	18.0 (1.8)	129.0 (5.4)	885.3 (11.5)
Other	11.7 (1.2)	104.8 (4.4)	1,042.1 (13.6)

Ownership	Employment (Millions)		
	1985	1990	1994
Industrial			
State-owned	89.9 (18.0%)	103.5 (18.2%)	148.5 (17.7%)
Collective-owned	33.2 (6.7)	35.5 (6.3)	32.1 (5.2)
Individual-owned	4.5 (0.9)	6.1 (1.1)	12.3 (2.0)
Other	0.4 (0.1)	1.6 (0.3)	7.5 (1.2)
Rural Labour	359.7 (74.6)	420.1 (74.0)	446.5 (72.6)

Source: *China Statistical Yearbook 1995*, Beijing: China Statistical Publishing House, 1995, pp. 84, 375.

process, as the state sector has stagnated, the private and collective sector has been mainland China's principal source of job creation (now accounting for more than 110 million jobs) and export generation. Hong Kong-funded ventures—which now number more than 250,000 across the Mainland—have been the dynamo behind a very large part of this growth and job creation. At the end of 1995, they accounted for a cumulative US$234 billion in contracted investment in mainland China— just under two-thirds of the total US$396 billion contracted since 1979. (See Table 3.4.) While this investment is concentrated in Hong Kong's Pearl River Delta hinterland, it has been so substantial that Hong Kong investors remain by far the largest investors in virtually every province in mainland China. For example, in Liaoning Province (close to Japan in China's north-east), Hong Kong investors account for 40 per cent of the US$16 billion in contracted foreign investment— more than twice the amount of investment from Japan. (See Table 3.5.) In Shandong, which has strong links with South

Table 3.4 Top Five Foreign Investors in Mainland
China

Country/Region	Contracted Foreign Direct Investment, Billions of US Dollars		
	Cumulative (1979–95)	1994	1995
Total	395.86	82.68	91.28
Hong Kong	233.60 (59.0%)	46.97 (56.8%)	40.81 (44.7%)
United States	33.06 (8.4)	6.01 (7.3)	7.47 (8.2)
Taiwan	28.75 (7.3)	5.40 (6.5)	5.85 (6.4)
Japan	27.52 (7.0)	4.44 (5.4)	7.59 (8.3)
Singapore	18.53 (4.7)	3.78 (4.6)	8.67 (9.5)

Sources: *China Statistical Yearbook 1996*, Beijing: China Statistical Publishing House, p. 597; *Almanac of China's Foreign Economic Relations and Trade*, Beijing and Hong Kong, various years.

Korea, Hong Kong investors account for 38 per cent of the province's US$28.3 billion in contracted investment—more than four times the total invested from Korea. Hong Kong has been the source of more than 50 per cent of the foreign investment committed to the Pudong area projects in Shanghai.

China's Jiangsu Province, which is not in Hong Kong's immediate hinterland, has received substantial press attention due to the investments by Singapore in the Suzhou and Wuxi township projects. In fact, Hong Kong is a much larger investor in the province than is Singapore. Out of contracted investment in Jiangsu totalling US$34 billion between 1985 and 1995, Hong Kong investors accounted for nearly one-half—about US$16.5 billion. There are no comprehensive comparisons with other international investors for this whole period, but in 1994, when Hong Kong investors accounted for investment of US$3 billion, Taiwan accounted for just under US$1 billion, the United States for less than US$900 million, Japan for less than US$850 million, and Singapore for just over US$750 million.[31]

Table 3.5 Top Foreign Investors in Selected Mainland Chinese Provinces

Cumulative Contracted Foreign Direct Investment, Billions of US Dollars

Liaoning (1985–95)		Shandong (1990–95)		Shanghai (1979–95)	
Investor	Investment	Investor	Investment	Investor	Investment
Total	16.10	Total	28.28	Total	34.27
Hong Kong	6.48 (40.2%)	Hong Kong	10.66 (37.7%)	Hong Kong	16.98 (49.6%)
Japan	2.99 (18.6)	Korea	2.46 (8.7)	Japan	3.26 (9.5)
US	1.77 (11.0)	US	2.35 (8.3)	US	3.12 (9.1)
Korea	1.16 (7.2)	Taiwan	2.26 (8.0)	Taiwan	1.78 (5.2)

Sources: Statistical Yearbook of Liaoning, Beijing: China Statistical Publishing House, various years.
Statistical Yearbook of Shandong, Beijing: China Statistical Publishing House, various years.
Statistical Yearbook of Shanghai 1996, Beijing: China Statistical Publishing House, 1996, p. 127.

Credit Lyonnais has identified 62 companies listed on the Hong Kong stock exchange that intend to invest almost US$20 billion in mainland China in the 1996 to 1998 period.[32] (Their short-list of firms is drawn from companies listed on the Hong Kong Stock Exchange, but excludes Mainland Chinese 'H-share' companies.) These same companies invested US$6.5 billion in 1992 to 1995, with another US$7 billion tied up in ongoing projects. While 58 per cent of this investment was in property development—which clearly matches Hong Kong's corporate strengths with mainland China's urgent needs—a further 38 per cent was in infrastructure-building, mainly energy and road-building.

The wide-ranging infrastructure projects undertaken by Hong Kong firms have included: the highly publicized investments by Gordon Wu's Hopewell Holdings in the 123-kilometre, US$2.3 billion Guangzhou–Shenzhen superhighway; investments by the power subsidiary Consolidated Electric Power Asia (CEPA) (sold by Gordon Wu to the United States power generation group, Southern Co., in October 1996) in power plants at Shajiao in Guangdong; the mass housing and bridge and road projects undertaken by Cheng Yu-tung's New World Development and its affiliate New World Infrastructure; and investments by Li Ka-shing's Hutchison group in ports in Shanghai and Yantian. From 1996 to 1998, Hutchison plans to invest US$1.23 billion in projects on the Mainland, with Hopewell planning to invest more than US$2.69 billion, and the New World Group planning investments of more than US$4.1 billion. Property development and infrastructure projects account for 96 per cent of the planned US$18 billion investment in the Mainland by Hong Kong's leading mainland China investors.[33]

Much of the rest of Hong Kong's investment on the Mainland has come in manufacturing, often by smaller investors not captured in the Credit Lyonnais survey. Factories with Hong Kong funding employ an estimated five million workers on the Mainland. Many of these factories are involved in export processing, in which the Mainland leases to a Hong Kong manufacturer the land and buildings needed for operation, and provides the labour force. The Hong Kong company supplies necessary equipment, which is regarded as leased to the project. Since ownership remains with the Hong Kong company, no tariff is paid on the import of the equipment. Raw materials and semi-manufactures can be imported tariff-free as long as the finished goods are re-exported after processing. By 1993, the output of Hong Kong-invested or contracted export-processing operations was on the order of US$36 billion[34], or more than three times recorded manufacturing output in Hong Kong.

Hong Kong is a crucial business services hub for mainland China. It is a complete business service centre for the Mainland and the logistics centre for much of South China. No community has deeper practical knowledge of how to do business in the world's most populous market, and Hong Kong's professional service providers are applying their expertise to facilitate business there. Many Hong Kong law, accountancy, and consulting firms have extensive office networks across mainland China which are able to provide practical, on-the-ground help. One leading accounting firm alone employs 200 people based in Hong Kong to perform due diligence on Mainland Chinese companies.

Hong Kong professional expertise is also helping mainland China develop its own business services sector from the ground up. The Mainland's embryonic professional associations for law and accountancy have turned to Hong Kong for guidance on curricula for law and accounting degrees, and for locally based training of Chinese lawyers and accountants in joint-venture law and international auditing practices. The Hong Kong Federation of Insurers is helping the Mainland's insurance companies in defining the structure and goals of a nation-wide insurance industry federation.[35] Principles of corporate governance are being disseminated on the Mainland through the efforts of the Hong Kong Institute of Company Secretaries, which has signed a memorandum of understanding with the Shenzhen Stock Exchange and offered seminars to Mainland corporate secretaries.[36]

Hong Kong also plays an important role as an intermediator for trade and investment between Taiwan and the Mainland. No direct trade or other direct forms of commercial or official contact have been allowed between Taiwan and the Mainland since the Communist victory in 1949, and the retreat of the Kuomintang to Taiwan. For many years, this stand-off was driven by fears on both sides over subversion and 'fifth-column' activism. Taipei allowed the resumption of indirect trade and travel in the late 1980s, though no direct shipping is allowed, nor are there direct air links. Since the opening of indirect trade and investment the authorities in Taipei have become more concerned about economic domination by the Mainland.

Over 3,000 Taiwan-controlled companies operate in Hong Kong, and an estimated 50,000 Taiwan nationals work in the territory. These companies account for the lion's share of the estimated US$25 billion Taiwan investment on the Mainland, and are the principal conduits for two-way trade of about US$20 billion per year. Hong Kong serves as the principal transit point for business and leisure travel by the Taiwanese to mainland China, all of it indirect. In fact, Hong Kong provides the role of transit point for much more than Taiwan–PRC travel. Overall, Hong Kong provides the entry or exit point for 80 per cent of the foreign business and leisure visitors to mainland China.

Hong Kong's firms have been a driving force not just in the Mainland's development, but also its emergence into a broader, integrated economy encompassing mainland China, Hong Kong, and Taiwan—an area known by international economists as the Chinese Economic Area or China Circle. There are three 'concentric layers' to the China Circle: the Greater Pearl River Delta as the first layer; Greater South China including Hong Kong, Guangdong, Fujian, and Taiwan as the second layer; and at the outer perimeter, Greater China including Hong Kong, Taiwan, and all of mainland China. Through the efforts of its dynamic firms, large and small, Hong Kong has emerged as the 'pivot' for the integration of these three layers into one of the world's dominant economic forces.[37]

THE CHINESE MAINLAND AS A DRIVER OF THE HONG KONG ECONOMY

Hong Kong's relationship with the Chinese Mainland, of course, has not been a one-way street. The Mainland has always exerted an important, if not decisive influence on the Hong Kong economy. Hong Kong's shifts from an entrepôt to a manufacturing enclave, and to a sophisticated provider of services and manufacturing activities, have been triggered by the closing and opening of mainland China's economy to the rest of the world. The Mainland has had a crucial direct role in the Hong Kong economy as well. The Mainland has long been a source of food, water, and staples for Hong Kong, so much so that in the last few decades the Mainland could have seriously crippled, and arguably taken over Hong Kong, simply by cutting off its water supply.[38] The economic opening that began in the late 1970s triggered a transformation of the Hong Kong economy that has left it more prosperous and more interdependent with the Mainland. At the same time, Mainland Chinese companies also have become major players in the Hong Kong economy in their own right.

More than 2,000 Mainland Chinese companies have opened operations in Hong Kong to compete in the Hong Kong economy, to win access to world markets, and in some cases to receive preferential treatment as 'foreign' investors back on the Mainland.[39] China's corporate presence permeates the economy, as shown by the long-standing presence in the territory of the 13 'sister banks' clustered around the Bank of China, one of Hong Kong's three note-issuing banks, and the massive state trading corporations like China Resources (controlled by the Ministry of Foreign Economic Relations and Trade, MOFERT), China Merchants' Steam Navigation (controlled by the Ministry of Communications), and China Travel (which has a monopoly of all cargo arriving in or leaving Hong Kong by rail). The giant conglomerate China International Trade and Investment Corporation (CITIC) has investments in most sectors of the economy, including Cathay Pacific Airways, Hongkong Telecommunications, and Ka

Wah Bank. Guangdong International Trust and Investment Corporation (GITIC), a corporate arm of the Guangdong government, is active in trading, manufacturing, and services. Other Chinese firms active in Hong Kong include provincial and municipal trading companies, and 22 'red *hongs*' listed on the Hong Kong stock exchange.

As more Mainland Chinese companies list in Hong Kong, they, too, are using Hong Kong as a springboard for foreign investment, using as financial intermediaries not just the Bank of China-linked 'sister banks,' but also building relationships with global investment banking groups like Salomon Brothers and Morgan Stanley. For example, Jiangxi Copper, mainland China's largest copper producer, plans a US$200 million initial public offering in Hong Kong in 1997—one of up to 20 Mainland companies that are likely to be allowed to list in Hong Kong. Datang Power plans a US$300–350 million offering in both Hong Kong and London, while China Eastern Airlines based in Shanghai hopes to raise US$400 million with offerings in Hong Kong and New York.[40]

Mainland China is now the fourth largest investor in Hong Kong. At the end of 1995, Mainland-backed firms registered in Hong Kong held assets valued at US$50 billion. Mainland-linked banks and financial services groups hold one-fourth of the territory's bank deposits and one-fifth of insurance premiums. They account for a quarter of the territory's cargo by volume, and almost one-eighth of all construction contracts. China's 'red *hongs*' account for almost 5 per cent of the market capitalization of the Hong Kong Stock Exchange, and with more companies planning to list in 1997 and beyond, this share is likely to rise rapidly in the future.[41] In addition, Chinese companies have a further US$20 billion or so invested in more than 5,000 affiliates around the world—with much of this investment intermediated through Hong Kong.[42]

The economies of Hong Kong and mainland China have developed increasingly close links in recent years and from an economic standpoint, their integration is very far along. The result has been a division of labour and symbiosis in which both have benefited. The Mainland has developed certain aspects of its economy far faster than would have been possible otherwise and Hong Kong has had the advantage of large demand for its goods and services and a supply base for its manufacturing industries. The two economies have become interdependent to an extent not usually understood in the West. Such interdependence is clearly one of Hong Kong's strengths, but at the same time constitutes a significant challenge, for if Hong Kong were to become 'just another Chinese city' as a result of this growing interdependence, then its distinctive strengths could be dissipated.

HONG KONG'S ROLES

As we have seen, Hong Kong and its firms have taken on many economic roles. Hong Kong has emerged as a packager and integrator of activities for the global economy, a leading source of foreign investment, a centre for overseas firms, the capital of the overseas Chinese business network, and a driver of the Mainland economy. In the process, Hong Kong firms have put themselves at or near the forefront of global trends toward virtual firms, dispersed manufacturing, boundaryless organizations, rapid response, and competing on capabilities transferable across businesses.[43] Hong Kong is evolving an economy based on managing information flows to its far-flung customers, to its regional investments, across its dispersed manufacturing networks, and between local and foreign operations of overseas firms. If, as the business gurus tell us, these are the keys to success in the future, then Hong Kong is well-positioned.

Hong Kong's roles also put it squarely in the centre of some of the most important economic interactions and trends in the world today. The territory—a home to Western multinationals and dynamic local firms, a nerve centre for Western investments in the region, and a matchmaker between demand in Europe and North America and sources of supply in Asia— is a place where Asia meets North America and Europe. As a packager and integrator of manufacturing activities and infrastructure projects, it is a place where the industrialized world meets the developing world. Hong Kong's roles as capital of the overseas Chinese business network, foreign investor, packager and integrator of management and services, and as a driver of the Mainland economy, make it a place where Asian interests come together and where mainland China interacts with the rest of the world. In short, Hong Kong is where East meets West, East meets East, North meets South, developing nations meet industrialized nations, and mainland China meets everywhere else. What is more, Hong Kong and its firms are not idle spectators at the great economic cross-roads of the world— they create or manage many of the important interactions.

NOTES

1   Amy K. Glasmeier, 'Flexibility and Adjustment: The Hong Kong Watch Industry and Global Change', *Growth and Change*, 25 (Spring 1994): 237.

2   Hong Kong Trade Development Council, *Hong Kong's Trade and Trade Supporting Services*, April 1996, p. 5.

3   Hong Kong Trade Development Council, 'Construction Giant Expands into Region', http://www.tdc.org.hk/hktrader/9606/9606p51.html.

4   See James Xiaoning Zhan, 'Transnationalization and Outward Investment: The Case of Chinese Firms', *Transnational Corporations*, 4, 3 (5 December 1995): Figure 1, p. 71; see also United Nations Conference on Trade and Development (UNCTAD), *UNCTAD World Investment Report 1995: Transnational Corporations and Competitiveness*, New York and Geneva: United Nations, 1995, p. 59.

5   Ezra F. Vogel, *One Step Ahead in China: Guangdong under Reform*, Cambridge, Mass.: Harvard University Press, 1989, pp. 56–7.

6   Authors' survey of multinational companies in Hong Kong, 1996.

7   Hong Kong is itself a significant market for some multinational firms, in such areas as banking and finance, engineering services, and luxury consumer goods.

8   Hong Kong Government Industry Department, *Report on the 1995 Survey of Regional Representation*, p. 9.

9   Ibid., p. 8.

10   Ibid.

11   Overall, Japanese firms are the leading foreign investors in Hong Kong's manufacturing sector, accounting for 34 per cent of total value, followed by firms from the United States (27 per cent) and China (10 per cent). Hong Kong Government Industry Department, *1995 Survey of External*

Investment in Hong Kong's Manufacturing Industries, December 1995, p. 1.

12 See, for example, Survey Research Hongkong Ltd. (SRH), *AmCham Business Confidence Survey: Management Report*, Hong Kong, November 1995, p. 10; see also Hong Kong Trade Development Council, 'Hong Kong as a Regional Sourcing and Distribution Base: Results of a Survey on Japanese Companies in Hong Kong', January 1996, p. 8.

13 Friedrich Wu and Sin Yue Duk, '(Overseas) China, Inc.', *The International Economy* (January/February 1995): 33–5, cited in Murray Weidenbaum and Samuel Hughes, *The Bamboo Network: How Expatriate Chinese Entrepreneurs Are Creating a New Economic Superpower in Asia*, New York: The Free Press, 1996, p. 24.

14 The great majority of overseas Chinese in South-East Asia, except for Thailand, Vietnam, Cambodia, and Laos, are Hokkien and Hakka who originated from Fujian Province, while in Hong Kong, the Cantonese predominate. Commonwealth of Australia, East Asia Analytical Unit, Department of Foreign Affairs and Trade, *Overseas Chinese Business Networks in Asia*, Sydney, 1995, p. 25.

15 Ronald Skeldon, 'Hong Kong in an International Migration System', in Ronald Skeldon (ed.), *Reluctant Exiles? Migration from Hong Kong and the New Overseas Chinese*, Hong Kong: Hong Kong University Press, 1994, p. 24.

16 Vogel, *One Step Ahead*, p. 57.

17 Kevin Rafferty, *City on the Rocks*, rev. edn., London: Penguin Books, 1991, Chapter 2, quoted in Michael Yahuda, *Hong Kong: China's Challenge*, London: Routledge, 1996, p. 32.

18 Weidenbaum and Hughes, *The Bamboo Network*, pp. 45–6, 48.

19 Ibid., pp. 43–4, and Commonwealth of Australia, *Overseas Chinese Business Networks*, pp. 167–8.

20 Commonwealth of Australia, *Overseas Chinese Business Networks*, p. 321.

21 Ibid., p. 176.

22 Weidenbaum and Hughes, *The Bamboo Network*, p. 46.

23 Commonwealth of Australia, *Overseas Chinese Business Networks*, pp. 198–9.

24 Ibid., pp. 166–7.

25 Ibid., p. 97.

26 John Naisbitt, *Megatrends Asia: Eight Asian Megatrends that are Reshaping the World*, New York: Simon & Schuster, 1996, p. 23.

27 Commonwealth of Australia, *Overseas Business Networks*, p. 97.

28 Naisbitt, *Megatrends Asia*, p. 23.

29 Based on first four months of 1996. Hong Kong Trade Development Council, 'Market Profile on Mainland China', http://www.tdc.org.hk/main/china.html, last updated 20 August 1996.

30 Hong Kong Trade Development Council, 'Economic & Trade

Information on Hong Kong', http://www.tdc.org.hk/main/economic.html#4, last updated 2 September 1996.

31   Hong Kong Trade Development Council, Research Department, citing various sources including *Jiangsu Statistical Yearbook 1996*, Beijing: China Statistical Publishing House, 1996, Table 15.11, p. 265, and *Almanac of China's Foreign Economic Relations and Trade 1996-97*, Hong Kong: China Advertising and Exhibition Co., Ltd., 1996, p. 262.

32   Credit Lyonnais Securities, Hong Kong Research, 'China Jump II: Hong Kong's HK$140bn China Jump', Hong Kong, March 1996, p. 1.

33   Ibid.

34   Yun-wing Sung; Pak-wai Liu; Yue-chim Richard Wong; and Pui-king Lau, *The Fifth Dragon: The Emergence of the Pearl River Delta*, Singapore: Addison Wesley Publishing Co., 1995, p. 229.

35   Hong Kong Trade Development Council, 'Industry Body Formed', *Hong Kong Trader: A TDC Newspaper*, http://www.tdc.org.hk/hktrader/9608/9608pb3.html.

36   Nick Tabakoff, 'Mainland Firms' Secretaries Get Training Boost', *Sunday Morning Post: Business Post* (29 September 1996): 5.

37   Yun-wing Sung, et al., *The Fifth Dragon*, p. 236.

38   William H. Overholt, *China: The Next Economic Superpower*, London: Weidenfeld & Nicolson, 1993, p. 134.

39   See *UNCTAD World Investment Report 1995*, p. 59.

40   Sophie Roell, 'Realism Enters Chinese Listing', *Financial Times* (9 September 1996): 31.

41   Hong Kong Trade Development Council, 'Market Profile on Mainland China', http://www.tdc.org.hk/main/china.html, last updated 20 August 1996.

42   China's outflows rose in 1995 to US$3.5 billion—behind only Hong Kong and Taiwan in Asia. According to James Xiaoning Zhan at the UNCTAD Division on Transnational Corporations and Investment, China's outward investment has averaged US$2.4 billion since 1990. See Zhan, 'Transnationalization and Outward Investment: The Case of Chinese Firms', Figure 1, p. 71.

43   See S. Davis and J. Botkin, 'Coming of Knowledge-Based Business', *Harvard Business Review*, 72, Reprint No. 94505 (1 September 1994); L. Hirschhorn and T. Gilmore, 'New Boundaries of the "Boundaryless" Company', *Harvard Business Review*, 70, Reprint No. 92304 (1 May 1992); C. K. Prahalad and G. Hamel, 'Core Competence of the Corporation', *Harvard Business Review*, 68, Reprint No. 90311 (1 May 1990); J. F. Rayport and J. J. Sviokla, 'Exploiting the Virtual Value Chain', *Harvard Business Review*, 73, Reprint No. 95610 (1 November 1995); and G. Stalk Jr.; P. Evans; and L. E. Shulman, 'Competing on Capabilities: The New Rules of Corporate Strategy', *Harvard Business Review*, 70, Reprint No. 92209 (1 March 1992).

4 ELEMENTS OF THE HONG KONG ECONOMIC SYSTEM

The economic system of each nation or region underpins the competitiveness of its firms and industries. Many of the elements of the Hong Kong system have been described in previous chapters. The purpose of this chapter is to highlight additional parts of the system that have contributed to the competitive success of the Hong Kong economy. Hong Kong's strong economic performance has been built upon several sources of advantage, including its location in the heart of the most dynamic economic area in the world, advantageous infrastructure and financial markets, and the development of clusters of related industries. The elements underlying these advantages are: favourable institutional structures that set and enforce clear rules of the game on a level playing field; motivated and hardworking individuals who continually strive for success; and a prevailing ethos that has fostered and stimulated economic development. The result has been a uniquely enterprising economy and culture.

INPUTS TO INDUSTRY

Hong Kong derives advantage in international markets from a select set of inputs. Prominent among them are its location and geography, its infrastructure, and its financial system. Since Hong Kong is natural-resource poor (not surprising, given its small size) it must import essentially all of its raw materials and energy—and most of its capital goods and many components for its industries. Hong Kong's ability to build a world-class economy, despite its lack of natural resources and its permanent shortage of land, springs in part from its success in capitalizing upon its endowments and using its limitations as a springboard for outward-looking strategies. Across its economic system, Hong Kong has repeatedly turned disadvantage into advantage.

Location and Geography

Hong Kong's strategic location for trade and its excellent harbour are the foundations on which many advantages have been built. The territory is ideally situated to serve as a sea and air hub for trade into and out of South China and East Asia and is within five hours flight of more than half of the world's population. (See Figure 4.1.) The harbour was the principal attraction of Hong Kong for the British traders who set up the Hong Kong colony one and a half centuries ago. Hong Kong's exceptional deep water access, critical for the present and future generations of cargo vessels, sets it apart from many ports in Asia, such as Shanghai and Bangkok, that do not have sufficient deep water capability to handle large, modern container ships. Hong Kong's location and natural landscape have provided advantages in sea cargo, air cargo, and tourism, as well as in the whole range of trade and investment-related activities involving mainland China and the region.

Because buildable land in Hong Kong is in short supply, Hong Kong is the most densely populated city in the world and its office rents and housing costs are very expensive by world standards.[1] Numerous reclamation projects carried out over the last century have added substantially to Hong Kong's usable land mass, but at a cost. Today, expensive waterfront land reclamation projects are under way on Hong Kong Island and Kowloon to help accommodate future development. The shortage of usable land and high cost of land in Hong Kong has had a direct impact on industrial development and firm strategies. It has discouraged land-intensive, heavy

Figure 4.1 Hong Kong's Location

Source: Cathay Pacific Airways.

manufacturing industries in favour of light manufacturing and services, has led to the use of flatted (multi-story) factories, and to the relocation of production processes to lower-cost sites in the Pearl River Delta and elsewhere.

Lack of land has forced Hong Kong and its firms to use land efficiently. High-rise office towers and apartment blocks dominate the skyline. Under the impetus of an acute land shortage and rapidly growing demand, Hong Kong's container terminal operators recently improved their throughput by 25 per cent in a single year, using innovative cargo management techniques without expanding their footprint. Similarly, limited space at the airport has caused innovation and improvement in Hong Kong's air cargo handling capability. HACTL (the sole cargo handler at Hong Kong's Kai Tak Airport) turned tradition on its head by arranging the air cargo handling system in its second terminal vertically rather than horizontally. In the process, it created one of the most efficient, if not the most efficient system in the world.

Infrastructure

Hong Kong has substantial infrastructure strengths in many areas, including its sea port, airport, and telecommunications system. Hong Kong's sea port is the world's busiest container port, handling approximately 12.6 million TEUs (20-foot equivalent container units, a measure of container throughput) in 1995, up more than 13 per cent from the year before, and more than double its throughput in 1991. Hong Kong also is 18 per cent more efficient on a per-berth basis than Singapore and twice as efficient as most ports in the United States. Though Hong Kong's port charges are expensive, services are considered reliable and efficient (with turnaround times of 12 hours), as are all the documentation procedures required for traded cargo. The port of Hong Kong has one of the densest route networks of any major port, allowing shippers to reach more destinations efficiently than from virtually anywhere else in the world.

Hong Kong's port operators are private entities that have

purchased the right by public auction or private tender to reclaim land, develop the facilities, and operate them. The three main operators, which operate Hong Kong's eight container terminals, will be joined by a fourth consortium when Container Terminal Nine (CT9) is opened. The private management by multiple operators in Hong Kong's port, which the government has supported as a way to ensure efficiency, is unique among the major ports of the world. A government agency, the Port Development Board, develops plans in consultation with industry experts to try to match port supply with cargo demand. Plans also have been drawn up for terminals Ten through Fifteen. The latest government projections place port traffic at 31 million TEUs by 2006 and 36 million TEUs by 2011.[2] In addition, a new river trade terminal for cargo arriving from ports along the Pearl River is expected to provide 800 metres of quay wall by 1999 and another 2,200 metres by the year 2000.[3]

Hong Kong's Kai Tak airport was the third busiest in the world for international passenger traffic and the world's second busiest for international air cargo in 1995. In 1995, Kai Tak handled 27.4 million passengers, up 8.7 per cent from 1994, and 1.46 million tonnes of cargo, up 12.8 per cent from 1994.[4] Hong Kong has perhaps the most extensive set of aviation links in the region. It is the home of three airlines: Cathay Pacific, the dominant international carrier; Dragonair, which flies to seven mainland China cities and seven other destinations in Asia; and Air Hong Kong, an all-cargo airline. A total of 60 airlines operate almost 2,700 flights per week between Hong Kong and 100 cities world-wide.

Kai Tak, a small airport located in the heart of crowded Kowloon and dating from the 1940s, has been outstripped by the airport infrastructures of many cities around the world. It is scheduled to be replaced in April 1998 by a major new airport at Chek Lap Kok. Until then, because Kai Tak has been operating at essentially full capacity, the rapid growth of the past decade will be constrained. Growth in passenger and cargo traffic is expected to jump thereafter. Chek Lap Kok will be able to handle 35 million passengers per year, and 3 million tonnes of air cargo when it first opens. The planned commissioning of a second runway in October 1998, and staged expansion of airport facilities thereafter, will enable the airport at Chek Lap Kok to handle 87 million passengers by the year 2040, along with 9 million tonnes of cargo.

The sophistication of Hong Kong's telecommunications and broadcasting infrastructure plays a key part in underpinning the territory's role as a headquarters hub, as a base for dispersed manufacturing, as a sourcing centre, and as a 'packager' of regionally coordinated services. Hong Kong is the first major city in the world to have an all-digital exchange infrastructure. It has more external telecommunications capacity than either Australia or Japan. This is largely due to immense investment by Hongkong Telecommunications, and its parent Cable & Wireless, in land lines to China, submarine cables, and communications satellites. Hong Kong is Asia's optical fibre hub, giving it huge regional advantages in terms of capacity. Hongkong Telecom has 15 commercial satellites under its management to provide dedicated services to multinational companies, international press organizations, and television channels.[5] Wharf Cable, Hong Kong's first cable TV operator and the world's single largest cable network, offers eleven of its 31 channels via optical fibre only. Hong Kong's STAR TV is the first commercial satellite broadcaster in Asia, reaching 53 countries across Asia and beyond.

With 680 lines per 1,000 people, Hong Kong has the highest teledensity in Asia, except for Japan. It is second to Japan world-wide in its rate of fax use (8.7 fax lines per 100 telephone lines). Approximately one-sixth of the population subscribes to radio pagers—the world's highest per capita rate. With more than one million subscribers to cellular phone services, Hong Kong has one of the highest levels of penetration world-wide.[6]

Because of Hong Kong's superb telecommunications infrastructure, international businesses based in the territory operate with unmatched ease and telecommunications providers offer cheaper international call rates than most competitors. The cost of making international calls is lower in Hong Kong than in Tokyo, Shanghai, Sydney, Singapore, and

Table 4.1 Top Ten Economies by Minutes of Outgoing International Telephone Traffic, 1995

Country/Region	Millions of Minutes	Minutes per Capita
United States	15,100	57.9
Germany	5,244	64.3
United Kingdom	4,111	70.4
Canada	2,870	98.2
France	2,630	45.4
Italy	1,908	33.4
Switzerland	1,739	248.4
Hong Kong	1,692	268.6
Japan	1,559	12.5
Netherlands	1,459	94.7

Source: International Telecommunications Map, produced by *The Financial Times* in association with Salomon Brothers, 'Survey on International Telecommunications', *The Financial Times* (19 September 1996): XXII.

Taipei (see Appendix, 'Telecommunications Costs'). It is not surprising, given Hong Kong's small size and the international orientation of its people and industry, that the territory's international telephone usage rates in 1995 surpassed, by far, those of the United States and Japan. (See Table 4.1). According to Hongkong Telecom, more than 450 overseas firms are using the territory as a hub for originating, terminating, and processing voice and data traffic, and transmitting such traffic to other places in the region.[7]

Hong Kong's telecommunications sector is developing at a rapid pace. The local fixed network, formerly operated under an exclusive franchise by the Hong Kong Telephone Company, was opened to competition in 1995. Within a year, three new operators—Hutchison Communications Limited, New T&T Hong Kong Limited, and New World Telephone Limited—entered the sector, and more are following. The mobile service sector also is expanding; the government plans to issue new licenses for personal communications and cordless access services. Liberalization of the sector is resulting in lower prices to the consumer, especially for international calls, and a broader range of service offerings. Annual investment in Hong Kong's telecommunications infrastructure is expected to total US$1.54 billion in 1996/7, not counting investments that follow upon the granting of new licenses in the mobile service sector.[8]

Capital and Finance

Hong Kong's capital markets are advanced and its capital flows substantial. Hong Kong's stock market—with 567 listed companies and a market capitalization of US$383 billion as of 30 September 1996—is the second largest in Asia after Tokyo and the eighth largest in the world in terms of market capitalization.[9] Hong Kong's volume of external banking transactions is the fifth largest in the world.[10] The territory boasts one of the world's most sophisticated financial markets and a very sophisticated financial services infrastructure.[11] Its banking and capital markets reduce the worry and the risk so often linked with cross-border business, and provide the leading location for raising funds for ventures across the region. The Hong Kong stock market offers international investors greater depth and liquidity than any other Asian market outside Japan. These strengths have made Hong Kong the ideal location for Hong Kong companies, Mainland Chinese companies, and a growing number of regional multinationals, to list and to raise capital. As of mid-November 1996, the Hong Kong Stock Exchange listed 22 Mainland (H-share) companies.

Eighty-five of the world's 100 biggest banks have a presence in Hong Kong. In total, about 500 foreign-owned licensed banks, restricted license banks, and deposit-taking companies have a presence in the territory.[12] Thomson Bank-Watch, the United States bank rating agency, recently identified Hong Kong as the home of the Asia–Pacific region's ten best performing banks in a 1995 survey of 300 banks based in 16 economies around the region.[13] In addition, 293 overseas securities and commodity trading firms, 122 overseas insurers, and 1,277 unit trusts and mutual funds operate in Hong Kong. In 1995, Hong Kong's foreign exchange market ranked fifth in the world, surpassing Switzerland, with an average daily turnover of US$91 billion.

In 1995, Hong Kong received about US$2.1 billion in inbound investment inflows, less than Thailand (US$2.3 billion), and significantly less than Indonesia (US$4.5 billion), Singapore (US$5.3 billion), and Malaysia (US$5.8 billion).[14] Hong Kong has slipped down the regional league table as a destination for investment inflows in recent years, largely for two reasons: large-scale investment in plant and equipment within the territory has declined; and multinational companies operating in Hong Kong increasingly tend to meet local investment needs by reinvesting locally generated earnings. Mainland China, of course, is in a league of its own, attracting US$37.5 billion in investment inflows in 1995 (almost 58 per cent of all foreign direct investment in Asia), up from almost US$34 billion in 1994.[15]

Hong Kong is Asia's leading centre outside Japan for raising venture capital, with total assets under management of more then US$8 billion as of mid-1996. Among the 15 venture capital funds launched in Hong Kong in 1995 (which raised altogether US$2 billion), eight were focused on enterprises in China, accounting for US$1 billion of the total. Just under three-quarters of the capital raised in 1995 went into property or infrastructure ventures, and the remainder involved consumer-related and industrial products.[16]

In terms of company financing, family funds and local banks have been key to the foundation and subsequent growth of many Hong Kong companies. Extended Hong Kong families often view themselves as a single economic unit, and often supply funds for the business ventures of their own members. The local banking sector also has played an important role. The Hongkong and Shanghai Bank (HSBC) has been particularly important in the territory's economic development, frequently backing large projects or enterprises, helping out local companies that might be facing difficulties, and operating almost as a development bank, among its other activities. This combination of sources is effective in making capital available to business: *The World Competitiveness Yearbook* ranked Hong Kong second world-wide in terms of the availability of venture capital for business development, after the United States; second world-wide (after Switzerland) in offering favourable costs of capital; and second world-wide (after Luxembourg) in the banking sector's positive influence on industry.[17]

Due to low tax rates for corporations and individuals, it is easier to accumulate retained earnings (or personal earnings) to finance new businesses and business growth in Hong Kong than perhaps anywhere else in the world. This has allowed some family companies and groups to grow quite large and to diversify into a wide range of businesses without diluting their control by issuing large amounts of equity or without amassing large bank debts. (See Appendix, 'Corporate Taxation'.)

Capital Goods and Components

It should be noted that Hong Kong produces relatively little in the way of machinery or capital goods. Heavy equipment, such as that used in major construction projects, or the cranes in the port, are imported mainly from Japan, or sometimes Korea. Machinery for light manufacturing industries, such as garments, textiles, and electronics, for example, is generally imported from Japan and Western Europe. One exception is injection moulding machines, in which a Hong Kong firm, Chen Hsong Machinery Co. Ltd, is a leader. Given Hong Kong's free-trade environment, and the prominence of Hong Kong in a number of industries, firms from the territory have had easy access to the world's best equipment and machinery, even if it is not produced in Hong Kong.

The development of a number of Asian economies, which have started out by importing equipment and machinery, has shown that economies do not need to be substantial producers of capital goods in order to succeed in a wide range of industries. The key is to have access to critical capital goods on terms and at prices equivalent to major competitors. Hong Kong does not have the history of land-intensive heavy industry or long-term industrial development necessary to succeed in most machinery industries. Since the territory's firms actually are major customers in the industries in which they tend to purchase capital goods, they are assured of relatively quick and comprehensive service. The lack of a local capital goods industry has actually proven to be an advantage in some cases. For example, since Hong Kong does not have local companies in communications switches and other large-scale computer and communications products, it has been free to buy the best equipment available, no matter where in the world it has been produced. In many other places, local firms must buy from protected 'national champions' no matter what the quality or cost.

Hong Kong firms also must import many, if not most, of the components that go into their manufactured products. Hong Kong's open trading environment and efficient logistics operations allow for quick and easy imports of components from anywhere in the world. Only in a few industries—such as electronics, where critical components can sometimes be in short supply—has this tendency to import been a significant disadvantage.

HONG KONG'S CLUSTERS

Hong Kong is the home of a number of dynamic 'clusters', or groups of industries that are related to each other, that draw upon common skill bases or inputs, and reinforce each other's competitive positions through dynamic interaction. This is particularly true in industries or activities that bundle, integrate, or package a wide variety of skills and inputs to create unique combinations. Among Hong Kong's leading clusters are: the property, infrastructure, and development cluster; the financial and business services cluster; the transport and logistics cluster; the light manufacturing and trading cluster; and the tourism cluster. In each case, several related businesses in which Hong Kong is world-class feed off each other and contribute to each other's advantage.

Property, Construction, and Infrastructure Cluster

Nothing could be closer to Hong Kong's economic heart than the cluster of property, construction, and infrastructure-related firms and the professional services that have grown up around them. The contribution of property and construction to GDP has averaged over 24 per cent since 1980, more than the contribution of the manufacturing sector as a whole (23.3 per cent).[18] During the period 1983 to 1992, over 60 per cent of capital investment in Hong Kong annually was in property.[19] It is estimated that more than 35 per cent of bank lending is to the property and construction sector, which surpasses by far the borrowing of any other sector in the economy.[20] Property and construction account for a bigger percentage of total stock market capitalization—estimated by one expert at 45 per cent—than anywhere else in the world.[21] As a result of two decades of escalating property values, property assets have provided much of the collateral for expansion and diversification by Hong Kong companies, both locally and overseas.[22]

A dynamic property, construction, and infrastructure cluster has developed, linking property development and construction groups with engineers, architects, surveyors, and interior designers. Hong Kong has around 1,400 firms engaged in a wide range of engineering and technical services, more than 500 firms active in real estate surveying, valuation, and consultancy, and around 400 architectural design firms. These three sectors as a whole employ an estimated 23,000 persons.[23] The sheer volume of work over the past two decades has been sufficient to make this cluster one of the most dynamic and expert of its kind in the world. As one leading architect noted, 'As an architect, I am involved with six or eight times as many projects as I would be back in the United Kingdom. This large flow of business gives us practical experience that few others can get.' Hong Kong also is an excellent school for the territory's engineering talent, which is considered better than that available elsewhere in Asia outside Japan.

Additional factors specific to Hong Kong have enhanced the

competitive strengths of its local property, construction, and infrastructure cluster. Intense cost pressures in the territory put unusual pressure on developers to complete buildings at speed and at minimum cost, while the territory's difficult building conditions (steep granite slopes and land reclamation) have been the impetus for technical rigour and innovations. In response, local building contractors have developed the ability to accelerate construction by 'suspending' buildings from deep pilings while land is still being formed beneath them, and by extending curtain-walling techniques. Such pressures also have been the impetus for local contractors to upgrade their management systems; more than one hundred Hong Kong contractors have been certified under the ISO 9000 quality management plans. Similarly, Hong Kong's architects have been forced to become extremely efficient in land economics and planning and design productivity.[24]

As Hong Kong's property companies have grown, they have extended their reach beyond Hong Kong's borders. These firms are significant developers on the Chinese Mainland, involved in projects ranging from hotels and shopping complexes to housing projects and port construction. In 1996, according to Credit Lyonnais Securities, property development and infrastructure combined accounted for 96 per cent of Hong Kong's planned investments on the Mainland, which have been valued at US$17.2 billion.[25] That year, the Hong Kong firms with the largest planned investments in property and infrastructure on the Mainland were New World Development, Hopewell Holdings, Henderson Land, Hutchison Whampoa, China Light & Power, New World Infrastructure, Hang Lung Development, and Sun Hung Kai Properties. New World Development's projects on the Mainland, for example, include toll roads, bridges, an airport in the city of Wuhan, and housing units in the northern port city of Tianjin.[26] Following New World's lead, Henderson China Holdings has announced that it will expand its portfolio of property investments on the Mainland by investing in a low-cost housing project in Tianjin.[27]

Hong Kong's firms also have become a significant force behind the private sector infrastructure building that has taken

Figure 4.2   Hong Kong's Infrastructure and Real Estate Cluster

Each entry represents a business in which Hong Kong is a leader on a global or regional basis

off across Asia over the past decade. Companies like Hopewell Holdings and its former subsidiary CEPA are now regional leaders in toll-road building and power plants. In September 1996, Hopewell announced a US$412.2 million joint venture to build and upgrade toll roads in the Philippines, the firm had completed a 350-megawatt power plant in the Philippines, and had contracted to build part of Bangkok's mass transit system.[28] Companies like Wharf Holdings and Hutchison Whampoa are involved in significant port development projects across the region. Great Eagle's Regal Hotels group, and the Hong Kong affiliate of the Malaysian-owned Shangri-La Group, are now significant investors in, and builders of hotels not just in Asia, but world-wide.

Hong Kong's property and construction firms have brought Hong Kong contractors and architects with them into China and throughout the Asia–Pacific region. As a result, Hong Kong contractors have two decades of experience in operating on the Mainland, directly or in joint ventures. Many Hong Kong contractors now have licenses issued by China's Ministry of Construction. More than half of Hong Kong's architectural design firms are engaged in projects outside Hong Kong, mostly in China, where they usually act as design consultants for local architectural firms due to foreign licensing requirements imposed by the Chinese government. (See Figure 4.2.)

Business and Financial Services Cluster

Hong Kong's extensive business and financial services cluster, which accounts for more than 26 per cent of GDP,[29] is a powerful source of competitive advantage, for the service firms themselves, for local and overseas firms operating in Hong Kong, and for a wide spectrum of user industries. This cluster includes legal services and accounting services as well as a dynamic financial services sector encompassing private banking, fund management, corporate finance, currency trading, insurance, venture capital finance, direct corporate investment, and stockbroking.

Hong Kong's business and financial services cluster generates advantages within the cluster itself and across the economy. Throughout Hong Kong's modern history, the financial sector has played a crucial role in channelling funds, both local and overseas, to productive areas in the economy. It finances Hong Kong's dispersed manufacturing and trading operations, complex property deals, and massive transport infrastructure projects. The business and financial services cluster as a whole has facilitated the growth of local firms, and attracted to Hong Kong foreign direct investment and regional headquarters of overseas firms. It also has generated managerial expertise for local and overseas firms.

Internal synergies between the parts of this cluster enhance the competitiveness of Hong Kong's economy. For example, the cluster's law firms have expertise in international taxation, which benefits the local banking sector, while their capabilities in corporate structuring and formation underpin the efficiency of Hong Kong's stock market and brokerage services. The cluster's 'due diligence' industry (the legal, financial, and accounting activities which try to ensure that information supplied by corporations to investors and potential investors is accurate) also promotes stock market transparency. Hong Kong's high concentration of fund managers generates better corporate reporting and more information on local and regional firms; this helps make the stock market more transparent, improves the local stock brokerage industry, and

99

provides deeper capital markets for local firms. The local fund management industry contributes to the development of the local stock market, prompting locally listed companies to improve their information disclosure practices for shareholders. This improved reporting discipline is of value to local companies, in due course, when they need to turn to international credit rating agencies as a precursor to issuing corporate bonds and other debt instruments. This is, in fact, part of a complementary process which has created a virtuous circle, since better information disclosure in the equity market also has been a factor in attracting more fund management business.

The high calibre of locally available business services enhances Hong Kong's allure as a place to operate a business. However, it is not the mere presence of one or another of these services that is so powerfully advantageous to businesses in Hong Kong. Rather, Hong Kong's advantage lies in the strength of its services cluster in its totality—accounting, legal, and financial services, as well as business infrastructure. It is this bundle of successful services that makes Hong Kong such an attractive and efficient place for overseas firms to locate operations, and also allows even small Hong Kong firms to be international in scope.

The complete menu of world-class business services readily available in Hong Kong is an advantage compared with most other cities in Asia and on the Mainland. Only Singapore and Sydney can offer comparable services strengths, and even these cannot be honed to the needs of small businesses, or to business on the Chinese Mainland as are those of Hong Kong.

The Hong Kong business service sector generates specific skills and capabilities that may be transferred to new areas, sometimes in ways that are not immediately apparent. For example, the financial services industry in Hong Kong has built up a reservoir of skills and expertise that has been transferable to cellular communications. Both lines of business are mass retail activities requiring the management of a 'branch network' of customer service outlets. Both require automation, within

Figure 4.3 Hong Kong's Business Services Cluster

Each entry represents a business in which Hong Kong is a leader on a global or regional basis

limits, to help control costs per transaction while remaining 'user friendly' to customers, and both give the operator scope to market different kinds of related services to its large customer base to increase profits at minimal cost. (See Figure 4.3.)

Transport and Logistics Cluster

Hong Kong has an extensive transport and logistics cluster, comprising air cargo, sea cargo, tourism, freight forwarders, and logistics-related services. In addition to its position as an air and sea hub, described above, Hong Kong has the world's largest and among the world's most technologically sophisticated communities of sourcing companies, freight forwarders, and trade financiers. Members of the Hong Kong Shipowners Association control a significant portion of the world's cargo fleet. Its members also include banks, maritime lawyers, adjusters, shipbrokers, shipbuilders, insurers, and surveyors. Hong Kong firms have substantial expertise in trade documentation, trade finance, and associated communications.

101

Figure 4.4 Hong Kong's Transport Cluster

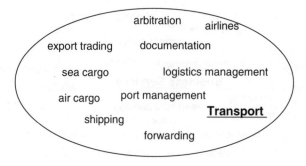

Each entry represents a business in which Hong Kong is a leader on a global or regional basis

Hong Kong's transport and logistics cluster has been linked together by location, history, and infrastructure. All the sectors within this cluster have benefited from the island's advantageous location, as well as its distinct history within the region. During this century, Hong Kong has enjoyed more continuous access to world markets and foreign customers than many of its neighbours. Hong Kong has also been free of some of the problems experienced by Taiwan, enjoying direct air and marine shipping links to, and unfettered business relations with, the Mainland.

Both the air and sea cargo sectors draw advantage from Hong Kong's specialized pool of legal expertise in the area of air and maritime regulations and dispute resolution (Hong Kong is an international arbitration centre for maritime disputes), as well as financial expertise in supplying finance and insurance for air and sea cargo. Hong Kong's logistics services also provide specialized support. Hong Kong's advanced communications infrastructure is another important source of advantage for the transport and logistics cluster, because shippers and customers often want up-to-the-minute information on the whereabouts and arrival times of aircraft and ships. One area in which Hong Kong does not have the regional edge, however, is electronic data interchange (EDI). In the 1980s, Singapore took the lead in developing an integrated

EDI system, TradeNet, that permitted trade documentation to be processed electronically, dispensed with the need for paperwork, and generated huge efficiency gains for agents, freight forwarders, shipping companies, port authorities, government customs agencies, and others. Compared with Singapore, Hong Kong pursued EDI half-heartedly and the lack of a strong EDI system is a disadvantage to Hong Kong's trading firms. (See Figure 4.4.)

Light Manufacturing and Trading Cluster

Hong Kong's light manufacturing and trading cluster comprises the four largest manufacturing industries in Hong Kong by export value—clothing, electronics, textiles, and watches and clocks—as well as plastics, toys, footwear, jewellery, and other consumer goods. This cluster derives powerful advantage from its critical mass. Hong Kong is headquarters to numerous garment, electronics, watches, jewellery, and toy manufacturers, as well as some 100,000 export trading firms. The manufacturing, trading, and logistical expertise of these firms feeds on itself in a virtuous circle. In an important sense, however, this cluster is built more around activities or functions—such as organizing the production chain, designing fashion-sensitive goods, and packaging and integrating inputs and components—than around specific product lines or even industries *per se*. What links together, and generates the extraordinary dynamism of Hong Kong's light manufacturing clusters, is not so much industry-specific investments or positionings, but the ability to develop supplier and customer relationships as well as the common ability to manage a particular type of operation. What might in individual cases look like opportunism and improvisation, hopping from industry to industry, is, in the aggregate, the accumulation of a set of skills that can be applied within and across industries. When viewed across the economy as a whole, this phenomenon reveals a meaningful pattern of competitive advantage.

The 'skills set' typical of the Hong Kong light manufacturing and trading cluster includes the ability to organize flexible

Figure 4.5 Hong Kong's Light Manufacturing and Trading Cluster

garments
jewellery
trade law
management services
Light Manufacturing and Trading
trade finance
export trading
watches   electronics
sea cargo
plastic products
air cargo
toys

Each entry represents a business in which Hong Kong is a leader on a global or regional basis

and efficient production, based on efficient subcontracting networks comprised mainly of small and medium-sized firms. It includes: strong interpretive design skills, such as the ability to interpret and anticipate consumer trends in major foreign markets; and world-class packaging and integrating skills, such as the ability to integrate far-flung sources of demand and supply world-wide into successful consumer products, and to create logistical solutions to sourcing, production, and distribution needs. (See Figure 4.5.)

Tourism Cluster

Another cluster of importance in the Hong Kong economy is centred on tourism, the hotel industry, and a range of tourism-oriented services such as retailing and restaurants. According to Hong Kong government sources, tourism accounted for just under 100,000 jobs at year-end 1992, while the Hong Kong Tourist Association claims rather ambitiously that tourism accounts for 350,000 jobs in the territory. Tourism earnings were estimated at US$9.6 billion in 1995, or 6.7 per cent of GDP, making Hong Kong the world's eighth leading tourism destination by receipts.[30] The territory, which attracted 10.2

million visitors in 1995, is easily Asia's leading tourist destination. In comparison, mainland China attracted 8.3 million international visitors, Singapore 7.6 million, and Thailand 6.6. million. In 1995, Hong Kong's 86 hotels boasted an average, year-round occupancy rate of 85 per cent, a level rarely matched anywhere else. In 1996, tourist arrivals increased to 11.7 million. Although Hong Kong is not the final destination for many of its visitors, the territory derives more revenue from tourism than any other centre in Asia.[31]

Hong Kong boasts one of the densest concentrations of upper-end hotels, restaurants, and retail shopping in the world. In the words of travel writer Robert Kane: 'No geographical space as compact as this one—anywhere—does better by hotels.'[32] Two Hong Kong hotels, the Peninsula and the Mandarin, are synonymous with the finest in luxury world-wide, and they face competition from more than 20 other luxury class hotels—including the Grand Hyatt, J. W. Marriott, Regent, Royal Garden, and the Island Shangri-La. Hong Kong's luxury class hotels are supremely service oriented and compete to meet the world's highest standards in design, construction, maintenance, decoration, staffing, and management. Hong Kong's restaurant sector is also rated among the best in the world.

Hong Kong's hotels, restaurants, and modern retail shopping centres function increasingly as complementary businesses. The city's new hotels have been developed as integral parts of larger retail developments and many generate a large proportion of their revenues through retail operations. To this end, their amenities are designed to be used by a wider public than just hotel guests: hotel lobbies, conference centres, and restaurants play a vital role in the public life. Dramatic examples are the lobbies of the Omni Hong Kong, Marco Polo, and Prince Hotels, which are integrated into the Ocean Centre Complex, one of Asia's largest shopping complexes. Another strategy of the luxury hotels is to offer high category restaurants among their amenities, aimed at the larger community as well as hotel guests.

Tourism is a powerful driver for local infrastructure

Figure 4.6 Hong Kong's Tourism Cluster

Each entry represents a business in which Hong Kong is a leader on a global or regional basis

development, in particular in providing Hong Kong with more and better luxury hotels and hotel services than are available almost anywhere in the world and in providing growth opportunities for the territory's property developers. It has enhanced the international character of the community by attracting foreign visitors, as well as workers and professionals for the hotel and restaurant industries, and has strengthened the local usage of English and Mandarin. The tourist cluster both contributes to and draws upon Hong Kong's role as a trade fair and exhibition hub and boosts its attractiveness as a destination for conference and incentive travel. Hong Kong's superior international telecommunications infrastructure and dense network of air passenger connections are an important foundation for this cluster. (See Figure 4.6.)

Links among Hong Kong's Clusters

One of the interesting aspects of Hong Kong's clusters is the extent to which they interact. The points of greatest overlap between Hong Kong's largest clusters tend to be sectors of the economy with very strong competitive positions in the relevant international markets. In trading, Hong Kong firms take

Figure 4.7   Links Between Hong Kong's Clusters

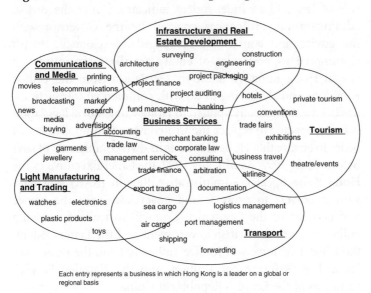

Each entry represents a business in which Hong Kong is a leader on a global or regional basis

advantage of the transportation and logistics cluster, the financial and business services cluster, and the light manufacturing cluster. The fact that Hong Kong is strong in all three clusters greatly strengthens the position of the Hong Kong traders. Trade finance is another activity that draws upon all three of the leading clusters. Tourism, particularly travel to Hong Kong for business, shopping, or conventions, would be another. Again, the interactions and intersections among Hong Kong's clusters provide substantial sources of competitive strength and make the individual industries more robust than they would be otherwise. (See Figure 4.7.)

HONG KONG'S LEGAL INSTITUTIONS

The role of the Hong Kong government has been described in Chapter 2. It is also worth noting the particular role of the Hong Kong legal system in fostering the territory's economic success. The Hong Kong legal system has been based on the rule of law and an independent judiciary. Under the British administration, ordinances enacted by the Governor with the advice and consent of the Legislative Council, British Common Law, and rules of equity are the main sources of law in Hong Kong. In addition, legislation from the United Kingdom, mostly having to do with commercial transactions, has been automatically applied in Hong Kong. Local legislation is being enacted to replace the United Kingdom-applied law in order to ensure that Hong Kong has its own complete set of laws before 1 July 1997. As of 1 July 1997, the Chief Executive of the Hong Kong Special Administrative Region (SAR) will have similar powers to propose and enact laws with the advice and consent of the Legislative Council. Instead of receiving authority from the British government and the Letters Patent, the Chief Executive will receive authority from the Basic Law, Hong Kong's future constitution, and the National People's Congress of the People's Republic of China.

The Hong Kong legal system has been characterized by the strict rule of law and judicial independence. No person or organization has been considered above the law and all have been subject to it. The judiciary has been independent of the executive and legislative branches and has been free to rule as it sees fit no matter the consequences for any individual, organization, or the government itself. The government has been bound by legal decisions and the legal system has been used to protect individuals against excesses of government, as well as society from the excesses of individuals. The International Covenant on Civil and Political Rights (ICCPR) and the International Covenant on Economic, Social, and Cultural Rights (ICESCR) have been applicable in Hong Kong since 1976. The 1984 Sino-British Joint Declaration on the Question of Hong Kong guarantees that the provisions of the two covenants will remain in force after 1 July 1997.

Hong Kong's legal system has been one of the major reasons for its success. Business people have known that agreements would be enforced. Individuals have known that they would be free from coercion and persecution by government. This has been important to the smooth operation of local business, to the attraction of Hong Kong for overseas firms (including firms from North America, Europe, and Japan, as well as overseas Chinese firms from elsewhere in Asia). Freedom of information, speech, and travel have been vital to a number of Hong Kong's industries, such as financial services, communications, trading, and tourism.

HONG KONG'S PEOPLE

As we have seen, Hong Kong's strengths derive from many elements of its economic system, including formal institutions created by government in its various guises. However, these formal institutional arrangements are only backdrops to the human story of Hong Kong's success. Hong Kong's economic strength rests on distinctly social and human ingredients, including powerful and society-wide agendas for personal success and a vibrant outlook on life focused on seizing opportunities and getting ahead. The Hong Kong Chinese are renowned for their optimistic business mentality, their strong work ethic, and their keen bargaining. Upward mobility is a vital force driving the Hong Kong people in all walks of life.

Hong Kong's labour force of 3.1 million people[33] is characterized by a can-do spirit, strong work ethic, willingness to invest in self-improvement, entrepreneurial drive, and business acumen. In the words of a human resources manager for a major multinational firm, 'the can-do attitude in Hong Kong is real and makes it an exciting place to do business.' Hong Kong's engineering industry has shown this spirit in developing novel solutions to pressing problems—for example, as mentioned above in this chapter, suspending buildings from piles while reclamation has proceeded, developing horizontal venting shafts for tunnels, and improving curtain-walling techniques, among others. The same has been true in air and sea cargo as mentioned above. The same is true of the many Hong Kong companies that 'accept unreasonable orders' but then deliver.

The Hong Kong work ethic is strong, as is its motivation for success. Most of the immigrants who streamed into Hong Kong in the 1950s and 1960s and found jobs in nascent local industries had no safety net. Most workers had limited skills with which to earn a livelihood, and were easily replaceable by the unemployed masses around them. To hold on to their jobs, they needed to be able to follow instructions and to work as hard as it took to get the job done.[34] This ethos has laid the foundation for work-force motivation in Hong Kong to the present day.

Hong Kong's labour market has relatively few of the frictions found in labour markets elsewhere. Real wages adjust as quickly, if not quicker than anywhere else in the world. Efficient signals and the lack of a substantial, public safety net encourage people to find jobs fast. In late 1995, for example, a demographic bulge due largely to immigration and Hong Kong people returning from abroad resulted in an unemployment rate of 3.5 per cent, a level virtually unheard of in Hong Kong, where unemployment has been well below 3 per cent for most of the 1990s. Within a few months, however, wages had adjusted, the labour market had absorbed the new entrants, and unemployment had returned to below 3 per cent.

Hong Kong's work-force is highly motivated for success. Upward social mobility is a powerful driver for business endeavour in Hong Kong. In modern times, within ethnic Chinese society, the upper strata of the social ranks have been open to newcomers. Wealth has been an important yardstick of rank, but not the only one. By the 1970s, highest social honours (such as appointment to the Legislative Council) were bestowed on local industrialists who had achieved wealth and distinguished themselves through service to the community.[35] Hong Kong's leading industrialists are generally seen as people not merely to envy, but to emulate. As one businessman observed, 'One Li Ka-shing every ten years is enough inspiration for the whole population.'

Historically, the generally transient nature of Hong Kong's population put a premium on business success. Hong Kong was a place to try to make some money quickly before moving on to somewhere else. This fostered a sense of self-reliance and responsibility. In this uncertain environment, the family unit and entrepreneurship reinforced each other. In Hong Kong, families have helped provide security in the absence of a safety net and provided the nucleus around which entrepreneurial firms were built. As early as the 1950s, enterprising workers left the textile and garment factories to set up their own small stores and production shops, building up significant subcontracting capacity in the textile and garment fields.[36] A similar growth of small subcontracting firms occurred in the watch industry and other light manufacturing sectors.

In the quest for success, Hong Kong entrepreneurs regularly put at stake their own reputations, and those of their families. The sense of personal and familial shame attached to failure is a powerful motive for success in building firms. However, there are no legal or social sanctions that prevent entrepreneurs, even those who have failed before, from trying new ventures and assuming new business risks, and in this respect, Hong Kong is one of the most entrepreneur-friendly places in the world. In response to the statement, 'In your country, risk-taking and individual initiative is fully supported and rewarded,' Hong Kong scored first among the world's major nations in the 1995 IMD *World Competitiveness Report*, above number two, the United States. As for other competitors within the Asia–Pacific region, New Zealand ranked fourth, Malaysia sixth, Taiwan and Thailand tied in seventh place, Singapore eleventh, Korea 29th, and Japan 47th of 48 nations (Russia ranked last).[37] This is one reason that entrepreneurial talent is so highly developed in Hong Kong and why the territory boasts an extremely dense concentration of entrepreneurs. The 1996 *World Competitiveness Yearbook* ranks Hong Kong's managers second in the world in terms of 'sense of entrepreneurship and innovation'.[38]

As a result, people in Hong Kong invest a great deal in education and self-improvement geared to increasing their career opportunities. Experts on the engineering industry noted the marked tendency for Hong Kong engineers constantly to take new evening courses to enhance their knowledge. Specialist training and courses offered by private and public institutions are often oversubscribed. In 1995, more than 1,400 persons took the Certified Financial Analyst course offered by a single university in Hong Kong, even though the CFA certificate is not a professional requirement in Hong Kong. That same year, roughly the same number of students took a similar course in the whole of Singapore, where the CFA is a professional requirement.[39]

Students in Hong Kong's tertiary institutions are selecting areas of study in line with the needs of the marketplace. University statistics on the distribution of graduating students by academic discipline do not show serious imbalances with the needs of industry and commerce within Hong Kong, as occurs in some other nations. Students (and their parents) keep abreast of labour output markets in choosing their lines of study and are heavily influenced by what they perceive their job prospects to be. Hong Kong's Career Expo, run by the Trade Development Council and the Labour Department and geared to information exchange for higher education, attracts one-quarter of a million persons over a three-day period each year.

The availability and quality of management talent is a strong competitive plus for Hong Kong, in part because people in Hong Kong are motivated to succeed and, in part, because managers in Hong Kong have greater experience than most in international business. Senior management in Hong Kong is more likely to have at least ten years of experience in international business than management in any other countries except Sweden and Switzerland.[40] This depth of international business experience stems in part from the highly international activities of Hong Kong's local firms as well as the dense concentration of overseas firms in Hong Kong. The overseas firms, in turn, rank Hong Kong highly in terms of the availability of professional, technical, and managerial skill.[41]

Perceptions and attitudes toward business in Hong Kong tend to support the dynamism of its economy. In Hong Kong, business is an important (perhaps the most important) part of everyday life. It is perceived as providing opportunities for self-improvement and prosperity. A visitor to Pacific Place, a leading shopping mall in the heart of central Hong Kong, on a Sunday in November of 1996 would have seen a sight not seen in many places. The main display in the centre of the mall was not an advertisement or artwork. The centre display was of the winners of a contest for the most professional and complete corporate annual report. More surprising perhaps were the scores of shoppers avidly pouring through the reports. When asked why they were spending their Sunday reading annual reports, the shoppers' most common replies were 'I want to learn from them' and 'Maybe I will find something to help me or my company.'

The Hong Kong view is that wealth is created through the productive efforts of individuals rather than bestowed by natural resources. Hong Kong people tend to believe they must rely on themselves for prosperity rather than on a paternalistic government. Competition is seen widely as a force for improvement, rather than a destructive force, and as essential to economic and personal prosperity. Government's role is widely seen as being to set clear rules of the game (such as property rights, contract enforcement, and transparent regulation), to provide basic infrastructure and indirect support (through education and training, for example), and to ensure separation of the public sector and personnel from the private sector. Hong Kong business people interviewed for this study tended to dismiss these attitudes as a given, assuming that such attitudes are found throughout the world. But our own work has shown that, in fact, Hong Kong attitudes toward business, wealth creation, competition, and government are markedly different from those in many other countries and are a very powerful engine of competitive advantage.[42]

Other observers have noted the nature of Hong Kong's ethos and the special business dynamism of Hong Kong's population. The 1996 *World Competitiveness Yearbook* ranked Hong Kong second out of 46 nations (after Singapore and ahead of Malaysia and Japan) in terms of the degree to which the values of society 'support competitiveness' (such as hard work, tenacity, or

113

loyalty).[43] The view from Singapore, which has adopted an immigration programme to attract Hong Kong people to 'boost its economy', is perhaps more telling. In the words of Lee Kuan-yew, the former Prime Minister of Singapore, Hong Kong people are 'superior, adaptable, flexible,' and capable of adjusting quickly 'to any condition in the world'.[44]

THE ECONOMIC SYSTEM IN PERSPECTIVE

Hong Kong has an economic system that is internally consistent and distinctive. No other economy in the world is quite like it. This system, which in many ways has combined aspects of East and West, has underpinned Hong Kong's prosperity. In fact, Hong Kong business talent cannot operate in a vacuum and does not always thrive under unfavourable business conditions in foreign countries. Hong Kong entrepreneurs who set up new businesses in Canada under that country's Business Immigration Program, for example, have faced difficult challenges posed by unfamiliar aspects of the Canadian economic system, including high taxes, high regulatory costs, and what they perceive as less positive attitudes toward work and enterprise among local employees.[45]

As one local businessman observed, 'Where else in this world is there such an agglomeration of like-minded people and a culture to support them? Yet the same people, transplanted, cannot thrive in Toronto—it is the wrong environment.' There is no single magic seed to be found in Hong Kong that drives success. Rather, success springs from multifaceted interactions within the Hong Kong environment. The nature and extent of the interactions have shaped a system characterized by balance and a set of combinations that have been counter-intuitive, but not counter-productive. These combinations have allowed Hong Kong to prosper. Hong Kong entrepreneurship thrives best in Hong Kong because of the local economic system, where its inputs, clustering, institutions, and ethos together support economic success.

NOTES

1   The total land mass of Hong Kong, including the New Territories, is 1,092 square kilometres, of which 0.2 per cent, or two square kilometres, has been developed for commercial use, 3.8 per cent for residential use, and 11.6 per cent for other uses. Hong Kong Government Information Services, Bob Howlett (ed.), *Hong Kong 1996*, 1996, Appendix 39, p. 468.

2   Hong Kong Port Development Board, *Hong Kong Port Cargo Forecasts 1995*, February 1996, p. 6.19.

3   Hong Kong Government Information Services, *Hong Kong Background Facts*, August 1996, p. 19.

4   Hong Kong Trade Development Council, 'Economic & Trade Information on Hong Kong', http://www.tdc.org.hk/main/economic.html#4, last updated 2 September 1996.

5   Hong Kong Trade Development Council, 'Hong Kong Beyond 1997: A Guide for Business', http://www.tdc.org.hk/beyond97/beyond.html.

6   Hong Kong Office of the Telecommunications Authority, 'Key Statistics for Wireless Services in Hong Kong', http://ofta.gov.hk/stats/statis/st95g261.html.

7   John Ure, 'Telecommunications', in Joseph Y. S. Cheng and Sonny S. H. Lo (eds.), *From Colony to SAR: Hong Kong's Challenges Ahead*, Hong Kong: Chinese University Press, 1995, pp. 432, 438.

8   Hong Kong Government Information Services, *Hong Kong Background Facts*, p. 34.

9   Data current as of 31 October 1996.

10   Hong Kong Government Information Services, *Hong Kong Background Facts*, p. 4.

11   *The World Competitiveness Report 1995* ranked Hong Kong's financial market as the world's most sophisticated, ahead of those of Switzerland, the United States, and the United Kingdom. IMD International and World Economic Forum, *The World Competitiveness Report 1995*, Lausanne, 1995, p. 532.

12   Hong Kong Government Information Services, *Hong Kong Background Facts*, p. 4.

13   Philippe Delhaise, 'Best Banks in Asia 1995', New York: Thomson Bank-Watch, January 1996.

14   United Nations Conference on Trade and Development (UNCTAD), *UNCTAD World Investment Report 1996: Investment, Trade and International Policy Arrangements*, New York and Geneva: United Nations, 1996, Annex Table 1, 'FDI Inflows by Host Region and Economy, 1984–1995', p. 227.

15   Ibid., p. 230.

16 'Guide to Venture Capital in Asia 1996/97', *Hong Kong Asian Venture Capital Journal* (November 1996): 59–60.

17 IMD International, *The World Competitiveness Yearbook 1996*, Lausanne, 1996, pp. 455, 449, 463.

18 Anthony Walker, *Hong Kong in China: Real Estate in the Economy*, Hong Kong: Brooke Hillier Parker, 1995, pp. 28–9, data based on years 1982 through 1991.

19 Ibid., pp. 34–5.

20 Ibid., pp. 36–7, based on the period 1984 to 1993.

21 Ibid., p. 31.

22 In the decade from 1986 to 1996, residential capital values rose fivefold from US$192 to US$979 per square foot, while over the same period, the capital value of prime offices rose sixfold from US$257 per square foot to US$1,602. Data from Colliers Jardine Research, *Asia Pacific Property Trends, Conditions and Forecasts*, Hong Kong: McGraw-Hill, July 1996, ed. X, pp. 59–67.

23 Hong Kong Trade Development Council, *Profiles of Selected Service Industries of Hong Kong*, March 1996 (March 1995 data).

24 K. K. Chan; C. K. Tsang; and Kenneth Lau, 'The Construction Industry Professionals, Their Contribution to Regional Development', Speech Given at the Conference, 'Building Strategic Partnerships for the Future', Singapore, 17 May 1996.

25 Credit Lyonnais Securities, Hong Kong Research, 'China Jump II: Hong Kong's HK$140bn China Jump', Hong Kong, March 1996, p. 1.

26 Erik Guyot, 'New World's Revamping Plan Signals Renewed Faith in China', *Asian Wall Street Journal* (19 September 1995): 3.

27 Elaine Chan, 'Henderson to Invest in Huge Tianjin Plan', *South China Morning Post: Property Post* (18 September 1996): 1.

28 Hong Kong Trade Development Council, 'Hopewell Helps 'Road to Development'', http://www.tdc.org.hk/hktrader/9607/9607p25.html.

29 This figure, for the year 1994, includes financing, insurance, real estate, and business services. Hong Kong Census and Statistics Department, *Estimates of Gross Domestic Product 1961–1995*, March 1996, Table 11, pp. 62–3.

30 World Trade Organization, private communication.

31 Hong Kong Tourist Association, *A Statistical Review of Tourism 1995*, Hong Kong, 1995, p. 19.

32 Robert Kane, *Hong Kong at its Best*, Lincolnwood, Ill.: Passport Books, 1992, p. 44.

33 Data current as of the third quarter of 1995. Hong Kong Government Information Services, Bob Howlett (ed.), *Hong Kong 1996*, 1996, p. 114.

34 Ezra F. Vogel, *One Step Ahead in China: Guangdong under Reform*, Cambridge, Mass.: Harvard University Press, 1989, p. 51.

35 Ibid., p. 55.

36 Ibid., p. 48.

37 IMD International, *The World Competitiveness Report 1995*, p. 635.

38 IMD International, *The World Competitiveness Yearbook 1996*, p. 515.

39 Authors' interview.

40 IMD International, *The World Competitiveness Yearbook 1996*, p. 518.

41 In a recent survey, these factors were rated favourably by about 80 per cent of overseas firms with regional headquarters or offices in Hong Kong. Hong Kong Government Industry Department, *Report on the 1995 Survey of Regional Representation by Overseas Companies in Hong Kong*, December 1995, p. 17.

42 Michael Enright, Antonio Francés, and Edith Scott Saavedra, *Venezuela: The Challenge of Competitiveness*, New York: St. Martins Press, 1996, pp. 437–40.

43 IMD International, *The World Competitiveness Yearbook 1996*, p. 581.

44 Reported in *The Straits Times*, 13 January 1990, and quoted in Chan Kwok Bun, 'The Ethnicity Paradox: Hong Kong Immigration in Singapore', in Ronald Skeldon (ed.), *Reluctant Exiles? Migration from Hong Kong and the New Overseas Chinese*, Hong Kong: Hong Kong University Press, 1994, p. 309.

45 Josephine Smart, 'Business Immigration to Canada: Deception and Exploitation', in Ronald Skeldon (ed.), *Reluctant Exiles? Migration from Hong Kong and the New Overseas Chinese*, Hong Kong: Hong Kong University Press, 1994, p. 116.

5 THE COMPETITIVENESS OF HONG KONG INDUSTRIES

As we have seen, the Hong Kong advantage derives from an economic system and unique combinations that allow Hong Kong and its firms to play an important role in the world economy. But aggregate advantages only contribute to prosperity if they are turned into advantages at the industry level—the level at which firms compete, customers are satisfied, and money is made. Aggregate prosperity is the result of competitive successes and failures across the whole spectrum of industries. In the case of Hong Kong, a small, open economy, this means that the territory's prosperity depends on the *international* competitiveness of its industries and economic activities. In this chapter, we turn to the industry level to analyse Hong Kong's position in international competition, and the drivers of competitive advantage and disadvantage in industries, by providing some brief profiles of the industries studied as part of our research.

METHODOLOGY

The methodology used in our industry studies employs a framework developed and improved in our ten years of similar work in 17 economies around the world.[1] Our work has shown that nations and regions around the world succeed in industries in which the local environment provides superior market

Figure 5.1   Drivers of Competitiveness at the Industry Level

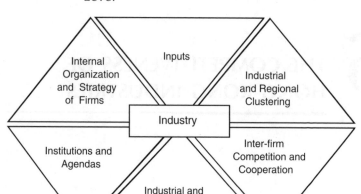

incentives, pressures, and capabilities to innovate and improve, as compared with their competitors in international markets. To understand the dynamics of competitive advantage at the industry and regional levels, we must first understand the industry itself. In particular, we must identify the relevant market (both product market and geographic market), the relevant customers, and the relevant competitors. This allows us to determine the key competitive variables and success factors for the industry, or more simply put, what it is that a company, any company, has to do to address the relevant market, to serve the relevant customers, and to beat the relevant competitors. This step is absolutely critical. No approach to understanding the competitiveness of industries that does not start with an understanding of the nature of the industry is of much use in the real world.

Once we understand what it is that a company has to do well, the question becomes how supportive or unsupportive is the local environment in fostering advantages in those key competitive variables and success factors. We call the major features of a national or regional economy that contribute to the competitive success or failure of local firms the *drivers of competitiveness.* (See Figure 5.1.) For example, the *inputs* available locally—such as natural resources, location, geography, human skills, expertise, technology, capital, infrastructure, capital goods, and produced inputs—can provide advantages to local firms if the nation or region has access to inputs of higher quality or lower cost, or if it can obtain them more quickly or with greater customization than those found in relevant competitor nations or regions. Firms benefit when local *industrial and consumer demand* sends signals that allow or force them to develop skills and capabilities that can be exploited in the international marketplace. This can be due to the presence of large or advanced local demand, demand from local operations of overseas firms, or superior access to advanced foreign demand obtained through trading blocs or original equipment manufacture (OEM) relationships. The *internal organization and strategy of firms* can help or hinder performance in a particular industry. There are certain organizational forms and strategies that work well in particular industries and some that tend to work well in particular nations and regions. Nations and regions tend to succeed in those industries which employ the same organizational forms and strategies that also work well in the nation or the region. In addition, no national or regional source of advantage will be turned into advantages in the marketplace unless firms do so.

Inter-firm competition and cooperation each can be a source of competitive advantage. Competition among local firms, with the local operations of overseas firms, and in the international marketplace can all provide the pressure for firms to invest, innovate, and improve. Inter-firm cooperation can also be an important source of advantage, particularly when small and medium-sized firms find ways to cooperate to achieve scale economies beyond the reach of any one firm in certain activities.

Industrial clustering[2] is a source of advantage where local world-class firms can provide knowledge spillovers, complementary products or services, or have similar requirements that help build a strong supplier base. Clustering is particularly important in industries that provide a complex bundle of goods and/or services.

A nation's or region's *institutions* and *agendas* also influence the competitiveness of its firms and industries. Governmental institutions, legal institutions, political institutions, educational institutions, social institutions, and community institutions all have their impact. Underlying institutions and agendas are sets of perceptions, attitudes, and beliefs that influence the ways in which people deal with each other and do business. These could include, for example, notions about the nature of wealth creation, the desirability of competition, the role of business and government, individual or collective responsibility, and sources of competitive advantage. They can provide sources of advantage or disadvantage for an economy as a whole as well as for individual industries.

Each of the profiles in this chapter has been chosen to illustrate particular aspects of the Hong Kong system. Space considerations preclude us from profiling more than four industries and even these profiles are abstracts. At the end of the chapter, we will take an overview of the complete set of industries studied in order to further identify the patterns of advantage for the Hong Kong economy.

THE HONG KONG SEA CARGO INDUSTRY

For much of the last 150 years, Hong Kong and its economy were defined by its seaport. Hong Kong's rise as a trading post, its annexation by Britain, and its emergence as an entrepôt were all based on its natural location and geographic advantages. Today, those natural advantages are still present, but in addition the Hong Kong sea cargo industry has built its strength on expertise, investments, growing demand, aggressive corporate strategies, a cluster of supporting industries and services, and favourable institutional arrangements. Hong Kong has become the world's busiest container port, with a throughput in 1995 of 12.6 million TEUs (20-foot equivalent units, a measure of containers) compared with 11 million in Singapore.

The Industry

The sea cargo industry provides cargo handling, shipping, and support services to the maritime trade. In Hong Kong's case, the relevant market is for the shipment of goods into and out of Hong Kong and mainland China, which accounts for about 85 per cent of all cargo through the port of Hong Kong. The port of Hong Kong is principally a container port (or a port for shipping goods that can be packed into containers) although it also does handle significant quantities of bulk cargo (raw materials, grain, steel, other commodities, and heavy manufactured goods). The relevant competitors for the Hong Kong industry are ports that can or could handle the same business. This means that the main competitors or potential competitors are other ports on the China coast—such as Yantian just north-east of Hong Kong, or Ningbo near Shanghai. Other ports that potentially could act as transhipment centres for China trade include Kaohsiung in Taiwan (Asia's third leading container port with 1995 throughput of 5 million TEUs), if direct shipping links between Taiwan and mainland China are established, Pusan in Korea, and a few others. Although the ports of Hong Kong and Singapore are often compared in terms of throughput and efficiency, Singapore is too far away to address the same market or to serve the same customers as the port of Hong Kong for the vast majority of its business.

The key competitive variables and success factors for the sea cargo industry include location, access to deep water, advanced container terminal infrastructure, and transportation to and from the port. Increasingly sophisticated customers look for the route density (how many other ports can be reached from a given port), efficiency and reliability of service, the ability to track containers at any point in their journey, and low cost. The cost of using a port consists not only of the direct handling fees of the cargo terminal or transfer operator, but also the cost of pilots, supplies, and most importantly, the cost of delays and downtime. The efficiency of the port operation itself depends on the investments made in infrastructure, in management

123

skills, and on increasingly sophisticated software and procedures used to optimize throughput.

Advantageous Natural and Created Inputs

Hong Kong benefits from the best natural harbour within hundreds of kilometres up or down the Chinese coast and an ideal location for the port that links South China with the rest of the world. The harbour is a superb natural input with few equals in the world. Across the entire Chinese coastline, only a few locations have comparable deep water access, and for reasons of history they have not developed the infrastructure needed for direct containerized shipping to the West.[3] This location has been enhanced by heavy investment in infrastructure—including the creation of eight large container terminals (built and operated by private sector firms) and development for land access to and from the port (by the government). Hong Kong's physical port infrastructure is far superior to other ports along the Chinese coast. New road and rail access routes are currently under construction.

Hong Kong benefits from extremely advanced port management skills, especially investment analysis and software skills for optimizing the flow of containers through the large terminals. Hong Kong port operators themselves are involved in managing the major port projects in mainland China. Hong Kong also has easier access to capital and a far superior communication system than the relevant competitors. In produced inputs, it has no real advantage in terms of purchasing cranes and other hardware, most of which come from abroad.

Burgeoning Demand for Port Services

Demand for port services in Hong Kong has grown dramatically in the last several years as the South China region has become a substantial exporter and importer of goods. Most of the cargo from China that goes through Hong Kong originates within a day's drive of Hong Kong, in Guangdong

Province. The Guangdong economy has been growing at an annual rate of 12 per cent or more for a decade and trade into and out of the province has been growing even faster. Hong Kong itself is the most trade-dependent economy in the world. The result has been growth in container throughput of 13 per cent a year from 1985 to 1995 for the port of Hong Kong. To give some perspective, in the 1993 to 1995 period, Hong Kong handled as much additional demand each year as the total capacity of some of the largest container ports in the United States. This growth in demand has put substantial pressure on port operators to improve their operations and efficiency. This pressure has been intensified by delays in bringing Container Terminal Nine (CT9) on stream. Hong Kong has an unmatched route network, driven by its large demand. This will become even more important as larger next generation container ships are likely to make only a few stops.

The customers of the port operations, large shipping companies and the retailers that hire them, are global in nature. These customers exert substantial pressures for speed, efficiency, and reliability of port services. These pressures are exerted everywhere and are not unique to Hong Kong. The fact that a great deal of the production of South China is geared toward export markets and is produced by Hong Kong-connected firms means these companies are comfortable bringing cargo into and out of Hong Kong. Some shippers, citing the efficiency and reliability of Hong Kong's port, even bring cargoes from central and northern China to Hong Kong for shipping.

A Vibrant Cluster

Hong Kong has developed a strong cluster of industries related to sea cargo over its 150-year period as a major sea port. The territory is unmatched in the expertise provided in marine insurance, evaluation and assessment of marine damages, trade finance, letters of credit, trade documentation, and logistical support. These services facilitate the rapid completion of logistical transactions crucial to on-time performance by shippers and has contributed to Hong Kong's advantage over smaller ports in the region. Hong Kong is an arbitration centre for maritime dispute resolution, an area in which its legal community has great expertise. Since shippers and customers often want up-to-the-minute information on their cargo, Hong Kong's position as a hub for international telecommunications provides additional advantages. It will be very difficult for the relevant competitor ports to develop nearly the same supporting structures for the sea cargo industry.

Private Sector Strategies

The fundamental fact about the strategies of the container terminal operators and other cargo handlers in Hong Kong is that they are private sector strategies. Unlike most ports in the region, the port of Hong Kong is privately operated by franchisees that have developed their own facilities and manage for profitability. This is very different from most Asian ports, which are operated as government services with other goals. One result has been aggressive investment strategies in which the private companies have pumped hundreds of millions of dollars into their operations in recent years. Industry sources estimate that Hong Kong's port handles an average of 550,000 TEUs per berth (with one facility actually handling one million TEUs per year at a single berth). In comparison, Singapore's port handles on average 450,000 TEUs per berth per year, while in the United States and Europe, operators rarely handle more than 225,000 TEUs per berth per year.[4]

The profit motive has provided a powerful incentive for the port operators to improve their operations to cope with rapidly expanding demand. Recently, to serve increased demand, the operators made substantial investments in facilities and improved computer systems, which allowed them to increase productivity at the average berth by around 25 per cent in a single year. When asked if productivity would have improved so much if it had been managed by government, any government, one industry expert simply laughed.

Of the three major terminal operators, Hongkong

International Terminals (HIT) and Modern Terminals Limited (MTL) are general user, container handling terminals. Sea-Land, a consolidator of less-than-container-load trucks, performs much of its consolidation work for its US parent, an international shipping firm. HIT, controlled by Hutchison Whampoa, operates ports in the United States and the United Kingdom, holds a concession for cargo handling at Shanghai, and is developing the new deep water port at Yantian. MTL, partly owned by the Swire Group and by Wharf (Holdings) Limited, is expanding handling capacity in Hong Kong and has been exploring investments in container operations at the port of Shekou in the Pearl River Delta.[5]

Limited Competition and Cooperation

Hong Kong's container port has more internal competition, with three major terminal operators and many smaller 'mid-stream' operators (that transfer cargo ship to ship without it coming to rest within a land-based terminal), than most ports in the world. Although the competition is not considered particularly fierce (not surprising when demand has been outstripping supply), there is competition to keep customers and competition that limits pricing behaviour. The operators also engage in some cooperative activities. One operator, for example, has an arrangement under which another takes any overflow from its terminal.

Government as Referee

The Hong Kong government does not directly build or operate port facilities, as do governments in Singapore and in many other ports in the region and around the world. Nor does it set rates or regulate the terminal operators' rate of return. The philosophy has been to let the private sector develop port facilities as private profit-making ventures, in the belief that private firms with profit motives are more likely to provide efficient services than the public sector.

The supply of port facilities is managed in an attempt to track demand and to ensure that private sector firms can make a reasonable profit on their investments. The Hong Kong government charges the operators substantial fees for the right to reclaim or redevelop land at the terminal facilities. These fees are said to contribute to high prices at the port, even though the government takes its fee in a lump sum. The 'trigger point' system in which Hong Kong tries to match port development with supply is a very different strategy from that of Singapore, for example, where the government tends to build facilities ahead of demand and then tries to use low prices to fill capacity.

Hong Kong's status as a free port means that there are no lengthy customs procedures for cargo coming into or out of Hong Kong, at least on the Hong Kong side. This is offset somewhat for the trade with China due to customs delays and inefficiencies at that end. Hong Kong's strong legal system means that firms can have greater confidence that papers and documents issued by Hong Kong banks and shippers are legitimate, and are issued in a transparent fashion, than for documents issued on the Mainland. Companies also can be confident that, contracts will be enforced in Hong Kong and that there are internationally recognized arbitration and dispute resolution mechanisms available, an important advantage over local competitors.

The Hong Kong government has tried to increase the competition in the port by inviting new entrants to participate in the new Container Terminal Nine. Disputes with Mainland officials over the make-up of the consortium that would operate CT9, which included Jardine Matheson, a company that has had a stormy relationship at times with Mainland officials, have delayed the construction of CT9, putting even more pressure on the existing terminals.

Sea Cargo in Perspective

Advantages in several of the drivers of competitiveness have allowed Hong Kong to become the busiest container port in the world and to handle some 60 per cent of China's trade. Natural advantages have been supplemented by management skills,

Figure 5.2 Hong Kong's Sea Cargo Industry

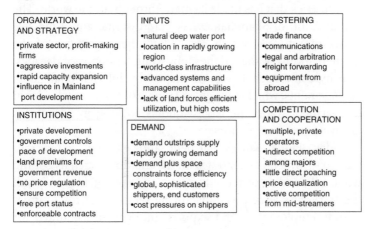

ORGANIZATION AND STRATEGY	INPUTS	CLUSTERING
•private sector, profit-making firms •aggressive investments •rapid capacity expansion •influence in Mainland port development	•natural deep water port •location in rapidly growing region •world-class infrastructure •advanced systems and management capabilities •lack of land forces efficient utilization, but high costs	•trade finance •communications •legal and arbitration •freight forwarding •equipment from abroad
INSTITUTIONS	**DEMAND**	**COMPETITION AND COOPERATION**
•private development •government controls pace of development •land premiums for government revenue •no price regulation •ensure competition •free port status •enforceable contracts	•demand outstrips supply •rapidly growing demand •demand plus space constraints force efficiency •global, sophisticated shippers, end customers •cost pressures on shippers	•multiple, private operators •indirect competition among majors •little direct poaching •price equalization •active competition from mid-streamers

enormous demand pressures, and the profit motive that drives firm strategies. The principal challenge to the port at present is managing growth and costs in the port. Shippers claim that Hong Kong's port charges are too high, that it is very expensive to bring cargo to or from Hong Kong, and that they are seeking alternatives. The operators counter that when relative efficiency and all other costs are factored in, Hong Kong is on par with other major ports in the region. And, they claim, shippers still use Hong Kong.

The closest alternative, Yantian, is under development, has a capacity of only 400,000 to 500,000 TEUs per year, and is being developed by HIT, one of the Hong Kong operators. In fact, all of the expansions planned in the Pearl River Delta region will add only as much capacity as Hong Kong has been adding every one to two years. High costs or not, the Hong Kong port has a series of advantages that are unlikely to be duplicated in the near future. (See Figure 5.2.)

THE HONG KONG GARMENT INDUSTRY

The garment industry is another of the quintessential industries of Hong Kong. It was the garment industry that initiated the development of Hong Kong's light manufacturing cluster, a set of industries that has made its mark throughout the world. The combination of Shanghainese skill and capital and a massive influx of refugees, which resulted in the emergence of the garment industry, shaped the Hong Kong economy for decades. The industry itself has been shaped by international quota arrangements, which have given Hong Kong, an early leader in the garment trade, the largest quotas, locking in advantages against newer competitors.

Today, Hong Kong's garment and garment accessories industry,[6] which concentrates on natural fibres such as cotton, wool, silk, and as of recently, ramie and similar fibres,[7] is still the territory's largest manufacturing sector in terms of gross output, employment, and exports. In 1994, it accounted for 5,628 factories, or more than 16 per cent of all of the territory's factories, and 140,000 local jobs, or 31 per cent of manufacturing employment.[8] Exports of garments made in Hong Kong accounted for almost 40 per cent of Hong Kong's domestic exports. Based on exports of garments produced in the territory, Hong Kong is the world's third largest clothing exporter, behind China and Italy, but ahead of Germany and Korea. If re-exports of garments from mainland China are taken into account, Hong Kong ranks first in the world in garment exports. When one considers the sum total of garment exports produced world-wide by Hong Kong interests, it is clear the Hong Kong companies occupy a dominant position in the world's garment trade.

The garment industry is a global industry; customers and competitors are found world-wide. The key competitive variables include flexibility, rapid response capabilities, reliable quality, and knowledge of markets and merchandise. The Hong Kong garment industry's major competitors are unrelated firms in mainland China and South and South-East Asia. Beyond this core competition, the identity of key competitors depends on the target market of individual manufacturers.[9] Hong Kong producers focusing on the US market see the Mainland, Mexico, and Central American nations as competitors, while those focusing on European markets compete with garment makers in Italy, Turkey, and some Eastern European nations.

Flexible Organizations and Strategies

The Hong Kong garment industry is characterized by a high incidence of family-owned firms and geographically dispersed manufacturing. Hong Kong's garment industry is uniquely dispersed across the globe. Virtually all Hong Kong garment manufacturers control factories in mainland China (due to cost pressures and quota regulations that require certain operations to be performed in Hong Kong and allow others to be performed elsewhere) and other countries in Asia. Many have production facilities as far afield as Africa, Europe, Latin America, and the Caribbean. At the same time, they keep management control, headquarters, and logistics in Hong Kong, allowing the firms to benefit from Hong Kong's strengths as a trading, communications, and transport hub.

The quota restraints that govern the world's trade in garments have had a profound impact on the strategies within Hong Kong's garment industry. Differences in quota rules on exports to the United States and to Europe have made it difficult for Hong Kong producers to sell to both markets. In essence, the quotas forced Hong Kong producers to prioritize, but then assured them a foreign market for their output. The great majority of Hong Kong manufacturers appear to focus on either the United States or Europe, with residual exports going to their second choice and to non-quota markets.

Hong Kong manufacturers have a strong reputation for quality, and for reliability in meeting product specifications and tight delivery deadlines. The flexibility of local manufacturers in responding speedily to fast-changing, fashion-driven demand is a rare strength, linked with the presence of a very large number of small and medium-sized factories (averaging 24 employees). This means companies have a reputation for being able to respond quickly whether orders are large or small, specialized, or requiring unusual materials.

131

Traditionally, this sector has shown a marked preference for original equipment manufacture (OEM, in which a manufacturer produces an item under contract to another company that sells it to the end user under the second company's brand) rather than branded production (in which the manufacturing company sells the product directly to the end customer under its own brand). This strategy, however, has limited the value added captured by Hong Kong firms on the garments they produce. Although Hong Kong garment manufacturers widely recognize that branded strategies potentially can yield a higher return on output than OEM production, many are dissuaded by the cost and time commitments required. There are, however, very notable exceptions. Episode, Giordano, Goldlion, Michel René, U-2, and Toppy stand out as Hong Kong clothing firms that have invested heavily in their own brand names.

Advantages in Light Manufacturing and Trading

The 'critical mass' of Hong Kong's light manufacturing and trading cluster, which encompasses producers of garments, electronics, textiles, watches and clocks, plastics, toys, footwear, jewellery, and other products, as well as more than one hundred thousand export traders, is a powerful advantage for Hong Kong's garment manufacturers. The cluster as a whole generates an ample and sophisticated supply of expertise, professional skills, and service inputs. Even where manufacturing has been shifted entirely from Hong Kong, garment companies continue to operate headquarters functions in Hong Kong, capitalizing on its strong port, air-cargo hub, and telecommunications infrastructure. Hong Kong's status as the 'one-stop shopping centre' for garment buyers world-wide has consolidated in the territory the functions of marketing, order processing, sourcing, design, product development, prototype making, and quality control. These activities are conducted, not just by the 5,600 garment manufacturers, but by many of its export traders, making Hong Kong one of the most convenient places in the world to perform these functions.

Input Challenges

Rising land and labour costs have weighed heavily on Hong Kong garment manufacturers and underlie the emigration of low-value-added processes to factories in mainland China. Although cost pressures lessened somewhat between mid-1995 and mid-1996, Hong Kong remains a high-cost environment. Shortages of qualified staff and high turnover rates are also a problem for many firms. Garment workers tend to be middle-aged, with most having no education beyond primary school. Young workers continue to prefer the white collar jobs available in the growing services industry to the blue collar factory work in new towns in Hong Kong's New Territories. Staff turnover rates of more than 100 per cent per year are not uncommon. This problem is aggravated by the reluctance of employers to train staff, or to pay higher wages to keep them, except at executive levels. As a result, skills remain low, and worker motivation is often poor. As of mid-1996, however, employers reported that workers were not job-hopping as much as before, and that the skill profile in the industry was improving. This was attributed in part to the cooling of the economy in general and the return from overseas of workers who had spent several years abroad to qualify for foreign residency.

Hong Kong historically has derived strong advantage from the local dyeing, weaving, knitting, and accessories industries. It remains home to more than 200 spinners, weavers, and other textile factories (down from 400 one decade ago). Local suppliers meet the entire local demand for knitted fabrics. Local supplies of thread, zippers, buttons, fasteners, belts, labels, and non-standard trims appear to remain substantial. However, weaving, bleaching, and dyeing operations, pressured by environmental concerns and high local costs, have been migrating to China, Malaysia, Taiwan, and elsewhere.[10] At present, only 10 per cent of the Hong Kong demand for yarn and woven fabrics is produced locally. This creates problems for Hong Kong garment producers, who find themselves under growing pressure in export markets for quick response to orders for simpler fashion garments, though under less pressure for complex garments with longer delivery times. The disadvantage of distance is partly offset by the fact that ownership and control of the weaving and dyeing firms often remain in Hong Kong after the production operations have moved elsewhere, and links with Hong Kong garment manufacturers remain strong.

Competition Influenced by Quotas

The international system of import quotas began in the late 1950s for textiles and was extended to garments in the early 1970s as a response on the part of industrialized countries to rapid increases in imports from less developed economies. The industrialized countries imposed the restrictions in order to reduce the impact of imports on their domestic industries. Quotas for a given product were largely based on past levels of import. Since Hong Kong was an 'early mover' in textiles and garments, it received some of the largest quota holdings in the world. In addition, Hong Kong firms used their expertise to develop the industry in new locations, often obtaining significant portions of the quotas when restrictions were imposed on the new locations.

The quota system has tended to secure long-term demand for early entrants but has made it difficult for late entrants to gain access to foreign markets. It also has discouraged head-to-head competition between firms because within particular quota categories, the quantum of sales was fixed. Instead, firms have tended to compete by seeking higher value added from each garment exported, by innovating in materials outside material-specific quota categories, and by seeking out export platforms whether inside quota regions, or in countries with quota preferences. Long-term customer relationships with market-mediated outcomes are the norm.

Emphasis on Foreign Demand

In the past, serving the home market has not given Hong Kong garment makers special knowledge, abilities, or expertise in competing in foreign markets. Although Hong Kong consumers of garments are powerfully fashion-conscious, they traditionally have preferred foreign brand garments, especially in high fashion. Only recently have some Hong Kong labels (mostly mass market) started to gain popularity at home. Instead, local firms were driven by the small local market to seek out and satisfy global demand, selling to the United States, Europe, and elsewhere. In the future, rapidly growing emerging markets of the Asia-Pacific region, including but not limited to mainland China, are major potential markets. Few non-Chinese manufacturers are able to capture as Hong Kong firms can the advantages and opportunities offered by China's demand for garments.

Business-Friendly Institutions

The business-friendly policies maintained consistently by the Hong Kong government over four decades have underpinned the strong performance of this sector in international competition. Low tax rates have been very important. The dispersed production strategies of Hong Kong garment producers have been made possible by the speed with which materials of different origins may be brought together in Hong Kong. This, in turn, owes much to the government's investments in communications and transportation infrastructure and its policy of maintaining a simple and open customs regime. The speed with which export licenses can be obtained (two days) also greatly aids export competitiveness.

Government policies also have contributed to rising costs. Tighter environmental controls have forced out a number of supporting industries, such as the dyeing industry. Flexible employment rules on the hiring and firing of workers have been a plus, but limitations on labour imports have closed the door to low-value-added manufacturing in Hong Kong itself. The use of imported labour or guest workers has been a contentious issue in Hong Kong. Industrialists, particularly those in the garment, construction, and low-wage service industries have pressed for a liberal labour importation scheme, claiming that

Hong Kong is at virtually full employment and is losing opportunities. Trade unionists, on the other hand, have generally been against labour importation schemes such as those operating in Singapore and Malaysia. In the garment industry, some have claimed that a lack of low-wage workers prevents Hong Kong from fully exploiting its quota position.

The Garment Industry in Perspective

The garment industry has long been a mainstay of the Hong Kong economy. Over the last few decades, Hong Kong firms have developed dispersed manufacturing capabilities that have allowed them to continue to compete in the international marketplace. Global quota rules, entrepreneurial firm strategies, and a business-friendly environment have enabled the industry to persist even in the face of rising costs.

Many managers in the industry, however, believe that rising costs, the planned dismantling of the global quota arrangements in 2005, more restrictive changes in US rules of origin, problems in obtaining and retaining skilled staff, and stagnant world prices will send the Hong Kong industry into a steep decline. This is likely to be true for the producers of low-priced goods. Hong Kong companies making high-value or complex garments, on the other hand, see no prospects of decline. Instead, they see Hong Kong factories being used to meet high-pressure orders where quality requirements and delivery deadlines are particularly rigorous. Managers who regard Hong Kong and South China operations as an integral whole are also bullish; several whom we surveyed spoke of this combination as a 'dream ticket'.

The further development of brands, a focus on niche markets, greater incorporation of new technologies, further penetration into Asian markets, and better use of relationships and communication technology hold out some of the best opportunities for the industry. In addition, as quotas are lifted, Hong Kong's advantages as a headquarters hub, a strategic centre, and as a 'packager' of services for importers are likely to continue to make Hong Kong the unchallenged 'one-

Figure 5.3 Hong Kong's Garment Industry

ORGANIZATION AND STRATEGY	INPUTS	CLUSTERING
•geographically dispersed manufacturing •Hong Kong logistics hub •local, family ownership •OEM, not branded focus	•deep merchandise and market knowledge •efficient port and airport infrastructure •proximity to Mainland labour and market •very high Hong Kong office and labour costs	•former spillovers from dyeing, weaving, knitting •accessories •now many activities offshore •migration a problem for some segments

INSTITUTIONS	DEMAND	COMPETITION AND COOPERATION
•open and simple customs regime •low taxation •government factor creation •restrictive labour importation policies •flexible hiring and firing	•local demand no advantage •firms seek out global demand •US and European demand saturated •Asia is the growth market	•quotas have influenced competition •long-term customer relations •market-mediated outcomes

stop shopping centre' for garments from the region. (See Figure 5.3.)

THE HONG KONG EXPORT TRADING SECTOR

Trading houses helped to establish Hong Kong in the middle of the nineteenth century and trading is vitally important to the Hong Kong economy even today. Export trading has become the entrepreneurial industry *par excellence* and the industry in which the packaging and integrating function of Hong Kong and its firms can be most clearly seen. Traditional intermediaries are complemented by Hong Kong firms, which match sources of supply with sources of demand on a global basis.

The Industry

In 1994, the Hong Kong-based activities of the import/export trade as a whole generated US$23 billion in value added,[11] or 18 per cent of Hong Kong's GDP, while service income from offshore buying and selling of goods amounted to an additional

137

US$6.63 billion.[12] Hong Kong's import/export trade accounts for approximately 106,000 firms and 520,000 jobs in Hong Kong.[13] Because Hong Kong is one of the world's great trading centres and is open to foreign trading firms, its import/export trading sector is highly cosmopolitan. Although Hong Kong hosts numerous Japanese, United States, and European trading companies, the Hong Kong industry is dominated by indigenous companies. This study will examine a subset of the import/export trade, the exporting of light consumer manufactures produced in Hong Kong, the Mainland, and/or third countries, either through Hong Kong or directly from offshore. The major products subject to this trade include textiles, garments, footwear, toys, travel goods and handbags, jewellery, and watches and clocks.

The services provided by Hong Kong's export trading sector range from traditional import/export functions, provided by small export trading companies, to sophisticated, high value-added services provided by Hong Kong's large export traders. The full range of activities offered by these firms includes: trade financing; sourcing raw materials and components; planning and managing production processes (including product design, packaging, quality control, and monitoring for timely delivery); and logistical services encompassing shipping arrangements, consolidation, scheduling, documentation, and customs clearance. In addition to Hong Kong-produced goods, many Hong Kong export traders are active in re-export trade involving outward processing on the Mainland of raw materials or semi-manufactures brought to China through Hong Kong. Hong Kong export traders also are engaged in subcontract processing on the Mainland or elsewhere—of materials or semi-manufactures not imported from Hong Kong—for export directly from offshore or via Hong Kong.

The traders' operations can vary from local to world-wide, as can the nature of the relevant competition. It is interesting to note, however, that the direct 'competitors' to Hong Kong's indigenous trading firms often have their operations in Hong Kong anyway. Indirect competition comes from light manufacturing industries in places where the Hong Kong traders are not active. The trading function also can be done in-house by specialized customers, such as a sports shoes or jeans producer but it is more difficult to handle for clients with a diversified buying need. Success depends on performance, information, and business acumen. It also requires the ability to respond rapidly to shifting signals in supplier and end markets, and to set a winning direction in a changing and uncharted environment. In the words of one industry member: 'The one constant in this industry is the need to respond to change.'

Dispersed Operations and Rapid Response Strategies

The geographic scope of the Hong Kong firms may be termed 'Hong Kong plus,' with Hong Kong headquarters overseeing widely dispersed operations. When China opened its borders to trade and investment in 1978, Hong Kong's traders and manufacturers saw an opportunity in the Mainland's vast and inexpensive labour pool for new sources of supply. Today, export traders headquartered in Hong Kong often have sourcing and/or manufacturing operations in low-cost locations on the Mainland, elsewhere in Asia, and beyond.

Hong Kong's export trading firms generally have headquarters in Hong Kong and flexible sourcing patterns focused primarily on the Asia-Pacific region. They rely on various arrangements to supply capital to the offshore concerns, including direct ownership of offshore manufacturing operations and the provision of working capital to manufacturers. Diversification of production operations allows the export trading firms to exploit the comparative advantages of other locations (such as low-cost labour and material inputs) and permits them to do far more business than otherwise would be the case.

Another source of advantage for this sector is its flexibility and speed in responding to changes in existing markets and in the general business environment. Firms enter and exit product lines and reconfigure sourcing patterns and strategies frequently. For the larger export traders, who employ 500 or more workers, identifying the best sourcing options requires the constant monitoring of shifting regional wage and productivity patterns, as well as agility in implementing new sourcing strategies. Flexibility in responding to production patterns permits the export trading firms to capture shifting cost advantages across the Asia-Pacific region and elsewhere.

Hong Kong's large export traders perform a variety of value-added services in addition to matching demand and supply. They provide credibility with suppliers, something most foreign buyers lack. They monitor work done by suppliers on their customers' orders, to make sure quality requirements and delivery deadlines are met. They also offer specialized manufacturing expertise, by working with suppliers or through their own manufacturing operations. As more retailers adopt 'just-in-time' inventory requirements, one large trader, Li & Fung, is offering expertise in 'planning their manufacturing, shipping and replenishment from start to finish' through 'just-in-time' replenishment hubs.[14]

Small export traders, which are often family-owned and operated firms, tend to engage in cost-based competition for a limited number of customers within a narrow product or geographic area (for example, men's shirts, or a small district in Guangdong Province). In June 1996, small export and import traders, with fewer than ten workers each, accounted for nearly 95,000 firms and 52 per cent of employment in the import/export trade as a whole.[15] These small export traders often are highly specialized, have in-depth knowledge of their product lines and suppliers, and can offer personalized service.

Advantages in Contacts and Capabilities

Apart from Hong Kong's harbour and well-developed infrastructure, some of this sector's strongest input advantages lie in specialized advanced capabilities, such as networking and interpretive product design. Hong Kong's large export traders have networks of informal relationships with factories and factory owners across Asia, sometimes numbering in the thousands. These networks of contacts and knowledge give

Hong Kong's traders unmatched expertise in finding the supplier or factory that can best meet their customers' needs. For example, one potential supplier might have the lowest cost structure, but might be weaker in a critical skill needed for the job or not have enough quota available for the intended export market; another on the opposite side of Asia, with higher costs but a superior skills base, might offer better quality or an ample quota. It is the job of the Hong Kong export trader to know all this. His information network helps get the products produced at cost, to specification, and on foreign retail shelves on time.

Hong Kong's export traders also have an acute understanding of consumer tastes in selected lines of merchandise, especially light manufactures with a fashion element, such as garments, watches, toys, and sporting equipment. Export traders often monitor the products that are successful in the major retail markets and suggest related concepts for the next season in ways predictive of consumer tastes, providing value for their clients. Their strengths are in interpretive, rather than original, design. Major shifts in fashion trends occur in the West, while Hong Kong traders elaborate and develop existing fashions. Geographic distance is an ongoing handicap to Hong Kong export traders, who have to work hard to keep abreast of retail market developments in the United States and Europe. Cross-cultural skills, including foreign language abilities, traditionally have been a strength for the Hong Kong export traders. The generally even distribution of English proficiency throughout the ranks of workers who have contact with foreign buyers facilitates deal-making and makes it easier to win customer trust.

Cluster Advantages

Hong Kong's export traders are an integral part of a larger light manufacturing and trading cluster firmly rooted in Hong Kong. These businesses together provide a critical mass of strategic knowledge, manufacturing expertise, and information networks for Hong Kong export traders. They also demand many of the same supporting services as the export traders, generating a critical mass of high quality services in every area needed by this sector (for example, trade finance, transportation, communications, insurance services, trade documentation services, advertising, market research, research and development, laboratory testing and product certification, product design, and exhibition facilities).[16] There is a positive, two-way dynamic at work. The supporting services generate advantages for local export traders while the latter provide strong and sophisticated demand which drives the service providers forward.

Indirect Competition

Competition in this sector is characterized by long-term, exclusive customer relationships with market-mediated outcomes. Firms tend to focus on different customers or segments, and there is limited direct competition to win customers away from each other. Although it is relatively easy to enter the industry, it often is difficult for new entrants to build up the supplier and information network, packaging skills, and proven track record required to service a large foreign retailer or importer. Many of the smaller export traders are destined to be niche fillers, holding onto customer relationships for as long as possible. Even among the larger firms, switching costs are high. Only a few export traders can handle very large customers, and one firm cannot handle large competing customers easily due to capacity constraints and potential conflicts of interest. The result is a certain amount of inertia in big customer accounts.

In recent years, some large retailers and importers have set up their own internal sourcing operations, creating a source of external competitive pressure for Hong Kong's export traders. The in-house sourcing strategy appears to be most successful among businesses with relatively narrow and well-defined product lines, which do not require as extensive an international supplier network. For businesses active in a variety of consumer products, the high cost of establishing and maintaining such a network often weighs strongly in favour of working with an export trading firm, rather than setting up an in-house sourcing operation. In addition, companies with in-house sourcing operations are coming up against the global corporate trend of keeping to core competencies and reducing costs through out-sourcing, which favours the use of trading companies.

Institutional Strengths and Entrepreneurial Agendas

Public institutions have been a source of competitive advantage for the Hong Kong export trading sector. Hong Kong's stable government, transparent administration, and low taxation have fostered an environment much more favourable to business dealings than many other places in Asia. Taxes are levied on Hong Kong-based income only, to the advantage of companies headquartered in Hong Kong with geographically dispersed manufacturing operations. The Hong Kong legal system provides for the effective enforcement of contracts—an essential element of the trading business. Hong Kong's free-trade regime and its expeditious system of export approvals facilitate trade flows. The government also safeguards the free flow of business information, which is critical to overall industry health. The Hong Kong Trade Development Council (TDC) provides strong information and logistics support for export traders, and organizes high-profile trade fairs at local exhibition facilities.

Social agendas have been a plus for this sector. Hong Kong's entrepreneurial drive attracts new entrants to the industry and keeps existing firms working hard. In consumer products, such as fashion, unknown entrants can rise quickly to prominence in world markets. The prospect of joining forces with one of tomorrow's market leaders can be a powerful incentive for new traders.

Export Trading in Perspective

Hong Kong's export trading industry is built on a series of distinct advantages, including unmatched access to the

Figure 5.4   Hong Kong's Export Trading Sector

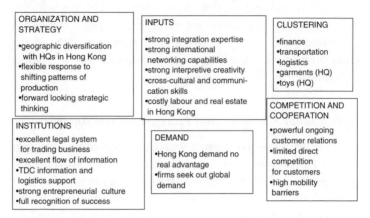

ORGANIZATION AND STRATEGY
- geographic diversification with HQs in Hong Kong
- flexible response to shifting patterns of production
- forward looking strategic thinking

INSTITUTIONS
- excellent legal system for trading business
- excellent flow of information
- TDC information and logistics support
- strong entrepreneurial culture
- full recognition of success

INPUTS
- strong integration expertise
- strong international networking capabilities
- strong interpretive creativity
- cross-cultural and communication skills
- costly labour and real estate in Hong Kong

DEMAND
- Hong Kong demand no real advantage
- firms seek out global demand

CLUSTERING
- finance
- transportation
- logistics
- garments (HQ)
- toys (HQ)

COMPETITION AND COOPERATION
- powerful ongoing customer relations
- limited direct competition for customers
- high mobility barriers

Mainland and to sources of demand and supply around the world. The sector contributes to the vibrancy of the whole economy. When one speaks to people in the industry, however, one hears a litany of problems. Hong Kong trading companies complain about the high costs of doing business in Hong Kong, the high costs of using the port of Hong Kong, and what they see as a diminution of cross-cultural and English language skills. Some claim they plan to move to Guangdong. Some firms report a shortage of recruits interested in working in trading. One executive commented, 'We almost have to take what we can get.' The skills base of workers hired directly from school is reported to be 'relatively low'. Workers expect annual inflation-insulating pay increases of between 8 per cent and 10 per cent, driving up operational costs. Studies show a lack of capital, managerial, and information resources on the part of small Hong Kong trading companies. A recent study sponsored by the Hong Kong Productivity Council, for example, found that small and medium-sized traders, in particular, are lacking in strategic awareness and planning.[17]

Despite these issues, there are no major apparent competitors for the Hong Kong trading industry at this time and no major apparent competition for Hong Kong as their location. A recent survey by the Hong Kong Trade Development Council indicates that a high percentage of trading and manufacturing firms with controlling headquarters in Hong Kong intend to remain in Hong Kong.[18] A large number of Taiwanese firms actually use Hong Kong as their base for sourcing activities. Firms from elsewhere in the world also use Hong Kong for the same reasons that Hong Kong firms have succeeded. The information networks, unequalled access to sourcing in mainland China, Asia, and elsewhere—and access to markets in Europe, North America, and elsewhere—still make Hong Kong the place where East meets West and East meets East for the export traders. This is what allows Hong Kong's export traders to package and integrate the activities of light manufacturing industries on a regional and global basis. (See Figure 5.4.)

THE HONG KONG FUND MANAGEMENT INDUSTRY

Hong Kong is one of the world's leading financial centres. A small, but interesting portion of the financial sector is the fund management industry, which is closely linked with other parts of the sector. Fund management is particularly interesting in the case of Hong Kong, given the fact that most fund managers in the territory are overseas firms and some other cities in Asia have tried to attract fund managers away from Hong Kong. It is an industry which requires very little capital investment and relies heavily on sophisticated international networks. It is hypersensitive to the free movement of capital, of information, and of people. As such, even though it accounts for a relatively small number of jobs in the territory, many regard it as 'a canary in the coal mine' in terms of the business-friendliness of Hong Kong's working environment.

The Industry

The key success factors in this industry are: the ability to win and hold investor confidence; superior market knowledge and investment acumen; superior fund performance; and the free flow of business information. A deep local market, a favourable

145

regulatory environment, high-quality communications infrastructure, and the presence of related services all contribute to a city's ability to become a centre for fund management.

In 1995, Hong Kong's fund managers collectively managed assets totaling US$94.2 billion, not including life insurance funds. US$33 billion of the total was in Hong Kong-authorized funds. Pension and non-pension institutional money accounted for 48.3 per cent of the total, and unit trusts around 37.5 per cent. The Singaporean fund management sector, Hong Kong's leading rival, is much smaller, with a total of US$46.8 billion under management at year-end 1994. Malaysia, another competitor, is further behind. Japanese fund managers focus almost exclusively on the domestic market, leaving Hong Kong as the leading Asian (and Asian time zone) centre for international fund management. The development of fund management in Singapore and Malaysia has been hampered by government 'monopolies' over the management of provident funds. Both governments, however, recently have committed to opening their provident funds to private sector managers. This liberalization is expected to open up an additional US$28 billion to private fund management in Singapore by the end of the decade.[19] This new policy, combined with a special incentive measure that will tax profits above a certain amount at 5 per cent, is reportedly attracting the attention of foreign fund managers in Hong Kong.

Overseas and Local Firms

The 45 registered fund management firms in Hong Kong, most of which are offices of firms headquartered in the United States or Europe, employ an estimated 3,000 persons. According to a survey by Hong Kong's Investment Funds Association, 86 per cent of the fund managers with a local presence have their regional headquarters in Hong Kong. One-third had their only Asian office in Hong Kong. Most of these firms use Hong Kong as a base for planning investment across Asia, principally on behalf of clients in the United States or Europe. The fund managers which could be defined as local (for example, HSBC

Asset Management or Jardine Fleming) also have powerful global links (HSBC with its own global network and Jardine Fleming with Robert Fleming of the United Kingdom).

Hong Kong's fund management industry emerged in the early 1970s when the only stock markets in Asia outside Japan that were open to international investment were Hong Kong and the Philippines. Hong Kong was the natural base from which to research companies listed on these exchanges, and to invest in them. Hong Kong's 'first-mover' advantage has been significant within the region. Three early entrants— Jardine Fleming, Schroders and Wardley (now HSBC Asset Management)—sought out local funds and still account for a dominant share of local fund management business.

United States-owned fund managers (nearly all the major US funds are represented in Hong Kong) arrived later on the scene in Hong Kong, driven largely by the desire for a base from which to manage business across the Asia-Pacific region, rather than out of any strong interest in local customers. Even today, the US fund managers based in Hong Kong are focused primarily on regional research and stock picking for the investment of funds raised in the United States, rather than on raising funds in the region, or competing for local pension fund business.

Some Hong Kong-based fund managers operate as integrated, multifunctional 'merchant banks', linking private banking operations, corporate finance, broking, and other related activities. Others operate as self-standing operations. For some, research and company visits are conducted 'in-house'. Others rely on broker research. Some regard it as essential to have a body of fund managers on the ground in Hong Kong, others keep them 'centralized' in cities like Geneva, Edinburgh, Chicago, and New York, maintaining little more than marketing arms in Hong Kong.

Small, but Growing Local Demand

Most of the fund management activity in Hong Kong is driven by demand in the United States and Europe, with local demand playing a much smaller role. Nevertheless, as Hong Kong's domestic funds grow in size and number, they are beginning to attract more international fund managers. If the Hong Kong government goes ahead with plans to establish a Mandatory Provident Fund, it is estimated that US$4 billion will be added annually to the local investment pool. Fund managers are attaching increasing importance to the Asia-Pacific region, in part because the body of savings available for investment in the region is rising rapidly. Hong Kong is well situated to serve regional demand because of its status as a hub for communications and financial and business services, and the depth of its stock market.

Hong Kong's attractiveness to fund management firms benefits from the proximity of pent-up demand on the Mainland, even though the Mainland has not opened up its market in this sector. Many fund managers say they maintain headquarters operations in Hong Kong in part because of the long-term potential for managing funds in mainland China. Such ambitions remain hypothetical, despite the enormous reservoir of savings seeking professional management in China. Mainland authorities show no sign at present of allowing foreign companies to manage indigenous pension or insurance funds, or to offer fund management products to retail savers; yet this expectation appears to be one of several important factors keeping 'waverers' headquartered in Hong Kong rather than Singapore.

Highly Skilled and High-Cost Inputs

Hong Kong's fund management industry has benefited from the fact that its firms draw expertise from all over the world. Location, transport, communications, and excellent business information also are strengths. But many fund managers complained about office rental and staffing costs, which are the highest in the region with the exception of Japan. This high cost is exacerbated by the 'prestige image' of fund management, which prompts managers to occupy prime office space, underwrite generous expatriate packages for senior staff, and offer some of the territory's highest salaries.

All fund management companies nevertheless noted that when *overall* costs were compared with other centres in the region, Hong Kong was not significantly different from main competitor centres such as Tokyo or Singapore. Factors such as low tax levels, cheap telecommunications costs, and competitive airline ticketing costs, all compare favourably in Hong Kong. Some noted that if costs escalated further, they would consider centralizing back to Europe or the United States, rather than to another Asia-Pacific centre.

While costs are without doubt a source of competitive concern—and have triggered the migration of a number of labour-intensive, back-office operations—fund management groups are less likely to be cost-conscious than companies in many other sectors in the economy. Once break-even costs have been covered, then new funds can often be managed without significant additions of staff or office space. The growth of a fund under management from US$200 million to US$500 million is likely to require minimal additional outgoing costs. One respected fund manager noted that if Hong Kong was used simply as a marketing and servicing centre, with back-office operations located elsewhere, a manager could break even with no more than US$700 million under management. A manager operating a full research and investment operation would require funds under management of at least US$2.1 billion to break even. While there is fierce pressure to surpass these break-even points, profits rise quickly once they have been passed.

With respect to the skills base, the local pool of appropriately skilled staff was generally seen to be deeper than anywhere else in Asia. Fund managers could not identify any specific shortcomings in Hong Kong's tertiary sector in terms of preparing graduates for careers in fund management, mainly because they regard their business as a 'mentor-mentee' profession where necessary skills are not easily learned in courses, nor measured by examination results. Many nevertheless felt there should be stronger formal endorsement for either the United States or United Kingdom professional qualification—the Certified Financial Analyst (CFA) from the United States was most strongly preferred. Some fund managers complained of a shortage of local staff able to 'think outside the box'. Others complained of poor general levels of competence in English language. Singapore generally won higher marks for language skills, but significantly lower marks for analysis, creativity, and risk taking.

Part of a Dynamic Business Services Cluster

The size and liquidity of Hong Kong's equity market is a key competitive advantage for this sector and an important reason why foreign fund managers chose Hong Kong as a regional base.[20] Not only is market capitalization higher in Hong Kong than anywhere else in Asia (outside Japan), but the depth of trading in individual stocks is greater than any other market. Asia fund managers thus have a larger proportion of funds under management invested in Hong Kong stocks than elsewhere, and as a result need to research local stocks closely and in large numbers. Hong Kong's fund managers are sophisticated users of information systems and legal services, favouring co-location with other financial service activities within the firm and within the region.

The fund management business itself plays an important role in maintaining the territory's pre-eminence as an integrating hub for financial services. It is integrally linked with stock broking, private banking, corporate finance, insurance, and a number of key professional services such as legal and accounting services, in which Hong Kong is strong. Perhaps most important of all, Hong Kong's fund management industry plays a vital role in encouraging locally listed firms to adopt 'best practice' accounting and reporting practices. This is important, not just for Hong Kong companies, but it also provides critical role models for Mainland Chinese firms as they seek to list in Hong Kong or elsewhere.

Important Institutional Benefits

All fund managers talked of the Hong Kong government's light but clear supervision of the financial markets in general, and fund management in particular, as a powerful source of competitive advantage. Great comfort was derived from the knowledge that regulation matched international best standards, but was barely felt in the daily operation of business.

The free flow of information, persons, and capital in and out of Hong Kong is seen within the industry as a critical source of competitive advantage. The fund management industry is unusually sensitive to the ability to obtain accurate information as speedily as is technologically possible, and to disseminate information with equal speed to clients. Hong Kong's free flow of information is seen as a distinct advantage over Singapore, where stock analysts often do not sign their reports and where key publications, such as *The Asian Wall Street Journal, The International Herald Tribune*, and *The Economist* have had their circulation restricted or even banned for periods for publishing articles that the Singapore government deemed inaccurate or inappropriate. Even though Hong Kong was generally regarded as having a deep pool of professional skills, the international nature of fund management and the value of transnational experience among employees puts an unusually high premium on the free international movement of staff in a wide range of positions within the firm.

Although Hong Kong's low tax rate is an advantage, some fund managers spoke of a lack of clarity in certain aspects of the taxation of funds under management as a source of concern. By contrast, Singapore has developed a clear and simple tax environment, which gives it an edge, even though taxes there are higher. Singapore also has a full array of double-taxation agreements with other countries, which Hong Kong lacks.

Active Competition Among Local Managers

Hong Kong's fund management industry is characterized by segmented competition within specialties. Most fund managers forecast that competition will increasingly focus on winning the right to manage the growing pools of savings across the Asia-Pacific region. Current competition thus involves a combination of efforts to demonstrate superior analysis of, and investment in, the markets of the Asia-Pacific region, and manoeuvring into position for opportunities to identify and capture regional sources of funds. This is one reason why local staff (as opposed to expatriates) are increasingly found among the ranks of multinational financial companies in Hong Kong.

In the domestic funds sector, fund managers talk of fiercely personal competition for the limited opportunities to manage these funds—fine margins are maintained by those currently managing funds in order to keep 'outsiders' at bay. Personal reputations are strongly identified with the success of a fund, and incomes correlate closely with performance. The competition for the local 'retail' market, however, appears limited to a comparatively small number of entrenched players, as potential entrants have considered it to be too small to justify the immense investment needed to capture a significant market share.

Fund Management in Perspective

Despite the attempts by other cities in the region to develop rival centres, Hong Kong remains the largest international fund management centre in Asia. Although Singapore has emerged as a strong competitor, limitations on free movement of staff, restrictions on free flow of information, and the lack of a critical mass of fund managers make it uncompetitive on a number of counts. In addition, its physical distance from mainland China makes it an inappropriate hub for tackling the Mainland market when the opportunity materializes.

The critical mass of fund managers and associated industries found in Hong Kong is unmatched in the region. Although some firms have moved part of their fund management operations to other centres, the vast majority have remained in Hong Kong. Given the importance of the Hong Kong equity market, the potential for further listings by Mainland companies, and the hope of future business on the Mainland, Hong Kong remains the location of choice. (See Figure 5.5.)

Figure 5.5 Hong Kong's Fund Management Industry

INPUTS	
ORGANIZATION AND STRATEGY •early mover advantages in the region •multinational ownership and control with diverse strategies	•hub strength in location and transport •deep pool of foreign and local skills •excellent business information •high rental and staff costs •uneven support staff skills (English)

ORGANIZATION AND STRATEGY
- early mover advantages in the region
- multinational ownership and control with diverse strategies

INPUTS
- hub strength in location and transport
- deep pool of foreign and local skills
- excellent business information
- high rental and staff costs
- uneven support staff skills (English)

CLUSTERING
- strong cluster of financial and other services
- deep local equity markets
- advanced stockbroking
- advanced computing, communications

INSTITUTIONS
- state-of-the-art regulation (UK)
- free movement of people, capital, information
- open door for foreign managers and practices
- flexible registration
- low tax rates

DEMAND
- local demand role in industry birth
- high regional savings levels
- local demand mostly not an issue
- demand from high-net-worth individuals

COMPETITION AND COOPERATION
- compartmentalized competition within segments
- highly personal rivalry based on reputation and performance

ADDITIONAL INDUSTRIES

The Hong Kong Air Cargo Industry

Hong Kong is the world's second leading centre for international air cargo after Narita Airport in Japan. In 1995, cargo throughput was 1.46 million tonnes after a decade of 11 per cent per year growth. Hong Kong's air cargo industry handles 20 per cent of the value of Hong Kong's external trade.[21] The vast majority of the trade is either sourced in or destined for Hong Kong or mainland China. Hong Kong Air Cargo Terminals Limited (HACTL) is the sole cargo handler at Hong Kong's Kai Tak Airport.

Hong Kong benefits from its role as the air hub for South China and as a leading hub airport for the Asian region. Expertise and reliability in air cargo handling is such that cargo from as far north as Shanghai and Beijing often comes to Hong Kong for air shipment. Since Hong Kong has been at the farthest distance from the West Coast of North America reachable non-stop, flights bound for points further into South-East Asia must stop in Hong Kong or elsewhere in the vicinity. HACTL is considered reliable and efficient by most customers. The growth of demand, and limited space at Kai Tak, has forced HACTL to come up with innovative solutions to cargo handling problems. HACTL built its second terminal vertically instead of horizontally and in the process dramatically improved efficiency. Many of the advantages of the sea cargo industry in terms of clustering of trade and logistics-related services also apply to air cargo. In addition, there is a close linkage of air cargo and passenger air services since roughly 60 per cent of air cargo in the region travels on passenger flights.

The new airport at Chek Lap Kok, scheduled to open in April 1998, is designed to remove many of the constraints facing the air cargo industry at Kai Tak. Capacity will be greatly enhanced and the airport will operate 24 hours a day. There will be two cargo handlers in the new airport in order to have competition to stimulate even better service. HACTL is investing US$1 billion in a state-of-the-art complex that will be the world's largest air cargo handling facility, with a capacity of 2.4 million tonnes of standard cargo and 200,000 tonnes of express cargo. Although the air cargo industry does not have some of the same natural advantages of the sea cargo industry (a unique geographic advantage), and there are new airports not far from Hong Kong, the combination of the skills, expertise, supporting services, and a dense route network, which could not be duplicated overnight, continue to make Hong Kong the centre for air cargo in the South China region.

The Hong Kong Electronics Industry

Hong Kong's electronics industry, which accounted for 27.7 per cent of Hong Kong's domestic exports in 1995 and exported roughly 90 per cent of its output, focuses primarily on producing consumer electronics for original equipment manufacture (OEM) customers. The industry performs its product development, marketing, design, and other high-value-added activities in Hong Kong, but has relocated the vast majority of its actual production work to the Pearl River Delta. Most of the firms are small, family firms that employ labour-intensive, cost-based strategies.

The Hong Kong industry benefits from talented designers and keen attention to fashion trends on the part of manufacturers. On the other hand, Hong Kong does not produce as many engineers as other economies in the region and the Hong Kong firms invest little in basic research. The Hong Kong industry imports most of its key components, packaging and integrating technologies and components sourced elsewhere into new products. This can be a problem when industry-wide shortages make obtaining components difficult. Firms in the territory have yet to take full advantage of Hong Kong-based demand, which is brand sensitive and very open to new products (one-fourth of Hong Kong consumers replace their television sets each year and many replace audio equipment, mobile phones, and other electronic goods just to have and be seen with the latest models). The Hong Kong government has initiated some support programmes to help firms develop and incorporate new technologies, but it has not targeted the industry as Taiwan, Singapore, and others have done and the dollar amounts spent on its support programmes are small.

Major trends in the industry include the further decentralization of production into the Pearl River Delta, the development of brands by some local manufacturers, and increasing sales of finished goods into the Mainland. Hong Kong firms remain at a disadvantage in capital and scale-sensitive component production, but they are better situated to compete in final goods market niches characterized by rapidly evolving consumer tastes. The potential for the development of branded manufacture for the Mainland market also could be substantial.

The Hong Kong Civil and Construction Engineering Industry

Hong Kong's civil and construction engineering industry is an example of the close interaction of local and overseas firms in Hong Kong.[22] Many of the leading 'Hong Kong firms' actually are the Hong Kong offices of overseas firms from the United

Kingdom, Australia, the United States, or elsewhere. In many instances the Hong Kong office is bigger than the 'home office' and is the headquarters for Asian operations. This history, the specialized nature of some projects, and an open door for foreign engineers, means that Hong Kong engineers frequently work with engineers from other nations or regions in a given project. According to some in the industry, this allows the Hong Kong firms to 'learn from the best'.

Hong Kong engineers are considered good to very good by regional standards. (They are 'streets ahead' of engineers from elsewhere in the region according to one manager). Hong Kong University's engineering programme is considered to be particularly good. The territory's engineers are considered fairly creative and adaptable. Hong Kong engineers are known for coming up with novel solutions to several pressing problems in the industry. Hong Kong-based demand has been an enormous plus for the industry. There have been a large number of major infrastructure and commercial development projects in the territory, including ten projects associated with the new airport at Chek Lap Kok, which have provided better on-the-job training than perhaps anywhere else in the world. At one point in the early to mid-1990s, for example, roughly 80 per cent of the world's dredging fleet was employed in Hong Kong. Rapidly increasing costs and land rents have placed a premium on the quick completion of projects, as has the private sector funding and ownership of many major projects. Hong Kong's difficult geological conditions have presented additional challenges to the engineering firms.

Hong Kong engineering firms have been stretched to their limits by the huge demand at home and therefore have not developed international markets to the extent one might expect. In addition, since the engineering market, at least for major projects, tends to be global, it is not good enough to be better than other engineers in the region because the relevant competition might be firms from the United Kingdom or the United States. High costs for Hong Kong engineers means it is not only cheaper to employ an engineer from the United Kingdom in mainland China than a Hong Kong engineer, it is often cheaper to employ a British engineer in Hong Kong than a Hong Kong engineer. Nevertheless, many Hong Kong engineering firms, either brought in by Hong Kong infrastructure and development firms or on their own contracts, are active on the Mainland and in the region. Continued infrastructure development in Hong Kong and in the region should keep the demand for Hong Kong engineers high in the short to medium term.

The Hong Kong Telecommunications Industry

Hong Kong's telecommunications market, excluding Internet services, is estimated at US$4 billion.[23] Per capita telecommunications revenues are among the highest in the world. Within Hong Kong, there are four fixed telecommunications network services operators, four cellular network operators (the number of mobile subscribers went from 500,000 to one million from mid-1995 to mid-1996 and service is even available inside the subway system), approximately 50 paging network services, and more than 80 Internet service providers. The high quality and low cost of international communications is an advantage for local and multinational firms in Hong Kong and is an important reason why so many multinational firms locate and choose to remain in Hong Kong.[24]

Heavy investments over many years have made the Hong Kong telecommunications system one of the best in the world. Hong Kong Telephone was an early investor in all-digital technology. Cable & Wireless, the British company that obtained a controlling stake in Hong Kong Telephone's successor Hongkong Telecommunications in 1989, had developed an extensive network of submarine cables centred on Hong Kong, giving the territory an advantage as a regional communications hub. Hongkong Telecommunications is moving into interactive multimedia services and is expanding in the Asia-Pacific region. Other Hong Kong telecommunications suppliers are active in the Mainland industry through lending and in value-added services. The strong transnational orientation of the local and overseas firms found in Hong Kong generates substantial demand for international services. Hong Kong's international calls are remarkable in that they are roughly evenly distributed across the day and evening,[25] a sign of the multitude of international destinations of calls. Since its founding in 1993, the Office of the Telecommunications Authority has spearheaded a deregulation process that has stimulated the growth of competition in the sector, reduced prices, provided more choices, and fostered greater technological diversity.[26]

Singapore and Sydney both have emerged as rival Asia–Pacific telecommunications hubs. Both have developed their telecommunications systems to bridge distances and to support service- and knowledge-based industrial development. Both can reasonably claim to match the excellence of Hong Kong's telecommunications infrastructure in terms of the range and quality of services available to local and multinational firms. Hong Kong, however, still can handle higher volumes of international traffic. It is still the home of more extensive demand and is still better situated to be a telecommunications hub for the Mainland and the region. The pace of deregulation, change, competition, and investment is picking up in the Hong Kong industry. If this trend continues, Hong Kong should remain as a major international telecommunications centre.

The Hong Kong Tourism Industry

Hong Kong's tourism industry derives strong advantages from Hong Kong's central location within Asia and its proximity to the Mainland, from Hong Kong's status as a major international business centre, and from its well-developed communications and transportation infrastructure. Between 1986 and 1995, visitor arrivals to Hong Kong increased by more than 150 per cent. Although Hong Kong attracts tourists from around the world, in 1995 around 80 per cent of visitors to Hong Kong came from the Asia–Pacific region, and they generated around 80 per cent of Hong Kong's US$9.6 billion in tourism receipts.[27]

Hong Kong's tourism industry is succeeding in attracting the type of tourist sought by destinations around the world—white-collar professionals, who spend not just in the local hotels, but also at local shops, restaurants, and attractions. In 1995, the average foreign visitor to Hong Kong spent much more on shopping than on his or her hotel bill.[28] Hong Kong's prices for clothing and accessories, on the whole, are no longer a bargain for many Western tourists but they continue to be a better buy than in Japan and elsewhere in the region where goods often are subject to substantial tariffs. Approximately 30 per cent of foreign visitors to Hong Kong in 1995 came on business, underlining Hong Kong's position as a business centre and a home for international exhibitions and trade fairs. Hong Kong's luxury hotels (the territory has one of the densest concentrations of luxury hotels in the world) try to outdo each other in every aspect of service and presentation, recruiting architects from New York to design showcase buildings, concierges from Switzerland, and chefs from France, the Mainland, and around the world. Many international chains have flagship hotels in the territory and two Hong Kong hotels, the Peninsula and the Mandarin, frequently appear in rankings of the world's best hotels.

The Hong Kong Tourist Association has voiced concerns about a shortage of hotel rooms and difficulties in hiring capable people. Hong Kong does not offer the relaxing vacation experience that some travellers desire. However, Hong Kong's position as a business centre, as a travel gateway to mainland China, as a free port, as a centre of attractions and events, and as perhaps the most cosmopolitan city in Asia are advantages that are not going to go away soon.

HONG KONG'S INDUSTRIES

In this chapter, we have briefly profiled some of Hong Kong's most representative industries. These industries, along with closely linked industries, account for 750,000 to 800,000 employees in Hong Kong and many more than that on the Mainland and elsewhere. They account for roughly 40 per cent

Figure 5.6   Activities Performed by Hong Kong Firms

	Firm Infra	HRM	Proc	RD	Tech Dev PD	TD	Logs	Ops	Mktg	Ser
Garments	HK	Both	HK	None	HK	None	HK	Both	HK	None
Electronics	HK	Both	HK	None	HK	None	HK	Elsewhere	HK	None
Trading	HK	Both	HK	None	HK	None	HK	Both	HK	HK
Fund Mgmt	Both	Both	HK	Elsewhere	Both	Elsewhere	HK	Both	Both	Both
Civil Eng	Both	Both	HK	Elsewhere	Both	Both	HK	Both	Both	Both
Air Cargo	HK	HK	HK	None	HK	None	HK	HK	HK	HK
Sea Cargo	HK	HK	HK	None	HK	None	HK	HK	HK	HK
Telecom	Both	HK	HK	None	HK	None	HK	HK	HK	HK
Tourism	HK	Both	HK	None	HK	None	HK	HK	Both	None

Legend: ☰ = Activity performed in Hong Kong | ▥ = Activity performed elsewhere | ■ = Both | ☐ = Activity not performed by Hong Kong firms

of GDP. Figure 5.6 summarizes the geographic distribution of activities performed by Hong Kong's firms, across the industries studied. It provides insight into how Hong Kong's firms in different sectors are distributing their activities across the entire value-added chain,[29]—from firm infrastructure, human resource management, procurement, research and development, product development, and technology development, to logistics, operations, marketing, and service. From this visual sorting of activities, several interesting patterns emerge. Certain industries are more amenable to geographic dispersal strategies than others. Air cargo and sea cargo, for example, are firmly location-based and are tied to Hong Kong across the entire value chain. Hong Kong's industries in general perform relatively little basic research and development, and in many instances whatever research and development occurs is carried out elsewhere. In contrast, product development is widely performed in Hong Kong. Hong Kong firms in the manufacturing industries studied in this project, garments and electronics, do not perform appreciable after-sales service.

Operations (either manufacturing or, for service industries, the actual provision of services) and human resources management show a relatively high degree of geographic dispersal. As we have seen from the industry studies, Hong Kong firms are increasingly pursuing dispersed manufacturing strategies, with operations in China, Asia, and globally, and therefore require some form of dispersed human resource management. This pattern underscores the role of Hong Kong's firms as packagers and integrators of economic activity regionally and globally. It also confirms recent findings by the Hong Kong Trade Development Council that the territory's manufacturing and trading firms draw upon a diversified production base that expands well beyond Hong Kong and the Mainland.[30]

Hong Kong emerges clearly as a centre for procurement, marketing, design, and logistics. Firms across the entire spectrum of industries studied in this project are choosing to locate these activities in Hong Kong because of the territory's powerful strengths as a transport and communications hub, its deep business services cluster, its powerful light manufacturing and trading cluster, and its specialized expertise. Hong Kong's powers of attraction are strongest precisely at the high-value points on the value chain. This is the result of a strategic rearrangement of activities across industries, from which Hong Kong has emerged as the centre of procurement, marketing, design, and logistics for a wide range of dispersed economic activity.

Figure 5.7 contains a skeletal summary of the areas of advantage in the representative industries. Even at this level, overall patterns that are reflective of the Hong Kong economy start to emerge. A single plus sign indicates a source of advantage in regional or global terms. Two plus signs indicate strong advantage, and three plus signs indicate a truly extraordinary advantage. The operative question is: Does this driver of competitiveness provide a source of competitive advantage in today's international marketplace?

The pattern that emerges offers several insights into the competitive positioning of Hong Kong's industries. The industries studied in this project show a relatively dense pattern of advantage. Most of the industries studied derive competitive

Figure 5.7 Sources of Advantage in Hong Kong Industry

	Inst	Inputs	Demand	Cluster	Strategy	Comp/ Coop
Garments	+	++		+	++	+
Electronics		+		+	+	
Trading	+	++		++	++	
Fund Management	++	+		+++		+
Civil Engineering		+	++	++		
Air Cargo	++	++	+++	++	+	
Sea Cargo	++	+++	+++	+++	++	
Telecommunications	+	+	++		++	
Tourism	+	++		++	+	

advantages in the relevant foreign markets in at least four of the six drivers, and also show strong advantages (indicated by at least two plus signs) in at least two drivers each. This indicates that these Hong Kong industries derive strengths from multiple aspects of Hong Kong's economic system. This is a positive sign for the health of Hong Kong's industries generally. In international competition, industries that enjoy broadly based strengths rooted in different aspects of their domestic economic system tend to be more robust than industries dependent on a single source of advantage.

All of the industries studied, for example, derive competitive advantage in the international playing field from local inputs, including basic natural endowments (such as location), and human inputs (such as expertise). These input advantages are reinforced in most industries by parallel advantages offered by the local clustering of firms, which provide related industry inputs and a critical mass of expertise. As we also have seen, some of Hong Kong's most dynamic industries occur at points in the economy where multiple clusters overlap. This suggests that cluster-related advantages in these industries are very deep, and that the input and other advantages within those clusters are mutually reinforcing.

Figure 5.7 also reflects deep and widely distributed

advantages in the area of firm strategy. In most of the industries studied, aggressive firm strategies are distinct sources of advantage in international competition. We see a broad mix of managerial and entrepreneurial firms, of local and overseas firms, and of hustle and commitment strategies across different sectors. We also see government and institutional structures as sources of advantage in most of the industries studied. This does not mean that government or its policies have been perfect, but it does mean that on the whole, the Hong Kong government's business and economic policies have placed Hong Kong firms in a strong or very strong competitive position *vis-à-vis* the relevant foreign rivals. In this regard, we have looked at the institutional and regulatory system as a whole, including low levels of government intervention, the provision of a level playing field and well-functioning judicial system, low corporate and personal taxation, and the open flow of goods, capital, expertise, and information.

Among the industries studied for this project, competition has had only a limited impact. In garments, this is the result of a system of international quota rules which obviated head-to-head competition for foreign market share. In export trading, it is a function of competing by forming new relationships. In other industries, such as sea cargo, it is a function of demand exceeding supply. The industries studied in this project do not reveal systemic cooperation among local firms in pooling activities that lend themselves to consolidation at the industry or district level.

Consumer and industrial demand emerge as competitive strengths in industries linked to Hong Kong's transportation, communications, and property/construction clusters. In these sectors, local demand tends to be both large and sophisticated. We have seen in several industries a dynamic where large and sophisticated users—of civil engineering services or sea cargo services, for example—pressure local service providers to find solutions to local input constraints, such as difficult building terrain or a shortage of cargo holding space. This pressure fosters the development of state-of-the-art technical and managerial innovations.

THE INDUSTRIES IN PERSPECTIVE

Many studies of the competitiveness of economies focus on macroeconomic aggregates and never delve into individual industries. But it is in individual industries that firms add value and create wealth. It is only at the industry level that we can see Hong Kong's unique combinations truly at work. The industry level is where we can best see the emergence of Hong Kong and its firms as packagers and integrators of economic activities, as foreign investors, as a home for overseas firms, and as drivers of the modernization of the Mainland economy. An understanding of the competitiveness of Hong Kong's industries underpins an understanding of Hong Kong's clusters and its economy.

So far we have focused on the past and present of the Hong Kong economy at the economy level, the cluster level, and the industry level. We next turn to the future of the Hong Kong economy: its opportunities, its challenges, its competitors, and its uncertainties.

NOTES

1 See, for example, Michael Enright, Antonio Francés, and Edith Scott Saavedra, *Venezuela: The Challenge of Competitiveness*, New York: St. Martins Press, 1996; Michael Enright and Rolf Weder, *Studies in Swiss Competitive Advantage*, Berne: Peter Lang, 1995; Graham Crocombe, Michael Enright, and Michael Porter, *Upgrading New Zealand's Competitive Advantage*, Auckland: Oxford University Press, 1991.

2 See Michael Enright, 'Why Local Clusters Are the Way to Win the Game', *World Link* (July/August 1992): 24–5.

3 Hong Kong Port Development Board, *Hong Kong Port Cargo Forecasts 1995*, February 1996, pp. 5.85, 5.42.

4 Interview with Hong Kong Port Development Board.

5 K. K. Chadha, 'MTL Throughput Hits Record High', *South China Morning Post: Business Post* (3 October 1994): 2.

6 This is a wider category than that in the tables of Chapter 1.

7 About 60 per cent of the sector is focused on cut-and-sewn garments, with just under 25 per cent focused on piece-knitted garments, and the remainder on fur and leather goods, gloves, hosiery, and clothing accessories.

8   Hong Kong Government Industry Department, 'Clothing Industry', in *1995 Hong Kong Manufacturing Industries*, 1995, pp. 41–57.

9   In 1995, 48 per cent of domestic exports of garments went to the United States, while Germany and the United Kingdom combined accounted for 20.8 per cent. Hong Kong Trade Development Council, private communication.

10 A representative case is Winsor Industrial Corp., for many years Hong Kong's largest listed textile firm, which in 1993 shifted cotton weaving and yarn dyeing operations to Malaysia, and in 1994 shifted bleaching and dyeing works to Heshan, Guangdong. Nicholas Reynolds, 'End of an Era Flagged as Garment Giant Crosses the Border', *South China Morning Post: Business Post* (24 May 1994): 3.

11 Hong Kong Census and Statistics Department, 'Principal Statistics for all Establishments by Major Industry Group, Industry Group and Sales and Other Receipts, 1994', in *Report on 1994 Survey of Wholesale, Retail & Import & Export Trades, Restaurants & Hotels*, August 1996, p. 16.

12 Hong Kong Trade Development Council, *Hong Kong's Trade and Trade Supporting Services*, April 1996, p. 14.

13 Hong Kong Census and Statistics Department, *Hong Kong Monthly Digest of Statistics* (September 1996): 16.

14 Gareth Hewett, 'Service with a Smile as Hong Kong Reverts to Playing Traditional Role', *South China Morning Post: Business Post* (5 May 1996): 12.

15 Hong Kong Census and Statistics Department, *Hong Kong Monthly Digest of Statistics* (October 1996): 16.

16 Hong Kong's Trade Development Council recently found that trading and manufacturing firms with controlling headquarters in Hong Kong are a strong source of demand for local supporting services. Hong Kong Trade Development Council, *Hong Kong's Trade and Trade Supporting Services*, pp. 17, 29.

17 KPMG Management Consulting Ltd. for the Hong Kong Productivity Council, *Moving Forward by Adding Value: A Study of Productivity in Hong Kong's Trading Sectors*, Hong Kong, January 1996, p. 9.

18 Hong Kong Trade Development Council, *Hong Kong's Trade and Trade Supporting Services*, pp. 17, 29.

19 Asia Pacific Economics Group, *Asia Pacific Profiles 1996*, Research School of Pacific and Asian Studies, Australian National University, South Melbourne: Pearson Professional [Australia] Pty. Ltd. (distr.), 1996, p. 280.

20 For example, the German insurer Allianz selected Hong Kong as its regional base for fund management in April 1996 because of the liquidity of the local equity market. See John Ridding, 'Allianz Expansion Puts Faith in Hong Kong', *Financial Times* (22 April 1996): 27.

21 Airport Authority Hong Kong, Press Release, 28 September 1995.

22 Hong Kong's leading professional association for civil engineers counts

more than 5,530 qualified members. Hong Kong Trade Development Council, *Profiles of Selected Service Industries of Hong Kong*, March 1996, p. 23.

23 Half of this demand is accounted for by international calls, and a further US$900 million by local and fixed calls. Cellular demand accounts for around US$600 million, while paging services account for another US$500 million. Demand is expected to quadruple in nominal terms in the coming ten years. Peter Tsang, Managing Director, New T&T, private communication.

24 In a recent survey, overseas firms operating in Hong Kong rated the territory's communications network as 'very satisfactory' (scoring 3.9 points out of a total of 4.0). The communications infrastructure was identified as an important contributor to these firms' positive outlook for their operations in Hong Kong for the next three years. Survey Research Hong Kong Ltd. (SRH), *AmCham Business Confidence Survey: Management Report*, Hong Kong, November 1995, p. 10.

25 Professor John Ure, University of Hong Kong, private communication.

26 John Ure, 'Telecommunications', in Joseph Y. S. Cheng and Sonny S. H. Lo (eds.), *From Colony to SAR: Hong Kong's Challenges Ahead*, Hong Kong: Chinese University Press, 1995, p. 410.

27 Hong Kong Tourist Association, *A Statistical Review of Tourism 1995*, 1995, pp. 5, 6, 14.

28 Ibid., p. 14.

29 For an explanation of the value chain, see Michael E. Porter, *Competitive Advantage*, New York: The Free Press, 1985.

30 Hong Kong Trade Development Council, *Hong Kong's Trade and Trade Supporting Services*, p. 5.

6 OPPORTUNITIES FOR HONG KONG

The various strengths and advantages apparent in the Hong Kong economy open up the potential to capture a range of opportunities both locally and in overseas markets that so far have either not been exploited, or have only partially been explored. Hong Kong and its firms are poised to benefit from numerous opportunities in China and in the Asian region. Further opportunities can be derived from leveraging the development of local demand within Hong Kong and by extending the internationalization of Hong Kong's service economy. Specific sectors examined as part of this study have their opportunities as well. Finally, the new opportunities available to Hong Kong firms might give them the option to expand their choice sets and to augment their traditional strategies.

OPPORTUNITIES ON THE CHINESE MAINLAND

The most significant opportunities for local companies are those in mainland China, which represents the single largest potential business and economic opportunity in the world today. China is not only the world's most populous nation, it also had the world's fastest growing economy over the last decade and a half by a significant margin (real GDP grew at a rate of 10.2 per cent per year from 1980 to 1990 and 12.9 per

Table 6.1 Cumulative Inbound Foreign Investment,
Selected Nations, 1989–1995

Country/Region	Cumulative Investment (Billions of US Dollars)
United States	239
China	122
United Kingdom	117
Singapore	27
Brazil	13
Indonesia	13
Japan	7
South Korea	6
India	3

Source: United Nations Conference on Trade and Development (UNCTAD), *UNCTAD World Investment Report 1996: Investment, Trade and International Policy Arrangements*, Annex Table 1, pp. 227–31.

cent per year from 1990 to 1994).[1] In the process, China's standard of living has improved faster for more people than at any time or place in world history. By World Bank estimates, the Chinese economy is already larger than that of Japan on a purchasing-power-parity basis.[2] If growth were to slow to 7 per cent per year, by 2006 mainland China's economy would have roughly the same purchasing power as the United States economy had in 1994. China, of course, faces many economic challenges, including an inefficient state-owned sector, a backward banking system, and inefficiencies due to poor planning, corruption, and nepotism. Its potential, however, has led more than one commentator to call China the next economic superpower.[3]

China also has joined the world economy. The Chinese Mainland has become the tenth leading trading economy in the world and its total trade has been growing at roughly three times the rate of total world trade. Its exports increased at a rate of 11.5 per cent per year from 1980 to 1990 and by 16 per cent per year from 1990 to 1994. Imports rose at a rate of 10 per cent and 24.8 per cent per year for the two periods.[4] Growth in output and trade from Hong Kong's Guangdong hinterland has been roughly twice that of the Mainland economy as a whole. The Mainland economy also has attracted an enormous amount of foreign investment, rising in a few short years to become one of the world's leading destinations for international investments. (See Table 6.1.)

In almost every area of business activity in which Hong Kong companies are involved, they stand in pole position to intermediate between international business, and the emerging market-oriented businesses of the Mainland. As hub for almost 2,000 multinational companies, for an estimated 3,000 Taiwanese companies, and for more than 2,000 Mainland Chinese corporations, Hong Kong has aggregated a huge critical mass of knowledge and experience about doing business in China (for foreign companies) and in the global markets (for Mainland companies keen to boost trade and attract investment). Hong Kong companies have unique practical experience of operating inside the Mainland economy. The country-wide reach of Hong Kong investors is worth re-emphasizing, since many acknowledge the importance of Hong Kong's impact on the Pearl River Delta or China south of the Yangtze without fully appreciating that Hong Kong is by a large margin the leading investor in almost every province and city in the country.[5] Counter-intuitively, this is as true in Liaoning, close to Japan, and Shandong, close to Korea, as it is in Shanghai or Fujian.

Up to now, responding to the priorities of China's national and regional leaderships, Hong Kong investment has been concentrated on export processing of light manufactures, on property, and on infrastructure-building. But as the Mainland economy matures and opens further to foreign investment, there will be opportunities to invest in machinery and other industrial goods manufacture, in food processing, distribution, and retailing, to identify just a few. Distribution and logistics, which are not well-developed on the Mainland and in which Hong Kong firms excel, could be a prime example.

In addition, if the Guangdong economy follows the path of the economies of Japan, Korea, or Taiwan, light manufacturing exports will create enough income to support the development of cities that will have substantial 'industrial' demand (demand for capital goods, building materials, construction inputs, and business services). Given the size of the population and economy, it will soon be economical to produce many of these inputs locally rather than to import them. To date, Hong Kong's export traders have been quite active in Guangdong. Soon, Hong Kong's import traders could have the same opportunities to set up facilities in South China, only this time to serve the local market. Since Hong Kong's import traders generally import machinery, industrial goods, and technological goods from the West or from Japan and sell them into the region, it might prove advisable to try to set up production joint ventures for these products in South China. The window of opportunity for Hong Kong firms might be limited, however, as more and more Western and Japanese companies develop their own contacts on the Mainland and increase the potential of bypassing Hong Kong altogether.

Vast opportunities are also likely to arise in China's tertiary sector. China's tertiary sector has been growing at 10.4 per cent per year since 1981, and now accounts for more than 31 per cent of GDP. Value-added in tertiary industries amounted to almost US$220 billion at the end of 1995. Just under 150 million people were employed in services—about 24 per cent of the national work-force. About 40 per cent of investment flows into the Mainland in 1995 were in the tertiary sector, with the largest sums focused on the financial sector (US$9 billion), telecommunications (US$6 billion), and tourism and transport (over US$2 billion).[6]

While such absolute numbers are large, Beijing recognizes that by international standards its services economy is underdeveloped. As a result, it is committed to speeding development of the sector. Growth is expected to continue at 11 per cent per year, with services accounting for 35 per cent of GDP by 2000, and generating a further 40 million jobs. Priority areas for development under the current Ninth Five Year Plan are commerce, trade, finance, insurance, tourism, real estate, warehousing, public amenities, catering, legal, accounting and business services, transport, telecommunications, public utilities, education, and scientific research.

Beijing already has liberalized a number of these service sectors. Foreign banks now have branches in more than 23 cities on the Mainland. They are effectively barred from engaging in local currency business, but are beginning to operate in a wide range of commercial banking activities. International insurance companies are operating on a pilot basis in Shanghai and Guangzhou. A number of pilot joint-venture retail enterprises have been set up, with foreign-owned chain stores now joining the fray in competition with an estimated 300 domestic retail chain operators. Other foreign service providers have set up joint ventures in real estate, civil aviation, and telecommunications.

It is clear that Hong Kong-based firms, whether owned by local entrepreneurs, Mainland Chinese, or foreign multinationals, are well positioned to tackle and capture these opportunities as they arise. Hong Kong-based law firms make up the bulk of around 60 foreign legal firms now approved to be set up in China.[7] At the same time, many Hong Kong-based accountants have established a presence on the Mainland, and are active in training Mainland accountants and auditors. They also are collaborating with Mainland institutions in setting up curricula and examinations for Chinese accountants.

As with accountancy, legal services, and banking, a wide range of Hong Kong-based service providers are already preparing to capture opportunities as they arise on the Mainland. For some, the geographical, cultural, linguistic, and family links with Guangdong and the Pearl River Delta will make this the preferred initial target market. But for many of the international firms based in Hong Kong, nation-wide strategies are being devised through wholly owned ventures and joint ventures with Mainland partners. For Hong Kong as a whole, these developments suggest a wide range of new opportunities for local service providers, and a further strengthening of the territory's pivotal role as Asia's strongest and most diversified service economy.

Hong Kong's role as a test site for products and services

aimed at the large Mainland market is also likely to provide a wide range of opportunities, underpinned by the many thousands of Mainlanders who visit the territory each year, and by the growing exposure of Mainland audiences to Hong Kong television programming. This will range from foods, fashion-wear, and consumer electronics to local films and pop music. Developing this potential will require concerted efforts by local and international manufacturers and their product design teams. It will also require the critical input of locally based advertising, marketing, and product designers who can combine their knowledge of, and connections with, multinational groups with their knowledge of the developing tastes of the Mainland consumers, and those of the new consumer markets of the region. Many of these opportunities are linked with the strength and vitality of the Cantonese culture, which Hong Kong people share with over 60 million Mainlanders in South China, and with the emergence of Hong Kong brands as leading-edge brands. Clearly, careful development of Hong Kong brands will play an important part in leveraging Hong Kong's value as test site. It is arguable that many companies in the territory have been slow off the mark in 'brand-building', and will need to dedicate more attention and resources to the issue if the territory's full potential as a test site is to be captured.

OPPORTUNITIES IN ASIA

If mainland China represents the largest single business opportunity in the world today, the rest of Asia must rank second. The emergence of Asia's economies has been the most important development in the last quarter of the twentieth century. Myriad opportunities arise for Hong Kong companies simply by riding the wave of regional economic growth, which remains by a wide margin the fastest of any region in the world. (See Tables 6.2 and 6.3.) Between 1980 and 1994, Asia increased its share of world output from 17 per cent to 26 per cent in nominal terms. During this period, Asian growth was nearly

Table 6.2 Economic Data, Selected Asian Economies

Country/Region	Population (millions) 1994	Per Capita GDP (PPP)[a] (US$) 1995	GDP (PPP)[a] (US$ bn) 1995	Average GDP Growth 1991–1995	Average Export Growth 1991–1995	GDP Growth 1996[b]	Export Growth 1996[b]	International Reserves (US$ bn) October 1996
Hong Kong	6.1	23,892	148	5.6%	14.8%	4.9%	10.6%	59.5
Singapore	2.9	23,565	70	8.6	16.2	8.3	10.1	72.2
Japan	125.1	22,200	2,782	1.2	0.4	3.9	8.7	211.0
Taiwan	21.6	14,295	304	6.7	6.4	5.1	7.3	85.2
South Korea	44.5	11,750	527	7.6	13.1	6.8	11.0	32.8
Malaysia	19.7	9,470	191	8.5	13.5	8.5	11.3	25.1
Thailand	58.0	7,535	454	8.5	14.6	8.5	12.8	38.8
Indonesia	190.4	3,705	724	6.9	12.6	6.8	11.2	14.7
China	1,190.9	2,935	3,587	11.8	17.4	9.6	7.2	90.8
Philippines	67.0	2,395	199	2.4	6.9	4.6	12.3	8.8

[a] PPP = purchasing power parity.
[b] Estimate as of October 1996.
Sources: Column 1, The World Bank; columns 2–3, The World Bank, *Asiaweek* (1 November 1996): 57; columns 4–7, DRI/McGraw-Hill, The World Bank; column 8, *Asiaweek* (1 November 1996): 57, *Far Eastern Economic Review* (31 October 1996): 64.

Table 6.3 Foreign Investment Inflows, Selected Host Economies, 1984–1995

Country/Region	Billions of US Dollars						
	1984–1989 (average)	1990	1991	1992	1993	1994	1995
World	115.4	203.8	157.8	168.1	207.9	225.7	314.9
South, East, and South-East Asia (incl. Japan)	9.9	21.6	22.5	30.7	46.7	54.5	65.0
(% of World)	(8.6)	(10.6)	(14.3)	(18.2)	(22.5)	(24.1)	(20.6)
China	2.3	3.5	4.4	11.2	27.5	33.8	37.5
Hong Kong	1.4	1.7	0.5	2.1	1.7	2.0	2.1
Indonesia	0.4	1.1	1.5	1.8	2.0	2.1	4.5
South Korea	0.6	0.8	1.2	0.7	0.6	0.8	1.5
Malaysia	0.8	2.3	4.0	5.2	5.0	4.3	5.8
Philippines	0.3	0.5	0.5	0.2	1.0	1.5	1.5
Singapore	2.2	5.6	4.9	2.4	5.0	5.6	5.3
Taiwan	0.7	1.3	1.3	0.9	0.9	1.4	1.5
Thailand	0.7	2.4	2.0	2.1	1.7	0.7	2.3

Source: UNCTAD, UNCTAD World Investment Report 1996, pp. 230–1.

twice that of the rest of the world economy. If present trends continue, by 2010, Asia will account for more than 40 per cent of world output.[8] While growth has in some economies been from a low base, this is no longer true in many countries in the region. Japan, Hong Kong, and Singapore are now among the wealthiest economies in the world on a per capita basis. After more than 20 years of growth averaging 7 to 8 per cent, standards of living in South Korea and Taiwan are now equal to those for many in Europe. Countries like Malaysia, Thailand, and Indonesia also now boast substantial middle-income populations with substantial consumer power. While average incomes on the Chinese Mainland remain low in nominal terms, strong economic growth in urban centres and in the country's coastal provinces have lifted incomes above US$1,000 per year for tens of millions of consumers. In addition, on a purchasing-power-parity basis, Chinese incomes are significantly higher. The steady lowering of tariff barriers around the region is beginning to provide unprecedented access to consumers in these markets—access beneficial to Hong Kong firms, with their particular strengths as a supplier of fashion-driven consumer products ranging from garments and consumer electronics to wrist-watches.

As the Asian economies grow, East–West (Asia with Europe and the Americas) and East–East trade and investment are increasing in importance. Trade flows between Asia and North America have exceeded those between North America and the European Union throughout the 1980s and 1990s. Trade to and from Asia and intra-Asian trade have been growing significantly faster than trade elsewhere, despite the North American Free Trade Agreement and the European Union's 1992 Programme. (See Figure 6.1.) In 1980, intra-EU trade was 3.7 times that of intra-Asian trade; by 1994, it was 1.5 times intra-Asian trade. In 1980, intra-Asian trade was 1.9 times that of intra-North American trade; by 1994, the figure was 3.2 times.

Investment flows from North America to Asia historically have been lower than those from North America to Western Europe, but recent data suggest that this may be changing. From

175

Figure 6.1   Growth in Trade, 1984–1994, 1990–1994

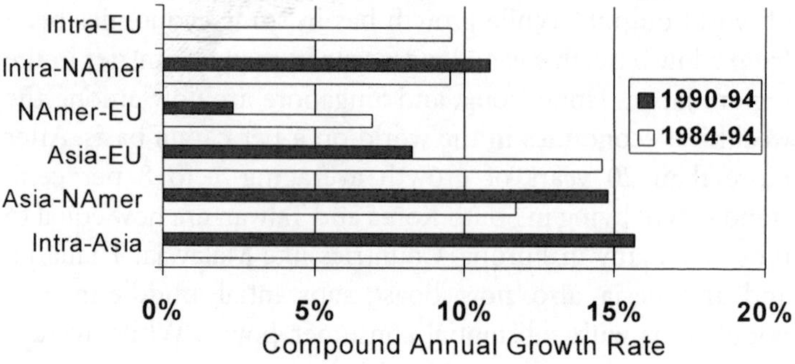

Source: Calculated from data in International Monetary Fund, *Direction of Trade Statistics Yearbook*,
Washington, D.C., various editions.

1990 to 1994, United States foreign direct investment stock in
the Asia–Pacific region grew at 6.6 per cent on average, a
significantly higher growth rate than that applicable to United
States foreign direct investment stock in Europe (4.4 per cent).
In 1994, United States investments in the Asia–Pacific region
earned higher rates of return (on average 12.1 per cent) than
those in Western Europe (on average 9.4 per cent).[9]

Intra-Asian flows of foreign direct investment have
accelerated very rapidly, with the Asian newly industrialized
economies (NIEs) emerging as new investors in other Asian
nations. In 1993, more than half of the total value of the foreign
direct capital stock in East and South-East Asia originated
from within Asia itself.[10] As more of Asia's nations reach a
certain level of affluence, and as formerly closed export-driven
economies become more open, intra-Asian trade and
investment are expected to rise rapidly over the next two
decades. As Asia's leading foreign investor and a centre which
accounts for nearly 17 per cent of all intra-Asian trade, Hong
Kong is poised to benefit from increased East–West and
East–East flows.[11]

As one examines the forces that underpin increases in Asia's
wealth, trade, and investment flows, so again they play to Hong
Kong's strengths. Take for example those trends described by
John Naisbitt in his recent book *Megatrends Asia*: a shift of

emphasis from nation states to networks; from traditions to options; from export-led economies to consumer-driven economies; from government-controlled to market-driven economies; from farms to 'supercities'; from labour-intensive activity to high technology activity; from male dominance to the emergence of women; and from the economic dominance of the West to a more equal balance between East and West.[12]

Naisbitt claims, 'The world is moving from a collection of nation-states to a collection of networks'[13] and that the overseas Chinese network will be the organizational model for business in the twenty-first century and the main driver of economic transformation of Asia. The rapid rise of the region's middle class has triggered a trend from export-led economies to consumer-driven economies. As more and more people (some estimate a billion by 2010) in Asia acquire significant purchasing power, Asian consumer markets for goods, entertainment, and travel will take off. 'Traditions to options' captures the shift from societies in which roles were prescribed to societies in which new-found affluence and openness allow greater scope for personal decision-making. 'Export-led to consumer-driven' is the transition from export economies in which consumption was often suppressed to the development of affluent middle classes in the region. 'Government-controlled to market-driven' is the trend toward a greater focus on economic well-being and openness than on ideology, as well as the growth of private enterprise and the privatization of government-owned businesses. 'Farms to supercities' involves migration from farms to major metropolitan areas.

Hong Kong is squarely at the forefront of, and ready to profit from, most of these trends. Hong Kong is poised to benefit from the shift from West to East. If the overseas Chinese (or eventually 'Chinese') business network is the organizational form of the future, Hong Kong is the headquarters location. Nowhere else is even close to its ability to link the overseas network and the emerging network of Mainland entrepreneurs. The implications for Hong Kong—as a location for company headquarters, as a meeting place for business in the region, and as a supplier of business services—is potentially staggering, especially when one realizes that in the absence of any real affinities among Asian nations, the overseas Chinese network provides the only truly functional transnational links in the region.

The movement to individual choice, market-driven societies, and consumer-driven economies also should benefit Hong Kong. Who in Asia knows the ins and outs of a market economy better than Hong Kong business people? Who is better at anticipating, recognizing, and then satisfying rapidly emerging consumer demand? Who is better positioned to profit from increased flows of trade and investment? Who is better positioned to benefit from increases in travel in the region, especially travel into and out of China? Who is better positioned to participate in the massive financing of development and infrastructure projects Asia will need in the next decades? Who is better positioned to help put together privatization deals in the region, or to invest in them? Urban planners from around the region already flock to Hong Kong to understand how it works. Who is better situated to provide advice, consulting, and engineering help to Asia's emerging metropolises?

These trends will give Hong Kong and its firms the opportunity to exploit their skills and capabilities over a wider field than has been possible to date. Of course not all aspects of these trends would be positive for Hong Kong. Many, for example, would claim that Hong Kong is behind in Asia's high technology boom.[14] (Hong Kong spends a far lower percentage of its GDP on research and development and lacks the position that Japan, Korea, Taiwan, and Singapore have in high technology industries.) New supercities might provide competition for some of the activities that Hong Kong has historically performed. If the rest of Asia becomes more like Hong Kong, then Hong Kong might be less distinctive in the future than it has been. Other centres also, Singapore for example, are well situated to benefit from many of the trends described. On balance, however, as long as Hong Kong is a leading indicator of trends in Asia, the territory and its firms should find substantial opportunities.

OPPORTUNITIES DRIVEN BY LOCAL DEMAND

Given the impressive growth potential of demand in the Mainland and other Asian markets, there is a strong temptation to be dismissive of local demand as a stimulus for Hong Kong companies. Yet there are opportunities to leverage capabilities developed in serving the Hong Kong market, and these have yet to be exploited. Historically, local demand in Hong Kong, for most goods, has been relatively small in world terms. Limited home markets have spurred Hong Kong manufacturers and traders to look overseas for business opportunities. Such was the case in the 1950s, when Shanghai refugees helped create Hong Kong's garment and textile industries and immediately looked to foreign markets. In the 1960s and 1970s, Hong Kong industrialists followed suit in a variety of light consumer goods, such as footwear, toys, watches, jewellery, travel goods, and handbags, where Hong Kong itself lacked a deep mass market.

As we have seen, however, several Hong Kong industries, such as export trading, shipping, freight forwarding, engineering services, and business services have benefited from a large and sophisticated local demand that forces them continually to improve. Hong Kong's export trading firms are sophisticated buyers of inputs and finished goods, as well as financial and logistical services. Hong Kong's shippers and freight forwarders are sophisticated purchasers of cargo and port services. Overseas firms in Hong Kong generally are a source of sophisticated demand for financial, logistics, legal, accounting, and other support services, as well as telecommunications, and have stimulated the provision of top-quality services by foreign and local companies. Demand within Hong Kong for engineering services for infrastructure and building projects is large in absolute terms and very sophisticated.

There are increasing opportunities for Hong Kong firms to benefit from the territory's growing consumer market as well. Rising wealth in the territory has crept up unnoticed on many local companies. Even today, few recognize that Hong Kong's market is not dissimilar from that of Switzerland, which has

179

a population of 7 million and per capita income (on a purchasing-power-parity basis) not far above that of Hong Kong—and Hong Kong is growing faster too. Hong Kong's consumer demand is often highly sophisticated despite its small size. Its consumers of consumer electronics are known to be 'status conscious and gadget crazy'. They value sophisticated new product features and enjoy experimenting with new product offerings. In Hong Kong, more than in most parts of the world, watches and even cellular phones are fashion accessories to be changed or 'upgraded' periodically.

Hong Kong consumers are also among the most brand-aware in the world and have a penchant for luxury items. They tend to favour foreign high-end brand names, which they associate with status. This tendency is at its most pronounced in the fashion segment, where there is a very marked preference for top French and Italian couture fashions among the high-income bracket. The high-end Hong Kong consumer would rather pay a very high premium for a European couture brand or label, even if he or she knows that it was made in Hong Kong, than the same garment with a Hong Kong label on it. The same tendency is also seen in consumer electronics and other products. The local preference for foreign brands has made it somewhat difficult for Hong Kong firms to leverage sophisticated demand in the local market into competitive advantages in international competition, as is often done around the world by firms with sophisticated home demand.

Hong Kong firms appear to be adapting to an increasingly important local consumer market in two ways: first, by capitalizing on the extraordinarily international fashion-sensitivity of Hong Kong consumers to provide a test site for retail goods before they are launched on global markets; and second by starting to develop local brands. The fact that a quarter of the territory's households appear willing to change their television every year (as mentioned in Chapter 5) allows television manufacturers to use Hong Kong to provide important signals to emerging tastes. They can quickly discover whether a new device or feature is likely to have consumer appeal. In other countries, where families change televisions every two, four, or even six years, such market research offers much less timely insight. This fashion-responsiveness can be found across the entire consumer spectrum in the territory. An unusually high proportion of Hong Kong families have multi-function telephones, multi-feature mobile phones and pagers, high-definition televisions, Nicam multi-language channel devices for televisions, laser-disc players, home computers, and fax machines at home as well as in the office. This explains why the territory has become home to over 80 Internet server companies in just a few years. At the same time, some Hong Kong fashion houses are developing their own brands and their own marketing systems in the West, such as Episode, which has stores in Knightsbridge (London) and on Fifth Avenue.

Hong Kong also is taking on an important role as a test market for mainland China. In some ways, Hong Kong has been an entry point for the Mainland market for many decades. Even during the Mainland's most reclusive and xenophobic days, Hong Kong was used as a source of quality international products, ranging from bathroom equipment to Western drugs and medical equipment. More recently, this role has expanded rapidly and become much more sophisticated. Many Western food companies have learned that Hong Kong is an ideal test-market for food products to be targeted at the region's Chinese consumers. As Hong Kong's media have become more important influences across South China, and in particular in the Pearl River Delta region, so the cachet attached to products used or advertised on Hong Kong television has helped to pave the way into the large Mainland Chinese consumer market.

So far, the unusual fashion-consciousness of Hong Kong's consumer market is understood only anecdotally. It is nevertheless distinctive enough to have made the territory a testing location for many local and international consumer goods companies, and suggests that local Hong Kong demand is significantly more important than mere numbers would imply. Clearly, opportunities exist for local and international companies to exploit further Hong Kong's potential as a test site.

SPECIFIC SECTORAL OPPORTUNITIES

A wide range of opportunities are arising that are specific to individual industries and activities in the Hong Kong economy. These were readily apparent in those areas we studied in detail, but without doubt are also apparent in other sectors too. There is potential for garment manufacturers to play a more potent role in the creation and development of new fashion trends. Many Hong Kong companies are well placed to hone skills and technologies that enable the fastest possible response to buyers' orders. These factors are likely to be of great importance as competitors in locations such as the Caribbean or Eastern Europe, which are so much closer to primary consumer markets, reach higher levels of production sophistication, and in their own right become speedier in meeting orders. Perhaps most important of all, Hong Kong manufacturers have substantial potential to develop own-brand garments for sale both in Western markets, and also in the emerging consumer markets of Asia. A few Hong Kong companies, such as Goldlion, Giordano, and Shanghai Tang, have already begun to establish such brands. Many others are equivocating on whether or not to develop them. All are tempted by the opportunity that brands offer to create consumer loyalty and to command a brand premium. But at the same time, they are wary of the costs involved in buying or establishing brand identity, and the limitations imposed on future strategic options once a brand has been established. This choice is a clear example of how hustle and commitment strategies are beginning to meld for many Hong Kong manufacturers as they become more substantial and influential in the global apparel market.

Few of Hong Kong's electronics manufacturers are yet in a position, as are many garment manufacturers, to consider developing global or regional brand identities. They play a smaller role in the world's electronics markets. With few exceptions, they have lacked the resources and the will (and the government support) to develop technologies that would put them among the world's brand leaders. They nevertheless have a number of distinctive opportunities to retain competitiveness into the future, based on their well-honed responsiveness to fast-changing consumer tastes. A number of local and regional electronics groups have come to recognize that the 'fast-turn', 'just-in-time' demands characteristic of the apparel industry are becoming applicable to their own industry, and that many aspects of their product are as seasonal and fashion-driven as the market for garments. They are increasingly pursuing upstream and downstream investment in strategic alliances with foreign companies to tackle weaknesses and develop synergies. In particular, Hong Kong electronics groups are well placed to leverage themselves in the Mainland Chinese market—as partners to fast-growing Mainland manufacturers, as partners to international companies seeking access to the Mainland market, and in their own right as suppliers into the Mainland market. They have potential to provide prototyping and beta-testing capability, in particular to the growing community of science-based industries on the Mainland which possess the technological capacity to compete internationally, but lack the knowledge of global markets that would enable them to respond effectively to changing consumer tastes.

For the territory's 100,000-plus trading companies—which range from substantial local and Western multinationals, to Japanese *sogo shosha*, to thousands of one- or two-person enterprises—the local clustering of skills and knowledge needed for effective regional sourcing gives an immense competitive advantage into the future. Opportunities arise for further diversification of sourcing, and for adding value by intensive application of information technology in the role they play between factory suppliers and retail outlets in Western and regional markets.

Analysis of the territory's port operations suggests that the future growth of import and export activity in Hong Kong's South China hinterland will maintain strong pressure on the port to develop services as rapidly as is physically possible. Much is said of the threat of diversion of cargo to other Mainland ports, in particular if and when Taiwan resumes direct trade with the Mainland. But even the most ambitious port development projects along the Guangdong, Fujian, and

Zhejiang coasts will only be able to offer in the first decade of the next century as much ultimate capacity as Hong Kong's current annual growth in container throughput. Sooner rather than later there will have to be a slowdown in the physical addition of new berths, but this is likely to be due to increasing local environmental concern over continuous expansion of container port facilities, rather than any abatement in demand. Port operators likely will have to make a virtue of this necessity by applying organization and management techniques and the latest technologies to intensify the throughput of each berth. Hong Kong's terminal operators are already planning productivity enhancements to raise the annual operating capacity of Container Terminals One through Eight by 17 per cent by 1998.[15] This immense and growing demand pressure is likely to keep Hong Kong port operators at the cutting edge of their industry in competitive terms, enabling them to bid for contracts to operate ports elsewhere, or perhaps to 'franchise' their methods. Already, Hong Kong's leading operators have won contracts to operate new coastal and river ports in China. One, Hongkong International Terminals (HIT), already operates a port in the United Kingdom and several in China. Again, the fast growth of the Asia–Pacific region is likely to make the area fertile for such opportunities in the future, particularly as governments privatize port operations and open contracts up to international competitive tender.

Our analysis of the activities linked with air cargo suggests the promise of a similar range of opportunities. The growth of demand for air cargo services is expected to be huge, driven by the economic dynamism of Hong Kong's Pearl River Delta hinterland, the region's increasing engagement in international trade, and buyer pressure for steadily tighter delivery deadlines. Hong Kong also is likely to remain a hub for a number of air cargo operators drawing cargo from the region, or distributing into it, adding to 'local' demand growth as a driver for development of the industry.

Hong Kong's new airport at Chek Lap Kok, due to open in 1998, will allow the introduction of state-of-the-art air cargo handling equipment and methods. The long-time monopoly of

Hong Kong Air Cargo Terminals Limited (HACTL) at Kai Tak will be broken, with a second air cargo consortium due to enter the fray at Chek Lap Kok, undoubtedly providing a competitive stimulus to services offered at the airport. Both of these developments are likely to force steadily higher levels of efficiency from the territory's air cargo operators. So, too, will the very high costs of operating at Chek Lap Kok. Airport charges have yet to be fixed, but it is already clear that the Hong Kong government, anxious to recoup some of the immense cost of building the airport from reclaimed land north of Lantau Island, intends to impose charges that will be high by international standards. Air operators have expressed alarm over the competitive challenge that would be generated by high airport charges. But if, as in the past, the air cargo operators develop efficiencies which enable them to continue to offer competitively priced services, they are likely to remain at the competitive cutting edge in terms of cargo handling methods and logistics, and ought to be in a strong position to 'export' these methods as and when opportunities arise to compete for air cargo handling contracts at airports across the Asia–Pacific region.

Local and regional opportunities for Hong Kong-based civil engineers are also extensive, in spite of the competitive challenges described earlier. While their costs are high, Hong Kong-based civil engineers possess a combination of unusual strengths which can be leveraged with great effect both in China and across the Asia–Pacific region. First, they have a vast body of work experience, given the mass of infrastructure-building that has occurred in Hong Kong over the past two decades. Second, they have rare experience of work in technically difficult or distinct circumstances—constructing high-rise buildings on land reclaimed from the ocean, and on precipitous granite slopes. Third, given Hong Kong's severe cost pressures, they are under extraordinary pressure to work at speed. Finally, they have extensive experience of build–own–operate (BOO), or build–operate–transfer (BOT) infrastructure contracts, which are likely to play a significant part in infrastructure-building across the region in the decades ahead.

For Hong Kong's telecommunications operators, new opportunities are emerging at a rapid rate, driven by technological developments as well as regional liberalization of telecommunications services. Hong Kong also is blessed with a unique optical fibre linkage across the region, endowed by Cable & Wireless, the United Kingdom company which controls the territory's one-time telecommunications monopolist, Hongkong Telecommunications. Many new entrants to the market have appeared over the past year, providing a wide range of services. Many of these are subsidiaries or affiliates of United States or European companies, and it is as yet open to question whether these companies will choose to tackle regional opportunities directly, or through affiliates based in the region. Hong Kong is by far the region's largest user of international telecommunications services, and thus has a clustering of skills, technologies, and critical mass efficiencies which can be applied effectively in other markets across the region. Nevertheless, the pace of technological change in this sector, coupled with the integration of telecommunications with information technology and media developments, makes it difficult to predict the future shape of the industry, and the role likely to be played by Hong Kong-based players. In principle, the burgeoning population of Hong Kong companies providing telecommunications and telecommunications-linked services should be well placed to capture Mainland and regional opportunities.

Finally, for Hong Kong's fund managers, substantial opportunities exist locally, across the Chinese Mainland, and for providing services and products to the wider Asia–Pacific region. The prospect of the Hong Kong government establishing a compulsory pension programme, the Mandatory Provident Fund Scheme, coupled with the emerging strength of similar schemes across the region, points towards strong growth for the fund management industry in general. This will be enhanced as the size and liquidity of regional stock markets grow, and as the massive United States, Japanese, and European mutual fund industries raise the international weightings of their portfolios. Hong Kong's fund management companies are at the fore in developing regional and China funds, and have a clustering of local strengths which augur well for managing a substantial proportion of the growing sums being channelled into the region, and for providing the hub for the regionally integrated operations of global fund managers. This sector is nevertheless sensitive to perceived risks associated with the transfer of Hong Kong from British to Chinese sovereignty in 1997, so it is possible that at least some of the growth in regional opportunities arising during the years spanning the transition will be channelled through other regional financial centres.

In addition to the sectors investigated specifically as part of this study, it also is useful to identify growth industries in the region. An extensive search of on-line databases for newspapers and periodicals turned up repeated references to high growth prospects for seven industries in Asia: business outsourcing, computers and electronics, entertainment and media, health care, information technology hardware and software, infrastructure, and tourism. Although others might come up with slightly different sets, these industries would rank high on any systematic list. What is interesting is that Hong Kong is either a regional leader or close to being a regional leader in all but two of the seven (computers and electronics, and information technology hardware and software). Though many people would not consider the other five 'high tech' industries, they are high growth industries and Hong Kong and its firms are well-positioned in them.

OPPORTUNITIES ARISING OUT OF THE INTERNATIONALIZATION OF SERVICES

In addition to opportunities in existing areas of strength, Hong Kong has the potential to develop new strengths through further internationalization of its service sector. Hong Kong's services sector is extraordinarily strong in the Asia–Pacific region. The sector is relatively larger, more diverse, and is developing faster than perhaps anywhere else in the region. It also is a bilingual one—perhaps the only fully bilingual service sector spanning the Chinese speaking and English speaking worlds. As a result, locally based services providers appear to be particularly well placed to capture opportunities that are beginning to arise across the region for cross-border trade in services.

There is ample opportunity for Hong Kong to extend its position as a regional services centre. Its clustering of expertise in trading services, financial services, accounting, legal, and other services for Chinese markets has been attracting an increasing number of regional headquarters, which in turn create even greater demand for servicing the activities of subsidiaries and affiliates dispersed across the region. Technological developments—in particular in telecommunications, computing and information technology—are making it easier for many companies to centralize many functions, and to control low-value-added, back-office activities that have been shifted to cheaper locations. The same technological changes are enabling service providers to circumvent regulatory barriers to delivery of their services across borders—whether this involves software companies delivering solutions to corporate problems over the Internet, or over a telephone line, or a design group sending designs by fax.

Additionally, the freedom of access to Hong Kong's own market for European and American services professionals is likely to generate many options for strategic alliances which capitalize on the technological and system strengths of Western professionals, and the efficiency and regional reach of Hong Kong partners—a highly competitive combination for tackling opportunities. The territory's services strengths make Hong Kong an attractive strategic ally as companies plan seriously how to build close and strong links with the world's fastest growing region.

Particular services areas come immediately to mind as sources of early opportunities, ranging from communications, import–export, and transport services to the media, advertising, market research, financial services, business services, and the gamut of consulting services. While the potential for banking and financial services, brokerage, and import–export services is by now widely understood, areas of opportunity in media services and civil engineering remain to be properly explored. As indicated earlier, Hong Kong is Asia's most dynamic media and communications centre. Its role as a communications hub and a marketplace for communications and entertainment companies is unrivalled in the region.

Hong Kong-based engineers, designers, architects, surveyors, and developers in the region are now using Hong Kong as their base to tackle the growing opportunities on the Chinese Mainland, and in Asia's other fast-growing economies—in particular Thailand, Vietnam, Malaysia, and Indonesia. While we have some reservations about the ability of such companies to export their services directly from Hong Kong rather than through affiliates based elsewhere in the region, it can be argued that this clustering of professionals has distinct strengths which provide the basis for careful exploration of export opportunities.

Hong Kong in addition has the potential to become a regional leader in services areas that have yet to be harnessed. In principle, Hong Kong has the potential to become a significant supplier of medical services to the region, and to become a hub for educational services. On the contrary, however, Hong Kong sustains a significant but unquantified deficit in these services, due at least in part to lack of competition in the sectors.[16] Quite modest reform could unleash the potential to reverse this outflow, enabling local medical and educational institutions to 'sell' services to the region. In Hong Kong, these areas have not been treated as businesses and the difficulties in internationalizing the services are largely bureaucratic.

Hong Kong's medical system is considered to be one of the best in Asia. The leading local hospitals have internationally high reputations in a number of areas of medical practice and research, including infectious tropical diseases. The medical profession in Hong Kong is self-regulating and has erected numerous barriers to entry for foreign doctors and medical services. Even the most highly skilled foreign doctors with degrees from the world's leading medical institutions have to undergo three years of training in Hong Kong before they can practice locally. Similar restrictions exist in the nursing profession, reducing the pool from which nurses can be drawn.

The public sector accounts for 90 per cent of hospital services, leaving a very small private sector with limited facilities and in which private doctors do not have access to public hospital facilities. This combination of forces has prevented Hong Kong from developing a regional medical services role and has restricted supply in the private sector. Instead of Hong Kong being a major destination for patients from the region, thousands of Hong Kong people travel to Europe or the United States for medical treatment each year.

In the education sector, standards compare favourably with other countries in the region, but in certain respects the government's historical monopoly has constrained development. At the primary and secondary levels, where most schools in the public sector are run by voluntary agencies on a publicly subsidized basis, government regulation has prohibited schools in the private sector from raising tuition fees in order to improve the quality of education offered, preventing them from competing against schools in the public sector.[17] The tertiary education sector lacks a strong contingent of privately owned and operated colleges and universities to act as a competitive stimulus to the public institutions of higher education. In 1993, international education brought US$1.1 billion in foreign revenues to Australia and US$1.09 billion to Canada. In the same year, the United States ran a trade surplus of US$6 billion in tertiary education and received an additional US$3.6 billion in related spending by international students.[18] By 1995, fees and expenditures by foreign students added roughly US$2 billion to the Australian economy.[19] One might ask why these nations should obtain such huge export earnings from its educational sector and Hong Kong hardly any.

Asian students accounted for 48 per cent of the 1.2 million students studying abroad in 1990. According to IDP Education Australia (a marketing body for Australia's colleges and

Table 6.4 International Student Enrollment Projections by Source Region, 2000–2025

Country/Region	Thousands		
	2000	2010	2025
China	143	318	849
Hong Kong	41	50	57
India	82	181	501
Indonesia	37	77	170
Japan	54	60	75
Malaysia	46	62	87
Philippines	13	31	61
Singapore	15	21	26
South Korea	58	76	80
Taiwan	65	87	108
Thailand	23	46	126

Source: The Australian Academy/IDP Education Australia, published in *Asian Business* (September 1996): 62.

universities), 50 per cent of the 2.8 million international students expected in 2010 and 59 per cent of the 4.9 million international students expected in 2025 will come from Asia.[20] (See Table 6.4.) China is expected to be the largest source of international students as demand for higher education dramatically outpaces supply. As the centre of gravity in economic and geopolitical terms moves toward Asia, so eventually will education services. Hong Kong, with its location, its educational tradition, and English language instruction, could benefit enormously in the process.

Even greater potential exists in the area of management and business training and education—tapping the territory's immense reservoir of international managers and entrepreneurs both as educators and as students on MBA and other business programmes. Evidence of this potential is already clear in the number of young Hong Kong executives who study on MBA and business programmes in the United States, Canada, Australia, and the United Kingdom. It is also clear in the number of 'satellite' courses offered in Hong Kong by numerous business schools. Top flight local programmes could become strong competitors in this marketplace.

There are unquestionably some barriers to the internationalization of Hong Kong service industries. Some Hong Kong service operations are domestically oriented because of the need for local delivery of service. Others are domestically oriented because multinational service firms might have no interest in having their Hong Kong affiliate enter markets already covered by sister affiliates. This is a particular issue for Hong Kong's banking and finance, fund management and insurance, accountancy, legal services, civil engineering, and even telecommunications sectors where multinationals dominate. In many nations, service industries are protected by barriers to trade and investment (which were reduced only slightly by the 1994 Uruguay Round agreement on global trade liberalization). Across the Asia–Pacific region, many services remain the domain of national or municipal monopolies, often government-owned or subsidized. Others, like medicine, the law, accountancy and architecture, are subject to highly protective rules drawn up by local professional associations, or, like civil engineers, architects, and other consultant professionals, face information requirements that can hinder outsiders from competing with local companies.

In spite of these highly cautionary notes, many Hong Kong services companies can remain confident that expanding opportunities are likely to arise in markets across the region in the decade ahead.

EXPANDING STRATEGIC CHOICES FOR FIRMS

As Hong Kong companies evolve and mature, and fresh opportunities arise, it is fruitful to consider a wider range of strategic choices to capture these opportunities. In addition, as more and more Hong Kong residents call Hong Kong home and become less interested in returning to ancestral homes or moving elsewhere, some of the transient mentality that has limited certain strategies might diminish. As Hong Kong-based firms develop sources of supply and markets on the Mainland and in the region, they might finally find themselves with sufficiently stable, or substantial, supply and demand to undertake strategies that rely on investments in technologies, brands, physical assets, and personnel.

Massive demands on the Mainland and the region for infrastructure and development might well make investments in technology developments in these industries more attractive to Hong Kong firms. As sizeable technology-based industries develop on the Mainland, they might provide the critical mass of demand for technology development in other industries that has been lacking and has limited investment in technology development in Hong Kong to date. Many Hong Kong firms have acted to transfer technology in light manufacturing industries to the Mainland and elsewhere, and there is no reason to believe that Hong Kong cannot expand the range of industries in which it provides similar services. On the other hand, Hong Kong and its firms also are well situated to be involved in the commercialization of technologies developed in South China or elsewhere on the Mainland.

As demand in Hong Kong, the Mainland, and Asia expands, there will be additional opportunities for Asian brands to take their place alongside Western brands. Given the strength of Hong Kong's market research capabilities and the fast response to changing consumer demand exhibited by many Hong Kong firms, Hong Kong seems to be a natural for this type of business, both for Hong Kong firms and for overseas firms.

In recent years, Hong Kong firms have been expanding their investments in automation, information systems, and communications hardware. The development of facilities and operations on the Mainland and elsewhere has allowed many Hong Kong firms to escape the limitations imposed by the limited land and labour available in Hong Kong itself. Though these 'foreign' facilities often employ significantly more people than the Hong Kong facilities they might have replaced, this does not mean that many firms have fundamentally changed the nature of their investments or lack of investments in physical assets. As export processing with leased facilities is replaced by joint ventures, more and more Hong Kong companies are faced with the prospects of increasing their investments in physical assets.

Finally, as family-run firms begin to professionalize their managements, as other firms depend on the skills of well-educated professionals, and as the requirements of doing business in Hong Kong become more demanding, there will be ample scope for firms to invest more in their key people and in the organization. Although this might be viewed primarily as a challenge, the growth in the Hong Kong economy and the options that Hong Kong companies have going forward also make it an opportunity.

THE OPPORTUNITIES

The combination of many natural and 'manufactured' advantages has created in Hong Kong a strong and resilient economy that should be favoured by the likely future direction of most key global economic trends. There are many specific opportunities for Hong Kong and its firms in individual industries and in the region. They suggest that Hong Kong has a promising future as one of the world's most versatile and prosperous economies. But opportunities by themselves do not create prosperity. Opportunities must be seized if they are to be of any use and there are others who are in the process of identifying many of the same opportunities identified by people in Hong Kong. Hong Kong will prosper—just so long as it can continue to meet its own internal challenges, to out-compete its competitors, to exploit optimally its many advantages, and to deal with the political and economic uncertainties that must inevitably arise during the territory's transition from British to Chinese administration. So it is to these separate issues that we must now turn in the coming chapters.

NOTES

1   World Bank, *From Plan to Market: World Development Report 1996*, New York: Oxford University Press, 1996, p. 208.

2   Calculated from data in the World Bank, *World Development Report 1996*.

3   See, for example, William H. Overholt, *China: The Next Economic Superpower*, London: Weidenfeld & Nicolson, 1993.

4   World Bank, *World Development Report 1996*, pp. 216, 208.

5   See Chapter 3, Table 3.5.

6   Hong Kong Trade Development Council, *The Opening of China's Tertiary Sector: Latest Development and Outlook*, May 1996, pp. 23–9.

7   Hong Kong Trade Development Council, 'Economic Relations between Hong Kong and China', July 1996, p. 4.

8   Calculated from data in World Bank, *World Development Report 1996*, pp. 210–11.

9   United Nations Conference on Trade and Development (UNCTAD), *World Investment Report 1996*, Fact Sheet No. 2, 24 September 1996.

10 Asian Development Bank, *Asian Development Outlook 1996 and 1997*, Hong Kong: Oxford University Press, 1996, pp. 196, 201.

11 Hong Kong Trade Development Council, 'Economic & Trade Information on Hong Kong', http://www.tdc.org.hk/main/economic.html#4, last updated 2 September 1996.

12 John Naisbitt, *Megatrends Asia: Eight Asian Megatrends that are Reshaping our World*, New York: Simon & Schuster, 1996, pp. 14–16.

13 Ibid., p. 23.

14 See United Nations Conference on Trade and Development (UNCTAD), *1996 UNCTAD Trade and Development Report*, New York and Geneva: United Nations, 1996; see also James Tien, 'The Brains Revolution but not Quite', *Hong Kong Echo Magazine*, 8 (Summer 1996): 54–5.

15 Hong Kong Port Development Board, *Hong Kong Port Cargo Forecasts 1995*, February 1996, pp. 5.76–5.77.

16 Private communication with a Hong Kong government official.

17 Richard Y. C. Wong, 'Understanding Competition in Hong Kong', reprinted from *HKCER Letters*, Hong Kong Centre for Economic Research, 20 (May 1993): 4.

18 Cris Prystay, 'Boom in University "Twinning" Across Asia', *Asian Business* (September 1996): 60.

19 Gary Silverman and Trish Saywell, 'Cramming Classes', *Far Eastern Economic Review* (14 November 1996): 28.

20 Prystay, 'Boom in University "Twinning" Across Asia', p. 60.

7 HONG KONG'S ECONOMIC CHALLENGES

Hong Kong's economy faces many challenges. In this chapter, we will focus on the economic and business challenges and will leave those associated with the change from British to Chinese administration for a later chapter. Hong Kong's economic transformation has left the economy stronger and more prosperous, but it also has created a number of internal economic challenges to its present and future competitiveness and prosperity. Key among these challenges are the costs incurred by companies doing business in Hong Kong, the need for improved work-force development, the competitiveness of the relatively protected non-traded sector, the future viability of past strategies, challenges surrounding technology development and utilization, the challenges associated with continuing to attract and retain the operations of overseas firms, the challenges of economic interaction with the Mainland, and challenges regarding the sustainability of government policy. These challenges are present and would have to be dealt with, with or without the 1997 transition. If anything, the uncertainty and pressure put on Hong Kong by the transition to Chinese administration makes it even more important that these challenges be met.

COST PRESSURES

One of the most frequently discussed issues concerning Hong Kong's present and future competitiveness is that of costs. Hong

Kong's residential and office rental costs are widely known to be among the most expensive in the world. The territory's reputation as a shopping paradise has been dented as retail rental costs have been carried through into the price of most retail items. Visitors from Japan might find Hong Kong's retail prices attractive by comparison with Osaka or Tokyo, but few from the United States or Europe are likely to find bargains matching those available at home. High levels of inflation— passing 10 per cent for several years in the past decade (see Table 7.1)—have added to cost pressures, and have been an inevitable consequence of pegging the local currency firmly to the United States dollar (the currency of a slower growing economy) since 1983. Fierce competition for skilled professional and managerial staff has lifted wage levels at a pace significantly higher than inflation. About 66 per cent of overseas firms with regional headquarters or offices in Hong Kong have encountered problems with high staff costs, according to a 1995 survey.[1] Manufacturers competing in global markets have been unable to pass these higher costs on into the prices charged for exported products, and so have seen margins squeezed. These factors together have contributed to the exodus of production lines and some back-office operations, have created anxiety over the territory's cost-competitiveness, and have prompted some companies to consider relocating headquarters and office activities to other centres in the region.

Before examining these concerns in detail, it is worth emphasizing that rising costs, though always a concern for individual companies, might not be as much of a concern for an economy as a whole. After all, the economic goal of a nation or region should be an economy with high wages and high asset values. If higher costs mean higher real wages and higher living standards, then they can be a good thing, delivering to the population some of the rewards of the territory's economic success. If cost increases are outpaced by increases in productivity, then the competitiveness of firms and industries can be enhanced in spite of rising nominal input costs. However, unless cost increases are matched by increases in productivity in existing businesses or migration to

Table 7.1 Inflation and Exchange Rates, Selected Economies

Country/Region	Average Change in Consumer Prices				Exchange Rate[b] Index, 1986 = 100 November 1996	CPI Index, 1986 = 100 Nov. 1996
	1971–80	1981–90	1991–95	1996[a]		
Hong Kong	8.7%	8.2%	9.2%	5.4%	101	215
China	1.1	7.8	11.6	8.1	42	293
South Korea	16.5	6.4	6.6	5.2	107	184
Malaysia	6.0	3.2	4.1	3.7	102	138
Singapore	7.4	2.3	3.0	1.2	155	127
Taiwan	11.1	3.1	3.6	2.2	138	135

[a] Annual rate as of 14 November 1996. All CPI measurements are in local currencies.
[b] Shows movement of US$/local currency. Numbers greater than 100 represent an appreciation of the local currency versus the US dollar. Numbers below 100 show a depreciation.
Sources: Asian Development Bank, *Asian Development Outlook 1992*, Hong Kong: Oxford University Press, 1992, pp. 296 and 308; Asian Development Bank, *Asian Development Outlook 1995 and 1996*, Hong Kong: Oxford University Press, 1995, pp. 247 and 257; *Far Eastern Economic Review* (14 November 1996): 84–85.

Table 7.2 Real Wage and Productivity Growth, Hong Kong, 1983–1993

Sector	Average annual change in real wages	Average annual change in labour productivity
Manufacturing	1.7%	4.2%
Wholesale, retail, export/import, restaurants, and hotels	1.7	3.0
Transport, storage, and communications	3.7	2.2
Financing, insurance, real estate, and business services	4.1	2.9
Community, social, and personal services	3.2	2.3

Source: S. K. Chan, 'The Enhancement of Productivity of Hong Kong's Human Resources', Speech Given to the Hong Kong Institute of Human Resources, 1995 Pay Trend Seminar, 3 November 1995, p. 3.

higher productivity businesses, the cost increases hurt competitiveness. Rough estimates of the productivity of different sectors of the Hong Kong economy indicate that in a number of sectors, wage increases outstripped productivity gains in the 1983 to 1993 period, which suggests that cost competitiveness in these sectors might have been declining. (See Table 7.2.)

A series of cost comparisons undertaken for this study (see Appendix) indicates that Hong Kong's rental costs for office space are very high, roughly comparable to those found in Tokyo, somewhat higher than those found in Singapore, comparable to those in Shanghai, and substantially higher than those found in Taipei or Sydney. Costs for a basic expatriate manager compensation package were lower than in Shanghai, higher than in Singapore, and substantially higher than in Sydney and Taipei. In a number of cost areas, such as air travel throughout Asia and telecommunications costs, Hong Kong compared quite favourably. When one factors in the advantages of the territory's low personal and corporate tax rates and simple tax system, Hong Kong's costs are on par with many cities in the region on an after-tax basis. In addition, Hong Kong's infrastructure and amenities are far superior to almost all other comparable cities in the region, with the exception of Singapore and Sydney.

Certain factors underlying Hong Kong's high cost base appear logical and perhaps even inevitable. The limited availability of land, which makes the territory by far the most densely populated urban area in the world, suggests not only that Hong Kong will continue to have high land, property, and rental costs—but that it ought to have, if factors of production are being allocated properly in the economy. The physical squeeze on land supply is aggravated by the distinctive mountain terrain that makes it impossible to build on much of the territory's land. Even where construction is possible, it is often expensive because of the engineering challenges of building high-rise structures on steep granite slopes. Some of this squeeze has been ameliorated by the reclamation of hundreds of hectares of land around Hong Kong's Victoria Harbour. But environmental considerations limit the amount of land that can be reclaimed and reclamation costs are such that this has done little to lower the average cost of property.

There are similarly logical reasons for the comparatively high labour costs. Hong Kong has quite strict limits on labour immigration, originating from a need during the 1950s and 1960s to control the influx of Chinese families seeking refuge from turbulence on the Mainland. These limits remain firmly in place today, and are unlikely to be relaxed through the transfer to Chinese sovereignty in 1997. They have led to a consistently tight labour market, in particular among the unskilled and semi-skilled, which has generated a steady upward pressure on remuneration packages. Singapore has responded to similar pressures by instituting a massive guest worker programme that employs some 300,000, in a state where total population is only around 3 million.[2] In addition, while Hong Kong has a well-educated, professional work-force, and a highly flexible set of policies linked with recruitment of expatriate professionals, the rapid structural transformation of Hong Kong into a knowledge-based metropolitan economy (as well as some loss of professionals to migration) has led to intense competition for skilled professionals. Interestingly, this is a problem that has become regional, as other economies in the region have also grown strongly. For example, Singapore companies faced with similar shortages of skilled personnel in a country with a labour force less than half the size of Hong Kong have often sought to recruit staff in Hong Kong, only adding to the competition for skilled personnel in the territory, and adding further upward pressure on remuneration packages—both in Hong Kong and in Singapore. Throughout Asia, similar shortages are leading to similar cost pressures.[3]

High costs have meant that certain activities are not competitive in Hong Kong. The exodus of production-line work already has been noted, but other activities have been affected as well. When Cathay Pacific decided to relocate its data centre, it found it could obtain land near Sydney at one per cent of the cost of land in Hong Kong.[4] The Hongkong and Shanghai Bank has placed back-office processing activities in Guangzhou. When Unisys relocated to Singapore, it gave high costs in Hong Kong as a major reason. Hong Kong government data show, however, that overall far more multinational firms have been setting up regional headquarters and offices in Hong Kong than have relocated away from Hong Kong.[5]

Given the inevitable nature of some of the cost increases in Hong Kong, the challenge is to make sure that no costs are added artificially. Although incomes are high today and unemployment is low, Hong Kong cannot be complacent. If costs get to the point where a substantial number of firms leave, Hong Kong could be worse off. Once firms go through the time and trouble of planning and executing a move, they will not return if Hong Kong's costs fall by 5 or 10 per cent. Increasingly, costs with respect to Asian cities are not the only relevant comparisons. Some firms have moved or will move activities to the United States, Canada, Australia, or elsewhere if Hong Kong's costs get too high. The challenge for Hong Kong-based firms is to ensure that they remain as cost-effective and efficient as possible. The challenge for government is to ensure that the levers it controls be used to moderate rather than exacerbate the problem.

In property, the challenge to government is to manage the substantial influence it has on costs in the territory appropriately. Since the Hong Kong government owns essentially all land in Hong Kong, it has a major influence on the price of commercial and residential real estate. This influence has been documented in an extensive study of the residential property market by the Hong Kong Consumer Council, an independent consumer watchdog group. The study, undertaken in the summer of 1996, highlighted the powerful role the government plays in determining prices in the sector— as a supplier of land leases, as the determinant of zoning policies, and as the fixer of rules that determine mortgage lending.[6] The supply of land for development in Hong Kong is strictly controlled, with revenues deriving from property and construction, including the sale of leases, accounting for more than one-third of all government revenue.[7] High costs, slow rezoning and redevelopment approvals, and limited vehicles for financing sales of older properties have contributed to the very high prices paid for office and residential property in Hong Kong. One might question a policy that on the one hand extracts such high land premiums from commercial and some residential developments, and on the other hand provides public housing for more than half of the population. As Hong Kong becomes more affluent, one might think of a time when less intervention might provide a more efficient market equilibrium. In the short run, there is reason to believe that the efficiency of the land market might be improved through faster rezoning (there are several areas in which vacant properties zoned for 'industrial use' might be rezoned for office or residential use), faster redevelopment approvals, and a better financing system for older properties (to increase the efficiency of the secondary property market).

The very high cost of acquiring leases, and then developing residential or commercial buildings, has created enormous barriers to entry and has served to concentrate the Hong Kong property industry in the hands of a few property developers. The Consumer Council summarized: 'Whilst new entrants have emerged, no new firms became major players (i.e. capable of producing 5 per cent or more of the annual supply of new private housing) in the market after 1981.'[8] The Consumer Council suggested that although there was no evidence of cartelization in the sector, its oligopolistic nature raised concerns, given the tendency of the large property companies to build up large land banks and to release units onto the market in small lots. Even so, Hong Kong's large developers appear to be among the most efficient in the world, and have an international reputation for being successful at completing projects cost effectively, at high speed, and to very high specifications.

CHALLENGES OF WORK-FORCE DEVELOPMENT

The requirements for the Hong Kong work-force have changed with the economy. When Hong Kong was primarily a low-cost manufacturing centre, the main requirements for the work were minimal qualifications, a certain skill level, and the ability to follow directions. Progressive waves of unskilled immigrants could meet these job requirements as long as they were willing to work hard. Today, and into the future, the requirements of Hong Kong's knowledge-based economy include high qualifications, advanced and specialized skills, and the ability to think independently and make decisions. This change, combined with strong local and regional growth, has vastly increased Hong Kong's need for skilled human resources. The shortage of workers with first-rate skills and abilities will become more acute unless local education and training challenges are met.

Hong Kong's ability to educate and to train the 'knowledge' workers of the present and the future depends on whether the education and training systems, designed to meet different requirements in the past, can adjust to meet the requirements and imperatives of the territory's new economic structure. Despite advances in education and vocational training, many top-tier firms are dissatisfied with products of the local education and training systems. Managers from several top-tier local and overseas firms interviewed for this project are keen to hire entry-level, first-tier management talent from among Hong Kong's university graduates, but feel that few of these graduates appear to have the requisite abilities. These firms find only small numbers of suitable candidates, even from the very best local universities.

The ability to solve problems creatively and independently is highly sought by leading firms. Managers with international supervisory experience tended to rate graduates of Hong Kong's tertiary sector as above average or superior for Asia, but nevertheless it is relatively rare to find a local recruit who can suggest fresh ways to solve problems. Similarly, the communication and self-presentation skills of entry-level workers from Hong Kong schools also are a source of frustration for prospective employers. As one manager explained, a candidate's academic discipline is irrelevant if he or she cannot present himself at an interview.

Traditionally, the cross-cultural capabilities and widespread diffusion of proficiency in English among the local population was one of Hong Kong's major advantages. The current sentiment among employers, however, is that the general level of East/West cultural awareness and communications skills among Hong Kong youth is declining. Executives with international experience tend to rank the English skills of Singaporean workers above those of Hong Kong workers and also emphasize that English proficiency on the Mainland is rising fast compared with Hong Kong. In the words of a Japanese executive, 'When I arrived in Hong Kong in 1992, I expected the locals to speak better English. I was surprised that the English education by the British Government could be so poor. Singapore, in contrast, has been independent post-British rule, yet its English education is very good.' There are historical reasons for this difference. Hong Kong has a dynamic Cantonese culture and Cantonese is the language of first use and dominant use for most people, while in Singapore the government promoted English as a language of first use to defuse rivalries among diverse ethnic groups. One Hong Kong Chinese observer pointed to an ethnic resurgence in Hong Kong, a sense that 'we are all Chinese and who needs English'.

Whatever the reason, if Hong Kong is to retain its position as an important international business centre, widespread facility in English is a must. English is the language of international business and is quickly becoming the universal language of Asia. As Gordon Wu of Hopewell Holdings has said, English 'is the means we in Asia use to communicate with the world and with each other'.[9] The combined GDP of primarily English speaking nations world-wide is far above that of any other language (see Table 7.3). When one adds nations in which English is a strong second language, such as India, Scandinavian countries, Western Europe, and a number of nations in Asia, the economic dominance of English becomes overwhelming. Facility in English can provide access into the international business community, whereas a lack of facility can close doors. In addition, new employment in Hong Kong will come from lines of business where the need for English is paramount, including the international service sector, manufacturing-linked business services, and financial services.

Table 7.3 GDP by Principal Language, Selected Languages, 1994

Language	1994 GNP[a] (Billions of US$)	1994 GNP (PPP)[a] (Billions of US$)
English[b]	8,756	8,763
Japanese	4,332	2,645
German	2,085	1,588
Chinese (all dialects)[c]	1,088	3,455

[a] Refers to the GNP of nations in which the language is the dominant language.
[b] Major English speaking nations were the United States, the United Kingdom, Canada, Australia, and New Zealand.
[c] Includes mainland China, Hong Kong, Taiwan, and Singapore. The large discrepancy between the two columns for Chinese is due to estimates of purchasing power that far exceed nomimal GNP.
Source: Calculated from data in World Bank, *From Plan to Market: World Development Report 1996*, New York: Oxford University Press, 1996, pp. 188–189.

Despite government efforts, English language training in Hong Kong often leaves much to be desired. Local staff at the primary and secondary level often are not qualified and have opposed efforts to bring in expatriates to fill the void.

Although the flexibility of Hong Kong's labour market has been a plus, Hong Kong also has one of the highest employee turnover rates of the major economies world-wide. One of Hong Kong's large trading firms, for example, has experienced annual turnover of 35 per cent for mid-level staff and almost 80 per cent for more junior staff. Turnover is particularly high among younger workers within the first few years after entry into the work-force, in part because many aspire to strike out on their own after acquiring some experience. The period just after Chinese New Year has become particularly difficult with respect to turnover, as many people take their bonuses and then switch jobs. Employee turnover is generally high in the fast-growing economies of the region, and in regional terms, Hong Kong is not much worse off than some of its neighbours. In the 1995 IMD *World Competitiveness Report*, Hong Kong scored 47th out of 48 economies in terms of turnover, Singapore was 44th; Thailand 45th, and Malaysia 46th.[10]

The availability of people with more advanced skills will depend on Hong Kong's ability to educate and train people from Hong Kong to fill positions in the knowledge economy and to attract people from outside to fill voids that might exist. Given the structure of the Hong Kong economy and its firms (small firms with frequent turnover) and potential free rider problems (firms that do not invest in training poaching individuals from firms that do), calling on firms to spend more on company training is unlikely to resolve the issue. However, Hong Kong students and workers have shown that they react to market signals in their choices of course of study and personal investments in attending the numerous private training courses available in Hong Kong. This positive trait could be leveraged to the benefit of the economy as a whole if local firms would make a greater effort to manage their human resource needs on a long-term basis. If Hong Kong's firms are going to compete in the future 'knowledge' economy, by becoming highly efficient information processors, they must begin by knowing what staff they need, with what skills, how they can find and retrain them as needed, and how they can motivate them to work efficiently and train themselves for future roles. In-house career counselling and advice about training opportunities might be a more viable option for many Hong Kong firms than creating or increasing formal, in-house training programmes. Staff appraisal systems, coupled with career planning, could reduce labour turnover, and raise commitment, morale, and thus efficiency in the workplace. Once firms do this they will be better equipped to participate in discussions with the government and educators about what their educational needs are, regardless of whether they are funding education or training their own staff.

Government agencies have been attempting to ensure that the needs of the economy and the education and training options open to individuals are clearly communicated to interested parties. Of course, supply must react if demand is to be satisfied. Here is a place where Hong Kong's institutions should be ahead of the market. Substantial efforts have been made to identify the territory's manpower needs into the future.[11] These need to be translated into effective action in the training and educational communities. One response has been the rapid expansion of university education, from only a few per cent of the relevant age cohort to 18 per cent in seven years. Increased emphasis on vocational training has been another. In both cases, however, links with the needs of the economy have been at times tenuous. Tertiary institutions remain in large part aloof from industry, and vocational training tends to focus more on the manual production skills that have moved out of Hong Kong than on the manufacturing-linked activities and services the economy has created.[12] Increased participation by the private sector is one way of ensuring that this occurs. In general, the education and training fields would benefit from a stronger set of signals from the private sector to Hong Kong students and workers and from greater responsiveness to the demand on the part of the education and training systems.

Mainland China also poses human resource challenges to

Hong Kong. The Mainland will represent a significant demand for Hong Kong talent. Already, many thousands of businesses in Hong Kong are active on the Mainland and staffing up in Hong Kong for Mainland operations is a 'growing phenomenon', especially for managerial talent. Mainland businesses come to Hong Kong for management skills because the process of building a base of experienced managers is just starting in China. The Mainland already is absorbing a substantial amount of talent and will continue to do so even as it develops its own managerial class. Although Mainland concerns will continue their investments in Hong Kong as well, generating local demand for labour, the net flow over the long term will probably be outward. Equally important is the competitive challenge presented by the Mainland's work-force and education system. The Mainland's human resources are perceived by many Hong Kong businessmen to be very good and, more importantly, to be improving at a faster pace than Hong Kong's. The Mainland enjoys a much larger pool of raw talent from which to recruit, and as a result, the raw ability of the top candidates on the Mainland is considered higher. In addition, the Mainland Chinese, especially today's youth, take education very seriously and are actively learning about Western languages and culture. Employers also sense a growing complacency among Hong Kong youth that concerns many of the older generation, particularly those with first-hand experience with young Mainland workers who impress them as more willing to work hard. There is concern among education experts in Hong Kong that the Mainland work-force might surpass Hong Kong in a relatively short period of time, and that Hong Kong may be left with 'fewer qualified workers overpaid for their abilities' relative to the Mainland.

Hong Kong will not be able to train or educate all of the skilled people that it will need. In the past, corporations have been able to attract qualified people to Hong Kong. Though this practice can be expensive, the mixture of foreign and local talent has been an important benefit to both Hong Kong firms and the Hong Kong economy. As long as business prospects in Hong Kong are good, the quality of life is high, Hong Kong remains a cosmopolitan city, and Hong Kong remains open and friendly to outsiders, it should continue to be able to attract talent from abroad. In addition, more and more Hong Kong firms are taking advantage of new programmes to hire skilled people from the Mainland to fill important positions. A mixture of Hong Kong, Mainland, and foreign talent could be a very strong advantage going forward.

EMPLOYMENT CHALLENGES

The second part of the work-force challenge involves the opportunities for those who cannot be trained or retrained for the 'knowledge' economy. Historically, such people were employed in Hong Kong's labour-intensive, light manufacturing activities. It is unlikely that this outlet will be available for many in the future. As indicated earlier, most major metropolitan economies are losing their manufacturing employment. In addition, in order to preserve relatively unskilled employment in the manufacturing or traded sector in Hong Kong, a small open economy, one would need both to be competitive in world markets and to employ relatively basic skills that could not be developed just across the border, where labour is much cheaper. Needless to say, this represents at best a small set of opportunities. The likelihood is that the lesser skilled will be employed in the non-traded sector in Hong Kong, in activities such as construction, local transportation, maintenance, custodial, and personal services, or in immobile traded services, such as hotels, tourism, and goods handling. Nor is policy likely to be able to reverse this conclusion. As Leonard Cheng, Professor of Economics at the Hong Kong University of Science and Technology, has written, 'Any attempt to artificially strike a "balance" between manufacturing and service that is not based on Hong Kong's comparative advantage would be futile and unsustainable.'[13]

To date, the Hong Kong economy has been able to absorb workers displaced from manual production-line work while maintaining low unemployment. And in a real sense, the bulk of the transformation of the economy already has taken place. Manufacturing went from 42 per cent of employment in 1980 to 16 per cent in 1995. It simply cannot fall another 26 per cent in relative terms, and since the total number of 'lost' manufacturing jobs is larger than the total number of 'manufacturing' jobs in Hong Kong today, it cannot fall as much in absolute terms. In fact, Hong Kong faces shortages of workers in low-skill occupations and in traditional office occupations as well. The present generations of Hong Kong children and young adults have had the advantage of more schooling than prior generations. Families and individuals have a better idea of the skills they will need to prosper in the future. Young people have more options and they are opting out of manual and clerical occupations.

Edward Chen, the president of Lingnan College in Hong Kong has argued, however, that immigration from the Mainland could swell the ranks of the unskilled beyond the capabilities of the Hong Kong economy to employ them. By agreement with the Mainland, Hong Kong increased the number of immigrants allowed in from the Mainland from 105 per day to 150 per day in July 1995.[14] Over a period of years, immigration at this level (more than 50,000 a year) could have an important impact depending on the skill levels of the newcomers. Of course, if higher levels of legal immigration were allowed, or if illegal immigration became a major issue, the potential problem could be exacerbated. Policies to control the border, and perhaps to allocate immigration slots based on a 'points' system as Canada and Australia have done, would allow Hong Kong to turn immigration from the Mainland into an economic boon—not just for Hong Kong, but for the Mainland as well—rather than a drain. Otherwise, continued flexibility in the labour market is likely to be the most promising path to incorporating new members of the work-force.

Another potential concern for the future involves whether the loss of manual production work will take away the 'first rung' of the ladder for some people entering the work-force. The vitality of Hong Kong's entrepreneurial economy over the past 40 years has been fuelled in part by the steady arrival of migrants from the Mainland, most of them unskilled, but all determined to build a secure future for themselves in more stable surroundings. It is important to examine how this reservoir of entrepreneurship will be replenished as an increasing proportion of the local population aspires to professional and managerial careers, and as the transformation of the domestic economy will make it harder in the future to absorb the same large numbers of unskilled immigrants as in the past. Evidence to date indicates that there is little slackening in Hong Kong's entrepreneurial spirit so far.

CHALLENGES FOR THE NON-TRADED SECTOR

The non-traded sector influences the competitiveness of an economy in two ways: it provides key inputs and services to the traded sector and contributes to its success or failures in international markets. The non-traded sector also contributes directly to the standard of living found in a nation through the efficiency and productivity with which its activities are carried out. By definition, the non-traded sector comes under less direct pressure from international competition than the traded sector. In most nations, it is therefore important that the local environment provide the competition and administrative regime necessary to keep the non-traded sector operating at peak cost-effectiveness and efficiency.

Despite Hong Kong's reputation for free and open competition, monopolies and oligopolies are found in its non-traded sector. Power, telecommunications, rail service, bus transportation, airport services, and port services have all been supplied by franchised monopolies or oligopolies. Property and supermarkets have been *de facto* oligopolies. In some professions, such as legal and medical services, licensing restrictions have been used to keep out the competition as well as the unqualified. The banking sector had an interest rate cartel for thirty years. While in many economies the prominence of monopolies and oligopolies would raise alarm signals over the efficiency of the sector, in Hong Kong it has generally not been viewed as a cause for concern. Only recently has a lack of competition in the non-traded sector surfaced as an issue.[15]

Traditionally, Hong Kong's advantages in light manufacturing and as a regional centre were large enough that the non-competitive delivery of non-traded services was not a matter likely to jeopardise the territory's competitiveness. But today, with a transformed economy that demands higher productivity in the service sector, increasing cost pressures, and tougher competitors, Hong Kong cannot afford to have a non-competitive non-traded sector. On balance, costs in the non-traded sector have become high, in part as an inevitable response to Hong Kong's high cost environment. While costs have risen, the quality of many services has nevertheless remained persistently high, partly because of biases deliberately built into the schemes of control of formally regulated monopolies and oligopolies, and partly because of pressures from customer industries. The question is whether prices, quality, or variety of services could have been better.

Hong Kong consumers traditionally have been served by monopolies in telecommunications and power (one company serving Hong Kong Island and a second serving Kowloon and the New Territories) operating under schemes of control that guaranteed profits equivalent to a fixed percentage of invested capital. This has resulted in generally reliable, if not top-of-the-line services at what has been considered a reasonable price. Hongkong Telecommunications which with its predecessor Hong Kong Telephone was the territory's monopoly telecommunications supplier until 1991, was required to connect new customers within one day, and for a fixed monthly charge provided all local calls free of charge. The power companies generally kept substantial excess generating capacity 'in reserve'. These services were relatively inexpensive compared to lower quality services provided elsewhere in Asia, but given the low overhead costs of serving the territory's highly geographically concentrated consumer base, the question is whether they were as inexpensive as they might have been.

The terms of the scheme of control and price capping

arrangements enabled Hong Kong to develop one of the most sophisticated telecommunications infrastructures in the world. Hongkong Telecommunications and others provided the critical mass to make substantial investments each year in the basic infrastructure (US$555 million in 1996 by Hongkong Telecommunications alone). Charges have historically remained low by comparison with many other economies. In 1996, Hong Kong's international telephone charges were the tenth lowest in the world and the lowest for Asia.[16] In addition, the policy decision to make local telephone charges 'free' once a monthly connection charge was paid has encouraged a massive proliferation of add-on telecommunications services, in particular fax, pager, and Internet communication. Our own study of comparative costs (see Appendix) would endorse the claim that telecommunications costs in Hong Kong compare favourably with most competitor locations—even before the surge in competitive cost-cutting in 1996.

But Hong Kong's demographics ought to allow the telecommunications providers not simply to offer competitively priced services. They ought to enable local operators to offer some of the lowest prices in the world. Few telecommunications operators have so many customers so densely concentrated in a tight, high-rise metropolitan area. Nor is there any necessity to invest heavily in linking small and remote communities dispersed over large geographical areas—as is the case in countries like China, Indonesia, the United States, or Australia. The effective removal of the Hongkong Telecommunications' monopoly of international voice traffic has led to a dramatic reduction in international telephone call charges. In addition, Hongkong Telecommunications has begun significant 'downsizing' to streamline costs in today's more competitive environment. The recent surge in competition has led to lower prices, and efforts at greater efficiency, but it suggests that services could have been delivered at lower cost in the past. The general consensus is that competition in telecommunications has reduced costs and raised service standards. Without its monopoly, however, Hongkong Telecommunications might not have made some of the investments that resulted in the world's most advanced fibre optic system. Even though competition appears to have stimulated greater efficiency, this past has given Hong Kong a high quality infrastructure base on which to proceed with telecommunications liberalization. The challenge will be to continue to drive down costs, improve the range of services, and keep Hong Kong among the world's most sophisticated telecommunications hubs.

A number of airport operations are monopolies or oligopolies, including airport catering, maintenance, and cargo handling. Although some customers complain about service quality and/or prices, they rate the overall service they receive as effective and efficient. Three main operators dominate container handling at the port, but they control only two-thirds of the container traffic through the port. In addition, even with few main operators and less than cut-throat competition, Hong Kong's port has a higher degree of competition than in most major ports around the world, where a monopoly service provider is the norm. Port users complain vehemently about the high cost of a number of port services, and actively seek alternatives, but port charges themselves have not stopped the break-neck growth of traffic through what has for several years been the world's busiest container port.

The Mass Transit Railway and the Kowloon–Canton Railway, both of which were funded largely out of government coffers and sovereign borrowing arrangements, have to operate as if they were commercial operations under strict schemes of control. The two rail systems, which carry over 3 million passengers each day (2.5 million on the MTR and over 630,000 on the KCR in 1995)[17] are recognized as being among the most efficient in the world, and play an important role in ensuring the fluid operation of the territory's transport infrastructure— whether in terms of getting commuters efficiently to and from work, or in terms of getting people and cargo to and from the Chinese Mainland by train.

In other sectors, restrictions on competition can have obvious and hidden costs. The banking rate cartel clearly resulted in lower rates for depositors. Less obviously, it hindered the development of the local portion of the banking industry and might have contributed to a lack of expertise on the lending side. The banking rate cartel was partially deregulated after a report by the Consumer Council in 1994, 30 years after the government had given the Hong Kong Association of Banks the right to fix rates. As a result, competition increased and banks introduced new products and services. The banks themselves actually became more profitable after the change. Savings rates, however, are still regulated. Continued rate setting is hardly what one would expect in a territory that is home to so many banks and to such a sophisticated financial sector. Relatively low deposit rates and relatively high lending rates insulated local banks for many years. Some observers suggest this might have hindered development of expertise on the part of some banks in seeking out and lending to new types of economic activity.

Historically, Hong Kong's legal services sector, which is self-regulating, had high barriers to entry for foreign practitioners. Foreign (non-British) firms were forbidden for practice local law or engage in court advocacy, measures designed to ensure that only British and Hong Kong firms were able to practice local law. A small number of local firms in the upper echelon of the market handled matters of importance involving local laws, primarily the conveyancing of property, and their small numbers in a closed market kept local legal fees high. As growing numbers of foreign firms chose Hong Kong as a base for international practices within the Asia–Pacific region, a bifurcated market for legal services developed, with foreign firms focusing on the region and local firms on Hong Kong. Legal fees in Hong Kong are reputed to be among the highest in the world. In 1996, the Hong Kong market rates for corporate legal work done by law firm partners ranged from US$390 to US$520 per hour, on par with London and higher than New York. World-wide, only Tokyo's rates were higher.[18]

Less obvious is the observation by some experts that the closed local market made many local lawyers insular and protective, not only of their positions, but also of particular ways of doing things. As a result, Hong Kong is saddled with an obsolete Companies Ordinance that imposes unnecessary burdens on companies and numerous other legal inefficiencies that a less insular legal community might not attempt to uphold so vehemently. Since 1994, bar admission procedures have been put in place allowing foreign lawyers, through examination, to qualify to practise local law as solicitors. Many foreign law firms headquartered in Hong Kong are availing themselves of this option. The mixture of foreign and local talent should have the effect of enhancing the Hong Kong legal profession, just as it has enhanced other professions in Hong Kong.

Recently, competition, or lack thereof, in food retailing also has come into the spotlight. The Consumer Council in Hong Kong claims that barriers to entry in the local supermarket sector are very high and have resulted in less choice for Hong Kong shoppers. Whether this is true or not is probably less important from the point of view of this study than the fact that certain international food groups keen to 'test' products for the China market have chosen to launch directly in (for example) Guangzhou or Shanghai rather than use Hong Kong's retail market, and have to deal with Hong Kong retailers. This represents an important lost opportunity for Hong Kong to consolidate a role as a test site for the China market, and a location for the brand leadership, marketing, advertising, and related services.

The extent to which Hong Kong's economy has been hurt in the past by lack of competition in the non-traded sector is debatable, but it has the potential to hurt the Hong Kong economy in the future. The rapid transformation of the telecommunications sector in response to the emergence of competition is a reminder of the great flexibility of the Hong Kong economy and gives hope that Hong Kong will avoid the 'Swiss disease'[19] in which a highly efficient and competitive externally oriented part of the economy comes over time to be hobbled by the closed nature of the internally oriented, non-traded part of the economy. It will be important that awareness of the consequences of a lack of competition for the competitiveness of the Hong Kong economy be raised and for government to be vigilant in ensuring that markets not be artificially skewed by limits on competition.

VIABILITY OF PAST STRATEGIES

The transformation of the Hong Kong economy has created new managerial imperatives. While many firms we studied had made substantial changes in their operations over the last several years, many others had not made the adjustments one would expect given the evolution of Hong Kong from a low-cost economy to a high-cost economy. Many have yet to adopt different practices with respect to their work-forces. Many have yet to incorporate modern information and management systems. Some Hong Kong firms will have to rethink the way they do business in order to improve efficiency and reduce the impact of generalised cost increases. In some instances, this will involve higher levels of automation; in others it will require greater investment in information handling technology; in others it might involve rethinking the way that products and services are delivered.

Many Hong Kong manufacturing firms have moved labour-intensive production activities to mainland China or elsewhere without changing the nature of the activities themselves. Many still operate the same labour-intensive processes as before, maximizing flexibility while minimizing investments in fixed assets or other long term investments. This has been the case for a number of watchmakers[20] and electronics firms, among others. As costs in Hong Kong's hinterland increase (wages across the border in Shenzhen rose by 24 per cent in 1994 and 11 per cent in 1995)[21] Hong Kong firms will either have to move on to other lower cost regions in China or elsewhere or reassess the labour-intensive strategies themselves.

Some believe that Hong Kong firms have simply put off the inevitable upgrading of production processes by moving into the Mainland and wonder if they will be able to continue to do so. They point out that the industries in which Hong Kong firms have decentralised production activities have been industries in which manufacturing was once located in Hong Kong. One manager told us, 'We [Hong Kong] were lucky in that the Mainland opened up while we still had the skills to transfer to new production locations.' Another reiterated the point, 'We have transferred activities we knew how to perform. If we do not achieve a position in new, high technology industries here in Hong Kong, then what will we have to transfer?'

There are related questions as to whether Hong Kong firms can follow their traditional 'hustle' strategies. As the Hong Kong companies grow and mature, they are faced with new sets of decisions and choices. In order to continue to improve their position, some are faced with the prospect of investing more in research and development, some are facing the prospect of investing more in hard assets, some are facing the prospect of investing more heavily in brands, and many are facing the prospect of investing more in human resources development. Similarly, there are concerns that some of the larger, managerial companies might have become more administrators of franchises than active creators and managers of opportunities. Other companies have run into some difficulties in succession and in maintaining individual control despite rapid growth and diversification.

In the future, there still should be ample room for Hong Kong's traditional commitment and hustle strategies. Given the revenues and incomes that flow through Hong Kong, commitments that provide strong positions to capture part of the flow for themselves are likely to remain viable. In addition, given the trends in the world economy identified earlier, hustle strategies will remain viable for many Hong Kong firms. Some of the commitment firms, however, will find that they have to hustle more to find new and better ways to serve their customers. Similarly some of the hustle firms will have to commit more to investments in technologies, people, and assets if they are to continue their growth. Some will succeed and some will fail. Fortunately, the fact that Hong Kong has been home to both types of firms means that each will be able to find many or most of the skills they need to extend their strategies in Hong Kong.

Many companies, on the other hand, need to rethink the way they use and train their workers. Many Hong Kong firms appear to use manpower inefficiently. Traditionally, labour was plentiful and cheap, and workers in large numbers were thrown on to projects. One manager told us, 'Fifteen years ago when we had a problem, we threw people at it. Today when we have a problem we still throw people at it. The trouble is that the people are more expensive than they were.' Hong Kong firms are making their employees work harder and harder, squeezing more out of whatever exists. In the words of one expert, 'We keep on squeezing more and more inefficiencies out of the system, but in terms of manpower productivity, no, we are not relatively efficient. Workers are not effectively used.'

Most Hong Kong entrepreneurial firms have little in the way of career development and spend little on worker training. Overall, Hong Kong firms invest far less in training than do their counterparts in such competitor nations as Japan, Singapore, and Taiwan, according to the IMD *World Competitiveness Yearbook*.[22] Large Hong Kong firms run by ethnic Chinese often prefer their entry-level workers to have a few years' experience in the workplace after university and do not recruit direct from universities.

The distinctive mindset of many Chinese-owned firms in Hong Kong discourages large investments in worker training. For these firms, training employees to produce more immediate profit makes sense, but training as a source of long-term profit or growth does not. This bias is deeply ingrained in the local business culture. Employers are unlikely to spend if spending does not help the bottom line immediately, while employees generally are averse to providing value to employers outside their strict terms of employment. This 'every man for himself' attitude shared by many employers and employees alike has fostered high turnover rates in recent years. Many local firms do not formulate long-term strategies for manpower, so employees must build their careers by moving from firm to firm. High turnover rates, in turn, discourage investments in worker training, since in many cases, those firms that do invest in training have difficulty retaining even the top 30 per cent of their trainees. In contrast, the leading *hongs* and overseas firms active in Hong Kong tend to have cultures strongly supportive of training and do invest heavily in it at the managerial entry level.

Finally, our investigations indicated that more and more Hong Kong companies are really in the business of handling information. This extends from the port operator that has to keep track of thousands of containers at every second, to the garment manufacturer that must be keyed in to the latest sales and inventory figures of its clients, to the fund manager that requires up to the second information on market trends and global economic conditions, to the trader that has to know the capabilities and availability of production sites around the region, to the developer and engineer that have to manage extremely complex schedules. Although we found a number of companies that realized they were essentially information handlers, we found many that did not. And even among the companies that acknowledged the importance of information, relatively few had actually organized their activities and operations around the information flows, or made maximum use of modern information and management systems.

TECHNOLOGY DEVELOPMENT AND UTILIZATION

On the whole, Hong Kong and its firms invest little in research and development. According to the Industry Department, Hong Kong's research and development expenditures equalled only 0.1 per cent of GDP, one of the lowest ratios in the world. One of the major reasons for this figure is the fact that Hong Kong firms do not tend to compete in industries that are research intensive. In the OECD nations, roughly 70 per cent of research and development expenditures are incurred in the aerospace, automobile, chemical, computer, defence, electronic components, and pharmaceutical industries. All of these industries are subject to substantial economies of scale in both research and in actually competing in the international market place. Given Hong Kong's small land area and relatively small economy, it is not surprising that Hong Kong is not a major competitor in these industries.

Another reason for low research and development expenditures is the short-term outlook of many of Hong Kong's light manufacturing and trading firms, which focus more on fashion and design than technology *per se*. Both the electronics and watches sectors have tended to import technology-intensive components and to respond to, rather than initiate, technological change. Few technology-intensive or innovative electronic components are developed locally, and most such components, such as Application Specific Integrated Circuits (ASICs) must be sourced from companies overseas. In watches, the Hong Kong industry imports most watch movements (the 'brains' of the watch) while excelling in the design and production of watch cases and bands, relatively low-technology components with a fashion element.[23] Hong Kong is one of the world's leading exporters of garments despite the fact that its garment industry historically has not been on the cutting edge in incoporating new technologies. Hong Kong companies like Johnson Electric, a world leader in micromotors, and VTech, the world leader in educational electronics, do substantial technology development, but these tend to be exceptions. Local firms that do conduct research do much of it outside Hong Kong, for example, in the United States, Switzerland, and Australia.

The Hong Kong government does not invest as much in public sector technology support or technology education as other governments in the region. In recent years, the Hong Kong government has increased its support programmes to industry with a wide range of programmes to promote the development and adoption of modern technologies. Some of the most prominent efforts are: the creation of the Hong Kong University of Science and Technology; the planned creation of a science park; and Hong Kong Productivity Council programmes to disseminate state-of-the-art technologies and improve managers' understanding of technology. The Hong Kong Productivity Council, a government agency, has in the recent past dedicated a great deal of effort in introducing manufacturers to new technologies linked with computer-aided design, computer-integrated manufacturing, three-dimensional design systems, automatic spreading systems, and simulation, but nevertheless concedes that the local use of these technologies is 'not widespread'.

Despite recent efforts, some in Hong Kong believe the territory missed the opportunity to develop high-tech industries in the 1970s and 1980s, when governments in Korea, Taiwan, and Singapore made massive efforts to attract or build such industries and call for additional government investments and tax breaks for 'high technology' companies. In some quarters, the paradigm appears to be that if government supports university research and science parks, then self-sustaining high technology development will take place. The trouble is that this flies in the face of international experience. Only a few of the world's great research universities have spawned substantial local development. For every MIT, Stanford, or Cambridge, there are dozens of University of Chicagos, Tokyo Universities, or Oxfords, world-class research institutions that have had little appreciable impact on local high technology industrial development.[24] Similarly, few science parks world-wide have created self-sustaining development of new high technology firms. Technologies get developed by firms under pressure and when old technologies have run out of steam. Our prior work in many countries has indicated that universities are best at providing trained people and support for existing firms and that science parks 'work' when they attract a critical mass of outside firms or are a vehicle for substantial subsidization. Even one of the most 'successful' science parks, Research Triangle in North Carolina, only began to develop local high technology firms decades after it was founded when some engineers that had been let go by the larger outside firms in the Triangle started businesses of their own.

Japan's initial forays into high technology industries came through restrictive technology licensing agreements, protected and explicitly carved up local markets, government orchestrated large-scale research projects, and some subsidies. Korea developed its high technology firms by giving preferential access to capital to the large *chaebol* and by keeping the Korean market relatively closed, protecting the profits of the *chaebol* in a significant portion of their businesses. There has been a clear understanding that the banks and the government would come to the rescue should bets placed on high technology industries turn out badly. Taiwan's government has directly engaged in industrial research and development itself and has chosen the technologies to be developed by the public and private sector. Singapore has invested substantially in local technological capacity, but it is still the foreign multinational firms, attracted by concessionary tax rates, infrastructure provision, and the overall business climate, that do the overwhelming majority of research and development in Singapore. So far, relatively little 'trickle down' development of note has taken place.

For Hong Kong, with its relatively few high technology firms, a government-led effort to develop high technology product industries to an extent that will make a difference would mean attracting high technology operations of overseas firms (probably with tax breaks or other inducements), substantially subsidizing local firms, or trying to close its markets. Although Hong Kong might be able to attract such firms based on the general business conditions present in the territory, and it certainly could do more than it has in this regard in the past, it is a 'seller's market' for the high technology firms with footloose facilities to locate and they tend to extract substantial concessions for locating a plant in a particular region or country. Hong Kong has not resorted to 'buying' industries or favouring particular companies in the past; one might question why it should do so now.

Our research indicates that technology development to improve the business infrastructure and technology development to improve business processes would have a far greater positive impact on the Hong Kong economy than promotion of high technology product industries. Hong Kong managers interviewed for this project identified substantial needs for individuals and firms that could develop engineering processes, write business process software, manage financial and control systems, create models for new financial securities, integrate communications systems hardware and software, package emerging technologies into new consumer electronics products, and exploit new networking technology. The pay-off to investments that create these skills, to satisfy existing demand from industries in which Hong Kong firms are trying to maintain leadership positions, is likely to be much greater than investments to target the same industries that are being targeted by a dozen other economies in Asia.

Instead of creating new technologies, Hong Kong firms are more likely to profit by scanning the world for existing technologies and combining them into new products. This actually reflects the rapidly changing nature of technology development world-wide. Increasingly, even companies like Intel, Silicon Graphics, Microsoft, Netscape, and others scan the world of science and technology to locate and pull together, package, and integrate multiple sources of technology from around the world, performing little basic research themselves, but creating new combinations of technologies and components to serve new needs. One part of the world is already coming to Hong Kong. Several Mainland technology based companies are opening Hong Kong offices or seeking Hong Kong partners to commercialize their own developments. Scanning and combining technologies requires a level of skill and training that would be a worthwhile investment for the territory.

CHALLENGES FOR ATTRACTING AND RETAINING OVERSEAS FIRMS

Fundamentally, continued economic growth in Hong Kong, on the Mainland, and throughout the Asia–Pacific region is the key factor which will continue to attract and retain the overseas firms which have been such an important part of the Hong Kong scene. Beyond vibrant economics, the challenge to Hong Kong lies largely in succeeding as a high value/high cost location, in preserving and upgrading the unique package of strengths that draws firms to Hong Kong, and in managing perceptions abroad.

The sensitivity of overseas firms to further increases in the cost of doing business in Hong Kong has been discussed above. For Hong Kong, the challenge will be to offer better value for money to overseas firms, in terms of infrastructure, supporting services, and human skills. To date, Hong Kong has had an important edge over competing locations in the Asia–Pacific region because of its dense concentration of services and skills. Critical mass will be less of an advantage in the future, as other first- and second-tier Asian cities develop as business centres. This makes it incumbent upon Hong Kong to offer higher value added across its service clusters. In the words of an executive of an overseas firm in Hong Kong, 'Hong Kong has to be the one to provide the unique skills, the people who come up with the ideas . . . the locus of higher-end value added in intellectual input.'

Western observers often express the fear that Hong Kong will become more Chinese and lose much of its lustre for foreign firms, without considering its multiple sources of strength as a location. Hong Kong's superb geographic location, strong transportation and communications infrastructures, and unsurpassed physical and networking access to the Mainland, are robust. A greater challenge lies in preserving many of the institutional advantages that distinguish Hong Kong today as a superb place to do business: the transparency and efficiency of government, the honesty of public administration, which frees firms to pursue business without concern for corruption, Hong Kong's effective legal system, and its openness to information and ideas. These are some of the most important advantages of Hong Kong over the Mainland as a place to do business in the opinion of overseas firms.[25] The challenge here will be to keep the personnel, expertise, and commitment to public service necessary to keep the ship of government on course and to continue to aspire to even-handed and world class regulatory regimes.

It will be important that Hong Kong keep aware of its standing relative to the major competing locations for overseas firms in the region, and clear communication with overseas firms located in Hong Kong can meet this need. Joint efforts by government and industry to conduct and compile surveys of overseas firms should be made to continually assess Hong Kong's position. The ongoing discussions that the Hong Kong government has with both local and overseas firm representatives is encouraging in this regard.

Shaping foreign perceptions of Hong Kong also will be an ongoing challenge. There is a discrepancy between the views of Hong Kong of overseas firms already operating here, and the many firms that are not. Overseas firms that are already here are conversant in Hong Kong's complex and unique strengths, while executives back at home, unless already lured by Mainland business prospects, are more likely to ask, 'Why Hong Kong?' Reports of political uncertainty surrounding the changeover to Chinese rule have coloured popular and business perceptions of Hong Kong in the West to an extent difficult to understand for many foreigners based locally. An important challenge to Hong Kong will be to get the message out to foreign business audiences of Hong Kong's unparalleled vibrancy, skills, strengths, and roles in the regional and world economy. Many of these challenges will be picked up in later chapters.

ENVIRONMENTAL CHALLENGES

There is widening concern that the quality of life in Hong Kong is deteriorating due to environmental problems and congestion, and that Hong Kong may be losing its attractiveness for multinational firms and foreign expatriates on this count. There is rising awareness that constant growth in so small a territory is beginning to take an environmental toll. Environmental amelioration nevertheless remains a relatively low governmental priority and a low business priority. Careful attention needs to be paid to this issue, in part because future competitiveness will rely on continued success in attracting international firms and executives to base and work in the territory. Also, many of Hong Kong's future environmental problems are likely to come from across the border, where officials are unlikely to bow to Hong Kong pressure to 'clean up their act' unless Hong Kong itself is leading by example.

Hong Kong's water system is currently capacity constrained, though improvements are under way. Nearly US$400 million is earmarked for expanding the water supply system to bring water from the Mainland, and several major water treatment works are under construction.[26] Although the sewage treatment department treated some 670 million cubic metres of sewage in 1995, up from 385 million in 1989, treatment of effluents dumped into Hong Kong harbour and nearby waters is inadequate and there is no quick solution in sight. A sewage disposal scheme is under construction to alleviate pollution in the harbour at a cost of US$1.2 billion, with maintenance and operation expenses to be paid by sewage charges that have proven politically unpopular among certain restaurant, factory, and business owners, and others.[27] The disposal of mud deposits and solid wastes generated by Hong Kong's large land reclamation works is an ongoing water quality control problem.

In recent times, Hong Kong's infrastructure projects, particularly the many large projects associated with the construction of the new airport, have developed through coordinated land usage plans. Hong Kong is left, however, with certain areas blighted by past commercial development, including older industrial areas with factory buildings in need of conversion, such as Kwun Tong, Cheung Sha Wan, and Kwai Chung, urban 'fringe' areas in the Yuen Long–Tuen Mun Corridor, and areas in the New Territories degraded by random usage of land for open storage.[28] In addition, the congested nature of Hong Kong creates ongoing infrastructure and environmental difficulties that are not easily abated. There are calls, and government proposals, for increased road construction and further expansion of the public transport system over the mid- and long-term.[29] Also under consideration are fiscal and administrative measures to manage the use of road space and land-use planning to rationalize commuting patterns and promote passenger rail transport systems.[30]

Poor air quality is an ongoing problem for Hong Kong. Air pollution is especially severe in the environs of local roadways, aggravated by the widespread use of sulphur-emitting diesel fuel by a wide variety of diesel vehicles, including taxis and trucks. Currently proposed pollution control measures include emissions standards for new vehicles and a conversion from diesel to petrol, but their implementation would require further policy approval. Operators of diesel-powered vehicles are strongly opposed to measures to reduce local reliance on diesel fuel.[31] Air quality modelling indicates that even if all proposed pollution control measures are implemented, vehicular emissions will be such by the year 2011 that Hong Kong probably will not be able to meet its statutory air quality objectives in some downtown areas.[32]

CHALLENGES OF ECONOMIC INTERACTION WITH THE MAINLAND

While the opportunities arising out of Hong Kong's close Mainland linkages are enormous, it would be wrong to ignore the associated dangers. The first is that closer links with the Mainland make Hong Kong more vulnerable to economic policies and shocks emanating from the Mainland, regardless of the change of administration. Hong Kong has been somewhat insulated from the effects of economic upheaval on the Mainland over the last few decades. Closer links mean less insulation and greater susceptibility to starts and stops in economic reforms, to struggles between Mainland cities and provinces over development priorities and strategies, and to the continued uncertainties of doing business with the Mainland. Despite its overall rapid growth, the Mainland economy has experienced several ups and downs and bouts of high inflation in the 1979–95 period. (See Figure 7.1.) Beijing has attempted in recent months to rein in Guangdong's attempts to push ahead economically.[33] It also has designated Shanghai to be the leader in developing a range of high technology industries and financial services.

229

Figure 7.1 China GDP Growth and Inflation, 1979–1995

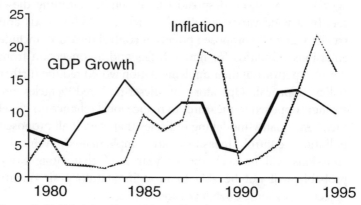

Source: The World Bank, *From Plan to Market: World Development Report 1996*, New York: Oxford University Press, 1996, p. 34.

Some Hong Kong firms still find doing business in mainland China fraught with difficulties. Giordano had several Mainland outlets closed after its founder, Jimmy Lai, wrote an anti-Beijing opinion piece. Hopewell has had difficulty in getting Mainland officials to pay the tolls on the Shenzhen–Guangzhou highway or to approve terms of other projects. Stories of extortion of Hong Kong business people by Mainland interests are well-known in the local business community.

Despite the difficulties of doing business on the Mainland, there is a very real possibility that many Hong Kong companies will become so preoccupied with Mainland opportunities that these could crowd out their distinctive transnational focus. If this were to result in Hong Kong becoming less 'international' or in valuable skills like English language skills being diluted, then Hong Kong's attractiveness as a location for regional and global multinationals could be damaged. At the same time, if Hong Kong's distinct characteristics were to blur, and its economic system came to be regarded as largely the same as that on the Mainland, then international companies would quickly bypass the territory and build relationships directly on the Mainland. As in so many other contexts, Hong Kong's greatest strength is in its uniqueness, or at least in the nurturing of the distinct characteristics that have in the past provided the basis of its attractiveness to international business.

It should be emphasised that by identifying this danger of turning inward, we in no way suggest any immediate evidence of an inclination to do so. On the contrary, there is probably widespread appreciation of the benefits that have arisen—and can arise in the future—from the internationalization of the economy. This involves not simply an appreciation of the additional earnings that can be generated by internationalization, but of the spill-over effects that arise from Hong Kong being the preferred meeting point for transnationally organized companies, of the enhanced sophistication that comes from Hong Kong people being exposed to executives from other cultures and nationalities, and of the competitive stimulus and higher quality of overall service that comes from the multi-cultural mixing that occurs in Hong Kong. It is also recognized that the territory's openness and internationalness has contributed to a general empathy towards Hong Kong, its people, and the principles that underpin its economic system (a matter of no small significance during the present unprecedented transition), and to demand-pull for Hong Kong goods and services. Even so, however, some companies are viewing Hong Kong as a place to access China opportunities, but Singapore or other centres as places to access other Asian opportunities.[34]

SUSTAINABILITY OF GOVERNMENT POLICY

There are also questions over whether the future Hong Kong SAR government, in the face of increasing pressures from local interests, will be able to continue the colonial government's relatively hands-off strategy for the economy. Calls for direct intervention in support of the manufacturing sector have been heard in Hong Kong for many years. In a 1982 pamphlet entitled, 'The Economy in the 1980s: Can Hong Kong Afford Not to Have a Growing Manufacturing Industry?', the Federation of Hong Kong Industries (an association of manufacturers) remarked, 'The conclusion is that we cannot continue to sustain or improve the quality of life of our citizens without a growing manufacturing sector.'[35] This was followed by a call for government to become much more active in supporting 'industry' (read 'manufacturing'). Despite the fact that manufacturing according to the Federation's definition (manufacturing employment in Hong Kong itself) has declined substantially and Hong Kong's prosperity has skyrocketed, there are continued calls for government support of 'industry'.[36]

The sustainability of past strategy, or at least the non-interventionist position taken with respect to much of the economy, might be far more a political question than an economic question. Hong Kong's economy has prospered under the present policy arrangements and there is no evidence that it would have fared any better under a different policy regime. However, there is substantial pressure on the government to change its economic and business strategy to one more like that of Singapore or Taiwan or Korea from within Hong Kong itself. While there is nothing new about this pressure, what might be new is a political environment in which resisting such pressure would be more difficult. Some individuals have used the discussions surrounding Hong Kong's political and economic future to push their genuine belief that a more interventionist government would help Hong Kong's economy. Such a vision, one should add, is more familiar to officials on the Mainland than Hong Kong's traditional approach. Whether a Special Administrative Region administration will resist such pressure to the same extent as the colonial administration remains to be seen.

The new administration would benefit from the type of clear communication essential to understanding the most pressing needs and concerns of the executives of local and overseas firms. The executives interviewed for this study have identified several priorities for the Hong Kong government going forward. Almost without exception, they have their eyes on the basics. They urge the future administration to keep corporate tax rates low and the Hong Kong currency pegged to the United States dollar. They urge it to keep the legal system and government bureaucracy strong and free of corruption and to guard against cutting corners, eliminating process, or changing staffing. They want experienced judges to stay in Hong Kong. They are counting on future administrations to maintain the free flow of information and freedom of reporting on business and economic matters. With respect to all these issues they are clear and unequivocal, because experience has shown them where Hong Kong's strengths lie.

In terms of economic policy, we see no need for a dramatic change in strategy, but we do see a need for the extension and perhaps better execution of the existing market-oriented strategy and a continued emphasis on providing the physical, technological, and human infrastructure needed to continue to progress. Of particular importance will be investments to ensure that the Hong Kong work-force has the language, communication, professional, and multicultural skills that will be required for the work-force of the future.

With regard to greater government intervention in the economy, it is not clear that Hong Kong will benefit from precedents of government showing particular favouritism to particular industries or types of companies. If such a precedent is set, it is not hard to imagine it being used to justify entirely different types of favouritism in the post-1997 economy. We believe that the Hong Kong government and public service need not be apologetic about its traditional stance, but it could be more articulate. A few years ago in response to a question in the Legislative Council 'How does positive non-intervention differ from doing nothing?' the Financial Secretary at the time responded by referring the questioner to a six page document written several years before. How much better it would have been if the response had been either, 'It means that government does not interfere in those decisions best left to the private sector,' or better yet 'It means that in Hong Kong people are free to succeed.'

CHALLENGES TO SPECIFIC HONG KONG INDUSTRIES

Individual Hong Kong industries also face challenges: some have problems that are more pressing than '1997', whereas others are more concerned with the potential consequences of the changeover. The most immediate issue facing Hong Kong's garment industry involves the recent United States decision to change its rules of origin to focus on assembly (where the garment is assembled) rather than cutting (where the patterns are cut). The announced change in policy, if carried through, could have severe negative repercussions, since it will require a reworking of the value chains that were set up to be consistent with the old rules. Hong Kong firms also face the challenge of maintaining their position after the international quota system, which essentially locked in Hong Kong's market position in the industry, is dismantled in 2005.

Hong Kong electronics companies face rising costs in their Pearl River Delta facilities. They are weaker technically than the firms in other nations and must import most sophisticated components, which at times can put them at a competitive disadvantage. Several other governments in the region protect or support their electronics industries much more than Hong Kong's government, placing some Hong Kong firms at a disadvantage and driving down overall industry profits.

Challenges in the export trading sector involve controlling costs and improving management and information systems. Increasing pressures to 'supply just in time' to far away markets will put pressure on existing management systems and might necessitate the further dispersal of production sites. Individual traders also face challenges associated with individual product lines and the continued competitiveness of their sourcing sites or networks.

The most important challenges facing the fund management industry in Hong Kong involve the state of the post-1997 administration regarding the regulation of the financial sector, free flows of information, and the perceptions of foreign investors that Hong Kong in some way might not be a 'safe place' for their money to be managed. Geographic dispersal of the fund management business due to the growth of other financial centres (some with extensive government support) and 'insurance policy' diversification could lead to a diminution of Hong Kong's relative strength. The critical uncertainties for fund management would be whether the free flow of professionals, capital, and information continue; whether Hong Kong's quality of life can be maintained; and if its regulatory environment will be at the cutting edge after it is separated fully from that of Britain.

Hong Kong's engineering firms face the challenges of exploiting the vast opportunities in Hong Kong, mainland China, and Asia over the next several years. High costs and a lack of willingness on the part of some Hong Kong engineers to take on projects outside of the territory might limit their ability to grasp opportunity. The fact that the Hong Kong companies often must compete against the world's best, even for projects at home, creates a constant source of challenge.

Challenges in sea and air cargo involve the high costs of doing business in Hong Kong and the emergence or potential emergence of new competitors. Shippers are actively seeking out alternatives to Hong Kong due to high costs. Surface transport costs and infrastructure requirements outside the port and airport themselves also are issues for the cargo handlers. If the recent disputes over the development of the new airport at Chek Lap Kok and CT9 (Container Terminal Nine at Hong Kong's port) are a portent of things to come, then the industries could perform at something less than their full potential. Equally troubling are statements attributed to some Mainland-linked people in Hong Kong that Mainland ports and airports should be developed before those of Hong Kong. Such statements are at best short-sighted since the further development of Hong Kong's airport and port facilities will benefit the whole South China region, not just Hong Kong.

The greatest challenges for the Hong Kong tele-communications industry involve the need to continue to invest and improve in a more competitive local environment and to stay ahead of other centres in the region who wish to become telecommunications hubs. The ownership structure of Hongkong Telecommunications also creates some challenges since the parent company might wish to keep opportunities outside of Hong Kong for itself and restrict the Hong Kong firm's options. Uncertainties involve the evolution of the local regulatory environment, the outcomes of competition being set up by deregulation, and the extent to which the Mainland market will be opened to Hong Kong firms.

CHALLENGES TO HONG KONG'S FUTURE COMPETITIVENESS

Hong Kong faces several challenges stemming from its economic make-up and the economic transformation that it has undergone. These challenges would be there regardless of the transition of administration on 1 July 1997. The transition, however, has both overshadowed these issues and provided a rationale to reassess the economy of Hong Kong at its core. We believe it necessary to identify these economic challenges as clearly as possible. It would be ironic if the transition of administration were to go smoothly only to have the Hong Kong economy fare poorly because the economic fundamentals failed to receive the attention they require.

Our study suggests that the challenges and opportunities that Hong Kong and its firms face do not call for dramatic changes in strategies, but that they do call for these strategies to be extended and better executed. There is a tendency among some in Hong Kong to look at the investments that other nations or regions in Asia made in the 1970s and 1980s to develop their economies and to suggest Hong Kong should make similar investments in the 1990s and beyond. We prefer to look at the investments that the same nations or regions and others are making to point toward the year 2000 and beyond. These are investments in opening economies to trade and investment, in reducing government's direct role in industry, in deregulation, in fostering competition, in encouraging individual initiative, in fostering the information infrastructure of the future, and in making a location a good operating centre for local and overseas firms. This is the economy of the future for some; it is the economy of the present for Hong Kong.

There are, however, many areas in which Hong Kong's competitiveness can be preserved or improved. As a relatively small economy, Hong Kong will always be at somewhat of a disadvantage in terms of locally supplied inputs to industry. To date, Hong Kong and its firms have recognized this fact and have made a virtue out of necessity. Hong Kong has proven that an economy does not have to supply all, or even most, of the components, technologies, capital goods, and even labour that its firms need, as long as it has access to competitive supplies from elsewhere, has the ability to package and integrate inputs from diverse sources, and constantly works to identify new demands and identifies or creates new sources of supply. Hong Kong also has been distinctive in its ability to develop world-class skills, capabilities, and know-how in some areas and to combine them with world-class skills, capabilities, and know-how imported from abroad. The appropriate focus throughout should be to build on the unique aspects of Hong Kong to develop distinctive Hong Kong ways of doing things, ways that will be mostly likely to succeed in the Hong Kong context, and will be most difficult for others to match.

NOTES

1 Hong Kong Government Industry Department, *Report on the 1995 Survey of Regional Representation by Overseas Companies in Hong Kong*, December 1995, p. 20.

2 Murray Hiebert, 'It's a Jungle Out There', *Far Eastern Economic Review* (25 April 1996): 58.

3 'Underpowered', *The Economist* (9 March 1996): 6.

4 William Mellor, 'Capital Cities: Sydney: New South Asia', *Asia, Inc.*, 5 (August 1996): 28.

5 Hong Kong Government Industry Department, *Report on the 1995 Survey of Regional Representation*, pp. 6, 11.

6 Hong Kong Consumer Council, *Report on Hong Kong's Private Residential Property Market*, Hong Kong, July 1996.

7 During the period 1984–93, revenue related to property and

construction ranged from 28 per cent to 45 per cent yearly, with an average for the period of 33 per cent. Anthony Walker, *Hong Kong in China: Real Estate in the Economy*, Hong Kong: Brooke Hillier Parker, 1995, p. 51.

8   Hong Kong Consumer Council, *Report on Hong Kong's Private Residential Property Market*, Executive Summary, p. 5.

9   Quoted in William McGurn, 'English in Asia: Money Talks', *Far Eastern Economic Review* (21 March 1996): 40.

10   IMD International and World Economic Forum, *The World Competitiveness Report 1995*, Lausanne, 1995, p. 646.

11   See, for example, Hong Kong Vocational Training Council, *1994 Demand and Supply Report on Technical Manpower of Major Hong Kong Industries*, Hong Kong, January 1995.

12   Segal Quince Wicksteed Ltd., 'Strategic and Organisational Review of the Vocational Training Council: A Final Report to the Secretary for Education and Manpower', Hong Kong, 1996.

13   Leonard K. Cheng, 'Trade and Industry: 1997 and Beyond', in Joseph Y. S. Cheng and Sonny S. H. Lo (eds.), *From Colony to SAR: Hong Kong's Challenges Ahead*, Hong Kong: Chinese University Press, 1995, p. 192.

14   Hong Kong Government Information Services, Bob Howlett (ed.), *Hong Kong 1996*, 1996, p. 396.

15   See, for example, Hong Kong Consumer Council, 'Achieving Competition in the Liberalised Telecommunications Market', Hong Kong, 14 March 1996, and Hong Kong Consumer Council, 'Assessing Competition in the Domestic Water Heating and Cooking Fuel Market', Hong Kong, 1995; see also Dermot Tatlow, 'Hong Kong's Free-Market Myth for Service Industries', *Executive* (September 1996): 24.

16   IMD International, *The World Competitiveness Yearbook 1996*, Lausanne, 1996, p. 480.

17   Hong Kong Government Information Services, *Hong Kong 1996*, pp. 235–6.

18   John McGrath, 'When Less is More?', *International Financial Law Review 1000*, 1997 edn. (October 1996): pp. x–xi.

19   A term coined by Michael Enright based on his prior work in Switzerland.

20   Amy K. Glasmeier, 'Flexibility and Adjustment: The Hong Kong Watch Industry and Global Change', *Growth and Change*, 25 (Spring 1994): 238.

21   Non-management salaries paid by joint ventures and cooperatives in Shenzhen, based on a survey by Watson Wyatt Hong Kong Ltd.

22   IMD International, *The World Competitiveness Yearbook 1996*, p. 568.

23   Glasmeier, p. 239.

24   Manuel Castells and Peter Hall, *Technopoles of the World*, London: Routledge, 1994.

25 Survey Research Hong Kong Ltd. (SRH), *AmCham Business Confidence Survey: Management Report*, Hong Kong, November 1995, pp. 10, 13.

26 Hong Kong Government Information Services, *Hong Kong Background Facts*, August 1996, p. 14

27 Hung Wing-tat, 'The Environment', in Stephen Y. L. Cheung and Stephen M. H. Sze (eds.), *The Other Hong Kong Report 1995*, Hong Kong: Chinese University Press, 1995, pp. 353–4.

28 Hong Kong Government Planning Department, *Consolidated Technical Report on the Territorial Development Strategy Review '96*, 1996, pp. 31, 43; Hong Kong Government, Planning, Environment, and Lands Branch, *A Consultative Digest, Territorial Development Strategy Review '96*, 1996, p. 73.

29 J. J. Wang, 'Transport', in Stephen Y. L. Cheung and Stephen M. H. Sze (eds.), *The Other Hong Kong Report 1995*, Hong Kong: Chinese University Press, 1995, p. 335.

30 Hong Kong Government Planning Department, *Consolidated Technical Report on the Territorial Development Strategy Review*, p. 32.

31 J. J. Wang, 'Transport', in *The Other Hong Kong Report*, p. 356.

32 Hong Kong Government Planning Department, *Consolidated Technical Report on the Territorial Development Strategy Review*, p. 100.

33 Economist Intelligence Unit, *Business China Briefing: Economic Outlook—Guangdong*, Hong Kong, February 1996, pp. 5–6.

34 See, for example, Salil Tripathi, 'Capital Cities: Singapore Swing', *Asia, Inc.* (February 1996): 40.

35 Federation of Hong Kong Industries, 'The Economy in the 1980s: Can Hong Kong Afford Not to Have a Growing Manufacturing Industry?', Hong Kong, 1982, p. 1.

36 See James Tien, 'The Brains Revolution but Not Quite', *Hong Kong Echo Magazine*, 8 (Summer 1996): 54–5; see also the examples cited in Tang Shu-hung, 'The Economy', in Joseph Y. S. Cheng and Sonny S. H. Lo (eds.), *From Colony to SAR: Hong Kong's Challenges Ahead*, Hong Kong: Chinese University Press, 1995, pp. 117–50.

8 THE COMPETITION

Once there were only two international business cities of note in the Asia–Pacific region—Tokyo and Hong Kong—and Tokyo was focused primarily on the Japanese domestic market. Today, this situation has changed. The rapid rise of Asian economies has been linked with the emergence of new business centres. Singapore has become a world-class business city. Taipei, Seoul, Kuala Lumpur, and Bangkok have become far more economically important and business-friendly. Shanghai is attempting to regain its position as the leading city in the Orient, while other Chinese cities, such as Shenzhen, Tianjin, Dalian, and Ningbo are coming up from almost nowhere. Improved transportation and communications, as well as an increased focus on Asia, have made Sydney a viable 'Asian' business city. Even former backwaters like Manila and Jakarta are becoming attractive bases for domestic firms and reasonable locations for overseas multinationals seeking Asian locations and markets.

Hong Kong and its firms might have more opportunities today than ever before, but they also have more competition than ever before. Hong Kong can no longer assume that its attractiveness as a base of operations for local and overseas firms will go unchallenged, or that its lead in infrastructure, regulatory environment, and transcultural capabilities can be taken for granted. Greater opportunities will not result in greater prosperity for Hong Kong if the territory loses out to

Table 8.1 Selected Indicators: Hong Kong and Regional Competitors, 1995

Indicator	Hong Kong	Singapore	Taipei	Shanghai	Sydney
Population (million)	6.3	3.0	3.3	9.5	3.6
GDP (billions of US$)	142	85	NA	29	116[a]
GDP per capita (US$)	23,200	26,400	12,419[b]	812	19,333[a]
GDP by sector (%)					
Primary	0.2[c]	0[d]	3.5[b]	2.5	4.2[a,d]
Secondary	16.4[c]	36[d]	36.3[b]	59.6	18.3[a,d]
— Manufacturing	9.2[c]	27[d]	33.0[b]	55.9	14.7[a,d]
Tertiary	83.4[c]	64[d]	60.2[b]	37.9	77.5[a,d]
Competitiveness Ranking (IMD 1996)	3	2	18[b]	26[b]	21[b]
Economic Freedom Ranking (Heritage Foundation 1997)	1	2	8[b]	126	18[b]

[a] Regional figures.
[b] National figures.
[c] Figures for 1994.
[d] Figures for 1993.
Source: Compiled by the authors. Population, GDP, and per capita GDP were taken from different sources and might not agree.

regional competitors. In this chapter, we have chosen to focus on four cities—Singapore, Taipei, Shanghai, and Sydney—in order to understand some of their strengths and weaknesses with respect to Hong Kong. The four represent different types of competition, or competition for different sets of businesses or activities, and therefore offer different perspectives on the competitive position of Hong Kong. (See Table 8.1.)

SINGAPORE

Singapore, perhaps the city most often compared with Hong Kong, shares many similarities with the latter. Both have been British colonies; both developed as trading enclaves; and both have very successful economies. Despite the similarities, Singapore and Hong Kong have followed very different development paths. Singapore's government has managed its economic development with a firm hand and has relied on overseas multinationals to build the economy. In the 1960s and 1970s, it focused on attracting the assembly activities of manufacturing firms, and large oil refining and chemical installations. In the 1980s, additional investments in education and infrastructure were undertaken to make Singapore a 'total business centre' for overseas firms. In the 1990s, the Singaporean government has attempted to attract financial service and transportation services companies and the regional headquarters of overseas multinationals. Overseas companies have been attracted by low rates of taxation, infrastructure provision, co-investment by the government, transparent regulation, law and order, and an educated, disciplined work-force.

Singapore is located in the centre of the ASEAN area (a region with a population of over 420 million) and along the major shipping routes between the Middle East and Pacific destinations. Singapore's population, at around 3 million, is roughly half that of Hong Kong. Per capita GDP was US$26,400 on a nominal basis and US$23,400 on a purchasing-power-parity basis in 1995, close to Hong Kong's US$23,200 and

243

US$23,890 respectively. Singapore's economy has been one of the world's most successful economies over the last few decades, with a growth rate of 8 per cent per year for nearly 30 years, inflation of less than 4 per cent per year for the last 25 years, a strong currency, low unemployment, and an enviable foreign reserve position. The Singaporean economy was rated the second most competitive in the 1996 IMD *World Competitiveness Yearbook* and the second freest economy by the United States-based Heritage Foundation in 1995 and 1996. As of 1996, Singapore has formally achieved 'developed country' status according to the Organization for Economic Cooperation and Development (OECD).

In 1995, financial and business services was the leading sector of the Singaporean economy, accounting for 27.4 per cent of GDP. Singapore is a regional financial centre, a location for several overseas multinationals, and a major logistics centre. Manufacturing accounted for 25 per cent of 1995 GDP. Singapore's leading manufacturing industries include electronics, petroleum and chemical products, fabricated metal products, and transportation equipment. Singapore is a very trade-dependent economy, with a trade-to-gross domestic product ratio of 290 per cent. According to the World Trade Organization, Singapore is the world's twelfth largest exporter and thirteenth largest importer. Its major exports are: electronics (particularly computers and peripherals); consumer and industrial products; petroleum and petrochemical products; and precision machine tools and optics. Electronics account for 70 per cent of domestic exports and roughly half of GDP, making Singapore vulnerable to downturns in the electronics industry.[1]

Singapore has had a very stable political environment, with an effective and efficient government controlled by a single political party, the People's Action Party (PAP), since independence from Britain in 1959. Singapore is rated as having extremely low political risk, an excellent legal system for business, and a reputation as the least corrupt place in Asia.[2] The most distinguishing feature of the Singaporean economy is the direct role taken by its government.

Singapore's Economic Development Board (EDB) provides economic development policies, marketing activities to attract foreign investment, missions to attract skilled manpower, support for technology development, and incentives (tax, financial, assistance in obtaining financing) for overseas firms. As a result, in 1995, there were approximately 4,000 multinational companies with operations in Singapore. Overseas firms account for the vast majority of manufacturing (four-fifths of value added, two-thirds of employment, and three-quarters of fixed investment),[3] as well as most of the internationally oriented part of the financial services sector. In 1993, ten of Singapore's top 100 companies (by sales) were state-owned, 61 were owned by foreign firms, and 29 were domestically owned.[4] Despite numerous government programmes to promote technology development in Singapore, there is rather limited indigenous technology development. Most of the important technology development in Singapore is done by overseas multinationals, which themselves usually do only a small portion of their total technology development in Singapore.

The Singapore government has invested heavily in its infrastructure ahead of demand so that infrastructure would not be a limiting factor in attempts to attract foreign firms. Singapore's port, the world's second busiest container port and the busiest port in terms of total tonnage of containerized and non-containerized cargo, is presently undergoing a major expansion. Changi Airport, which handled 21.6 million passenger movements and one million tonnes of air freight in 1994, is being expanded to a capacity of more than 30 million passengers per year. Singapore has become a regional communications centre based on its world-class communications infrastructure. The state provides industrial infrastructure, including industrial parks and factories with all facilities. The Singapore government runs the port and the airport, is the largest local developer of industrial properties, controls the principal airline (Singapore Airlines) and the telecommunications monopoly, and has wide-ranging commercial interests in banking, leading manufacturers,

245

shipping, marine industries, engineering, ship repair, finance, and other industries.

The Singapore government has extended its policies in recent years to promote Singapore as an international business hub through programmes designed to attract regional headquarters, improve logistics, develop communications and information systems, and provide a more attractive lifestyle. Multinational corporations are given tax breaks and incentives to locate regional headquarters activities in Singapore. Compaq, for example, reportedly was able to pay for its headquarters office lease entirely through the tax breaks it received in return for establishing its regional operational headquarters in Singapore.[5]

The EDB has attempted to 'regionalize' the Singaporean economy by investing in industrial parks in Suzhou and Wuxi (in the Yangtze Delta close to Shanghai) in China, the Hi-tech Industrial Estate in Thailand, the Bangalore Information Technology Park in India, an industrial park in Vietnam, and several complexes in Indonesia. The EDB also has begun co-investing with promising local companies and multinational firms with operations in Singapore. The idea is for the EDB to extend relationships with partners into the Asian region and reduce their risks by providing equity capital and low-interest loans.

Singapore has benefited from a highly skilled work-force. English language training is excellent, which is considered a major plus by multinational companies operating in Singapore. The Singaporean work-force repeatedly has been ranked first in the world by organizations such as the Institute for Management Development (IMD) and the Business Risk Intelligence Service (BERI). Singapore gets singled out for its emphasis on productivity, education and technical training, and for upgrading its work-force for higher value-added industries.[6] Increased expectations, however, have led some managers to conclude that the work-force is spoiled and prone to turnover.[7] Executives interviewed for this study indicate that there is a 'nine-to-five' mentality that makes it difficult to get the Singaporean worker to take initiative or put in extra efforts for the good of the company. This contrasts with Hong Kong where employees are willing to work long hours as long as they are compensated, and where, if they are out of the door at exactly five o'clock, it is often because they have another job or a class to go to.

There are some negative aspects to the Singaporean strategy. The same paternalistic system that plans the economy tends to hamper entrepreneurship and restrict information flows. With government and foreign companies taking the lead role in the economy, local private sector entrepreneurship is not nearly as developed as it is in Hong Kong. Government efforts to foster entrepreneurship have had little impact to date. Restrictions on publications such as *The Economist, The Asian Wall Street Journal, Far Eastern Economic Review,* and *The International Herald Tribune* (publications that contain information useful to companies) have resulted in limitations on information flows and self-censorship. This is a distinct negative for many multinationals and for industries that thrive on individualism and on information flows, such as many creative industries and financial service industries like fund management.

Singapore in Perspective

Singapore has had a very clear economic development strategy which it has executed successfully. There are pressures on that strategy today, however. A severe labour shortage has resulted in wage increases of 70 to 100 per cent over five years in many industries. This situation, combined with rents that doubled in some places from 1994 to 1996, makes Singapore one of the more expensive places to do business in Asia. Labour shortages have been eased through a guest worker programme that brings approximately 300,000 Malays each working day to work in Singapore's factories and hotels.[8] In total, foreigners account for 20 per cent of Singapore's work-force.[9] Increasingly, Singapore matches capital and technology from North America, Japan, and Europe with labour from Malaysia and Indonesia, which makes it potentially vulnerable to firms that do not need the intermediary. Its reliance on the electronics industry leaves it subject to downturns and competitive pressures from all the other nations in Asia that are trying to develop their own electronics industry. In addition, some of Singapore's neighbours are investing in their own ports and logistics networks to try to reduce their dependence on Singapore.

To its credit, the Singapore government has identified these shortcomings and is acting to mitigate them. The regionalization strategy hopes to expand the economy in the face of labour shortages and spiralling costs within Singapore, to obtain a friendly hinterland, and to reinvest Singapore's huge foreign reserves in ways that do not further strengthen the Singapore dollar or drive up local inflation. The co-investment strategy is an attempt to make sure that multinational firms still maintain key activities in Singapore despite rising costs.

Singapore and Hong Kong

Singapore poses a direct competitive threat to Hong Kong in attracting the regional headquarters and offices of overseas multinationals, certain financial service activities, communications and media industries, and the convention business, among others. Singapore has tried to use the uncertainties surrounding the change of administration in Hong Kong to attract multinational firms, fund managers, and transportation companies from Hong Kong. A lavish advertising campaign has been run in Hong Kong publicizing Singapore's quality of life, strategic business location, and political stability.[10]

In other industries and activities, Singapore and Hong Kong might be rivals, but not direct competitors. The vast preponderance of air and sea cargo handled in Hong Kong, for example, have either their source or destination in Hong Kong or mainland China. Singapore is not a real competitor for this business. The two ports can be compared in terms of throughput and efficiency, but are not directly competing. In a wide range of businesses, Singapore is a natural hub for logistics and trade in South-East Asia, whereas Hong Kong is a natural hub for business and investment into and out of China and the rest of Asia.

Singaporean and Hong Kong interests often work together. Singapore is Hong Kong's fifth largest trading partner and Hong Kong is Singapore's fourth leading trading partner. Hong Kong firms are active investors in Singapore and Singapore firms are active investors in Hong Kong. Hong Kong and Singapore have collaborated to support APEC efforts to open up the Asia–Pacific region further to trade and investment and have signed a repurchase agreement to help support each other's currency in the event of a speculative attack.

In comparing Hong Kong and Singapore, one is struck by the fact that both represent successful and self-consistent, but almost completely different systems. The Singaporean system is extremely well suited to attracting multinational manufacturing operations and activities in which government intervention or paving the way is decisive. Singapore also has been extremely good at marketing its attributes to the international business community. Though less exciting than Hong Kong, Singapore also is less congested, less polluted, and has greater scope for outdoor leisure activities. Hong Kong, on the other hand, has a much more vibrant entrepreneurial environment and much better information flows. The fluid, do-it-yourself nature of the Hong Kong economy makes the territory's business people capable of operating almost anywhere, while Singapore's more paternal system often leaves Singaporean business people at a loss when they have to deal with some of the ins and outs of doing business in the rest of Asia. Hong Kong has a huge natural hinterland with close cultural and economic ties, something Singapore will never have. The fundamental difference between the two systems, however, is that the firms that are the backbone of the Hong Kong economy develop their core competitive advantages in Hong Kong and the firms that are the backbone of the Singaporean economy develop their core competitive advantages elsewhere.

The result is that Hong Kong has a much larger financial sector, is a larger media and communications hub, and has more than twice as many regional headquarters as Singapore, all without direct government intervention. Hong Kong is the source for nearly ten times as much foreign investment, though Singapore gets more press attention for its regionalization strategy. Hong Kong and its firms have been packagers and integrators of economic activities, consistently increasing output by shifting to higher productivity activities within Hong Kong. Singapore has been the intermediary between foreign capital, foreign technology, and local (but now increasingly foreign) labour, achieving higher output by attracting more inputs. Hong Kong, on the other hand, has increased output by increasing the productivity with which its resources have been employed.[11]

There is no room for Hong Kong to be complacent, however. Singapore has developed into a world-class business city with infrastructure that has matched or exceeded that of Hong Kong. It has made the extensive investments in upgrading its labour force that Hong Kong needs to make. It also is increasingly applying the same tactics it has used successfully to attract manufacturing activities to Singapore in attempts to attract other firms and activities that formerly would have considered Hong Kong a natural home. Hong Kong has not faced this type of concerted effort to attract economic activities away from the territory before and has never developed a governmental strategy to deal with or counter such moves. Some firms, such as Unisys and CS First Boston have moved significant operations from Hong Kong to Singapore, but these have been isolated instances rather than part of a major trend. Competition from Singapore, however, shows that Hong Kong cannot simply assume that it will retain its position as Asia's leading business hub, and that it will have to meet external as well as internal challenges to do so.

TAIWAN/TAIPEI

Taiwan, and its leading city Taipei, have emerged as major economic success stories. Taiwan has grown from poverty at the end of the 1940s to become a modern and relatively wealthy economy. Japan occupied Taiwan from 1895 to 1945 and only a few years after the Japanese occupation was ended, the Kuomintang (KMT) under Chiang Kai-shek fled to Taiwan after their defeat in the Chinese Civil War.

In the 1950s, the KMT's economic development programme focused initially on improving agricultural productivity and developing import substitution industries with the help of the United States Agency for International Development. In the 1960s, the strategy shifted to one of export promotion of light manufacturing industries. This was followed in the 1970s by a second wave of import substitution, this time in upstream industries such as steel, chemicals, and shipbuilding. Foreign investment began to come to Taiwan in the mid-1960s when US electronics companies began setting up facilities in Taiwan to obtain lower costs than those available in Japan. Japanese companies followed suit shortly thereafter. By the 1980s, Taiwan ran enormous trade surpluses that caused a substantial appreciation in the New Taiwan dollar (NT$) and a burgeoning foreign reserve position.[12] The 1980s and early 1990s saw a transition away from labour-intensive manufacturing into higher technology products. Taiwan itself emerged as a major foreign investor. In 1995, the Taiwanese government announced its plan to become an Asia–Pacific regional operations centre, a programme to develop the island as a major provider of business services.

Taiwan, with a population of 21 million, is located off the south-eastern coast of the Chinese Mainland, separated from Fujian Province by the Taiwan Strait, which is 130 kilometres wide at its narrowest. Taiwan's location makes it an ideal place to access the central coast of mainland China, or rather it would if political conditions would permit. Taiwan's location along or near several major shipping routes between the Americas and Asia and within Asia, itself has helped stimulate its shipping and cargo industries. Greater Taipei, with a population of 3.3 million, is located at the north end of the island and is within a one- to two-hour flight of Hong Kong, Seoul, and Tokyo.

Taiwan's 1995 GDP of US$260.8 billion in 1995 made it the

world's eighteenth largest economy. Its per capita GDP of US$12,419 in 1995 was 47 per cent lower than that of Hong Kong.[13] Taiwan's foreign exchange reserves broke the US$100 billion mark for the first time in mid-1995, but fell to the neighbourhood of US$85 billion in mid-1996 after tensions surrounding Taiwan's presidential elections and Mainland military exercises in early 1996. By 1995, half of Taiwan's work-force of 8.9 million was employed in the service sector and another 30 per cent was employed in manufacturing.[14] Leading industries have included the textile industry and the computer and peripherals industry. Taiwan is the fourth leading producer of computers and related products in the world and the world leader in the production of computer monitors, notebook computers, motherboards, keyboards, scanners, and computer mice.

Taiwan was the world's fourteenth largest trading economy in 1995. Its foreign trade increased from US$50 billion in 1985 to $215 billion in 1995, with exports of US$111.7 billion and imports of US$103.6 billion. The leading export destinations were the United States, Hong Kong, and Japan, while the leading sources of imports were Japan and the United States. Taiwan's leading exports in 1994 were electronics and machinery (40.6 per cent), textiles and textile articles (15 per cent), and transportation and transportation products (5.5 per cent).[15]

Since the early 1980s, Taiwan has been undergoing an economic transition from agriculture and light manufacturing to scientific, technological, and service industries. A chronic shortage of labour and higher wages have caused many Taiwanese companies in labour-intensive manufacturing industries to move their production sites to mainland China and other locations in the Asia–Pacific region. In many instances, orders are taken in Taiwan, produced on the Mainland, and shipped from the Mainland directly to the customer without ever touching Taiwan. Taiwan saw a net reduction of between 300,000 and 400,000 manufacturing jobs in the years 1987 to 1995 (a similar magnitude as the decline seen in Hong Kong, though in an economy with three times

Hong Kong's work-force). Textiles, garments, footwear, food processing, and even consumer electronics saw particularly significant declines. In 1994, 11 per cent of all local garment manufacturers closed. Exports of footwear decreased by 37.7 per cent in the same year and by 18.8 per cent in 1995.[16]

The combination of private sector entrepreneurship and management, and hustle and commmitment strategies found in Taiwan is closer to that found in Hong Kong than anywhere else in Asia. Taiwan's private sector accounts for around four-fifths of its industrial output. Taiwan is similar to Hong Kong and unlike Singapore in that it is the home of thousands of small entrepreneurial firms and several large, indigenous private sector multinational firms. Unlike Hong Kong, Taiwan's multinationals include some major manufacturing firms, such as Formosa Plastics, Acer, and Tatung, that have developed their own markets, brands, and in some cases, technologies. Like Singapore, Taiwan is the home of a substantial number of manufacturing operations of foreign multinationals, particularly in the electronics industry.

Taiwan also has had a prominant state sector. In 1994, 18 of the 100 largest companies in Taiwan (and six of the top ten, including the monopoly oil company, the power company, the leading bank, the telecommunications company, and the tobacco and wine monopoly) were owned by the Taiwanese government. Ten of the top 100 were majority-owned by foreign firms. Eleven of Taiwan's twelve top financial institutions were owned by the government. Although many foreign banks have offices in Taiwan, only three of the top 50 financial firms were majority-owned by foreign firms.[17]

Taiwan's infrastructure is considered good by regional standards. Kaohsiung, Taiwan's leading seaport, is the third busiest container port in Asia. In 1994 it handled 4.9 million TEUs (20-foot equivalent container units) of container traffic and 68.5 million metric tonnes of cargo. Taipei's Chiang Kai-shek Airport, Taiwan's major international airport, handled the bulk of the island's international traffic of 37 million passengers and 880,000 tonnes of cargo in 1994. A $1.08 billion expansion programme will double its capacity by December 1997.

Taiwan's land transportation has been considered good by regional standards. In Taipei, however, a new mass transit rail system has become a nightmare of delays and cost overruns and has yet to reduce the congestion in the city. Telecommunications services are provided by the Directorate General of Telecommunications (DGT), which has been both a state-owned company and the telecommunications regulator. The DGT is in the process of extending fibre optic service, developing enhanced services, and providing Internet access. Despite progress, multinational managers in Taiwan frequently complain about poor phone services and a lack of responsiveness on the part of the DGT.

The Taiwanese work-force is considered hard-working and skilled. The 1996 IMD *World Competitiveness Report* ranked Taiwan fifth out of 48 economies on employee motivation and entrepreneurship, but only nineteenth on the ease of obtaining skilled labour.[18] Massive investments in education have dramatically improved literary and skill levels. Historically, many of the tens of thousands of Taiwanese students who went to college overseas stayed abroad after completing their studies. In recent years, however, many have returned to help power a high technology boom in Taiwan.

Most research and development in Taiwan is done by private companies. In addition, the Taiwanese government's National Science Council coordinates government research activities in a wide range of technologies and industries. Taiwan's Hsinchu Science Based Industrial Park has been in operation since 1979 and a second science park is under development. By 1994, there were 165 firms located at Hsinchu Park with total sales of US$6.7 billion. Hsinchu provides some subsidies for research and development and financial incentives to locate in the park for selected companies. Hsinchu is near two major universities and the Industrial Technology Research Institute, the main government research institute, which carries out medium and long term research projects sponsored by the government and private industry.

Taiwan's political situation and its relationship with the Chinese Mainland have shaped its development. The

Kuomintang ruled Taiwan under martial law from 1949 until 1987. Other political parties were outlawed and restrictions were placed on the press. In 1987, Taiwan began down the road to democracy which culminated with the first direct election of a Taiwanese president in 1996. Virtually all contacts between Taiwan and the Mainland were cut in 1949 and remained so until 1979 when Deng Xiaoping announced a shift in Beijing's Taiwan policy toward 'peaceful reunification' rather than the 'liberation of Taiwan'. At that time, the Mainland called for direct links with Taiwan in mail, transportation, and commerce, with an eye toward eventual reunification under a 'one country–two systems' framework. Taiwanese officials rejected Deng's proposals and six years later announced their own plans to approve indirect mail, transport, and commerce. Although Taiwanese officials purport to support increased contact with the Mainland, there is a constant fear that economic overreliance on the Mainland could leave Taiwan at a disadvantage in cross-Straits negotiations. In 1993, for example, the Taiwanese government instituted its 'go south' strategy in which it encouraged local firms to invest in South-East Asia instead of mainland China to reduce dependence on the Mainland and to improve relations with growing South-East Asian nations. According to Taiwan's Mainland Affairs Council, roughly 10 per cent of Taiwan's 1994 trade was with the Mainland, including 17.2 per cent of exports (US$16.02 billion) and 2.2 per cent (US$1.86 billion) of imports.[19] Mainland officials claim that Taiwan is the second leading external investor in mainland China after Hong Kong.

In 1995, the Taiwanese government announced its plan to make Taiwan an Asia Pacific Regional Operations Centre.[20] The APROC plan seeks to carve out a major role for Taiwan as a base of operations for local and multinational firms to develop their Asia–Pacific business by building on its manufacturing base, supply of high technology manpower, geographical position, managerial skills, network of local enterprises, and cultural similarities with mainland China. The programme is to consist of several steps, the first of which involves deregulating the economy to make it more open and attractive to domestic and foreign firms by reducing tariffs, deregulating the service sector, and revising laws and regulations to facilitate the free movement of goods, services, people, capital, and information. The focus would then shift to specific programmes designed to improve Taiwan's position in manufacturing, sea transportation, air transportation, financial services, telecommunications, and media.

Efforts to support manufacturing include plans to remove restrictions on foreign investment, simplify the procedures for investment review, transfer defence technology to the private sector, establish more business-oriented research and development organizations, and set up 20 to 30 intelligent industrial parks. Sea transport and air transport are to be improved by developing Kaohsiung into a transhipment port (with a special offshore zone for transhipments to mainland China), infrastructure expansions and improvements, and greater private sector involvement in port and airport services.

Financial markets are to be stimulated by relaxing restrictions on capital flows, financial institutions' operations, the establishment of new bank branches, and the development of several new financial markets. Efforts to establish Taiwan as an attractive location for regional telecommunications services involve gradually liberalizing the telecommunications sector, developing Taiwan into a switching hub, and upgrading services. Taiwan also aims to become a centre for Chinese language media by removing restrictions on employing Mainland performers and shooting films on the Mainland and by creating a media park in northern Taiwan for movies, television production, and post-production.

Taiwan in Perspective

Taiwan has had a very successful economy, but it faces a number of challenges. Its unresolved political status continues to hamper its economic development. In 1996, Mainland missile tests and naval exercises closed down shipping lanes and caused a flight of capital. Taiwan is unlikely to be admitted into the World Trade Organization until the Mainland is admitted. Nor is it likely to achieve much success with its APROC programme as long as direct links with the Mainland are forbidden. The APROC programme also requires an almost complete about-face for a government that has heavily regulated the economy, kept certain industries in the public sector, and limited the role that foreign companies could play. It remains to be seen if the government can force through the reforms that will be necessary in order for Taiwan to become an attractive regional operating centre.

Taiwan and Hong Kong

Taiwan is in many ways behind Hong Kong as an international business centre: Taipei is not a cosmopolitan city on par with Singapore or Hong Kong or even potentially with Shanghai and the Taiwanese economy is not characterized by the same transparent markets found in Hong Kong. Nevertheless, if Taiwan's political status is resolved in a peaceful manner, it could become a more direct competitor to Hong Kong than Singapore or Shanghai. Taiwan's geographic position makes it a potential competitor for Hong Kong's sea and air cargo businesses, particularly if direct air and sea cargo links are allowed between Taiwan and the Mainland. Taiwan's location could be far better than Singapore's for an offshore financial and business centre serving mainland China.

Under the best of circumstances, however, Taiwan appears to be at least a decade away from being able to challenge Hong Kong's financial service industries and other business service activities. For example, Taiwan lacks the experience, the openness, the transparency, the critical mass, and the cosmopolitan nature that would be necessary to become a major international financial centre. In a 1995 report, *Taipei as a Regional Financial and Funding Centre*, the Joint Banking Committee of the American Chamber of Commerce and European Council of Commerce and Trade stated, 'Taipei, frankly, is not well placed geographically to compete with Singapore as a financial centre for South-East Asia, nor, at present, is it well placed politically to compete with Hong Kong as the financial centre for "Greater China".[21] The report suggests that Taiwan should develop its domestic financial markets before it attempts to become an international financial centre.

Taiwan is a successful capitalist economy located in the heart of East Asia and just off the coast of mainland China. Its political circumstances and regulatory systems prevent it from competing directly with Hong Kong at present. At the same time, the relationship between Hong Kong and Taiwan is, and will remain, far more complex than that of competitors or complementors. Hong Kong has been the intermediary point for the bulk of trade, investment, and travel between Taiwan and the Mainland. The development of direct links with the Mainland would take away some (but not all) of the Taiwan-Mainland business that is now mediated through Hong Kong. More importantly, it would start Taiwan down the road to developing into a true regional business centre, rather than a manufacturing enclave with an insular service sector. Some aspects of the future of Taiwan–Hong Kong interaction after 1 July 1997 remain to be clarified. Taiwan appears to have determined that Hong Kong will be treated as a special case and therefore not subject to its ban on direct links with the Mainland. The Taiwanese government has decided to keep its offices in Hong Kong after 1 July 1997. In fact, it has decided to step up its efforts to promote exchange and cooperation between Hong Kong and Taiwan.[22]

SHANGHAI

Shanghai, mainland China's leading industrial city, has provincial status and an extensive metropolitan area. Opened to Western concessions by the Treaty of Nanking in 1842, Shanghai's location in the Yangtze Delta combined with Western and Eastern influences eventually made it the leading city in Asia. By the 1930s, Shanghai was China's leading manufacturing centre, its leading port, and its leading financial centre. The city was the epitome of pre-war Chinese capitalism and the scene of its greatest excesses. After the end of the

Chinese Civil War, Shanghai was turned into mainland China's leading heavy industrial centre, satisfying China's domestic demand and providing a substantial portion of national revenue. By 1978, the province of Shanghai ranked first among China's provinces, accounting for 8 per cent of total national income, 13 per cent of gross industrial output, and 30 per cent of exports. Historically, Shanghai had an uneasy relationship with the national government, which always has been wary of Shanghai's economic and political power. The city became a cash cow, with 87 per cent of the revenues it generated between 1949 and 1983 taken by the central government, a higher percentage than elsewhere in China.[23] As a result, needed investment in infrastructure and urban development was delayed.

In the 1980s, Shanghai took a back seat as special economic zones in Guangdong and Fujian were opened to foreign investment and trade. Guangdong's GDP passed that of Shanghai (at the provincial level) in 1983 and by 1994 was more than twice that of Shanghai. By 1990, Shanghai provided only 4 per cent of national income and 5.5 per cent of industrial output and had fallen from first in provincial GDP in 1978 to tenth in 1990. Its share of China's exports fell from 30 per cent in 1978 to 7.5 per cent in 1994.[24] Shanghai was one of the 14 coastal cities and towns declared open in 1984, but its development did not take off until the opening of the Pudong area of Shanghai in the late 1980s and after the emergence of political leaders, such as Jiang Zemin, China's president, and Zhu Rongji, its vice-premier, both of whom are former mayors of Shanghai.

Pudong, designed to be a 'socialist Hong Kong', will have a financial district, an export-processing area, a free-trade zone, and a high technology park.[25] Pudong represents another stage in the Mainland's development process that began with the opening of special economic zones in the late 1970s. The opening of the Pudong area of Shanghai for investment and development signalled the return of Shanghai to the forefront of Mainland economic planning. Plans to make Shanghai the 'dragonhead' of development of the Yangtze River Basin include the development of an international financial centre, export processing, business services, and high technology industries.

Today, Shanghai is the scene of one of the world's most ambitious development projects and fastest growing metropolitan economies. In 1995, Shanghai's GDP was on the order of 246 billion yuan (around US$29 billion). Per capita income among urban families grew at a real rate of 9.1 per cent per year from 1991 to 1995 to reach 6,822 yuan (US$812) in 1995.[26] Shanghai achieved double-digit growth in the 1990s, including a rate of more than 14 per cent from 1992 through 1995.

Shanghai has an excellent location near the mouth of the Yangtze River, bordering the East China Sea and facing the Pacific Ocean. The city is in the centre of China's industrial heartland, the most densely populated and wealthiest portion of the Mainland, and is only a one- to two-hour flight away from Beijing, Hong Kong, Seoul, and Tokyo. Shanghai itself is home to 13 million people, the Yangtze Delta to 77 million, and the Yangtze River Basin (extending 3,000 miles up to Sichuan Province) to 360 million. Shanghai's location makes it a major port for bulk cargo such as grain, raw materials, steel, and other commodities and a major transhipment centre. Sandbars in the river, however, prevent Shanghai from handling the fourth or fifth generation container ship traffic in which Hong Kong specializes. Shanghai handles only one-tenth the number of containers handled by Hong Kong.[27] Shanghai's Hongqiao Airport served 7.5 million passengers in 1994 and 11 million in 1995.

Several major infrastructure projects associated with the Pudong development have reached completion, including two bridges, two cross-river tunnels, highways, roads, harbour development, a water plant, gas works, a sewage treatment plant, a power plant, and a communications system. A new airport also is planned for Pudong. It has been estimated that Pudong's initial infrastructure requirements will cost a total of US$10 billion, most of which is intended to come from overseas.[28] Shanghai faces substantial infrastructure challenges in communications, transportation, water, sewerage, and industrial infrastructure. The old part of the city, Puxi (as opposed to the newly opened Pudong) is hindered by fragmented land usage in which virtually every district of the city has industrial, commercial, residential, and even agricultural areas. Activities that logically should be co-located are scattered, resulting in duplication and inefficient transport.[29] This was one of the major reasons why development is now being focused on Pudong, which had always been a relatively empty area of marshes and agricultural holdings. The eventual redevelopment of Puxi will probably entail greater challenges than the building of Pudong.

Shanghai has a largely industrial economy. In 1994, manufacturing accounted for nearly 50 per cent of output, down from nearly 75 per cent in 1980. The tertiary, or service sector accounted for nearly 40 per cent, up from 21 per cent in 1980. Six industries—steel, autos, petrochemicals, energy, telecommunications, and computer products—accounted for 45 per cent of gross industrial output in 1995.[30] Other prominent industries include machinery, shipbuilding, instruments, and polymers. Light manufacturing is represented by watches, cameras, radios, fountain pens, glassware, textiles, and apparel.

Shanghai has been the epitome of the Mainland's state-planned economy. From 1980 to 1995, however, the portion of gross industrial output accounted for by the state sector fell from 87.2 per cent to 37.5 per cent. The figure for collective firms increased from 11.6 per cent to 18.6 per cent, while that of cooperatives, private firms, and foreign-funded ventures rose from 1.1 per cent to 44 per cent.[31] State enterprises answer either to the central government or to one of the levels of local government in a complex set of reporting relationships. In the mid-1980s, many were urged to become independent companies, but did not take well to seeking their own customers and negotiating for their own inputs. Many continue to lose money, but are kept running with cash infusions from the state. Many are saddled with the so-called 'triangular debt' problem in which factories cannot pay back their debts because other factories are not paying them.

The reform of foreign investment regulations in the 1990s precipitated a dramatic rise in the number of foreign-invested companies in Shanghai. Special policies to attract investment include: special tax holidays; foreign operation of retail outlets; exemptions from duties; fewer licensing requirements; reduced regulation; circulation of foreign currency; and special provisions for repatriating earnings. The number of foreign-invested enterprises with total investment of $US10 million or more in Shanghai was 298 in 1994, up from 205 in 1993, and 18 in 1991.[32] Shanghai received approximately as much foreign investment in 1994 as it did during the entire 1980s.[33] According to a survey of foreign investors in 1995, the number one reason they invested in Shanghai was access to the local market (51 out of 81 responses).[34] The foreign investors surveyed were generally satisfied with their Shanghai partners, local employees, relations with the municipal government, and communications, but were less satisfied with the price of real estate, inflation rates, amenities for expatriate managers and their families, and availability of raw materials.[35] They identified transportation, bogus and inferior products (intellectual property and trademark protection), corruption, and efficiency of administrative bureaux as the items that required the most immediate improvement.[36] Another issue for the foreign investor has been costs. Though labour costs are low, rents for office space and housing in Shanghai can exceed those for much higher quality spaces in Hong Kong.

The Shanghai work-force is large and skilled by Mainland standards. Productivity is generally higher in Shanghai than elsewhere on the Mainland, despite the fact that the capital stock is typically older than that found in other areas in the nation. Wages are low by international standards. Prevailing wages for a manufacturing worker in a foreign-invested company in Shanghai in 1995 were only on the order of 10 per cent of those for a manufacturing worker in Hong Kong.[37] In addition, Shanghai exhibits a phenomenon common on the Mainland, where skilled manual workers often are paid more than knowledge workers, making the latter a downright bargain.

Shanghai is relatively advanced with respect to its educational system compared with the rest of the Mainland. By 1993, 21 per cent of the 18- to 21-year-old cohort was enrolled in tertiary education in Shanghai, with a target to raise the figure to 30 per cent by 2000.[38] Shanghai is the home of 52 colleges and universities. Institutions like Tongji, Fudan, and Jiaotong are among China's top universities. Shanghai ranks second only to Beijing on the Mainland in terms of the proportion of professionals in the work-force. It also ranks second to Beijing within China in terms of the number of science research institutes, technical employees, engineers, and scientists engaged in research and development.[39] Shanghai is the home of a government-sponsored, high technology park and a variety of research programmes in computers, software, biomedicine, microelectronics, optics, and other areas.

Shanghai in Perspective

Shanghai's rapid development has led some to believe that the city will outpace Hong Kong, Tokyo, and Singapore and become the leading city in Asia. Shanghai is an enormous city in the heart of the greatest untapped market of the world, but that by itself will not make it a major international centre. Despite its recent progress and growth, it is unlikely that Shanghai will displace any of the other centres in the short to medium term.

Shanghai is still hindered by a national legal system that is ranked among the least transparent in Asia by international surveys. The city also faces the heavy regulatory burden associated with a history of a planned economy and an incomplete process of economic reform. State-owned enterprises weigh down the economy, receiving massive subsidies, retaining priority access to raw materials, inputs, and skilled personnel, and influencing the competitiveness of related industries. Shanghai's history of state ownership has meant that entrepreneurship is not as well-developed there as it is in Hong Kong, or even in Guangdong. The decision to go into business for oneself in Shanghai can be a difficult one, since state enterprises often control access to education, health care, and housing. According to some observers, a legacy of anti-bourgeoisie purges and the Cultural Revolution also has created risk aversion and occupational inertia among many inhabitants.[40]

Shanghai's industries have evolved behind protectionist barriers that have made them inefficient on average. In recent years, Shanghai has attracted foreign investment geared toward the domestic, rather than the export market, a very different pattern from the export-oriented industrialization of Guangdong. Export-oriented activities will only be profitable if they can meet international quality standards and prices. Import substitution and protection, on the other hand, can give rise to industries which are not competitive in international terms. Shanghai's automobile joint venture with Volkswagen, for example, produces vehicles at a cost that is twice the international price, and is only profitable because of trade barriers. China will have to cut tariffs if it wishes to enter the World Trade Organization (WTO) and, according to experts, many of Shanghai's companies could go bankrupt if it does.[41]

The development planned for Shanghai, based on high technology industries and services, will be much more difficult to execute than that of Southern China, where relatively simple light manufacturing has been the main engine of growth. The expertise, capital, and market know-how for the development of Southern China has come largely from Hong Kong, which is less favourably situated geographically and in terms of its own skill base to play as comprehensive a role for the type of development planned for Shanghai. In addition, the personal freedoms and free flows of information critical for this type of development are chronically hampered in Shanghai.

Shanghai and Hong Kong

Although there are some industries and activities in which Hong Kong and Shanghai compete, the overall picture appears to be more one of complementarity than competition. Shanghai often is mentioned as a potential competitor for Hong Kong as a shipping centre and a financial centre, but the prospect of real competition appears to be well into the future. Some 90 per cent of Sichuan's trade, for example, goes through Hong Kong, even though Sichuan is on the upper Yangtze River. Similarly, the bulk of Wuhan's trade goes through Hong Kong even though ships of 5,000 deadweight tonnes can go from Shanghai to Wuhan by river.[42] In addition, Hong Kong specializes mostly in containerized cargo, whereas Shanghai is largely a bulk cargo port.

Shanghai has the largest stock exchange in mainland China, representative offices of approximately 90 foreign banks, and emerging markets for metals, short-term finance, securities, and foreign exchange swaps, but it presently lacks the skilled people, infrastructure, regulatory environment, and supporting services to become a major international financial centre. Shortcomings in the national banking system, and a lack of sophisticated macroeconomic tools associated with market economies, limits the attractiveness of financing Mainland companies, and hinders attempts to open up the financial sector further. Political pressures are still brought on local banks to fund money-losing, state-owned enterprises. There is no inter-bank fund market and foreign banks are not allowed to do business in the local currency, the Renminbi. China's specialized banks have refused to move their headquarters to Shanghai because credit is allocated centrally in Beijing.[43] Listings on the Shanghai Stock Market often are politically motivated, leading to low-quality issues and keeping many of the better state-run companies off the market (not to mention the total absence of listings for privately held Mainland companies).[44] Pricing restrictions on issues further hamper the Shanghai market.[45] Given these features, it will be some time before Shanghai can compete with the major financial centres of the world.

Shanghai is a major potential competitor to Hong Kong in the realm of attracting headquarters of the China-related operations of multinational companies. Shanghai is a natural location for companies that see both business and political benefits in locating China headquarters on the Mainland. One also might argue that Shanghai is attracting some investment that might otherwise have gone into Southern China. Such investments are less likely to generate ancillary benefits to Hong Kong than if they had been made in Guangdong. Similarly, while some worry that Shanghai will be favoured over Hong Kong after China assumes administrative control over Hong Kong, another factor might be that Shanghai will be favoured over Guangdong and that less benefit will accrue to Hong Kong. Historically, it was Shanghai that was the economic and business centre and Guangdong that was the poor peripheral region.

The danger for Hong Kong is not that Shanghai will catch up. In the long run, China has ample room for several great economic cities. If Shanghai catches up with Hong Kong, that implies a direction and pace of economic reform on the Mainland that would benefit the whole region. In this context, Shanghai's growth would be a source of trade, a market for goods, a customer for Hong Kong service providers, and a profitable investment for Hong Kong firms. (Hong Kong has been by far the largest external investor in Shanghai, accounting for more than 50 per cent of the external investment in Shanghai since 1979. By the beginning of 1994, the cumulative stock of Hong Kong-contracted investment in Shanghai was US$13.2 billion.[46] Another $5 billion was added in the first three quarters of 1994.[47] These investors obviously will benefit if Shanghai's development continues at a rapid rate.) The danger for Hong Kong is not that Shanghai will catch up, but that in some way Hong Kong would be dragged down either intentionally or unintentionally.

Shanghai itself will continue to be both helped and hindered by its location in the heart of mainland China. It will remain the great potential market and industrial engine of the Mainland. It remains a centre of science, technology, education, and manufacturing for the Mainland. At the same time, it will be limited by the pace of the Mainland's economic reform and its own inward orientation. Hong Kong should be able to continue to maintain its advantages with respect to export processing, transportation, international trade, international finance, regional headquarters, international communications, and other internationally oriented parts of the economy. The development of Shanghai shows that mainland China can and will develop more than one great economic city and that Hong Kong interests actually have the potential to benefit substantially from the process. Shanghai's development also highlights the fact that Hong Kong and its firms provide far more than just a 'gateway' and, in fact, are playing a critical role in economic development throughout the Mainland.

SYDNEY/NEW SOUTH WALES

Sydney might be considered an unusual choice as a potential competitor to Hong Kong. Historically, Australia tended to focus its attention on the British Commonwealth and North America rather than Asia. In recent years, however, Australia and the Australian government have made substantial efforts to integrate the nation more into the Asian region and to become an Asia–Pacific centre for business. Sydney has entered the competition with a combination of low costs, a technically skilled work-force, attractive quality of life, and government incentives designed to lure the regional headquarters of multinational firms.

Sydney, with a population of 3.6 million, is Australia's oldest and largest city. It is located in the state of New South Wales, whose population of just over 6 million is approximately that of Hong Kong. New South Wales' 1995 GDP of US$116 billion was about 17 per cent below that of Hong Kong, as was its per capita GDP of US$19,333. Sydney is squarely in the Asia–Pacific region with respect to time zones, but is far from other Asia–Pacific centres (an eight-hour flight to Singapore and a ten-hour flight to Hong Kong).

Sydney is the business and financial hub of Australia and New South Wales. It is the base for nearly half of the top 500 companies in the Australia/New Zealand area, three-quarters of the area's leading banks, and three-quarters of Australia's leading information technology firms. Other leading industries in Sydney include tourism, educational services, and manufacturing. Tourism earnings are expected to increase substantially in the year 2000 when Sydney hosts the Summer Olympic Games. Sydney is the principal Australian location for two-thirds of the over 160 overseas firms with regional headquarters in Australia. As of 1995, approximately one-quarter of the regional headquarters were for professional service firms and one-quarter were for information technology firms.[48]

In 1993/4, primary production (mostly agriculture and mining) accounted for 4.2 per cent of New South Wales' GDP. Manufacturing accounted for 14.7 per cent, utilities for 3.6 per cent, and services for 77.5 per cent.[49] Roughly three-quarters of the exports of New South Wales go to the Asia–Pacific region. In 1995, manufactured goods accounted for 32 per cent of the state's exports, compared with 16 per cent each for mining and agriculture, and 36 per cent in services (19 per cent in tourism alone).

Sydney's transportation and communications infrastructure is considered excellent. Transportation is relatively easy and roads are unclogged. In 1995, Sydney had direct flights to 152 destinations and nearly 300 international departures a week. Sydney has one of the three best telecommunications systems in the region (the other two being Singapore and Hong Kong) and competitive telecommunications costs. Given the nature of modern communications networks, where any geographic position on the network can be as good as any other, Sydney is a contender for the regional operations of communications and data-intensive activities. As a result, companies like IBM, Cathay Pacific, and others have set up regional data processing operations in Sydney. *The Straits Times*, a Singaporean newspaper, actually transmits some articles to Sydney for editing before they are sent back to Singapore.[50]

One of Sydney's major attractions has been its relatively low costs for labour, office space, warehousing space, factory space, communication charges, and living costs. According to ECA Limited, in 1995, the annual salaries of supervisors, systems analysts, accountants, engineers, and plant managers in Sydney were on the order of one-third lower than Hong Kong, Singapore, and Taipei and half as much as Tokyo. Rents for central business district office space in Sydney can be on the order of half or less than half of those of other Asia–Pacific cities. Housing rental costs can be on the order of one-fifth those of Hong Kong or Singapore and the cost of living can be one-third less than that of Taipei, Hong Kong, or Singapore.[51]

Australia's adult literacy rate of 99 per cent is equal to that of Japan and higher than most other places in the Asia–Pacific region. With English as the primary language, it is not surprising that English language fluency in Australia is higher than most places in the Asia–Pacific region. The presence of people from many Asian nations (a quarter of Sydney's population was born outside of Australia) and active language programmes in schools have dramatically improved Asian language proficiency in Australia in general and in Sydney in particular. Companies like American Express and Novell have cited the wide variety of language skills available in Australia as an important reason for setting up operations in Sydney instead of Singapore or Hong Kong.[52] Australia has an excellent education system, which has been turned into a big business in its own right, earning US$2 billion in international student fees in 1995. The overwhelming majority of this revenue came from Asian students attracted by Australia's quality of instruction, English language environment, pleasant surroundings, and an aggressive marketing campaign.[53]

Sydney's technical skills are considered good. A history of scientific education and demand for engineering of some of Australia's leading industries (such as mining) have made the nation home to a large number of well-trained scientists and engineers. Australia's number of computers per capita ranks among the highest in the world.[54] This combination, along with English language fluency (the dominance of the United States in computer software has meant that virtually every major computer operating system uses English language syntax, giving native English speakers an advantage in computer programming) gives Australia advantages in computer software and data processing in the Asia–Pacific arena. Skilled scientists, engineers, and programmers often can be hired at salaries up to one-third less than their counterparts in Hong Kong.[55]

One area in which the Australian work-force does not compare well with others in the region is industrial relations. A history of strikes and labour unrest have hurt Australian industry and have made it less than an ideal place for foreign investors. The power of labour unions has declined somewhat, though substantial reforms of labour laws have yet to be achieved. Since the early 1980s, the number and seriousness of industrial disputes have lessened dramatically, though labour difficulties are more of a concern in Australia than in Hong Kong, Singapore, Taiwan, or many other places in the region.

Australia is a politically stable democracy with a well-developed, independent legal system, based on the British Common Law System. Rule of law is respected, information flows freely, and personal liberties are upheld. In fact, Australia often has been viewed as a safe haven by people from less stable parts of the Asia–Pacific region. Australia in general, and Sydney in particular, both score very highly in surveys of quality of life, generally well ahead of Singapore, Hong Kong, Tokyo, Taipei, and other Asia–Pacific centres. Sydney bills itself as having the Western lifestyle desired by North American or European expatriates. It has a pleasant climate, low population density, many outdoor activities, and several cultural amenities. Sydney also has a reputation for being an open city, tolerant of different nationalities. In recent years, it has encouraged immigration on the part of people with investment capital or skills that could contribute to the Australian economy.

In the 1980s and early 1990s, the Australian government began to open the economy more to international competition and began to reduce what had become a bloated and inefficient welfare state. Starting in 1993, the national and local governments began an initiative to attract the Asia–Pacific regional headquarters of overseas firms by targeting 700 firms that might possibly set up a headquarters in Sydney and then offering tax concessions and other inducements. As part of this plan it also began streamlining immigration procedures for expatriate employees. By 1996, some 67 new headquarters had been attracted to Australia, most of these to Sydney. The national and local governments also made improving local competitiveness a key priority. Debate continues about the nation's tax structure, which is not nearly as attractive to overseas firms as those found in Hong Kong or Singapore. Other aspects of the regulatory environment are considered as generally favourable or neutral toward businesses such as financial services and telecommunications.

The Australian government has placed great emphasis on education and training, both to improve its own work-force and as an export earner. It is one of the few nations in the world to unify the tasks of education and training into a single department, the Department of Employment, Education, and Training (DEET). DEET has actually gone into business itself, consulting to a wide range of clients in Central Asia, Eastern Europe, and the Asia–Pacific region. The Australian government also sponsors research centres and company-based technology development through direct funding and tax incentive schemes.

Sydney in Perspective

Sydney has made aggressive efforts to become part of the Asia–Pacific region and to a certain extent has succeeded. The city has been benefiting from regional growth and from increasing contact with the more dynamic Asian economies. Sydney's distance from the centres of gravity of the Asia–Pacific region, however, limits its abilities to integrate into the Asian market and can be a decisive point for an overseas firm. In one example, after an exhaustive study, Compaq determined that Sydney had better technical expertise for its operations, but that Singapore was closer to where the action was in Asia.[56] For Sydney-based firms it means that the best strategy for serving East and North-East Asian markets often is to create an 'Asia–Pacific' office of their own further north.

Sydney has become a reasonably strong competitor for

location independent businesses, such as communications and data processing, and will benefit as the number of location independent businesses increases. Sydney is a particularly interesting alternative for Western multinationals with non-location sensitive businesses, or for companies preferring to start out in a more 'Western' setting before diving into the markets of Asia. The city also is becoming an interesting alternative for the 'back-office' operations of firms headquartered in Hong Kong, Singapore, Taiwan, and elsewhere in the Asia–Pacific region, where distance might not be so important, but being in a nearby time zone is. This is interesting in that if, as we believe, the ability to process information is critical to the future of many Hong Kong businesses, then the fact that a number of firms view Hong Kong as a less attractive place to process information, for whatever reason, is a cause for some concern.

Sydney and Hong Kong

For the most part, it is easier to see Sydney as complementary to Hong Kong rather than as competing with it. Australia and Hong Kong already have a number of ties. Australia has been a leading destination for Hong Kong students and emigrants in recent years. Some of the emigrants have stayed in Australia and some have returned to Hong Kong after obtaining an Australian passport. Many of the estimated 20,000 people who fly between Australia and Hong Kong each week are 'astronauts' who commute to work in Hong Kong each week and then return to spend the weekends with their families in Australia.[57] Australian firms find Hong Kong an easy place to do business and an excellent base for the China market. In 1994/5, Hong Kong accounted for 19 per cent of the profits recorded by the overseas subsidiaries of Australian firms, second to neighbouring New Zealand which accounted for 56 per cent.[58]

Sydney is not likely to compete for the bulk of Hong Kong businesses, or for its position as a packager and integrator of manufacturing, financial, and service activities for mainland China and the Asian region. Nor is it likely that Sydney could become a real centre of the overseas Chinese, or Chinese, business networks to the same extent as Hong Kong, Singapore, Taipei, or Shanghai. Sydney provides an interesting perspective on Hong Kong because in many ways—in its 'Westernness', its technical capabilities, its low costs, and its more relaxed lifestyle—Sydney provides features that Hong Kong does not.

HONG KONG'S COMPETITION

The nature of competition among regional centres in the world economy is changing. Many of the managers we interviewed for this study said that increasingly they do not face simple 'either/or decisions' (for example, whether to locate in Hong Kong or in Singapore). Instead, they increasingly tend to have operations in a number of Asian cities and they face decisions about which activities to locate in different places. The result is a more sophisticated and varied set of criteria for industrial location decisions. At the same time, the emergence of new centres and the development strategies of others provides a more complicated competitive environment.

Much of the 'competition' to date has been indirect rather than direct. Shanghai and Sydney might be more complementary than competing with Hong Kong, at least in the short to medium term. In many areas, Singapore and Hong Kong are rivals, but not direct competitors. Taiwan's political situation has made it difficult for Taiwan to become a direct competitor with Hong Kong. Both Hong Kong and Taiwan have benefited from the role that Hong Kong has played in facilitating trade and investment between Taiwan and the Mainland. And, of course, regional development is not a zero-sum game. All of the cities profiled have benefited from the increased trade and investment flows in the region and from each other's economic growth.

Some of the contrasts between Hong Kong and the places profiled in this chapter are relatively stark. Singapore, Taiwan, and Shanghai each have development programmes managed by governments that are far more activist than that of Hong Kong.

273

Even Sydney's government is more involved in active direct marketing to leading overseas companies and in the promotion of particular businesses or types of businesses than the Hong Kong government. Shanghai and, to a lesser extent, Taiwan, lack the transparency and level playing field of Hong Kong. Singapore, Shanghai, and, to a lesser extent, Sydney, lack the entrepreneurial drive found in Hong Kong. Singapore, Sydney, and, at least for now, Taiwan, lack the close, direct, fluid ties with a large hinterland.

The four 'competitors' profiled in this chapter have each attempted to develop a clear positioning. Singapore has positioned itself as the safe, certain (as opposed to 'uncertain' Hong Kong), regional partner for overseas multinationals. Shanghai is trying to position itself as the natural commercial, financial, and industrial centre of the world's most populous nation. Sydney has positioned itself as the low-cost, technically capable, pleasant lifestyle option for Western multinationals. Taipei wishes to position itself as the springboard to East Asia for local and overseas manufacturing and service firms.

Some regional competitors are trying to match certain aspects of Hong Kong. Singapore is trying to develop through government policy the type of hinterland and entrepreneurship that Hong Kong has naturally. Taiwan is trying to deregulate its economy (making it look more like Hong Kong's) and thereby make it more attractive as a centre for multinational companies and for business services within the Asia–Pacific region. Shanghai is trying to build a 'socialist Hong Kong' in Pudong, using a land leasing policy like that of Hong Kong to fund development. Both Taiwan and Singapore are taking close aim at industries and activities in which Hong Kong traditionally has been strong—Singapore with its targeting of financial service firms, transportation companies, and regional offices of multinational companies, and Taiwan with its APROC focus on air cargo, sea cargo, media, communications, and financial services.

On the other hand, there are areas in which the 'competitors' are comparable or superior to Hong Kong. Singapore and Hong Kong usually are neck-and-neck in most categories in international surveys of economic competitiveness or factors that affect competitiveness. Singapore and Sydney have transparent governments, neutral legal systems, and excellent infrastructure. Shanghai's hinterland has historically been a more important force in the Chinese economy than Southern China, Hong Kong's hinterland. Taiwan's location, while not quite as favourable as that of Hong Kong, is not that far off. For some activities, such as the physical production stage of manufacturing and as a centre for technology development, Hong Kong lags behind the others.

Hong Kong's regional competitors are unlikely to 'out-Hong Kong' Hong Kong any time soon. After all, Singapore does not serve quite the same markets, Taipei has its political isolation to deal with, Shanghai is still far behind, and Sydney is far away. More importantly, each would have to dismantle significant portions of its present economic system in order to truly copy Hong Kong. To match Hong Kong's hinterland, Singapore would have to integrate itself with neighouring Malaysia and Indonesia to a much greater extent than is possible and Sydney would have to move out of Australia. To match Hong Kong's entrepreneurial drive, Singapore and Shanghai would have to reduce drastically the importance of government in the economy and place decision-making firmly in the hands of the private sector. To match Hong Kong's service industries, Taiwan would have to end its prohibition on direct trade and travel to the Mainland and would have to deregulate its markets more than it presently envisions. To match the cosmopolitan nature of Hong Kong, Shanghai would have to allow free flow of information, reduce restrictions on foreign firms, improve transparency of administration, and substantially improve its infrastructure. To match Hong Kong's incentives to succeed, Sydney, Shanghai, Taipei, and Singapore would have to slash corporate tax rates, personal tax rates, social security tax rates, and other taxes. None of these moves would be easy.

Even if Hong Kong's competitors would find it difficult to 'out-Hong Kong' Hong Kong, each of the four does point out areas in which Hong Kong could be vulnerable. Sydney shows that Hong Kong's costs are very high by world standards and that Hong Kong is losing (or has lost) cost competitiveness for non-location-sensitive business. Shanghai reminds that there are cities closer and more integrated into the heart of the Chinese Mainland than Hong Kong. Singapore shows that there are world-class business cities ready to benefit from Hong Kong's uncertainties or if Hong Kong should falter. Taiwan shows that there are other entrepreneurial economies with close ties to mainland China and that there are potential competitors for Hong Kong's position as an international centre serving China and East Asia.

The competitors are narrowing the gap or the perceived gap. And when it comes to corporate location decisions, perceptions become reality and perceptions of Hong Kong are not as favourable as they once were. But the optimal response for Hong Kong is not to copy the policies of others or to move artificially into businesses in which others are stronger with strategies better attuned to other systems. The optimal response for Hong Kong is not to become 'less like Hong Kong' but to become 'more like Hong Kong' by capitalizing and building upon precisely the features of the territory's economy that others find the hardest to duplicate and then by making sure that it markets its attributes so that perceptions match reality.

Hong Kong derives critical advantages—from its location, connections to networks, private sector entrepreneurship, commercial infrastructure, clustering, transparent and business-friendly institutions, and unique combinations—for its roles as a packager and integrator of economic activities, as a foreign investor, as a home for overseas companies, and as a driver of the mainland China economy. None of the cities profiled in this chapter, nor any of the other cities in the region, are ready to displace Hong Kong in any of these roles at any time soon.

NOTES

1   Emily Thornton, 'Bitter Pill', *Far Eastern Economic Review* (31 October 1996): 58–9.
2   Republic of Singapore, Economic Development Board, 'Singapore Poses

Least Political Risk: PERC Survey', http://www.sedb.com.sg/biz/other/others14.html and Republic of Singapore, Economic Development Board, 'Singapore Has Least Corruption in Asia: PERC Survey', http://www.sedb.com.sg/biz/other/others10.html.

3   Republic of Singapore, Economic Development Board, 'Year in Review 1994', http://www.sedb.com.sg/annual95/review.html.

4   Dun and Bradstreet, *Key Business Directory of Singapore*, 1993/4 edn., Hong Kong, 1993.

5   Salil Tripathi, 'Capital Cities: Singapore Swing', *Asia, Inc.* (February 1996): 42.

6   Republic of Singapore, Economic Development Board, 'Singapore's Business Climate', http://www.sedb.com.sg/biz/other/others.

7   Philip Coggan, 'Survey of Singapore', *Financial Times* (8 February 1996): vi; see also Tripathi, 'Capital Cities: Singapore Swing', p. 38.

8   Ahirudin Attan, 'Need to Make Employment Benefits Attractive', *Business Times* (24 July 1995): 20.

9   Murray Hiebert, 'It's a Jungle Out There', *Far Eastern Economic Review* (25 April 1996): 58.

10   Tripathi, 'Capital Cities: Singapore Swing', p. 38.

11   See The World Bank, *The East Asian Miracle: Economic Growth and Public Policy*, New York: Oxford University Press, 1993.

12   Chi Schive, *Taiwan's Economic Role in East Asia*, Washington, D.C.: Center for Strategic and International Studies, 1995, p. 12.

13   See Republic of China, Government Information Office, 'The Republic of China at a Glance', Taipei http://www.gio.gov.tw/info/glance/index.html.

14   Ibid.

15   Republic of China, Government Information Office, 'The Economy', *Republic of China Yearbook 1996*, Taipei, 1996, p. 154.

16   Ibid.

17   China Credit Information Services, *The Largest Corporations in Taiwan, 1994*, Taipei, 1994, pp. 20, 289, 296–301.

18   IMD International, *The World Competitiveness Yearbook 1996*, Lausanne, 1996, pp. 550, 515, and 578.

19   Republic of China, 'The Economy', *Republic of China Yearbook 1996*, pp. 155–6.

20   Republic of China, Government Information Office, 'Taiwan: An Initiative into the Next Century: A Plan for Building Taiwan into an Asia–Pacific Regional Operations Center', http://www.gio.tw/info/.

21   The Joint Banking Committee of the American Chamber of Commerce and European Council of Commerce and Trade, *Taipei as a Regional Financial and Funding Centre*, Taipei, 1995.

22   Republic of China, 'Hong Kong and Macau', *Republic of China Yearbook 1996*, http://www.gio.tw/info/.

23   Chen Minzhi, *A Study of Shanghai's Development Strategy*, Shanghai:

Shanghai renmin chubanshe, 1985, cited in Peter T. Y. Cheung, 'The Political Context of Shanghai's Economic Development', in Y. M. Yeung and Sung Yun-wing (eds.), *Shanghai: Transformation and Modernization under China's Open Policy*, Hong Kong: Chinese University Press, 1996, p. 79; see also Ho Lok-sang and Tsui Kai-yuen, 'Fiscal Relations between Shanghai and the Central Government', in Y. M. Yeung and Sung Yun-wing (eds.), *Shanghai: Transformation and Modernization under China's Open Policy*, pp. 154–7.

24   Peter T. Y. Cheung, 'The Political Context of Shanghai's Economic Development', pp. 52–4; Sung Yun-wing, ' "Dragon Head" of China's Economy?', in Y. M. Yeung and Sung Yun-wing (eds.), *Shanghai: Transformation and Modernization under China's Open Policy*, p. 195.

25   Rupert Hodder, 'Industrial Location', in Y. M. Yeung and Sung Yun-wing (eds.), *Shanghai: Transformation and Modernization under China's Open Policy*, Hong Kong: Chinese University Press, 1996, p. 241.

26   Shanghai Internet Trading and Consultancy, 'Economic Structure' and 'Living Standards', http://china-window.com/shanghai/shbf.

27   Yeung, 'Introduction', *Shanghai: Transformation and Modernization under China's Open Policy*, p. 17; Sung, ' "Dragon Head" ', pp. 174–8.

28   Anthony G. O. Yeh, 'Pudong: Remaking Shanghai as a World City', in Y. M. Yeung and Sung Yun-wing (eds.), *Shanghai: Transformation and Modernization under China's Open Policy*, Hong Kong: Chinese University Press, 1996, p. 288.

29   Hodder, 'Industrial Location', pp. 227, 235, 237.

30   Hong Kong Trade Development Council, 'Market Profile on Shanghai Municipality', Hong Kong, 28 October 1996, p. 1.

31   Shanghai Internet Trading and Consultancy, 'Economic Structure', http://china-window.com/shanghai/shbf.

32   Shanghai Internet Trading and Consultancy, 'Investment', http://china-window.com/shanghai/inves/tu4.html.

33   Y. M. Yeung, 'Introduction', *Shanghai: Transformation and Modernization under China's Open Policy*, p. 11.

34   Nyaw Mee-kau, 'Investment Environment: Perceptions of Overseas Investors of Foreign-funded Industrial Firms', in Y. M. Yeung and Sung Yun-wing (eds.), *Shanghai: Transformation and Modernization under China's Open Policy*, Hong Kong: Chinese University Press, 1996, Table 10.6, p. 256.

35   Ibid., Tables 10.8, 10.9, pp. 260, 262.

36   Ibid., Table 10.10, p. 269.

37   Ibid., pp. 256–7.

38   Grace C. L. Mak and Leslie N. K. Lo, 'Education', in Y. M. Yeung and Sung Yun-wing (eds.), *Shanghai: Transformation and Modernization under China's Open Policy*, Hong Kong: Chinese University Press, 1996, p. 386.

39   Nyaw, 'Investment Environment', p. 257.

40   Wong Siu-lun, 'The Entrepreneurial Spirit: Shanghai and Hong Kong

Compared', in Y. M. Yeung and Sung Yun-wing (eds.), *Shanghai: Transformation and Modernization under China's Open Policy*, Hong Kong: Chinese University Press, 1996, p. 34.

41 Sung, ' "Dragon Head" ', pp. 187–9.

42 Ibid., pp. 174–8.

43 Ibid., p. 194.

44 James Leung, 'Beijing Stifles Shanghai Dream', *Asian Business* (October 1995): 24–8; Sung, ' "Dragon Head" ', pp. 194–5.

45 Ibid.

46 *1995 Statistical Yearbook of Shanghai*, Shanghai: China Statistics Publishing Co., 1995, p. 105.

47 Yeung, 'Introduction', p. 17.

48 New South Wales Office of Economic Development, 'New South Wales (NSW) Competitiveness Report', http://www.srd.nsw.gov.au/comprep/p39a.HTM.

49 Ibid.

50 William Mellor, 'Capital Cities: Sydney: New South Asia', *Asia, Inc.*, 5 (August 1996): 28–9.

51 New South Wales Office of Economic Development, 'New South Wales Competitiveness Report', http://www.srd.nsw.gov.au/comprep/.

52 Mellor, 'Capital Cities: Sydney: New South Asia', p. 30; see also New South Wales Office of Economic Development, 'Sydney: Being Clever Matters', http://www.srd.nsw.gov.au/rhq/clever.htm.

53 Gary Silverman and Trish Saywell, 'Cramming Classes: Supply of College Places Doesn't Meet Demand', *Far Eastern Economic Review* (14 November 1996): 28.

54 IMD International, *The World Competitiveness Yearbook 1996*, p. 472; see also IMD International and World Economic Forum, *The World Competitiveness Report 1995*, Lausanne, 1995, p. 602, cited in 'NSW Competitiveness Report', http://www.srd.nsw.gov.au/comprep/P16A.HTML.

55 Mellor, 'Sydney: New South Asia', p. 29.

56 Tripathi, 'Capital Cities: Singapore Swing', p. 38.

57 Mellor, 'Sydney: New South Asia', p. 31.

58 Phillip Ruthven, 'Australia's Positioning Within the Asia–Pacific', in ICIC Pty. Ltd., *Australian Enterprise Report*, http://www.icic.com.au/aer/articles/137.html.

9 1997 AND HONG KONG'S UNCERTAINTIES

Through most of this book, we have not focused explicitly on the issues surrounding the transfer of administration from Britain to China that will take place on 1 July 1997. This is not intended in any way to minimize the importance of the transition or to minimize the challenges that it will bring to Hong Kong and its economy. However, we have been surprised at the tendency of articles and speeches purporting to assess Hong Kong's economic future to focus almost exclusively on political issues and virtually to ignore the economy, or to give a short list of economic facts and figures and then dismiss them as meaningless. It appears that a number of people are going to wake up on 2 July 1997 only to realize that their preoccupation with the issues of political institutions has left them ill-prepared to tackle critical economic issues. We have become firmly convinced that in order to get a clearer picture of Hong Kong's economic future, through the transition and beyond, we had to explore the competitiveness of the Hong Kong economy and its industries, its advantages and disadvantages, its opportunities and challenges.

Hong Kong faces many uncertainties and people in Hong Kong have many concerns. The most obvious and important of these uncertainties are related to the transfer of control from Britain to China. But these are not the only uncertainties or challenges the economy faces and it would be a mistake to allow a preoccupation with '1997' to obstruct proper analysis and discussion of other uncertainties. It is hard to predict what the details of the outcomes might be. There is little historical precedent for the reincorporation of a territory with such an advanced economy into a nation with a less advanced economy, and there is little precedent for the arrangements under which this reincorporation will take place. The one thing of which we can be sure is that any detailed prediction will be wrong, at least in some respects. Nevertheless, the uncertainties and concerns exist and should be placed in an appropriate context.

HONG KONG'S CONCERNS

In the course of our interviews and workshops, a number of concerns have been voiced with respect to Hong Kong's political and economic future under Chinese administration. The main areas of concern include the rule of law, a level playing field for businesses and individuals, corruption, individual rights, the future of democracy, emigration, immigration, the potential for capital and companies to leave, economic autonomy, and political autonomy.

Hong Kong's legal system has been closely modelled on the British Common Law system. The prevailing ethos has been that of most Western nations, where the legal system plays an important role in providing checks and balances against certain acts of individuals and against the arbitrary exercise of power on the part of the government. The judiciary, appointed by the Governor but on recommendation of an independent Judicial Service Commission, has been considered independent of government influence. Laws and the judiciary on the Mainland, on the other hand, often are considered as subject to the authority of the Communist Party rather than the other way around. Although the Basic Law provides for the appointment of judges by the Chief Executive of the Hong Kong Special Administrative Region (SAR), many Hong Kong-based executives are worried that the rule of law will be replaced by the rule of officials and that the Hong Kong judiciary will cease to be independent and even-handed, particularly when Mainland companies or individuals are involved.

A lack of even-handedness could be a severe blow for the Hong Kong economy. Part of the attraction for Hong Kong, Western, and overseas Chinese firms has been the fact that Hong Kong has been a neutral playing field with a sound legal base. In Hong Kong, the government as a whole and government officials and civil servants as individuals generally have not had direct interests in private firms or in specific business dealings. The Mainland, despite recent reforms, has a history of state intervention and limits on private enterprise that is very different from the Hong Kong experience. Government officials on the Mainland often head major corporations. Conflict of interest boundaries that might exist in many countries between their governmental and business roles at best are blurred. Relatives of government and party officials often are given important posts in industry. The lack of separation between the state and business on the Mainland means that in many cases the main regulator is a business competitor. This is disquieting to some firms in Hong Kong which fear that unfair advantage might be taken by companies linked to Mainland political interests.

In Hong Kong, the Independent Commission Against Corruption (ICAC) and the administration have worked to weed out the corruption that was widespread in the territory in the 1960s and early 1970s. As a result, international surveys have concluded that Hong Kong has one of the least corrupt governments in the region. This, in turn, has helped to foster Hong Kong's free-wheeling, entrepreneurial, and information-intensive economy. Mainland China, on the other hand, in international surveys typically ranks among the most corrupt places in the world in which to do business. State ownership, the pervasive power of government and government officials, and the lack of an independent judiciary all have contributed to corruption on the Mainland. The problem has been underlined by the efforts of Mainland leaders to rein in corruption in recent years. A public opinion poll conducted in mid-1996 on the Mainland by the State Commission for Restructuring the Economy found that many people believed that 'corruption was one of the biggest problems facing the country', and 'the further spread of corruption could lead to the demise of the [Chinese Communist] Party and the country'. Confidence in the Mainland government's anti-corruption plan increased from 44.6 per cent in 1994 to 56.2 per cent in 1996.[1] Needless to say, there are fears in the Hong Kong business community that corruption will spread from the Mainland to the Hong Kong SAR after the change in administration and erode Hong Kong's business infrastructure.

People in Hong Kong have traditionally enjoyed a number of personal freedoms, such as freedom of expression, freedom of the press, freedom of travel, freedom of assembly, and freedom of religion. Hong Kong has had very clear laws concerning contracts, property rights, and other economic activity. These freedoms and laws have been enforced to protect both citizen and society. Although the Basic Law guarantees personal freedoms and rule of law, and extends international human rights conventions to Hong Kong, sceptics note that some of the same language found in the Basic Law also is found in the constitution of the People's Republic of China, where it is not necessarily upheld. Many of the freedoms that people in Hong Kong have taken for granted are not taken for granted on the Mainland nor in other countries in Asia. There are concerns that some of these freedoms, particularly freedom of expression, might be either curtailed, or in the case of free expression, limited by self-censorship. Mainland pronouncements that the Bill of Rights instituted by the British colonial administration in 1991 would be modified or repealed have added to the concern, particularly in light of the criticism that the Mainland has received from international human rights groups on its record regarding personal freedoms.

There also are concerns over the future of democracy in Hong Kong after 1 July 1997. Chinese plans to abolish the Legislative Council (Legco) elected in 1995 on 1 July 1997, and to replace it with an appointed provisional legislature until new elections can be held, have been widely reported in the West. In addition, leaders of the pro-democracy movement, which won the majority of the geographically based Legco seats in Hong Kong's 1995 election, have been excluded from the discussions on the territory's future held by Mainland representatives. This has contrasted with the reception that the same leaders have received in the United States and the United Kingdom. For a Western public brought up to equate democracy with freedom and personal liberties, the 'end of democracy' in Hong Kong is a seemingly ominous sign.

In the 1980s, the Western press reported on an exodus, or 'brain drain' from Hong Kong of 60,000 people a year; this was taken as a sign of a loss in confidence on the part of many in Hong Kong about the impending change in administration. The number of Hong Kong residents with the right of abode elsewhere has been estimated at between 500,000 and one million by various sources.[2] Many, if not most of the people with the right to live elsewhere are from the ranks of the managerial, professional, and middle classes. If conditions in Hong Kong were to deteriorate, a significant number of the people critical to the territory's prosperity in theory could leave. An exodus of expatriates would mean the loss of overseas companies and further wide-ranging economic impacts.

If emigration has been considered a potential problem, immigration has been considered an equally important potential problem. Given Hong Kong's relatively low birth rate and stable death rate, changes in the territory's population are largely governed by net migration. Until 1980, the Hong Kong government followed a 'touch base' policy in which people from the Mainland who reached the urban centres and found accommodation were allowed to stay. Starting in 1980, illegal immigrants from the Mainland have been repatriated upon discovery. Since that time, Hong Kong has relied on at least the tacit cooperation of Mainland authorities to control the border. Even though the Basic Law gives the SAR administration the right to determine who can enter Hong Kong, with the exception of the children of people from the territory, there are questions about the extent to which the new administration will be able to enforce the border. Authorities in neighbouring areas of China seem to believe that the border will not be enforced, as do a number of young people from Guangdong reportedly ready to 'march into Hong Kong' to sample its lifestyle after the transition.[3] That such false impressions have been left uncorrected is a source of concern. Planning documents for land use in Hong Kong aim to provide for a population in the year 2011 of between 7.5 million and 8.1 million.[4] Some in Hong Kong have taken these reports as evidence that the government expects a mass inward migration after 1997. Uncontrolled immigration would place a severe strain on Hong Kong's infrastructure and social services and result in a substantial deterioration of the quality of life found in the territory. Even controlled migration could create challenges as indicated in an earlier chapter.

There have been concerns about the movement of companies and capital out of Hong Kong as well. Roughly half of the companies listed on the Hong Kong Stock Exchange have a foreign domicile, or legal place of incorporation. Many have moved their domicile in the last 15 years. Some of the companies, such as Jardine Matheson and the Hongkong and Shanghai Bank, have been fixtures in Hong Kong for more than a century. In addition, many of Hong Kong's leading business people have placed significant portions of their assets outside of Hong Kong. If such people, with their wealth and connections on the Mainland, do not 'trust in Hong Kong's future', then some would say, why should anyone else?

There also are concerns that the economic guarantees found in the Basic Law—including the call for economic autonomy, a separate and convertible currency for Hong Kong, the control of Hong Kong revenues by the Hong Kong SAR, no remittances of tax revenues to the Mainland, and the continuation of the capitalist system for 50 years—will not be honoured. Milton Friedman, for example, has stated that he does not believe that the Mainland will allow the Hong Kong dollar to circulate for more than two years after the transition, whereas others believe that the Mainland will find Hong Kong's US$60 billion in international reserves too attractive to leave alone. In *Red Flag Over Hong Kong,* Bueno de Mesquita, Newman, and Rabushka predicted that Hong Kong's free-market system would not survive for a decade.[5]

On the political side, there have been questions—about the nature of the selection process of the Chief Executive and the Provisional Legislative Council (both selected by an electoral college of 400 people from Hong Kong appointed by Beijing); about the SAR government's future relationship with Mainland officials; and about the role of the Chinese Communist Party in Hong Kong, among others. Although the Chief Executive designate Tung Chee-hwa has promised to uphold Hong Kong's interests and status, some believe that the SAR administration will have no choice but to do the Mainland's bidding after the handover. Another question mark involves the precise functions of the New China News Agency (Xinhua), the unofficial consulate of the People's Republic of China in Hong Kong, the Hong Kong and Macau Affairs Office of the PRC government, and other agencies of the National People's Government after the changeover. Many wonder what influence if any they will exert over the day to day running of the Special Administrative Region.

CONCERNS IN CONTEXT

Although many of the concerns identified above are addressed in the Basic Law, which is to be the constitution of Hong Kong after 1 July 1997, this might be of little solace to some. There are those who believe that all the negotiations since 1982 over the future of Hong Kong have been hopeless; others believe that mainland China simply will not understand Hong Kong and therefore will engage in activities that will prove detrimental to Hong Kong regardless of its intentions. A number of the moves and statements made by Mainland officials have been taken as ominous signs in the West, though, once again, perception and reality in Hong Kong often differ and some of these moves and statements appear in a different light when placed in their appropriate context.

This context includes an unfortunate poisoning of the

relationship between the British and Chinese sides after the Tiananmen Square Incident of June 1989. Until that time, the British and Chinese sides had their differences, but had appeared to make significant progress on many of the issues facing Hong Kong and its future. The Tiananmen Square Incident created difficulties on both sides. Hundreds of thousands of supporters of the Tiananmen Square democracy movement protested in Hong Kong and sent money and supplies to the Tiananmen demonstrators. Mainland officials began to view Hong Kong as a source of dissent and a potential base for subversives. The British colonial administration rushed to institute several *faits accompli* before the handover to improve business confidence in the territory and to change its political landscape. Among the British moves were the announcement of a series of massive public works projects including the new airport at Chek Lap Kok and the acceleration of direct elections of members of the Legislative Council. Cooperation between the two sides diminished dramatically.

In the West, reports about Hong Kong and its imminent demise have become commonplace, even as the property and stock markets rise to new heights. Pronouncements from the Mainland regarding the planned replacement of the Legislative Council, disagreement between the Mainland and Britain over the Court of Final Appeal, Mainland requests for civil service loyalty and dossiers, delays over financing of the new airport, delays in receiving approval for Container Terminal Nine, and the exclusion of the Democratic Party from membership in committees discussing the future of Hong Kong provided a gloomy media picture of the Mainland and its intentions. The local context, however, has been somewhat more varied.

The main disagreement between the British and Chinese with respect to Hong Kong's future legal system was over the composition of the Court of Final Appeal, a Hong Kong-based court that would replace the British Privy Council as the final appeals court for the Hong Kong judiciary. The final bone of contention, over the number of foreign judges permitted to sit on any individual case, was finally resolved in mid-1995. Most observers failed to note how extraordinary it would be for any foreign judge to sit on the final appeals court in any jurisdiction. The Bill of Rights and related ordinances passed by the colonial administration in 1991 and thereafter withdrew from the Hong Kong government some of the more draconian tools that it had at its disposal to clamp down on civil unrest and corruption. Though in some ways the new laws simply confirmed the freedoms that people in Hong Kong had enjoyed under the colonial administration, the timing left much to be desired. To the outsider, it appeared that the colonial administration was trying to change laws that it could be trusted with, but felt that a future SAR administration could not be trusted with. Regardless of the merits of the changes, this was not something that the Chinese side could accept with equanimity, particularly after the support provided by some groups in Hong Kong to the Tiananmen demonstrators.

Democracy in Hong Kong also has a particular history. Relatively few people in the West reading the reports of the 'imminent demise of democracy' in Hong Kong realize that Hong Kong has never had a democracy. For 150 years, the colonial administration ruled Hong Kong without the benefit of an elected legislature nor a Bill of Rights. Even the legislature that was elected in 1995, the first in which a majority of seats was elected by something approaching universal suffrage, received its ultimate authority from the Governor of Hong Kong and therefore from the Queen of England. In the negotiations that culminated in the 1984 Joint Declaration of the United Kingdom and China concerning the future of Hong Kong, the Chinese side envisioned an executive-led SAR system modelled on the British colonial administration and a Legislative Council chosen 'by election'. The Chinese side did not accept that it would be bound to any particular form of election and expected to be able to participate in defining Hong Kong's electoral forms. Again, regardless of the merits of the case, the imposition of the new electoral system was viewed by Mainland officials as a breach of the process under which they believed major decisions regarding Hong Kong's future would be made.

The Basic Law (approved by the National People's Congress

of the People's Republic of China in 1990) itself calls for election of the Legislative Council with a gradual increase in the number of directly elected members and a gradual decrease in the number elected by a Hong Kong-based electoral college. The Basic Law calls for the eventual election of both the Legislative Council and the Chief Executive by universal suffrage of Hong Kong citizens, something that has never happened under British administration. The Mainland has promised a return to an elected Legislative Council in 1998, a fact often overlooked in the West. The Western media also tends to underplay the fact that 1 July 1997 will mark the first time anyone from Hong Kong will be in a position of true executive authority in the territory (other than temporary stints when a British governor has been out of town). During the past 150 years, locals have never had a say in who would be governor.

The movement of corporate domiciles, individuals placing assets offshore, and people from Hong Kong obtaining foreign travel documents should be viewed as what they are, insurance policies that help them manage uncertainties. No one would claim that buying fire insurance means that the purchaser's house will burn down, or that it will burn down on 1 July 1997. Similarly, the acts of changing corporate domiciles, placing assets offshore, and obtaining foreign travel documents do not ensure or even foretell the 'death of Hong Kong'. Insurance in the face of uncertainty is simply prudent risk management done to protect individuals or shareholders in case of unforeseen problems. Changing a corporate domicile does not change where the company does business, where its assets are invested, or where its people are employed. If it did, the state of Delaware (a favourite corporate domicile in the United States) would be the most populous state in the United States. Nearly all of the Hong Kong companies that have changed corporate domiciles are still alive and well and growing in Hong Kong.

Although some observers note that Li Ka-shing, Hong Kong's second richest man by most estimates, has moved a significant portion of his assets to a trust outside Hong Kong,[6] they fail to note that Li is still heavily invested in Hong Kong and mainland China and that Lee Shau-kee, Hong Kong's richest man, is invested almost totally in Hong Kong and mainland China. In fact, a striking feature of the holdings of many of Hong Kong's tycoons is that they are far less geographically diversified than the holdings of individuals with similar net worths in other parts of the world. Nor does the movement of capital offshore put much of a dent in the Hong Kong financial services business. Since Hong Kong-based fund managers, for example, largely manage the Asian portfolios of North American or European institutions, 'flight' capital from Hong Kong has not had a material effect on their business.

Emigration has not been all that it has appeared either. An increasing number (at least 12 per cent) of the Hong Kong people who emigrated from the territory in the decade prior to 1994 already have returned.[7] Many others are expected to return as soon as they have lived abroad long enough to obtain foreign travel documents. Such documents are their own personal insurance policies that would allow them to leave Hong Kong if conditions deteriorated, or if they simply wanted a change of scene. The emigration picture gets more interesting when one notes that more people were actually immigrating to Hong Kong than emigrating from Hong Kong during the entire period of the so-called 'brain drain'. In 1992, for example, when the emigration of up to 80,000 Hong Kong Chinese received world attention, more than 94,000 people immigrated legally to Hong Kong.[8] As 1997 approaches, there are substantially more expatriates in Hong Kong than there were just a few years ago. The expatriate population of Hong Kong has more than doubled in size since 1989, growing on average at a rate of 12 per cent annually.[9]

Emigration also must be put into historical perspective and regional perspective. Hong Kong always has been a place with substantial emigration. For many, it has been a stopping place on the way from the Mainland to somewhere else. As a result, Hong Kong people always have been mobile. In this, there has been little new in the 1980s and 1990s. The rapid economic growth and social change found within the wider Asian region has stimulated almost unprecedented mobility (apart from forced refugee migrations earlier in the century). Modern world history has shown that heightened population movement is a normal offshoot of economic development, and East Asia as a whole, including Hong Kong, is no exception. Less attention in the West has been paid to the emigration of the highly educated and skilled from other fast-growing Asian economies such as South Korea, Taiwan, and Singapore. While concern over the change in administration in 1997 does play a part in some decisions to emigrate from Hong Kong, overall outflows of population from Hong Kong also fit within the larger pattern of the expansion of Asian businesses and activities world-wide. As one expert has indicated, Hong Kong and other Asian economies have developed to the point where many citizens can move easily into and out of other developed regions.[10]

Finally, the fact that 'insurance' has been obtained for companies, assets, and individuals might decrease rather than increase the possibility of the deterioration of Hong Kong. Once such insurance is obtained, the companies, assets, and people can stay in Hong Kong as long as conditions do not deteriorate substantially. Furthermore, the knowledge that companies are housed elsewhere, assets are offshore, and individuals can leave quickly, might put a brake on counter-productive behaviour on the part of Mainland officials or the SAR administration. Both surely would know that a sudden exodus of companies, assets, and people would hurt the economies of both Hong Kong and the Mainland. Ironically, the very insurance cited as a lack of confidence in Hong Kong by some could help it weather minor to medium-sized storms in the future.

The conclusion that the Mainland will find Hong Kong's reserves 'irresistible' is essentially a statement that the Mainland will find Hong Kong more valuable as a victim of plunder than as a thriving, growing source of trade and capital for the Mainland. Hong Kong's reserves of US$60 billion might seem attractive, but they are dwarfed by the capital and trade that Hong Kong supplies to the Mainland. Between 1980 and 1995, Hong Kong has been the source of US$234 billion in contracted foreign direct investment.[11] Any attempt to 'pillage' the Hong Kong treasury surely would be met with resistance from Hong

Kong interests and Mainland enterprises with significant Hong Kong operations. More importantly, any such attempt would cause the Mainland to lose all credibility with respect to foreign investors and foreign firms with plans to do business on the Mainland. As attractive as US$60 billion might be, it is not nearly as attractive as continued international investment emanating from or organized through Hong Kong by an international community that is watching the situation in Hong Kong with great interest.

On the political side, there are those who predict that the entire 'one country–two systems' arrangement will unravel shortly after the change in administration. In an article titled 'The Death of Hong Kong', for example, Louis Kraar predicted that Beijing would control Hong Kong directly, that 'one country–two systems' would be a sham, and that Hong Kong's role as a vibrant international commercial hub was 'indisputably dying'.[12] Others have claimed that the Mainland values stability over economic growth and that as a result it will control Hong Kong to the latter's detriment. Such a conclusion, however, rests on an assumption that Mainland officials believe that 'control' could be best exercised in a heavy-handed manner from the centre, rather than through local autonomy in Hong Kong. Hong Kong has never been a difficult place to govern when it has been governed benignly. Close adherence to 'one country–two systems' might prove to be the most effective way to keep Hong Kong a peaceful place and at worst a mild administrative headache. More heavy-handed approaches might be more likely to ensure that Hong Kong spiralled out of control rather than remained 'under control'.

It is important to note that Hong Kong has been vulnerable to the Mainland for decades. In the 1920s and 1930s, the Nationalist Kuomintang government began seeking the return of Hong Kong, but put aside the issue when Japan invaded China. Several observers and former diplomats claim that if the Kuomintang had won the civil war, it would have demanded the return of Hong Kong in the 1940s. The Communists decided not to press for Hong Kong's return after their victory because their leadership decided that Hong Kong could be more useful under British administration, at least for a time. During most of the last 50 years, it would have been difficult for Britain to hold on to Hong Kong if China decided to march in or, even more simply, to turn off the water.[13]

The Basic Law, which will serve as the constitution for the Hong Kong Special Administrative Region for the first 50 years after the changeover, was written by Mainland Chinese officials with the help of two committees—the Basic Law Drafting Committee and the Basic Law Consultative Committee—both of which had wide representation from Hong Kong. The United Kingdom was not represented.[14] This means that the Basic Law should be understood as China's document, not a vestige of the colonial administration that will be overturned at the first opportunity as a matter of course. In Article 5, the Basic Law sets forth the fundamental principle that 'The socialist system shall not be practised in Hong Kong.' It goes on to provide for a continuation of many of the most important features of Hong Kong's way of life: a market-oriented economy with a separate convertible currency, the use of common law, freedom of religion, freedom of speech, freedom of travel, free trade, and free capital movements. It even mandates low tax rates, calls for the maintenance of the features that make Hong Kong an international finance centre, outlaws currency controls, and places control of business and financial regulation firmly in the hands of the Special Administrative Region.[15]

One might argue, of course, that what China gives China can take away. The ultimate interpreter of the Basic Law is the National People's Congress of the People's Republic of China, which also has the authority to amend the Basic Law. National Chinese laws can be extended to Hong Kong if there is a state of emergency and some of the wording of the Basic Law seems ambiguous. But it is hard to believe that the time and effort devoted to writing the Basic Law and obtaining input from Hong Kong interests would have been expended to create such a document, and such a statement of intentions to the rest of the world, if the intention was not to honour it. Members of the Preparatory Committee (a group put together to advise the

Mainland on the transition) interviewed for this study—including several leading Hong Kong academics, business people, and professionals—believe they have had an important influence on the way Hong Kong will be governed after 1 July 1997. The idea of 'one country–two systems' was originally developed by Deng Xiaoping as a formula under which Taiwan would be reunified with the Mainland. After the initial success of the economic linkages between the Mainland and Hong Kong, Deng was quoted as saying that the 'two systems' aspect should go on for 100 years, not just 50.

SCENARIOS FOR HONG KONG'S ECONOMIC FUTURE

Ultimately, each individual, group, or firm must decide how to face its own uncertainties. One tool that has been applied to the case of Hong Kong's economic future is scenario analysis. In scenario analysis, which has been widely used to assess uncertain political or economic situations, a set of different potential futures are identified and their logical conclusions worked out. The scenarios should be reasonable, different, and internally consistent if the technique is to yield the greatest insight. Several authors have developed scenarios to address Hong Kong's potential economic futures. Most such observers develop a trend, or 'most likely' scenario based on the present trajectory of the Hong Kong economy and a pessimistic scenario in which the Hong Kong way of life deteriorates substantially after 1 July 1997. Some observers add an optimistic scenario, which tends to be a minor variation on the trend scenario.[16] We prefer scenarios that use existing cities as examples of what Hong Kong might be, depending on the outcomes of the key uncertainties identified above.

Hong Kong as Hong Kong

The 'Hong Kong as Hong Kong' scenario involves more or less a continuation of the status quo in the territory with respect to:

the rule of law; a level playing field for individuals and companies; relative freedom from corruption; an independent judiciary; continued individual freedoms; strong local SAR governments; emigration and immigration that conform to historical patterns; no significant flight of capital or firms or individuals; substantial economic autonomy; and substantial political autonomy. The 'Hong Kong as Hong Kong' scenario postulates somewhat closer ties with the Mainland, but with the 'two systems' aspect of 'one country–two systems' dominating, so that Hong Kong would retain much of its 'insulation' from events on the Mainland.

The economic manifestation of such a scenario would include the continuation of Hong Kong's independent fiscal structure and currency, continuation of the free market and market-determined prices, and free trade in goods and services. In this view, Hong Kong would retain its status as an international financial and business services centre. The economy would continue to be robust, with manufacturing, finance, trade, transport, business services, and tourism leading the way. Hong Kong would face only limited competition from other cities, since Mainland cities would not progress so fast as to displace Hong Kong, and other cities, such as Singapore, would not be positioned to fill the same roles.

The 'Hong Kong as Hong Kong' scenario envisions a future in which the Joint Declaration and the Basic Law would be adhered to closely, the rationale being that they were carefully crafted and that China tends to respect international agreements. The scenario also postulates that it is in China's economic interest to maintain Hong Kong's separate status to allow Hong Kong to continue as a source of foreign exchange, loans, and investment for the Mainland and that the potential for eventual reunification with Taiwan along similar lines would be a major incentive for the Mainland to make 'one country–two systems' work. Further underpinning this scenario is a view that if Hong Kong's autonomy were compromised, China would lose political goodwill in the international community and would lose any chance of reunifying with Taiwan on a peaceful basis. In addition, it rests on the notion that Hong Kong itself could be a major liability and extremely difficult to rule if autonomy were compromised.

In the 'Hong Kong as Hong Kong' scenario, economic growth in the medium term is likely to be somewhat below its average for the last decade and somewhat below the faster growing economies of the Mainland and the region. The reasoning would be that a focus on keeping the barriers between Hong Kong and the Mainland might cause some strains and might drive some economic opportunities away to other cities in China.

Hong Kong as Shanghai

Another scenario is one in which Hong Kong quickly becomes just another Chinese city with no more privileges or special status than Shanghai, or any other Mainland city. The 'Hong Kong as Shanghai' scenario envisions such circumstances as: a sharply limited rule of law for matters affecting Mainland interests; no level playing field; substantial corruption; a judiciary controlled by the Mainland; suppression of individual freedoms (particularly of press, expression, and academic freedoms); future SAR governments run or controlled by Mainland officials; emigration of nearly anyone who could get out; immigration of nearly anyone who could get in; a substantial exodus of capital and firms; limited economic autonomy; and little political autonomy. In the 'Hong Kong as Shanghai' scenario, Hong Kong would wholly lose its 'insulation' from any instability, economic or otherwise, on the Mainland and would become subject to the same controls and problems as other Mainland cities.

The economic manifestations of the 'Hong Kong as Shanghai' scenario would be: the abolition of the Hong Kong dollar; the siphoning off of Hong Kong's reserves and taxes for the Mainland; restrictions on Hong Kong's market economy; price setting rather than market pricing; the erosion of Hong Kong's position as an international business city; and a dramatic reduction in its attractiveness as a financial centre, as well as collapses in Hong Kong's stock and property markets. In this view, government efficiency would decline, entrepreneurs and professionals would leave and take their capital if they could, and institutional changes would hinder the emergence of a new generation of entrepreneurs.

The 'Hong Kong as Shanghai' scenario relies on the premise that the Mainland government and the Chinese Communist Party would be more concerned with political control than with economic growth and would be willing to sacrifice prosperity (certainly Hong Kong's prosperity) if it conflicted with the consolidation of power. Hong Kong's economic role would be subordinated to the needs and priorities of Beijing. Such a scenario would reflect China's history of centralized control and the seeming inconsistency of 'one country–two systems' with an authoritarian political culture. Once the United Kingdom pulls out of Hong Kong, the argument goes, any agreements concerning Hong Kong could not and would not be enforced by an outside entity, rendering them useless. The 'Hong Kong as Shanghai' scenario posits that the Mainland would have a poor appreciation of Hong Kong and a poor appreciation that a free lifestyle backs up its economic success. This view also dismisses the validity of the argument that the Mainland will make 'one country–two systems' work in Hong Kong to serve as a model for eventual reunification with Taiwan. Finally, the 'Hong Kong as Shanghai' scenario would postulate that the reform of the Mainland economy is limited at best and would not go much further due to perceived political costs.

In the 'Hong Kong as Shanghai' scenario, Hong Kong would start from a sounder base than Shanghai, but its lead over Shanghai would be reliant on central policy priorities. After all, Hong Kong has a better natural port, a more developed financial system, is more cosmopolitan, and is not saddled with the state-owned enterprises and inefficient land-use patterns of Shanghai. Even if Hong Kong loses much of its international flavour and focuses inward, its international heritage would still be an advantage. This scenario, however, would involve a severe disruption of Hong Kong's way of life and economic system, particularly if developing Shanghai or other centres took priority over preserving Hong Kong.

Hong Kong as Singapore

'Hong Kong as Singapore' is a mixed scenario, with attributes of both the 'Hong Kong as Hong Kong' and the 'Hong Kong as Shanghai' scenarios. In the 'Hong Kong as Singapore' scenario, Hong Kong would be governed more like Singapore, with more regulation, less freedom of expression and information, more state paternalism, more favouritism for state companies, and a shift from firms with British links. Laws would continue to reflect the international character of Hong Kong and English would still be widely used in business. In this scenario, Hong Kong would lose part of its 'insulation' from events on the Mainland.

In this scenario, there would continue to be respect for private ownership and property rights in Hong Kong, the market would remain the ultimate arbiter of economic outcomes, the economy would continue to be far more open than that of the Mainland, and the Chinese Communist Party would be less visible and more restrained than on the Mainland. The Hong Kong dollar would remain a separate and convertible currency. Although there would be significant scope for independent action in Hong Kong, Mainland interests would dominate in many instances. Local views would be canvassed, but important decisions would be made centrally in Beijing. The scenario posits less autonomy than promised under the Joint Declaration or under British rule, though it does allow for distinctions between Hong Kong and the Mainland.

The 'Hong Kong as Singapore' scenario postulates that the Mainland understands the benefits it derives from Hong Kong, but would pursue both economic and political goals by engaging in the maximization of economic benefits while retaining political control. The result would be gradual and controlled economic progress, but not at a level that would occur if Hong Kong kept its distinct system intact. In this view, 'one country–two systems' would be difficult, but not impossible. There would be some brain drain and capital flight, but other individuals and investors would come to take advantage of the economic opportunities. The Mainland would learn about Hong Kong, would be accommodating to Hong Kong, and failures in implementing policies would not cause dramatic economic decline.

Although in this scenario there would be greater economic control and restrictions on individual activities, as in Singapore, the economic results would not be as good as in Singapore. The Singaporean government has had decades of managing the local economy and building advantages based on what foreign customers and companies want. In the 'Hong Kong as Singapore' scenario, there would be no such experienced hand guiding economic development and it is unlikely that decisions would be made as much for public gain as they are in Singapore—and if they were, they would probably be made for the economic benefit of mainland China, not Hong Kong. In Singapore, of course, decisions are made for the economic benefit of Singapore. Predicting an economic growth rate in such a scenario is extremely difficult, since it would depend on how much the Mainland would give to Hong Kong in terms of new investment and how much it would take away in terms of flexibility and entrepreneurship.

Hong Kong as London and Tokyo

The existing scenario analysis for Hong Kong is interesting and identifies a number of key uncertainties and concerns. The tendency to look only at a limited number and set of scenarios, however, limits the usefulness of the scenario analysis technique as it has been applied in the Hong Kong case. Much of the value of the technique comes from identifying scenarios that might not be immediately obvious or fit into preconceptions. In this regard, it is interesting that although pessimistic scenarios discussed in the context of Hong Kong include near economic meltdown, optimistic scenarios generally assume only a slight modification of the status quo. The observer is left to conclude that the status quo is the best that can be hoped for. In particular, the optimistic scenarios of analysts generally do not include futures in which the change in administration coincides with a substantial economic boom. This is due to a tendency to look at Hong Kong as a relatively isolated, maturing service economy rather than the main economic city of South China and the principal regional city of Asia. In other words, much has been made of the importance of the 'two systems' aspect of the future arrangements for Hong Kong. Much less has been made of the potential advantages that could arise out of the 'one country' portion.

There is a scenario in which Hong Kong does significantly better than the status quo. In the 'Hong Kong as London and Tokyo' scenario, Hong Kong would become not just the leading international centre in Asia for business services, finance, and overseas firms (London), it also would become the leading city of a vibrant, growing, industrially powerful area of 100 million people or more (Tokyo). Such a scenario would start with the 'Hong Kong as Hong Kong' scenario from above and add to it much closer interaction with a growing hinterland and a leadership role in the emergence of the South China economy as well as a leadership role in intra-Asian trade and investment. Hong Kong would lose its insulation from at least part of the Mainland, but that would not matter so much because Hong Kong would be leading, rather than following, regional development.

Analysts point out that it would be foolish to ignore the possibility that China will follow a similar economic development path as Japan, Korea, and Taiwan.[17] If it does, or even comes close, Guangdong is likely to be at or near the forefront of its development. Many already are calling Guangdong the 'fifth dragon'.[18] In addition to its role as an international centre, Hong Kong, under the 'Hong Kong as London and Tokyo' scenario, could well find itself as the principal economic city of the fastest growing part of the fastest growing major economy of the fastest growing region in the world. If it did, then Hong Kong's economic potential could go far beyond that posited in even the most 'optimistic' scenarios in the literature. The growth of Hong Kong's existing industries would be supplemented by substantial additional 'hubbing' activities and augmented by the growth of Hong Kong as a cultural centre and a medical and education centre serving the Asia–Pacific region.

SCENARIOS AND ECONOMIC GROWTH

Predicting actual growth rates for the Hong Kong economy is problematic given the strong influence of external conditions, such as regional growth and even United States interest rates (given the peg of the Hong Kong dollar to the United States dollar). The rank ordering of growth potential under the different scenarios, however, is not that difficult. The 'Hong Kong as London and Tokyo' scenario would involve significantly higher growth than any of the others and the 'Hong Kong as Shanghai' scenario would involve significantly lower growth. The 'Hong Kong as Hong Kong' scenario is likely to involve faster growth than the 'Hong Kong as Singapore' scenario—partly because it is more likely to preserve the territory's entrepreneurial spirit, and partly because Hong Kong is just better at being Hong Kong than it is at being Singapore.

BEYOND SCENARIOS

Scenario analysis helps us identify different potential futures and the key uncertainties that will shape those futures. This approach is useful, particularly to the external investor, but scenario analysis alone is less useful for those who stand to gain or lose the most in the transition—the people of Hong Kong. Most of the talk and writing about the transition, particularly in the West, fails to take into account the fact that Hong Kong individuals and organizations can influence the outcomes of the uncertainties and ultimately the scenario that results. Hong Kong and its people have had their own relationships and dealings with the Mainland for decades. Over the last several years, Hong Kong interests have shown themselves quite capable in their dealings with both the British Administration and Mainland agencies and officials. Mainland officials have sought advice on Hong Kong's future from people from Hong Kong in the Preparatory Committee and through other formal and informal channels, and frequently have followed the advice. After the transition, when the SAR administration is run by people from Hong Kong, they will have greater scope to deal with the Mainland directly than has been the case before. As the people who have the most to gain, and the most to lose, from the transition, the people of Hong Kong also have as much responsibility as anyone in making sure that the transition works and that it results in a favourable scenario. Adding to the complexity is that while both Hong Kong and the Mainland would benefit the most in economic terms from the 'Hong Kong as London and Tokyo' scenario, Hong Kong and Mainland interests might differ in terms of their second best outcomes. In particular, Hong Kong might prefer 'Hong Kong as Hong Kong', in which it keeps its international roles and cosmopolitan character, while some on the Mainland might prefer 'Hong Kong as Singapore', in which some of Hong Kong's potential is lost, but the system that results is more familiar and more directly dependent on the Mainland. This highlights the need for Hong Kong to actively manage its relations with the Mainland. The task is to influence the uncertainties faced by the territory so as to achieve the best possible outcome.

MANAGING THE RELATIONSHIP WITH THE MAINLAND

The largest questions regarding Hong Kong's future involve the nature of the future relationship between Hong Kong and mainland China. The nature of the relationship is carefully spelled out in the Basic Law, but there remains considerable scepticism about how the answers on paper will be implemented in reality. If the main issue is whether the Mainland will allow the persistence of 'a high degree of autonomy' in Hong Kong, then it is useful to understand how that autonomy could be undermined and how the latter could be prevented.

Hong Kong's autonomy could be undermined or reversed if the Mainland decided to interpret the Joint Declaration and the Basic Law in ways that do so no matter what people in Hong Kong do. This is unlikely in the short run given the arguments above. If the Mainland did not 'pull the plug' on Hong Kong when it was under British administration, there is no obvious reason why it should do so after Hong Kong reverts to Chinese administration. In the longer run, there is a potential that some Mainland interests would find the system inconvenient and work to overturn it or undermine it. But the Mainland is not a monolith and the reality of competing interests might help Hong Kong keep its special position. Perhaps more likely than direct attempts to undermine Hong Kong would be mismanagement of the relationship due to a failure to understand Hong Kong's unique attributes. The question, here, however, is not whether Mainland officials have a complete understanding of Hong Kong, but whether they recognize the extent to which they lack such a complete understanding.

An interpretation of the Basic Law that ran counter to what is generally understood or expected in Hong Kong also could lead to the decline of the territory and a substantial loss of face for the Mainland leadership. Perhaps more to be feared is the gradual erosion of autonomy that would occur if favouritism became widespread and the rule of law diminished, bringing about a 'death by a thousands cuts' of 'one country–two systems'.

Another way in which Hong Kong's autonomy might be undermined is if Hong Kong-based interests attempt to have Mainland officials reverse or influence Hong Kong SAR decisions. There have been recent reports of Hong Kong business people approaching Mainland officials to reverse decisions made in Hong Kong in the run-up to the transition. Such actions—although perhaps encouraged by the vacuum that has existed in Hong Kong, with the British colonial administration's time limitations, and with Beijing viewed as the representative of the future SAR administration—set an unfortunate precedent. If Hong Kong interests do not respect the authority of the SAR in the future, why should anyone else?

The SAR administration will have to assume and assert its rightful authority over Hong Kong-specific affairs if it is to successfully maintain its autonomy. It will be critical for the SAR administration to convince Hong Kong-based entities, Mainland organizations with activities in Hong Kong, and foreign organizations with activities in Hong Kong to subject themselves to the authority of the SAR administration for activities carried out within Hong Kong. In addition, the Hong Kong community, in particular the business community, might consider ways to sanction local interests or Mainland interests that try to go around the SAR administration. The Hong Kong business community might wish to consider the value of making 'one country–two systems' work for them, and how those who might undermine the arrangement should be treated.

Hong Kong has extensive economic interaction with the Mainland and will have even greater interaction in the future. The form and extent of these contacts also will influence the territory's economic future. Hong Kong interests can influence the nature of these contacts in many ways. They can engage their Mainland counterparts on issues of mutual concern, such as regional infrastructure, environmental issues, and trade. They can negotiate for greater access for Hong Kong-based service firms and investors on the Mainland. They can work to market the combination of Hong Kong and the Mainland as an attractive location for local and foreign firms, which could set up headquarters and management operations in Hong Kong and manufacturing operations on the Mainland. Hong Kong interests also can provide greater access to selected Mainland professionals, students, and managers who would benefit from greater interaction with Hong Kong. Finally, Hong Kong interests can market the 'one country–two systems' policy on the Mainland as well to ensure that it retains the support of key constituencies.

It is clear that Hong Kong-based companies can benefit from the territory's symbiotic relationship with the Mainland as it is defined by the 'one country–two systems' principle at the heart of the Sino-British Joint Declaration. International companies operating in Hong Kong, or partnering Hong Kong groups, will be beneficiaries of Hong Kong's separate legal and constitutional status, and not encumbered by China's higher tax rates, bureaucratic procedures, and operating environment. Hong Kong-based operations will be able to provide extensive technical support to affiliates operating on the Mainland—ranging from training to quality control. By capturing the advantages that prevail on both sides of the border, both Hong Kong and Chinese companies will be well placed to optimize competitive advantages and minimize joint costs.

Many fail to recognize that the 'one country–two systems' arrangement and closer links with the Mainland also provide an expanded choice set for policy that influences the economy. Disagreements between the Mainland side and the British side in the details of the transition and the nature of government in Hong Kong after the transition have made it difficult for government entities in Hong Kong and on the Mainland to seek joint gains. One could imagine substantially greater scope for marketing the Hong Kong–Guangdong combination to overseas firms: Hong Kong for headquarters activities and Guangdong for manufacturing activities. One could imagine a vastly expanded presence of agencies such as Hong Kong's Trade Development Council, Productivity Council, and Vocational Training Council on a fee-for-service basis beyond the present borders of Hong Kong. One could imagine greater interaction to address issues of common concern, such as the environment, than is the case today. One could imagine a greater intake of top-flight students from the Mainland, sponsored by Hong Kong, overseas, or Mainland companies and organizations, into Hong Kong educational institutions.

MANAGING HONG KONG'S RELATIONS WITH THE REST OF THE WORLD

After 1 July 1997, Hong Kong will still have substantial interaction with the rest of the world. The nature of this interaction will influence its economic future. After all, Hong Kong is a major trading nation and a major source of foreign investment for the Asian region. Its firms have become more internationally oriented as the territory has become a regional business centre. The challenge will be for Hong Kong to maintain its status as an international city and to raise its profile in the international community without overstepping its authority under 'one country–two systems'. The Mainland government has stated that:

The Hong Kong Special Administrative Region Government may on its own, using the name 'Hong Kong, China,' maintain and develop relations and conclude and implement agreements with foreign states and regions and relevant international organizations in the appropriate fields, including the economic, trade, financial and monetary, shipping, communications, tourism, cultural and sports fields.[19]

The Chinese and British have agreed that Hong Kong can maintain separate membership in organizations such as the World Trade Organization (WTO), the Asia Pacific Economic Cooperation forum (APEC), the Asian Development Bank, and dozens of other international organizations that do not restrict membership to sovereign states.[20] The United States and Canada have laws providing for the separate treatment of Hong Kong under specific circumstances. In the United States, the Hong Kong Policy Act of 1992 provides for: the treatment of Hong Kong as distinct from China for the purposes of United States domestic law; the continuation of international agreements of which Hong Kong is a party but the Mainland is not; and the treatment of Hong Kong as a separate territory in economic and trade matters.[21]

Despite the legalities of the situation, there are uncertainties about how Hong Kong will be viewed by foreign governments and business people. The United States has already indicated that if Hong Kong's autonomy is not respected, Hong Kong might be viewed simply as part of China for purposes of textile quotas and trade restrictions. Whereas a certain amount of this posture could indeed help Hong Kong, too much of it certainly would not. In recent years, Hong Kong politicians and officials have lobbied strongly for the retention of most-favoured-nation (MFN) status for China on the basis that removing it would cause irreparable harm to Hong Kong. Hong Kong officials will only be able to continue to lobby in this manner if they are seen as representing a separate constituency from that of the Mainland.

There also is the potential that multinational companies will no longer distinguish between Hong Kong and the Mainland. Not too long ago, the chairman of Daimler-Benz indicated that he viewed Hong Kong as just another part of China for business planning purposes. If managers do not perceive a distinction between Hong Kong and the Mainland, they will be tempted to bypass Hong Kong completely in order to set up operations in the Mainland's major population and commercial centres. If this occurs, Hong Kong could lose much of its attraction as an international economic and financial centre. Hong Kong clearly has an educational task ahead if it is to convince foreign governments and the headquarters staff of multinational companies that there is a distinction between Hong Kong and the Mainland.

It also will be important that Hong Kong retain its identity in international organizations consistent with 'one country–two systems'. Keeping its place in the Asia Pacific Economic Cooperation forum (APEC) and the World Trade Organization (WTO) will allow Hong Kong to retain its voice in these important fora. Similarly, Hong Kong will be better able to take advantage of its financial strength and business-friendly environment if international financial rating agencies and risk assessment studies consider Hong Kong as a separate system from that of mainland China. Finally, it will benefit Hong Kong to maintain a place in the statistical tables of multilateral organizations and in economic assessments by organizations such as the World Economic Forum, the Heritage Foundation, and others. While this last point might seem unimportant, the economic advantages of the 'one country–two systems' arrangement will be lost if Hong Kong is perceived as just another part of China by the international business and economic community. An absence of reliable information on Hong Kong would make it more difficult to distinguish Hong Kong from the Mainland. Hong Kong should, therefore, actively seek a position and profile consistent with 'one country–two systems' and should be forthcoming with information and statistics for multilateral agencies, risk assessment studies, and groups that provide comparative business and economic information. Only in this way can it prevent being lost in the shuffle after 1 July 1997.

Hong Kong should find ready allies for its efforts in this regard on the Mainland. After all, mainland China has benefited, and hopes to continue to benefit, from Hong Kong's status as an international financial centre, its role as a home for local and overseas companies, and its ability to act as a regional and global business centre. The Mainland also might welcome a relatively cost-free opportunity to demonstrate its commitment to the 'one country–two systems' arrangement. In the case of multilateral agencies, Mainland support might be necessary in order to ensure that Hong Kong does not disappear from international statistical tables and information sources.

Hong Kong's task in terms of its international relations will be more complex in the future than it has been. Once the glare of attention surrounding '1997' has worn off, it will be more difficult for Hong Kong to have an active international profile to the same extent as Singapore or other sovereign nations. Historically, there has not been a clear 'Hong Kong message' carried to the rest of the world. In the past, impressions of Hong Kong abroad have been generally favourable and perhaps it has not needed to keep a high international profile. Given the lack of understanding about Hong Kong in many parts of the world, and the business decisions and investments that can be influenced by inaccurate perceptions, the absence of such a message in the future could be costly.

MANAGING HONG KONG'S INTERNAL ADMINISTRATION

The skill and transparency of the new SAR administration will be of paramount importance in the post-1997 Hong Kong. Since 1841, executive authority in the territory has been in the hands of representatives of the British government. Thus, one of the most difficult political and administrative jobs in recent memory will be undertaken by someone by definition with no executive experience in government. The new administration should be aided by the Hong Kong civil service, the vast majority of which is expected to stay on after 1 July 1997. The Hong Kong civil service has been widely praised for its professionalism, efficiency, and honesty. An aggressive policy of localization has left capable Hong Kong locals in the most important positions. Incumbents in the most senior positions are well-known and respected within Hong Kong, on the Mainland, and elsewhere.

If Hong Kong is to continue to prosper, it will need institutions that support its capitalist system and way of life. This entails governmental and legal institutions that support the rule of law, personal freedoms and personal safety, and the enforcement of contracts and property rights. It entails institutions that provide for the free flow of information, goods, and capital, and institutions that deal even-handedly and fairly with all. It requires maintaining a high-quality administration that acts transparently in a professional, honest, and non-intrusive fashion. It also requires a continued separation of public and private interests. It implies clear policies enforced in both Hong Kong and on the Mainland to maintain the integrity of the border. Finally, it entails an administration that both assumes and asserts its rights and obligations under the Basic

Law, that puts the welfare of Hong Kong first, and that is willing to engage the Mainland on issues of concern to Hong Kong.

One important feature of Hong Kong that the new SAR administration will have to take into account is a growing political awareness on the part of people in Hong Kong. For much of its history, Hong Kong has been a home to immigrants and transients more concerned with survival and basic economic well-being than with political enfranchisement. Many were not in a position to question the colonial administration. The colonial administration, which formed policies in consultation with representatives of major groups in Hong Kong society, was considered relatively benign, individual rights were generally respected, and most Hong Kong people appeared rather disinterested in politics.

Today, however, Hong Kong is no longer the same immigrant, transient society it once was. A new generation born and raised in Hong Kong has come onto the scene. This generation has grown up in a more affluent and stable Hong Kong than that of its parents. A significant number of its members are well-educated professionals familiar with Western-style political institutions. It is natural that this generation would put down roots and consider Hong Kong a permanent home, and that it would have greater political aspirations and concerns than earlier generations of Hong Kong people. It also is natural that some would feel there was potentially a great deal to lose in a transition of administration. In this context, desires to move beyond consultation to direct representation have been natural consequences of social evolution. These tendencies might have been accelerated by the electoral system introduced by Governor Christopher Patten in the early 1990s, but it would be a mistake to conclude that the new system alone created them. The SAR administration will be faced with a political arena in which Hong Kong people of goodwill have different opinions—as to the best way to manage the territory, as to governmental priorities, and as to the best way to safeguard their freedoms and prosperity. Hong Kong as a whole faces its uncertainties as a relatively immature body politic without firmly established norms of behaviour for governing parties or opposition groups and parties. Hong Kong will benefit if the new SAR administration finds ways to accommodate the interests of representative groups and individuals within Hong Kong. This approach, in addition to fostering a more cohesive society, and a Hong Kong truly governed, not only *by* Hong Kong people, but *for* Hong Kong people, would also bring purely economic benefits. If Hong Kong is to continue to grow and prosper, it will need dynamic and prosperous professional communities committed to the territory's future. In other words, the professional groups from whose ranks the leaders of Hong Kong's main political groups are drawn are precisely the groups that will be needed to play a greater role in Hong Kong's future economic development.

Taking legitimate interests into consideration, however, does not mean that the new administration should cave in to every pressure group or special interest. One advantage of the colonial government has been that it has been run by people largely without local interests. This has made it relatively easy for the colonial government to resist pressures from special interests and develop a reputation as a neutral referee. It might take special efforts for the new administration comprised of Hong Kong people to ensure that it avoids falling prey to local pressures. The important matter will be not so much that every interest is accommodated in policy, but that different views can be voiced and due consideration given before decisions are taken. Hong Kong has a long history of consultative government in which dissenting views have been heard. There is no obvious reason why it cannot continue this practice into the future. The success of Hong Kong's internal political management will depend on whether various interests in the SAR can develop workable solutions to their differences within Hong Kong. If the interests can be managed in Hong Kong— either through the development of a genuine consensus within the SAR or through agreement to disagree, but not to take Hong Kong disagreements to Mainland officials for adjudication— then the chances of Hong Kong retaining autonomy are increased.

A more delicate problem might arise if Hong Kong became viewed as a base for activities hostile to the Mainland or if it became the site of extensive protests against the Mainland. Under such circumstances, there might be pressures for the SAR administration to take action or for the Mainland to intervene directly. The challenge going forward is how to retain the freedom of speech granted by the Basic Law in Hong Kong while reassuring the Mainland that Hong Kong is not a threat. Since 1949, Hong Kong has been seen by those on the Mainland as a potential base for subversion and such suspicions are unlikely to subside quickly. William Overholt has suggested that the only rational approach for Hong Kong is one of mutual non-subversion in which Hong Kong interests would not act to subvert the government on the Mainland and Mainland interests would not act to subvert Hong Kong's autonomy. Hong Kong, he claims, would come out the loser under any other approach.[22]

MANAGING EXPECTATIONS

There also is substantial scope for the people of Hong Kong to set the expectations for what constitutes a successful transition, particularly in the run-up to 1 July 1997. Goals—for economic growth, the stock market index, business confidence, particular economic policies (such as maintenance of an independent, convertible Hong Kong dollar), continued personal freedoms (as verified by the United Nations or another international organization), and others—can all be put on the table and publicized. The hurdle has yet to be set as to what constitutes a successful transition. If generally respected Hong Kong interest groups were to set forth criteria on which the transition could be judged a success, they would almost automatically become a yardstick by which the international community would judge success. This yardstick would set forth the challenge to both Hong Kong and the Mainland. In the absence of any clear statement of what constitutes success, virtually anything short of disaster could qualify.

OTHER IMPORTANT UNCERTAINTIES

It is well to remember that although much of the focus in Hong Kong and elsewhere has been on the change in administration, the Hong Kong economy faces other uncertainties that have nothing to do with '1997' *per se*. There are uncertainties about the state of the global and regional economies, and about internal administration in mainland China and in individual industries. Whereas Hong Kong cannot have a substantial impact on all of the uncertainties, it can at least influence some of them.

Hong Kong's economy is strongly influenced by the economic growth of the region. In 1996, several of the economies in the region experienced lower growth rates than in the past decade. Despite the relative slump, Asian economies were still outperforming those in the rest of the world. Obviously if regional growth were to slow dramatically, Hong Kong's economy would be negatively influenced. Although Hong Kong cannot control rates of growth in the region, Hong Kong firms and interests already influence the development of other economies in the region. Hong Kong manufacturers and traders are continually identifying new sources of supply and helping manufacturers in newly emerging economies enter the world economy. Hong Kong developers and infrastructure firms are providing the commercial and physical infrastructure necessary for development in the region. Hong Kong investors have a substantial influence on the development of mainland China and the ASEAN nations.

Hong Kong's economy is more dependent on trade and foreign investment flows than virtually any other in the world. This means that it is dependent on continued flows of goods and services in Asia and in the world. Anything that would hinder the Mainland's ability to trade, such as a failure to join the World Trade Organization (WTO), trade embargoes or disputes with the United States, or protectionism, would hurt Hong Kong. Hong Kong also could be hurt by a regional slowdown in trade and investment. Although Hong Kong is a small economy, it often has had influence in international trade negotiations and discussions. It has participated actively in the fora of the Asia Pacific Economic Cooperation (APEC), the General Agreement on Tariffs and Trade (GATT), and now the WTO. Hong Kong interests have lobbied the United States Congress against revocation of most favoured nation trading status for the Mainland.

Many uncertainties internal to mainland China have already influenced Hong Kong and will continue to do so in the future. Uncertainty surrounding China's future leadership after Deng Xioaping has affected a wide range of policies on the Mainland, including policies toward Hong Kong. According to some observers, in the jockeying for position among Mainland officials, none wishes to show any sign of weakness toward the British government or toward Hong Kong. As a result, domestic politics dictates that the safest course has been to react in a hostile manner to proposals by the British government or the Hong Kong colonial administration, even if such stands are damaging to China's image in Hong Kong or elsewhere.[23] The Mainland's relations with Taiwan, and disputes that have arisen over claims to the Spratly Islands (Nansha Islands) and the Diaoyu Islands also have created some concerns about China's intentions within the region.

Another uncertainty is the pace of economic reform that will be followed on the Mainland. The present leadership has clearly voiced its priority to ensure political stability, at the expense of economic growth if necessary. Although the pace of reform has varied since 1979, its direction has not. Money-losing, state-owned enterprises are still supported to the detriment of the rest of the economy. The banking system is still antiquated, and there is growing concern over the disparity of incomes among the provinces. The greater the stability and economic growth of the Mainland, the less likely it will be that it will seek to intervene in local Hong Kong affairs.

Hong Kong interests have exerted significant influence on the Mainland economy through their investments and through the provision of management and other services to Mainland operations. Hong Kong also has influenced Mainland economic policy through the advice and examples provided by Hong Kong people and by direct discussion and conversation. China actually changed the implementation of a capital gains tax designed to reduce real estate speculation after a group from Hong Kong urged the change. The result was a change in a Chinese tax to benefit Hong Kong developers.[24] Hong Kong advisors are currently helping to establish standards and rules of practice for the legal, accounting, surveying, and engineering professions on the Mainland. Here there is great potential to influence the shape of these industries into the future in ways that could benefit Hong Kong firms.

Hong Kong does face many important uncertainties and no one can know how all these uncertainties will play out. There is little precedent to guide the territory through its transition and there are substantial challenges beyond those posed by the change in administration. It is critical to place the uncertainties in context, to realize that people within Hong Kong actually have and have had significant scope to influence their own futures. Just as there are no guarantees of their success, there certainly are no guarantees of their failure.

NOTES

1   Quoted in Xiao Yu, 'Public Puts Hope in Future', *South China Morning Post* (5 October 1996): 10.
2   John Ridding, 'Fears of "Hollow" Hong Kong Grow as China Takeover Nears', *Financial Times: Weekend* (17/18 February 1996): 5.
3   Anthony G. O. Yeh, 'Planning and Management of Hong Kong's Border', in Joseph Y. S. Cheng and Sonny S. H. Lo (eds.), *From Colony to SAR: Hong Kong's Challenges Ahead*, Hong Kong: Chinese University of Hong Kong, 1995, pp. 261–91.
4   Hong Kong Government Planning Department, *The Final Technical Report on Territorial Development Strategy Review—1996, Part Three, Section A, Recommended Long-Term Strategy*, 1996, p. 29.
5   Bruce Bueno de Mesquita; David Newman; and Alvin Rabushka, *Red Flag Over Hong Kong*, Chatham, N.J.: Chatham House Publishers, 1996, pp. 114–19.
6   Ibid., p. 140.
7   Hong Kong Government Information Services, Bob Howlett (ed.), *Hong*

Kong 1996, 1996, p. 396; see also Yi-Hsin Chang, 'Opportunity Outweighs Fear as Expats Flood Hong Kong', *The Asian Wall Street Journal* (20 August 1996): 1.

8   The emigration figure excludes emigrants to the Mainland and Taiwan. Ronald Skeldon, 'Hong Kong in an International Migration System', in Ronald Skeldon (ed.), *Reluctant Exiles? Migration from Hong Kong and the New Overseas Chinese*, Hong Kong: Hong Kong University Press, 1994, pp. 31, 37.

9   Chang, 'Opportunity Outweighs Fear', p. 1.

10   Ronald Skeldon, 'Reluctant Exiles or Bold Pioneers', in Skeldon (ed.), *Reluctant Exiles?* pp. 3, 11–12.

11   *China Statistical Yearbook*, Beijing: China Statistical Publishing House, various years.

12   Louis Kraar, 'The Death of Hong Kong', *Fortune*, 131, 12 (26 June 1995): 42.

13   William H. Overholt, *China: The Next Economic Superpower*, London: Weidenfeld & Nicolson, 1993, p. 134; Ken Davies, *Hong Kong after 1997*, London: Economist Intelligence Unit Research Report, 1996, pp. 8–9; Jan Morris, *Hong Kong: Epilogue to an Empire*, London: Penguin Books, 1988, p. 274.

14   Richard Margolis, 'Countdown to 1997: Bumps in the Road', Hong Kong, Merrill Lynch, April 1996, p. 11.

15   People's Republic of China, Seventh National People's Congress, 'The Basic Law of the Hong Kong Special Administrative Region of the People's Republic of China', Hong Kong: One Country Two Systems Economic Research Institute, 1992, Chapters I, III, and V.

16   See, for example, Miron Mushkat, *The Economic Future of Hong Kong*, Boulder, Col.: Lynne Rienner Publishers, 1990; Ken Davies, *Hong Kong after 1997*, Economist Intelligence Unit Research Report, London, 1996; Ken Davies, *Hong Kong to 1994: A Question of Confidence*, Economist Intelligence Unit Special Report No. 2022, London, 1990; and Ian Perkin, 'Hong Kong in Transition: Economic Overview', *Hong Kong Echo Magazine*, 8 (Summer 1996): 12–13. We follow Mushkat's scenarios most closely.

17   See, for example, Overholt, *China: The Next Economic Superpower*, p. 45.

18   See, for example, Yun-wing Sung; Pak-wai Liu; Richard Yue-chim Wong and Pui-king Lau, *The Fifth Dragon: The Emergence of the Pearl River Delta*, Singapore: Addison Wesley Publishing Co., 1995, pp. 1–11.

19   'The Basic Law', Chapter VII, Art. 151, p. 51.

20   Hugh Davies, 'The Joint Liaison Group', *Hong Kong Echo Magazine*, 8 (Summer 1996): 31.

21   James T. H. Tang, 'Hong Kong's International Status', *The Pacific Review*, 6, 3 (1993): 208.

22   Overholt, *China: The Next Economic Superpower*, pp. 151–4.
23   Margolis, 'Countdown to 1997', p. 13.
24   William H. Overholt, 'Hong Kong's Financial Stability through 1997', Hong Kong: Bankers Trust Company, 20 March 1996, pp. 6–7.

10 GOING FORWARD

We started this book by claiming that things often are not what they seem in Hong Kong. In the last several chapters, we have seen that Hong Kong is not just a bridge, or a gateway, or an intermediary, that those terms do not begin to describe the role that Hong Kong plays in the local, regional, or world economies. We have seen that the 'decline' of Hong Kong manufacturing is not merely overstated, it is simply untrue. We have seen that Hong Kong is not a national economy, but a metropolitan economy, now closely linked with its natural hinterland. We have seen that in economic terms, Hong Kong already is well integrated with the Chinese Mainland. We have seen that, after negotiations between Britain and China, more democracy is planned for Hong Kong after 1997 under Chinese administration than has ever been the case under British administration. We have seen that, despite the harbingers of gloom and doom, the Hong Kong property and stock markets are up, more companies are setting up in Hong Kong than are leaving, and many people who left Hong Kong are returning.

ROBUSTNESS OF THE HONG KONG ECONOMY

In order to complete the picture of Hong Kong's economic future, we must examine the robustness of the economy, the robustness of its various economic roles, and the robustness of its various industries. Unless we break down the economy into its important components and understand those components, any attempt to look into the future becomes the economic equivalent of alchemy. The question is: How robust are the elements of the Hong Kong economy to potential shocks? A detailed examination indicates that they are robust indeed.

The fact that Hong Kong does not have a stand-alone service economy, but a strong manufacturing economy *and* a strong service economy, contributes to its robustness. A stand-alone service economy can fall under its own weight. After all, it is difficult for a territory's citizens to continue to prosper if they sell services only to each other. Hong Kong, of course, does not have a stand-alone service economy, it has a dynamic manufacturing economy that performs high-value, knowledge-intensive activities in Hong Kong and uses resources available elsewhere for physical production stages. It has a dynamic service economy that is integrated into, and plays a leadership role in, the fastest growing economic region in the world. The linkages that make this manufacturing and services economy strong are difficult to match and are likely to be robust even in the face of substantial shocks.

Hong Kong's 'unique combinations' of business and government, local and overseas firms, entrepreneurship and management, as well as hustle and commitment strategies also make the economy robust. The unique relationship between business and government means that the economy does not rely on the ability of government to 'pick winners', and this has allowed many strong Hong Kong companies to emerge. The presence of the territory's other unique combinations means that Hong Kong's prosperity does not rely on one type of firm, on one type of industry, or on one type of strategy. The elements of the combinations reinforce each other and they make the economy more flexible and resilient than other economies. This has always been the case in Hong Kong, and this is why Hong Kong has always been able to respond to past challenges. Although there will be temptation to alter the balance, the history of strong private sector firms in Hong Kong, both large and small, and the influence they exert, would not be easy to eliminate.

Hong Kong's strength as a packager and integrator of economic activities adds to its robustness. Intermediaries might be easy to replace or bypass, but initiators and instigators of economic activity are not. There always has been and always will be a need for firms and individuals who can match supply and demand. There always has been and always will be a need for firms and individuals who can put together new combinations of activities to serve rapidly changing markets. It has taken Hong Kong and its firms decades to build their capabilities to manage relationships in customer markets all over the world and production networks in Asia and elsewhere. This capability, this advantage, does not disappear overnight or get side-tracked easily. The fact that Hong Kong firms carry out the packaging and integrating function, not just in Hong Kong, not just on the Mainland, and not even just in Asia, diversifies their risk and makes them even more robust than they would be otherwise. Executives interviewed for this study did not see any other centre in Asia taking on a similar role in the foreseeable future. As one multinational manager put it, 'Singapore lacks the entrepreneurship and location, Taiwan is not cosmopolitan enough, and the Mainland is many years away.'

Hong Kong's other roles also contribute to the strength and resilience of its economy. According to every measure, overseas firms' commitment to Hong Kong remains high. One of the most striking findings of recent surveys is the high degree of commitment among locally based foreign firms to remaining in Hong Kong for the foreseeable future, and the number of foreign firms continuing to set up offices in Hong Kong. In a survey conducted in 1996 by the British Chamber of Commerce, 98 per cent of respondents predicted that their firms would still be in Hong Kong in the year 2000.[1] Surveys of German and Swiss firms carried out in the latter portion of 1996 told the same story. In both cases, the overwhelming majority of firms did not think that any place in Asia could really be considered an alternative to Hong Kong.[2]

Over 90 per cent of the more than 2,000 overseas firms surveyed by the Government Industry Department in 1995 had no plans to relocate their regional headquarters or regional offices outside Hong Kong.[3] The average number of new regional headquarters set up in Hong Kong per year increased substantially from the 1980s to the 1990s, with an average of 56 new headquarters established annually between 1990 and 1994.[4] The Government Industry Department Survey found that 230 new regional headquarters or offices had been set up by overseas firms from January 1994 to May 1995, while only six overseas firms had moved their regional headquarters or offices from Hong Kong during that period.[5] More than 90 per cent of those overseas firms with regional headquarters or centres in Hong Kong that responded to the 1995 the American Chamber of Commerce Business Confidence Survey planned to stay for at least the next three years.[6]

As a centre for the China business of overseas firms, Hong Kong is extraordinarily robust. It is a uniquely convenient location for doing business with the Mainland, in terms of its geographic proximity, unrivalled transport and communications linkages, and, in addition, the high concentration of Mainland entities physically present in Hong Kong. For overseas firms that need to plug into world-class infrastructure, services, and professional skills, Hong Kong is likely to remain unsurpassed as a foothold onto the Mainland. In the words of one Western executive, 'If your game is China, you have no alternative to Hong Kong. Hong Kong will always be better than taking the full risk and plunging into the Mainland.' Hong Kong is likely to be robust as the centre of the overseas Chinese network as well. In fact, growing links between overseas Chinese and Chinese firms, mediated through Hong Kong are likely to strengthen Hong Kong's position.

Hong Kong also is likely to retain its position as the leading source and conduit of foreign investment into the Mainland. No other centre has the combination of location and financial infrastructure, or local firms willing to sink hundreds of millions of dollars into Mainland projects. The robustness of Hong Kong in these roles reinforces the robustness of the economy as a whole. The fact that Hong Kong is the main base for Hong Kong, overseas Chinese, and Western investment (and associated transfers of technology and expertise) in mainland China means that the Mainland will think long and hard before it does anything that would severely hamper Hong Kong. The sheer magnitude of the investment capital that the Mainland could lose is enough on its own to give pause to anyone with other ideas.

The robustness of an economy also must be assessed industry by industry. And when one tries to determine by this method whether Hong Kong's competitive position—in the relevant markets, for the relevant customers, and against the relevant competitors—is fragile (and therefore likely to deteriorate substantially in the face of economic or political shocks) or is robust (and therefore able to withstand potential shocks), the findings point to the same conclusion: Hong Kong's industries are more robust than is generally assumed.

Since roughly 85 per cent of the sea cargo handled in Hong Kong has its source or destination in Hong Kong or on the Mainland, and the relevant competitors are Mainland ports and Kaohsiung in Taiwan, Hong Kong's position is likely to be resilient even to fairly major shocks. With respect to the Mainland, Hong Kong has better deep water access, superior infrastructure, superior expertise, far fewer regulatory and administrative barriers, far greater efficiency, and a denser route structure (which allows shippers to reach more destinations directly from Hong Kong). Costs in Hong Kong are high, but some of these, particularly those related to port handling charges, might be reduced if demand and supply were in better balance. In addition, there are not many other options. This will be particularly true for the next generation of container ships which will require greater minimum depths than the present generation of ships, minimum depths that Shanghai would not be able to provide without substantial dredging and construction. Kaohsiung could take some business away once direct Taiwan–Mainland shipping links are established, but Taiwan's Kaohsiung has its own problems with inefficiency, limited expansion capability, and the island's uncertain political state. Hong Kong has significant advantages versus the relevant competitors that are unlikely to be eroded significantly in the medium term. The industry is not likely to continue to grow at double-digit rates indefinitely, but it should maintain its strong competitive position. In order to stop the growth of the Hong Kong sea cargo industry in the next decade, one would have to virtually shut down the South China economy.

In air cargo, again the bulk of the business involves cargo sourced from or destined for Hong Kong or the Mainland. There is, however, more flexibility about where to put an airport than a major seaport and Hong Kong does not have the same natural advantages that it has in sea cargo. In air cargo, however, route density is critical and just because an airport is built does not mean that it will be able to develop a good route network, particularly for international connections which require negotiations with other nations. Hong Kong has built up its international connections and routes over decades. A competing airport would have to build up its own network and that can be extremely difficult. It is unlikely that the United States, for example, will allow a Zhuhai-to-Chicago route anytime soon. Even with high costs, Hong Kong should remain the air cargo hub for the region, a region that is poised for substantial increases in demand for air cargo and passenger services. In order to substantially hurt the Hong Kong industry, one would have to do something to substantially reduce regional travel as a whole.

Hong Kong's export trading industry would clearly be hurt by anything that reduces the Mainland's ability to engage in international trade. The larger trading companies, however, have extensive geographically diversified production systems and could shift their sources of supply if necessary. As long as Hong Kong serves as a regional information hub and logistics hub, in which it is relatively easy to obtain information about world markets and potential production sites, and as long as Hong Kong traders maintain good relationships with their buyers, the industry should be resilient at least to medium-sized shocks.

Even though the garment industry relies to a significant extent on Mainland operations and relatively labour-intensive strategies, the strong competitive position that Hong Kong firms have developed over the years should make the industry relatively robust. Given the substantial amount of production still carried out in Hong Kong and on the Mainland, however, loss of most-favoured-nation (MFN) status and changes in rules of origin could harm the industry. The garment manufacturers that have developed their own brands and who have diversified their sources of production would be less vulnerable.

Hong Kong's electronics firms have extensive operations on the Mainland. The Mainland is also the industry's largest single market. The industry is therefore dependent on the nature of mainland China's trade relations and is more dependent on the state of consumer demand on the Mainland than the other industries we have studied. The absence of local production of certain components makes the Hong Kong industry somewhat vulnerable to component shortages in periods of rapidly growing demand.

Hong Kong's position as an international communications hub should be relatively strong and resilient as long as the territory's firms continue to invest in the most modern technology and to develop the communications infrastructure. Hong Kong's demand for sophisticated communications services will continue into the foreseeable future. Its position as a communications and media centre could be hurt, however, if there were to be restrictions on the press or on information flows through Hong Kong. Hong Kong's civil engineering industry, which is dependent on often cyclical demand, just like everywhere else in the world, might not prove very robust should Hong Kong demand dry up and Mainland demand fail to materialize. The levels of demand in Hong Kong and on the Mainland, however, are expected to continue to be strong well into the next century, no matter what the exact details of the political and economic relations between Hong Kong and the Mainland. Similarly, infrastructure and property development will rise and fall with local and regional demand. If the Hong Kong economy were to hit very hard times, the property and infrastructure industries could be hurt substantially. The traditional equation of demand outstripping supply, however,

325

is likely to put a floor on Hong Kong property values and infrastructure requirements in the foreseeable future.

Lastly, we turn to an industry that one might expect would be among the least resilient to competitive pressures or shocks. Fund management is as mobile an industry as one could find. In theory, 50 or so Hong Kong-based fund managers could put their floppy disks in their pockets and their rolodexes into their briefcases and all leave Hong Kong on the same plane, effectively taking the industry with them. Millions or billions of dollars could be transferred by computer instantaneously. But even here, Hong Kong's position is more robust than it might appear. First, the fact that the industry could move so quickly means it does not have to, at least not until some serious event or series of events might trigger a departure. Ironically, because they can leave so easily, firms do not have to.

But if they did leave, where would they go? Singapore is the most logical place, but Singapore has high costs, skill shortages, and limits on access to information. In addition, Singapore is quite far away to use as an offshore financial centre for mainland China. If Hong Kong has problems due to the transition of administration, Shanghai is unlikely to be an attractive alternative. If the money managed in Hong Kong could be managed in New York or London, it already would be. The Hong Kong Stock Exchange has the second largest market capitalization in Asia. As more Mainland companies list in Hong Kong, this position is likely to be solidified further. Unless there is a massive crash in the Hong Kong market, large amounts of money will still be invested in Hong Kong-based and listed firms. And if the money is invested in Hong Kong, then unless there is a fairly dramatic turn for the worse in Hong Kong, fund managers will be in Hong Kong.

HONG KONG'S ROBUSTNESS IN PERSPECTIVE

Overall, in our view, the industries studied have present competitive positions, in terms of their advantages in

Figure 10.1 Position, Prospects, and Robustness of Hong Kong Industries

	Prospects		Robustness
	Position	Growth	
Garments	★★★	★	★★
Electronics	★★	★	★★
Trading	★★★	★★	★★★
Fund Management	★★	★★	★★
Civil Engineering	★	★★	★★
Air Cargo	★★★★	★★★★	★★★★
Sea Cargo	★★★★	★★★	★★★★
Telecommunications	★★★	★★★	★★★
Tourism	★★★	★★★	★★

addressing the relevant markets, serving the relevant customers, against the relevant competitors, that range from moderate (one star in Figure 10.1) to extraordinary (four stars). Their growth prospects range from moderate to extraordinary, and their robustness to at least medium-sized shocks should range from good (two stars) to extraordinary. This does not mean that the industries can stand up to every possible eventuality, but it does mean that, on average, substantial changes would be required to hurt them seriously.

This conclusion mirrors prospects for the economy as a whole. Hong Kong's economic structures, its roles in the world economy, and its industries give every appearance of being robust even to fairly significant change. The Hong Kong economy is not on a 'knife edge', nor at the edge of a cliff waiting to be pushed off. It is a strong, resilient economy that should be able to withstand even substantial difficulties or shocks. In the absence of near complete political meltdown or dramatic mishandling, Hong Kong should continue to prosper.

327

THE HONG KONG STORY

The obvious question that arises is: Why do our results appear to be so very different from reports of the imminent demise of Hong Kong? Repeatedly during our work, it has struck us that the Hong Kong we read about in the Western press often bore limited resemblance to the Hong Kong that we have come to know. One reason is the focus on the political aspects of the transition and the way these have been reported. Without the transition of administration, Hong Kong would not be in the news at all. We have been told by journalists that some Western publications would only run political stories about Hong Kong's transition, not economic stories about Hong Kong. Thus Hong Kong's economic success, its economic integration with the Mainland, and the spread of its influence throughout South-East Asia is ignored. This is at best short-sighted and at worst counter-productive. The best predictor of the relationship between Hong Kong and mainland China over the next two decades might well be the nature of the economic relationships that have developed over the last two decades. Given the economic value of Hong Kong to the Mainland in the past, present, and future, and the recent history of economic interaction between Hong Kong and the Mainland, one must understand the economic story that underlies the transition in order to understand the political story.

Some people cannot seem to imagine that transition to Chinese administration can bring anything but disaster. Every misstatement, every misunderstanding, every misstep becomes part of an ever downward spiral in which contrary evidence is either ignored or met with a knowing, 'But we know the *real* story now, don't we.' The world reads and hears about the concerns, but not the context, and not about the confidence in Hong Kong displayed by many. People who do not apply for Western travel documents or do not leave Hong Kong do not get much press. Nor do the thousands who are coming to Hong Kong or those returning to Hong Kong. The few companies that have left Hong Kong appear in the press. The many who are newly arriving do not. The 'death of Hong Kong' gets attention, the 'continued success of Hong Kong' does not.[7] Economic growth in Hong Kong has slowed in the 1990s and this has been reported accurately, but few seem to speculate on how many nations or regions could sustain a growth rate of 5 per cent or more per year in real GDP with such high levels of uncertainty.

Another reason external perceptions of Hong Kong do not match reality is a set of biases that creep into much economic analysis. There is a tendency around the world to overestimate the contribution of physical production activities and to underestimate the contribution that the high value-added activities of manufacturing and service industries can make to the prosperity of small economies, particularly metropolitan economies. Nowhere is this clearer than in the 1996 *UNCTAD Trade and Development Report*, which praises the development models of Singapore, Korea, Taiwan, and others, but concludes that the Hong Kong model has not been so successful because 'manufacturing' has declined.[8] It is unfortunate that multilateral agencies would not investigate deeply enough to understand the true nature of Hong Kong manufacturing, but the same bias can be found even within Hong Kong. At a recent workshop, the head of strategic planning for the Hong Kong office of a United States bank asked us whether Hong Kong could prosper if its 'real' industries (those that manufactured goods in Hong Kong itself) declined. We resisted the temptation to ask if banking was a 'real' industry or a 'fake' industry, or if the 155,000 people employed by Hong Kong's financial service sector contributed at all to the territory's prosperity. Market forces have shown Hong Kong and its firms that the territory's economic prospects would be sharply limited if they depended on production activities located physically in the territory, especially when these activities can be carried out just as easily and at lower costs in many other places in Asia. Market forces are showing Hong Kong and its firms that the territory's economic prospects could be extraordinary if it focuses on the high-value activities associated with manufacturing and on providing services of a variety and quality that cannot be found elsewhere in Asia.

There is a generalized bias toward overestimating the contribution of 'high tech' industries, as opposed to 'low tech' industries, to prosperity, despite the fact that the distinction between the two is at best blurred. After all, who wants to be in a 'low tech' industry? The truth is that there are many 'low tech' industries that have been or will be revolutionized by the application of modern technology. Furthermore there are many industries. Only a few of these industries are generally defined as 'high tech' and a good number of those are not very profitable in the first place. A small territory, such as Hong Kong, cannot and should not try to be in every industry or even every growth industry. It should be in industries in which its advantages and resources can be put to their most profitable use. Some of these industries might be considered 'high tech' while others might not.

Furthermore, Hong Kong's economy is more difficult to understand or explain than many others in Asia. Many in Hong Kong itself have difficulty in identifying precisely the reasons for Hong Kong's economic success. Observers searching for a single reason will be frustrated; but the absence of a single simple explanation does not make Hong Kong's performance any less impressive or any less robust. In fact, the more complex the web of advantages, the more difficult they are to duplicate and the more robust they are likely to be.

One example of this difficulty is the problem of explaining how an economy at least partially built on 'hustle' strategies can continue to succeed. It is easier to understand how a new factory, or patent, or brand (commitment strategies) can create value than it is to understand how a firm can continually be more attuned to the market and quicker to respond than its competitors (hustle strategies). The uncertainty surrounding such strategies does not sit comfortably with many Western managers or management experts. Not too long ago, one Western management guru came through Hong Kong and gave a talk on how Asian companies were going to have to stop 'improvising' and would have to stake out positions in particular industries and compete like their Western counterparts. One was left to wonder why it is that Asian economies are growing so much faster than Western economies and why some Asian economies already have per capita GDP and unemployment figures that would be envied in most Western nations.

Difficulties in getting the 'Hong Kong story' across have created complications for the Hong Kong government. It is easier to go to a government official in other places in Asia to get next year's economic plan than it is to put together the often conflicting signals found in a complex, market economy. It is easy for a government to appear decisive and proactive when it says it attracted a certain number of foreign companies that invested a certain amount of capital and created a certain number of jobs. It is much harder for a government to appear decisive and proactive when it says that it does not know how much capital flowed into or out of the territory and that it does not know which industries will grow in the future, but that as long as distortions are minimized and a strong infrastructure maintained, it is confident that there will be sufficient growth to ensure prosperity. The matter has been further complicated by the lack of a strong voice to spread the Hong Kong message. Before the naming of the new Special Administrative Region (SAR) administration, even though many government, business, and community leaders have spoken eloquently about Hong Kong, there was no one who could be said to be speaking with authority for Hong Kong.

Historically, it was not necessary to actively define and disseminate the Hong Kong story. People in Hong Kong simply went about their business. Today, however, Hong Kong's position as a major international economic centre depends on perceptions of Hong Kong in the territory, on the Mainland, and on the part of foreign companies and investors. In business and economics, perception is reality and the external perception of Hong Kong often is inaccurate. Thus, defining and disseminating the Hong Kong story is more important than ever before.

INTO THE FUTURE

Hong Kong faces many uncertainties, but it has prospered despite uncertainties in the past. Hong Kong historically had emerged from each past challenge stronger than before. With respect to the political risk associated with '1997' and beyond, it is important to note that Hong Kong has always been vulnerable to fluctuations on the Mainland. In many ways, the extensive negotiations and formalized documents describing life after the changeover provide greater certainty than Hong Kong has known in the last 50 years. In the past, it has never been known if Hong Kong would be annexed to China by force and if so when that might occur. Hong Kong people and outside investors always had to plan for the potential, however remote, that the worst would happen. Now at least there is a date, a plan, and the assurance of a peaceful handover. In an ironic sense, Hong Kong has been a victim of the known. Given the certainty that the change in administration would take place at a specified time, the various hopes and fears about the territory's future have had a focal point. It is arguable that the eventual death or retirements of President Suharto in Indonesia or Prime Minister Mahathir in Malaysia will bring more disruption of those economies than a transition that has been planned for 13 years.

Hong Kong has had 13 years to plan for the transition; 13 years to make sure that Hong Kong views and voices would have a major role in guiding the territory's future; 13 years to learn more about the Mainland; and 13 years to attempt to communicate the importance of maintaining Hong Kong's way of life to people on the Mainland and elsewhere. Along the way, Hong Kong people have handled themselves capably in discussions and negotiations with the Mainland and have shown themselves able to win substantial concessions in the economic and political spheres. They may well have greater scope to do so once the administration of the territory is turned over to the SAR government. Then Hong Kong interests might have a better platform to influence the outcomes of important uncertainties than a British administration that was never truly accepted by the Mainland. For its part, the Mainland has set up a variety of channels since 1984 through which to seek and listen to advice from Hong Kong people, and shows all signs of a desire to make 'one country–two systems' work. The reasons are not just economic, as important as those reasons might be. There will be pressure to live up to agreements that China has made in front of the entire world. There will be pressure on the Mainland to show that Hong Kong can thrive and be even more prosperous under Chinese rule than under colonial rule. There also will be pressure to make 'one country–two systems' work in Hong Kong as a potential precursor to reunification with Taiwan, and as a certain precursor to two events to occur in 1999: the return of Macau to Chinese sovereignty and the fiftieth anniversary of Communist Party rule in China.

Even the most optimistic observers believe that the transition from British to Chinese rule in Hong Kong will be trying. The Mainland and Hong Kong have existed under such different systems for so long that it is likely that there will be policy mistakes on both sides simply due to a lack of mutual understanding. There is little direct experience or precedent that Mainland officials and the SAR administration can call upon for guidance and the best of intentions could go awry. Undoubtedly, there are and will be individuals and groups on both sides who will try to use the transfer for their own benefit to the detriment of others. It should not be at all surprising if firms and individuals are circumspect in terms of their investment and spending behaviour until the political situation becomes completely clear.

In addition, it should be remembered that Hong Kong's economy faces other challenges as well. Many of Hong Kong's industries face uncertainties of their own, some linked to '1997' and some not. The findings of our study suggest, however, that Hong Kong's economy and its industries are likely to be able to ride out even relatively substantial storms. Hong Kong's economic integration with the Mainland has been taking place since 1979. It is very far advanced and has been one of the major, if not the major source of Hong Kong's growing prosperity over the last two decades. In the process, numerous links have been formed. Numerous practical problems have arisen and been solved. The path has not been smooth, but there has nevertheless been substantial progress.

The Hong Kong economy faces its challenges from a very

strong base, a fact often overlooked in the West. Hong Kong has faced challenges in the past and has succeeded despite war and occupation, inflows of refugees, armed conflict between China and the United States in Korea, the tensions of the Cold War, the upheaval of the Cultural Revolution on the Mainland, and rapid changes in the local economic structure. No one did or could fully have predicted or planned Hong Kong's successful reactions to past challenges. In fact, the 'death of Hong Kong' has been predicted many times and in circumstances which were arguably more difficult than those of the present, when the region is at peace and in the midst of unprecedented growth and prosperity. Just as in the past, no one can fully predict or plan Hong Kong's future today. But the brilliance of Hong Kong has always been its ability to rise to meet its challenges in ways that have made the territory stronger than before. To put it bluntly, those who have bet with Hong Kong in the past have won and those who have bet against Hong Kong in the past have lost.

The Basic Law and the Joint Declaration call for the preservation of Hong Kong's capitalist system and way of life for at least 50 years, but preservation should not mean stagnation. Among the most valuable aspects to preserve is Hong Kong's ability to adapt to changing circumstances. This ability is predicated on access to information from anywhere in the world, on the knowledge that the law will protect individuals and companies, and on the ability to evolve regulatory systems to keep up to date. What Hong Kong needs is a mixture of preservation that allows for change and change which allows for the preservation of prosperity. It is another Hong Kong irony that the aspects of Hong Kong most worth preserving are those that facilitate change.

The long period leading up to the transition has allowed Hong Kong to reassess what it is and what determines the Hong Kong way of life. It has allowed companies and individuals, both from Hong Kong and abroad, to critically assess the advantages and disadvantages, opportunities and challenges found in Hong Kong. While some have left, more have come and still more have stayed. Hong Kong's 'interesting times' have forced introspection in a place and among people not given to introspection. This has served to reduce the complacency that one might expect in an economy that has become affluent relatively quickly. It has not been a simple process, because the Hong Kong story is a complex story of adaptation, resilience, counter-intuitive combinations, and the opportunities provided by real market capitalism. This is what has made Hong Kong unique, and ultimately it is the uniqueness of Hong Kong that is its greatest asset. Hong Kong cannot prosper by being like other places. Its geopolitical situation will always be somewhat uncertain and its costs always will be high. Hong Kong adds value because it is unique. Maintaining and developing its unique attributes, its 'Hong Kong Advantage', will make its future as impressive as its past.

NOTES

1 Catriona Holland, British Chamber of Commerce Research Department, *Third Survey of Factors Affecting Members' Businesses in China and Hong Kong*, Hong Kong, 9 May 1996.
2 Private communications.
3 Hong Kong Government Industry Department, *Report on the 1995 Survey of Regional Representation by Overseas Companies in Hong Kong*, December 1995, p. 16.
4 Ibid., p. 6.
5 Hong Kong Government Industry Department, *Report on the 1995 Survey of Regional Representation*, pp. 5, 6, and 11.
6 Survey Research Hongkong Ltd. (SRH), *AmCham Business Confidence Survey: Management Report*, Hong Kong, November 1995, Charts 8 and 9, p. 9.
7 See Louis Kraar, 'The Death of Hong Kong', *Fortune*, 131, 12 (26 June 1995): 40–52.
8 United Nations Conference on Trade and Development (UNCTAD), *1996 UNCTAD Trade and Development Report*, New York and Geneva: United Nations, pp. 121–34.

APPENDIX
COST CHALLENGES

COST PRESSURES

One of the most frequently discussed issues concerning Hong Kong's present and future competitiveness is that of costs. Since costs are referred to so often in Hong Kong as a source of potential competitive weakness, we thought it necessary to conduct a serious comparative survey of costs in competitor locations—namely Tokyo, Shanghai, Singapore, Taipei, and Sydney.

Costs were assessed, as we thought they would be important to the headquarters operations of a regional or global multinational. Hence, when looking at corporate property costs, prime office space, rather than industrial land, was the basis of comparison. Attention was paid to expatriate costs, and to the costs of international operation—such as international direct dialing telephone charges, and the cost of business air travel.

These comparisons aimed to go beyond the usual headline analysis of prime office rental costs and expatriate salary packages to include other factors deemed by international companies to be significant in determining operating costs. In addition, since all companies ought, in principle, to be concerned above all with earning profits, the team examined tax environments economy by economy. Obviously, a number of unique factors will contribute to every company's tax liabilities, and hence after-tax profitability, but the analysis allows a general indication of how the contrasting tax regimes in place across the region are likely to impinge on a company's operations.

RISING COSTS—A REGIONAL PROBLEM

Rising costs are not unique to Hong Kong. Rapid economic growth over the past decade has squeezed resources and skills, and hiked costs in every economy in East and South-East Asia. All suffer to a greater or lesser extent from shortages of prime office space, of skilled professionals, and of adequate infrastructure—from roads, ports, airports, and mass transit systems to urban housing, power generation capacity, and basic telecommunications. It is arguable that among Asian hubs, only Hong Kong, Singapore, Sydney, and Tokyo have their infrastructural challenges under control. In other economies in the region, infrastructure bottlenecks have become increasingly severe, are now recognized as potential impediments to a high pace of future growth, and appear likely to get worse before they get better. It is also arguable that most of Hong Kong's competitors in the region—again with the exception of Singapore and Sydney—face greater, rather than fewer problems than Hong Kong in meeting future demand for the skilled and professional workers that underpin the knowledge-based activities to which they all aspire. Cost pressures are clearly a matter of concern to all economies in the region. At the same time, future competitiveness is likely to depend more on high and improving levels of productivity and efficient use of resources, than simply on the nominal cost of various inputs.

OFFICE RENTALS

Valid comparisons of office rental costs are problematical: What constitutes a 'prime' location?; Are premises of differing quality?; Is the rental based on 'gross' or 'net' usable area?; Are

Table A.1 Office Rental Costs, Average of Forecasted
Highs and Lows for June 1997, Selected
Cities

Location	Annual cost per square metre (US Dollars)	Location	Annual cost per square metre (US Dollars)
Hong Kong		Sydney	
— Central	1,153	— Central	477
— Wanchai	825		
— Causeway Bay	789	Taipei	
— Tsimshatsui	607	— Min-Sheng	478
		— Tun Hwa South	456
Shanghai		— Nanking-SC	401
— Huangpu	1,063	— Hsin-yi	397
Singapore		Tokyo	
— Raffles Place	938	— Maronouchi	1,123
— Shenton Way	801	— Toranomon	1,036
— Orchard Road	760	— Shinjuku	926
		— Kamata	707

Sources: Colliers Jardine; Conatus Limited.

they fully fitted?; Do comparisons take account of management
and other charges? It also is open to question whether tenants
are able to negotiate 'one-off' deals, depending on the amount
of space being contracted. In addition, the volatility of rental
prices means that comparisons must be constantly reassessed.

This study used data collated by Colliers Jardine in Hong
Kong, who provided a cross-section of 'prime' locations in each
of the markets compared, and a price range within each
location. Table A.1 gives an average of the highest and lowest
prices forecast in each location in mid-1997—many of which
are significantly higher or lower than actual average price levels
quoted at the end of 1996. In Hong Kong, for example, prices
have fallen from a peak at the end of 1993. So too in Shanghai,
where prices appear to have fallen from peak levels in 1995. But
in Sydney, Taipei, and Singapore, prices have risen steadily in
the recent past. The table shows that Hong Kong office real

339

estate is somewhat less expensive than Tokyo, but comparable locations in Sydney or Taipei would cost less than half of what they cost in Hong Kong. Perhaps surprisingly, however, the price differences between Singapore and Hong Kong are not substantial.

REMUNERATION PACKAGES

Remuneration packages were compared across the cities for a typical expatriate financial manager, a local sales manager, and a senior secretary. Where relevant, these packages include not just an employee's basic salary, but year-end or management bonuses, pension provision and housing allowances. Other aspects of remuneration—like international schooling for children, the provision of a car or club memberships, the provision of a domestic servant, medical coverage, the length of annual leave, and whether home leave is provided for an expatriate and his or her family—were also compared (see Table A.2). As far as the cost of top expatriate executives is concerned, Sydney clearly has a substantial advantage over other cities in the region—largely because of the comparatively low cost of local housing. Singapore also has a significant cost advantage over Hong Kong, due to the higher cost in Hong Kong of expatriate housing.

However, the balance of advantage shifts dramatically when the costs of local staff are compared. Singapore emerges as the most expensive location in the region, while Sydney loses much of the cost advantage apparent for expatriates. Not surprisingly, the cost of local staff in Shanghai is a fraction of the cost of equivalent staff in any other location. (See Table A.3.)

The comparison takes no account of taxes or other payments that have to be paid to the local government by an employer on behalf of an employee: in Singapore this can be a significant factor, given the substantial contributions employers have to make to an employee's Central Provident Fund. Nor do the comparisons take account of the length of the average working week (working on Saturdays is still common in some countries

Table A.2 Employment Costs, Expatriate Regional Manager, Thousands of US Dollars, Selected Cities, 1996

Item	Hong Kong	Shanghai	Singapore	Sydney	Taipei	Tokyo
Basic Salary	123–142	107–138	146–178	142	141–160	199
Year-end bonus	1 mo. (included)	20%–30%	15%–35%	20%	included	10%
Management bonus (discretionary)	20%–30%	50%–60%	10%–15%		20%–30%	
Housing	124–217	98–120	43–55	26–30	43	142
Basic Total	272–402	308–430	225–322	196–200	212–251	362
Car						
— Purchase	110–177	108–195	278–354	118–180	93–171	69–92
— Annual costs	4.6–6.2	1.0–1.4	3.0–4.4	1.8–5.3	1.5–2.7	2.6–3.9
Domestic help	Yes	Yes	No	No	Yes	No
Club	Yes	Yes	Yes	Sometimes	Yes	Sometimes
Home utilities	Yes	Yes	Yes	Sometimes	Yes	Sometimes
Children's education	International School	International School	International School	Local/Interntl School	International School	No
Medical Coverage	Family	Family	Family	Family	As for home	Family

Sources: Towers Perrin, Conatus Limited, Economist Intelligence Unit.

Table A.3 Employment Costs, Local Staff, Thousands of US Dollars, Selected Cities, 1996

Item	Hong Kong	Shanghai	Singapore	Sydney	Taipei	Tokyo
Sales Manager						
Basic Salary	78–88	4–6	75–92	59	53–62	127
Year-end bonus	1 mo. (included)	10%	20–50%	30%	16.67%	1–2%
Management bonus (discretionary)	15–25%	10%	0	30%	15–25%	0
Pension	5–10%	30%	19–22%	8–10%	2–15%	8%
Basic Total	89–110	6–9	89–138	77	62–78	141–142
Senior Secretary						
Basic Salary	26–29	3–4	25–28	32	17–20	59
Year-end bonus	1 mo. (included)	10%	10–15%	10–15%	0	16.67%
Management bonus (discretionary)	0–5%	30%	0	0	0–5%	0
Pension	5–10%	30%	20%	6–8%	2–15%	8%
Basic Total	26–31	5–6	27–33	32	17–21	65

Sources: Towers Perrin, Conatus Limited.

in Asia), annual holidays, or, perhaps most important of all, productivity levels. It is also worth emphasizing that the comparisons do not reflect take-home pay or the attractiveness of particular packages to individual employees, since they take no account of personal taxation. An employee in Hong Kong being taxed at a flat 15 per cent will clearly retain a far greater proportion of his or her basic salary than employees in other places. So too, an employee in Hong Kong earning the same basic wage as an employee in Singapore will retain more, because personal taxation is lower, and because he does not have to contribute 20 per cent of his income to the Central Provident Fund. At the same time, that same Hong Kong employee is under greater pressure to save for his or her own retirement.

AUTOMOBILES

Most multinational companies in Asia provide a car for key expatriate staff, and pay for operating expenses. Singapore is significantly more expensive than any other location in the region, as the government has used car pricing as a key lever to restrain traffic congestion. A family car in Singapore will cost between US$129,000 and US$187,000, while a luxury car will cost between US$278,000 and US$355,000. This is between two and three times the price of similar cars in Hong Kong, Shanghai, Taipei or Sydney, and is a quite extraordinary four times the price that would be paid in Tokyo.

Car operating costs do not diverge so strikingly, though Hong Kong appears to be up to twice as costly as other centres in the region. So too are petrol prices substantially higher in Hong Kong than elsewhere in the region, as the government has chosen this lever, rather than car prices, to restrain the proliferation of private car use. It is perhaps no surprise that the two cities in the region suffering severest space and population pressure have in place policies which make it expensive to own and operate a private car. Nor is it a surprise that both cities have superb mass transit transport systems, enabling the population such easy movement throughout the city that many feel no loss in not owning a car. Indeed, it is arguable that in both cities, a luxury car is much more a status and style statement than a functional requirement—which is, of course, another reason why so many multinational companies have no choice but to provide such luxury vehicles to expatriate executives.

TELECOMMUNICATIONS

There has been fierce competition in Asia for the title of leading telecommunications hub, as the discussion in Chapter 5 on telecommunications amply illustrates. Deregulation of national monopolies is occurring at a hectic pace, partly in response to business demands for a wider variety of services, partly because of a recognition that high telecommunications costs can be a serious impediment to business efficiency and competitiveness, and partly because telecommunications technologies are developing so rapidly that monopolies are becoming indefensible.

Table A.4 surveys the cost of calls using national service providers to a basket of typical destination cities. It shows Hong Kong's costs to be just over a third of Tokyo's, less than half the price of Shanghai, and an average of 20 per cent cheaper than those of Singapore, Sydney, and Taipei. This comparison takes no account of the fact that in Hong Kong, local calls are free once the monthly charge of US$12.68 is paid. The provision of free local calls, which is unique in Asia, has clearly been an attraction for companies operating in the territory. It has been a powerful stimulant for the growth of the local telecommunications infrastructure, and of the completion of all-digital exchanges in the 1980s. It has been a key factor behind the proliferation of fax and other add-on telecom services.

Such is the dramatic pace of liberalization occurring in the industry at present (in particular the proliferation of call-back and leased-line arrangements for international calls), however,

Table A.4 Telecommunications Costs, US Dollars, Selected Cities, 1996

	Hong Kong Standard rate	Lowest rate	Shanghai	Singapore[a]	Sydney	Taipei	Tokyo[a]
Monthly Fee	12.68	—	5.52	8.88	15.76	13.73	24.69
Local Calls	—		0.04[a]	0.01	—	0.04	0.03
International Calls							
Destination							
Beijing	1.23	1.14	0.12	1.70	2.06	1.25	3.04
Hong Kong	—	—	1.98	0.92	1.01	1.25	3.04
Jakarta	1.36	1.14	3.15	1.46	1.49	1.25	3.42
Shanghai	1.23	1.14	—	1.70	2.06	1.25	3.04
Singapore	1.23	0.56	2.95	—	1.01	1.25	3.42
Sydney	0.93	0.61	3.15	0.92	—	1.25	3.23
Taipei	1.02	0.71	1.98	1.70	1.73	—	3.04
Tokyo	1.02	0.68	2.18	1.35	1.35	1.25	—
London	1.14	0.66	3.55	1.28	1.01	1.68	3.61
New York	0.88	0.37	3.15	1.10	1.01	1.18	2.28
Average	1.12	0.79	2.47	1.35	1.41	1.29	3.12
Index	100	71	221	121	126	115	279

[a] Add government service tax or sales tax.
Sources: National service providers.

that comparison of the list prices from national service providers may soon have little relevance. As the table also shows for Hong Kong, call-back arrangements now being offered by at least four international telecom groups can, on average, strip a further 30 per cent from the standard charges incurred by an international caller using the territory's 'monopoly' international service provider, Hong Kong Telecommunications. No doubt, such arrangements are having a powerful influence on the cost of international telephone calls in all of the cities surveyed, but it may be some time before reliable comparative data are available.

Meanwhile, Hong Kong continues to be by far the region's leading source of international telephone traffic. The territory was the source of an estimated 1.7 billion minutes of traffic in 1995—higher than 1.6 billion minutes of outgoing traffic from Japan, almost three times the outgoing traffic from Singapore, and only just short of the 1.8 billion minutes of outgoing calls from the entire ASEAN region.

AIR TRAVEL

For many multinationals in Asia, air travel costs are substantial. One leading US bank in Hong Kong estimated that it had 50 staff travelling in the region at any one time, making air ticketing costs a key component of total operating costs. Of course, the cost of tickets is only one factor favouring one location over another. Just as important is the number of destinations served from the location, the frequency with which they are served, the ease of getting to and from a local airport, and the quality of service offered by airlines operating from the location. These have not been explicitly compared as this was exclusively a *cost* comparison, but it is clear that Hong Kong compares favourably with all cities in the region by these measures. Even Singapore, which would challenge fiercely the claim that Hong Kong is a superior hub on the grounds of ease of access to Singapore Changi airport, and the world-beating reputation of Singapore Airlines, cannot offer travellers the range of destinations and frequency of flights, particularly across the breadth of China.

Table A.5 shows that Hong Kong compares extremely favourably with other cities in the region in terms of the cost of air travel. Only Shanghai and Taipei offer flights that are cheaper than those from Hong Kong, and both cities suffer from limited route networks and limited flight frequencies— and, of course, the legal bar on direct flights between Taiwan and the Chinese Mainland. Hong Kong's price-competitiveness is particularly keen on long-haul routes. Flights to London from Singapore are 22 per cent more expensive, and from Sydney and Tokyo 45 per cent and 60 per cent respectively. Flights to New York from Singapore are almost 40 per cent more expensive than from Hong Kong, while from Sydney they are almost 80 per cent more expensive, and from Tokyo 20 per cent. Singapore is a cheaper base from which to serve Kuala Lumpur and Jakarta, as would be expected, but to Shanghai, Beijing, Tokyo and even Sydney it is significantly more expensive.

CORPORATE TAXATION

Corporate tax rates vary immensely, and it is in this area that Hong Kong offers companies advantages well beyond competitor locations in the region. Not only is Hong Kong's flat 16.5 per cent basic profits tax rate the lowest in the region, but the fact that it is simple, and levied only on local income appears to offer considerable attractions to companies based in the territory, or considering a domicile there. As Table A.6 shows, Hong Kong is also unlittered with any additional taxes, which lowers gross tax costs, and greatly simplifies the often costly and time consuming process of completing tax returns.

It is not possible to extrapolate from these different taxes to reach any one-line conclusion on how much more expensive other locations are compared to Hong Kong, since the different taxes will each have a unique impact on individual companies, but it can be concluded with some confidence that Hong Kong is significantly cheaper. The simplicity of Hong Kong's tax

Table A.5 Aviation Costs, US Dollars, May 1996, Selected Cities

	Cost of one business-class round-trip ticket					
	Hong Kong	Shanghai	Singapore	Sydney	Taipei	Tokyo
Destination						
Beijing	696	343	2,082	3,677	no flight	1,924
Hong Kong	—	664	1,481	3,796	418	1,644
Jakarta	1,424	no flight	669	2,666	1,617	3,148
Kuala Lumpur	1,119	no flight	290	3,070	1,272	2,749
Shanghai	492	—	1,909	3,602	no flight	1,352
Singapore	1,161	1,208	—	2,937	1,272	2,749
Sydney	2,557	2,899	3,168	—	2,791	4,529
Taipei	496	no flight	1,918	3,793	—	1,285
Tokyo	1,122	976	2,453	3,784	769	—
London	4,196	4,539	5,139	6,063	3,780	6,700
New York	3,805	3,725	5,274	6,807	3,117	4,954
Index	100	84	143	236	88	180
Index 2[a]	100	114	143	236	100	180

[a] Index 2 assumes that routes with no direct flights are routed through Hong Kong.
Source: Adapted from American Express information.

Table A.6 Corporate Taxation, Selected Cities, 1996

	Hong Kong	Shanghai	Singapore	Sydney	Taipei	Tokyo
Basic Tax	16.5%	33%	27%	36%	25%	37.5%
Basis	Local	World	Local/Remitted	World	World	World
Additional Taxes						
— Consumer Goods Tax		3–45%				
— Property Tax		18%				
— Provident Fund Tax			20% of salaries			
— Fringe Benefit				48.4% of value		
— Payroll Tax				4–7% of wages		
— Staff Welfare Tax					5% of paid in capital	
— Land Tax					40–60% of appreciation	
— Building Tax					3% of assessed value	
— Enterprise Tax						6.3% of net income
— Staff Tax						7.8% of net income
— VAT/Sales Tax		17%	3%	11–45%	5%	3%

Source: Adapted from Coopers and Lybrand information.

system also allows many companies to rely on the services of part-time book-keepers to maintain accounts, rather than employing their own auditing staff—a factor which unquestionably lowers costs and raises productivity by comparison with other locations.

COST COMPARISONS—THE CONCLUSIONS

For 'office-based' operations, Hong Kong's rental and basic personnel costs are among the highest in the region. In other key operating costs—in particular telecommunications and air travel costs—Hong Kong actually compares rather well with other cities in the region. Hong Kong's tax regime provides a substantial advantage for most firms, at least those interested in making money. The concessional tax rates offered in particular circumstances by the Singapore government compare favourably with Hong Kong's rates, but the fact that these are confined to specified areas of activity and have to be individually negotiated simply confirms, rather than contradicts the broad advantages provided by Hong Kong's low and simple tax regime.

The conclusion is, therefore, that the costs which attract the most headline attention—principally housing and remuneration—are not the only costs, and in many cases might not be the most important costs. On a total cost basis after tax, Hong Kong is more competitive than many outsiders realize. This provides one reason why such a large number of multinational companies continue to operate their regional headquarters from Hong Kong, and why so few local Hong Kong companies have been tempted to move their tax domicile away from Hong Kong. Hong Kong needs to be concerned about the 'headline costs', but it should be even more concerned about productivity levels, labour flexibility, improved efficiency in the land market, and the ability of companies to identify strategies based on the reality of operating in a high-cost economy.

BIBLIOGRAPHY

Almanac of China's Foreign Economic Relations and Trade, Beijing: China Statistical Publishing House and Hong Kong: China Resources Advertising Co., Ltd., various years.

Asia Equity, Robin Hammond (analyst), 'Hong Kong Banking Sector', Hong Kong, May 1996.

——, Osbert Tang (analyst), 'Company Update: Hong Kong Electric', Hong Kong, 4 July 1995.

Asia Pacific Economics Group, *Asia Pacific Profiles 1996*, Research School of Pacific and Asian Studies, Australian National University, South Melbourne: Pearson Professional [Australia] Pty. Ltd. (distr.), 1996.

Asian Development Bank, *Asian Development Outlook 1992*, Hong Kong: Oxford University Press, 1992.

——, *Asian Development Outlook 1995 and 1996*, Hong Kong: Oxford University Press, 1995.

——, *Asian Development Outlook 1996 and 1997*, Hong Kong: Oxford University Press, 1996.

Asiaweek (1 November 1996): 57.

Attan, Ahirudin, 'Need to Make Employment Benefits Attractive', *Business Times* (24 July 1995): 20.

Bhide, Amar, 'Hustle as Strategy', *Harvard Business Review*, 64, Reprint No. 86503 (1 September 1986).

Boston Consulting Group International, Inc., *Report on Techno-economic and Market Research Study on Hong Kong's Electronics Industry 1993–1994: Volume 2: Phase I Study—Industry Analysis*, Hong Kong: Hong Kong Government Industry Department, 1995.

Bueno de Mesquita, Bruce; Newman, David; and Rabushka, Alvin, *Red Flag Over Hong Kong*, Chatham, N.J.: Chatham House Publishers, 1996.

Business and Professionals Federation of Hong Kong, *Hong Kong 21: A Ten Year Vision and Agenda for Hong Kong's Economy*, Hong Kong, May 1993.

Castells, Manuel and Hall, Peter, *Technopoles of the World*, London: Routledge, 1994.

Chadha, K. K., 'MTL Throughput Hits Record High', *South China Morning Post: Business Post* (3 October 1994): 2.

Chan, Elaine, 'Henderson to Invest in Huge Tianjin Plan', *South China Morning Post: Property Post* (18 September 1996): 1.

Chan, K. K.; Tsang, C. K.; and Lau, Kenneth, 'The Construction Industry Professionals, Their Contribution to Regional Development', Speech Given at the Conference 'Building Strategic Partnerships for the Future', Singapore, 17 May 1996.

Chan Kwok Bun, 'The Ethnicity Paradox: Hong Kong Immigrants in Singapore', in Ronald Skeldon (ed.), *Reluctant Exiles? Migration from Hong Kong and the New Overseas Chinese*, Hong Kong: Hong Kong University Press, 1994, pp. 308–21.

Chan, S. K., Executive Director, Hong Kong Productivity Council, Speech Given to the Hong Kong Institute of Human Resources, 1995 Pay Trend Seminar, 3 November 1995.

Chang Yi-Hsin, 'Opportunity Outweighs Fear as Expats Flood Hong Kong', *The Asian Wall Street Journal* (20 August 1996): 1.

Chen Minzhi, *A Study of Shanghai's Development Strategy*, Shanghai: Shanghai renmin chubanshe, 1985.

Cheng, Leonard K., 'Trade and Industry: 1997 and Beyond', in Joseph Y. S. Cheng and Sonny S. H. Lo (eds.), *From Colony to SAR: Hong Kong's Challenges Ahead*, Hong Kong: Chinese University Press, 1995, pp. 175–95.

Cheung, Peter T. Y., 'The Political Context of Shanghai's Economic Development', in Y. M. Yeung and Sung Yun-wing (eds.), *Shanghai: Transformation and Modernization under China's Open Policy*, Hong Kong: Chinese University Press, 1996, pp. 49–92.

Cheung, Stephen Y. L. and Sze, Stephen M. H. (eds.), *The Other Hong Kong Report 1995*, Hong Kong, Chinese University Press, 1995.

Chew, Amy, 'Phone Wars', *Asiaweek* (4 October 1996): 43–4.

China Credit Information Services, *The Largest Corporations in Taiwan, 1994*, Taipei, 1994.

China Economic News Service (CENS), 'Taiwan Factbook', 1996, webmaster @www.cens.com>.

China Statistical Yearbook, Beijing: China Statistical Publishing House, various years.

Colliers Jardine Research, *Asia Pacific Property Trends, Conditions and Forecasts*, Hong Kong: McGraw–Hill, July 1996, ed. X, pp. 59–67.

Coggan, Philip, 'Survey of Singapore', *Financial Times* (8 February 1996): vi.

Commonwealth of Australia, East Asia Analytical Unit, Department of Foreign Affairs and Trade, *Overseas Chinese Business Networks in Asia*, Sydney, 1995.

Credit Lyonnais Securities, Hong Kong Research, 'China Jump II: Hong Kong's HK$140bn China Jump', Hong Kong, March 1996.

Crocombe, Graham; Enright, Michael; and Porter, Michael, *Upgrading New Zealand's Competitive Advantage*, Auckland: Oxford University Press, 1991.

Davies, Hugh, 'The Joint Liaison Group', *Hong Kong Echo Magazine*, 8 (Summer 1996): 30–1.

Davies, Ken, *Hong Kong after 1997*, London: Economist Intelligence Unit Research Report, London, 1996.

——, *Hong Kong to 1994: A Question of Confidence*, Economist Intelligence Unit Special Report No. 2022, London, 1990.

Davis, S. and Botkin, J., 'Coming of Knowledge-Based Business', *Harvard Business Review*, 72, Reprint No. 94505 (1 September 1994).

Delhaise, Philippe, 'Best Banks in Asia 1995', New York: Thomson Bank-Watch, January 1996.

Dun and Bradstreet, *Key Business Directory of Singapore*, 1993/4 edn., Hong Kong, 1993.

Economist Intelligence Unit, *Business China Briefing: Economic Outlook—Guangdong*, Hong Kong, February 1996.

Enright, Michael, 'Why Local Clusters Are the Way to Win the Game', *World Link* (July/August 1992): 24–5.

Enright, Michael; Frances, Antonio; and Scott Saavedra, Edith, *Venezuela: The Challenge of Competitiveness*, New York: St. Martins Press, 1996.

Enright, Michael and Weder, Rolf, *Studies in Swiss Competitive Advantage*, Berne: Peter Lang, 1995.

Far Eastern Economic Review (31 October 1996): 64.

——, (14 November 1996): 84–5.

Federation of Hong Kong Industries, 'The Economy in the 1980s: Can Hong Kong Afford Not to Have a Growing Manufacturing Industry?', Hong Kong, 1982.

Ghemawat, Pankaj, *Commitment: The Dynamic of Strategy*, New York: The Free Press, 1991.

Glasmeier, Amy K., 'Flexibility and Adjustment: The Hong Kong Watch Industry and Global Change', *Growth and Change*, 25 (Spring 1994): 223–46.

'Guide to Venture Capital in Asia 1996/97', *Hong Kong Asian Venture Capital Journal* (November 1996): 59–60.

Guyot, Erik, 'New World's Revamping Plan Signals Renewed Faith in China', *The Asian Wall Street Journal* (19 September 1995): 3.

Hewett, Gareth, 'Service With a Smile as Hong Kong Reverts to Playing Traditional Role', *South China Morning Post: Business Post* (5 May 1996): 12.

Hiebert, Murray, 'It's a Jungle Out There', *Far Eastern Economic Review* (25 April 1996): 58–61.

Hirschhorn, L. and Gilmore, T., 'New Boundaries of the "Boundaryless" Company', *Harvard Business Review*, 70, Reprint No. 92304 (1 May 1992).

Ho Lok-sang and Tsui Kai-yuen, 'Fiscal Relations between Shanghai and the

Central Government', in Y. M. Yeung and Sung Yun-wing (eds.), *Shanghai: Transformation and Modernization under China's Open Policy*, Hong Kong: Chinese University Press, 1996, pp. 153–69.

Hodder, Rupert, 'Industrial Location', in Y. M. Yeung and Sung Yun-wing (eds.), *Shanghai: Transformation and Modernization under China's Open Policy*, Hong Kong: Chinese University Press, 1996, pp. 225–48.

Holland, Catriona, British Chamber of Commerce Research Department, *Third Survey of Factors Affecting Members' Businesses in China and Hong Kong*, Hong Kong, 9 May 1996.

Hong Kong Air Cargo Terminals Limited, Press Release, 14 December 1995.

Hong Kong Census and Statistics Department, *Estimates of Gross Domestic Product 1961–1995*, Hong Kong, March 1996.

——, *Hong Kong Monthly Digest of Statistics* (1996, various months).

——, 'Labour Productivity in the Manufacturing Sector at Hong Kong, 1982–1993', *Hong Kong Monthly Digest of Statistics* (April 1996): FA4.

——, *Report on 1994 Survey of Wholesale, Retail & Import & Export Trades, Restaurants & Hotels*, Hong Kong, August 1996.

——, *Report on 1993 Survey of Wholesale, Retail & Import & Export Trades, Restaurants & Hotels*, Hong Kong, May 1995.

——, 'Trading Firms with Manufacturing Related Functions', *Hong Kong Monthly Digest of Statistics* (August 1996): FA1.

Hong Kong Consumer Council, 'Achieving Competition in the Liberalised Telecommunications Market', Hong Kong, 14 March 1996.

——, 'Assessing Competition in the Domestic Water Heating and Cooking Fuel Market', Hong Kong, 1995.

——, *Report on Hong Kong's Private Residential Property Market*, Hong Kong, July 1996.

Hong Kong Government Industry Department, 'Clothing Industry', in *1995 Hong Kong Manufacturing Industries*, Hong Kong, 1995, pp. 41–57.

——, *Consultancy Study on Hong Kong's Software Industry 1994–95*, Hong Kong, 1995.

——, 'Electronics Industry', in *1994 Hong Kong Manufacturing Industries*, Hong Kong, 1994, pp. 59–74.

——, 'Electronics Industry', in *1995 Hong Kong Manufacturing Industries*, Hong Kong, 1995, pp. 59–74.

——, *1995 Survey of External Investment in Hong Kong's Manufacturing Industries*, Hong Kong, December 1995.

——, *Report on the 1995 Survey of Regional Representation by Overseas Companies in Hong Kong*, Hong Kong, December 1995.

Hong Kong Government Information Services, *Hong Kong Background Facts*, Hong Kong, August 1996.

——, Renu Daryanani (ed.), *Hong Kong 1995*, Hong Kong, 1995.

——, Bob Howlett (ed.), *Hong Kong 1996*, Hong Kong, 1996.

Hong Kong Government Planning Department, *Consolidated Technical*

Report on the Territorial Development Strategy Review '96, Hong Kong, 1996.

——, *The Final Technical Report on Territorial Development Strategy Review—1996, Part Three, Section A, Recommended Long-Term Strategy*, Hong Kong, 1996.

Hong Kong Government, Planning, Environment, and Lands Branch, *A Consultative Digest, Territorial Development Strategy Review '96*, Hong Kong, 1996.

Hong Kong Office of the Telecommunications Authority, 'Key Statistics for Wireless Services in Hong Kong', http://ofta.gov.hk/stats/statis/st95g261.html.

Hong Kong Port Development Board, *Hong Kong Port Cargo Forecasts 1995*, Hong Kong, February 1996.

Hong Kong Provisional Airport Authority, 'New Airport Freight Forwarding Centre Developer Named', Press Release, 28 September 1995.

Hong Kong Tourist Association, *A Statistical Review of Tourism 1995*, Hong Kong, 1995.

Hong Kong Trade Development Council, 'Construction Giant Expands into Region', http://www.tdc.org.hk/hktrader/9606/9606p51.html.

——, 'Economic Relations Between Hong Kong and China', Hong Kong, July 1996.

——, 'Economic & Trade Information on Hong Kong', http://www.tdc.org.hk/main/economic.html#4, last updated 2 September 1996.

——, 'Hong Kong as a Regional Sourcing and Distribution Base: Results of a Survey on Japanese Companies in Hong Kong', Hong Kong, January 1996.

——, 'Hong Kong Beyond 1997: A Guide for Business', http://www.tdc.org.hk/beyond97/beyond.html.

——, *Hong Kong's Trade and Trade Supporting Services*, Hong Kong, April 1996.

——, 'Hopewell Helps "Road to Development"', http://www.tdc.org.hk/hktrader/9607/9607p25.html.

——, 'Industry Body Formed', *Hong Kong Trader: A TDC Newspaper*, http://www.tdc.org.hk/hktrader/9608/9608pb3.html.

——, 'Market Profile on Mainland China', http://www.tdc.org.hk/main/china.html, last updated 20 August 1996.

——, 'Market Profile on Shanghai Municipality', Hong Kong, 28 October 1996.

——, *Profiles of Selected Service Industries of Hong Kong*, Hong Kong, March 1996.

——, *The Opening of China's Tertiary Sector: Latest Development and Outlook*, Hong Kong, May 1996.

Hong Kong Vocational Training Council, *1994 Demand and Supply Report on Technical Manpower of Major Hong Kong Industries*, Hong Kong, January 1995.

Hughes, Richard, *Borrowed Place Borrowed Time: Hong Kong and its Many Faces*, rev. 2nd edn., London: André Deutsch, 1976.

Hung Wing-tat, 'The Environment', in Stephen Y. L. Cheung and Stephen M. H. Sze (eds.), *The Other Hong Kong Report 1995*, Hong Kong: Chinese University Press, 1995, pp. 343–59.

ICIC Pty. Ltd., *Australian Enterprise Report*, http://www.icic.com.au/aer/articles/.

IMD International, *The World Competitiveness Yearbook 1996*, Lausanne, 1996.

IMD International and World Economic Forum, *The World Competitiveness Report 1995*, Lausanne, 1995.

International Monetary Fund, *Direction of Trade Statistics Yearbook*, Washington, D.C., various editions.

Japan External Trade Organization (JETRO), *JETRO White Paper on Foreign Direct Investment 1996*, Tokyo, 1996.

Joint Banking Committee of the American Chamber of Commerce and European Council of Commerce and Trade, *Taipei as a Regional Financial and Funding Centre*, Taipei, 1995.

Kane, Robert, *Hong Kong at its Best*, Lincolnwood, Ill.: Passport Books, 1992.

KPMG Management Consulting Ltd. for the Hong Kong Productivity Council, *Moving Forward by Adding Value: A Study of Productivity in Hong Kong's Trading Sectors*, Hong Kong, January 1996.

Kraar, Louis, 'The Death of Hong Kong', *Fortune*, 131, 12 (26 June 1995): 40–52.

Kurt Salmon Associates for Hong Kong Government Industry Department, *1995 Techno-economic and Market Research Study on Hong Kong's Textiles and Clothing Industries*, Hong Kong, July 1996.

Law, Andrew; Shimomura, Kazushige; and Hutchings, Heather, 'Asia's Best Managed Companies: Hong Kong', *Asiamoney*, VI, 6 (July/August 1995): 14.

Leung, James, 'Beijing Stifles Shanghai dream', *Asian Business* (October 1995): 24–8.

Mak, Grace C. L. and Lo, Leslie N. K., 'Education', in Y. M. Yeung and Sung Yun-wing (eds.), *Shanghai: Transformation and Modernization under China's Open Policy*, Hong Kong: Chinese University Press, 1996, pp. 375–98.

Margolis, Richard, 'Countdown to 1997: Bumps in the Road', Hong Kong: Merrill Lynch, April 1996.

McGrath, John, 'When Less is More?', *International Financial Law Review 1000*, 1997 edn. (October 1996): x–xi.

McGurn, William, 'English in Asia: Money Talks', *Far Eastern Economic Review* (21 March 1996): 40–3.

Mellor, William, 'Capital Cities: Sydney: New South Asia', *Asia, Inc.*, 5 (August 1996): 28–33.

Mok, Victor, 'Industrial Development', in Y. M. Yeung and Sung Yun-wing (eds.), *Shanghai: Transformation and Modernization under China's Open Policy*, Hong Kong: Chinese University Press, 1996.

Morris, Jan, *Hong Kong: Epilogue to an Empire*, London: Penguin Books, 1988.

Mushkat, Miron, *The Economic Future of Hong Kong*, Boulder, Col.: Lynne Rienner Publishers, 1990.

Naisbitt, John, *Megatrends Asia: Eight Asian Megatrends that are Reshaping the World*, New York: Simon & Schuster, 1996.

New South Wales Office of Economic Development, 'New South Wales (NSW) Competitiveness Report', http://www.srd.nsw.gov.au/comprep/p39a.htm.

——, 'Sydney: Being Clever Matters', http://www.srd.nsw.gov.au/rhq/clever.htm (last modified 21 June 1996).

Nyaw Mee-kau, 'Investment Environment: Perceptions of Overseas Investors of Foreign-funded Industrial Firms', in Y. M. Yeung and Sung Yun-wing (eds.), *Shanghai: Transformation and Modernization under China's Open Policy*, Hong Kong: Chinese University Press, 1996, pp. 249–72.

Overholt, William H., *China: The Next Economic Superpower*, London: Weidenfeld & Nicolson, 1993.

——, 'Hong Kong's Financial Stability through 1997', Hong Kong: Bankers Trust Company, 20 March 1996.

People's Republic of China, Seventh National People's Congress, 'The Basic Law of the Hong Kong Special Administrative Region of the People's Republic of China', Hong Kong: One Country Two Systems Economic Research Institute Ltd., 1992.

Perkin, Ian, 'Hong Kong in Transition: Economic Overview', *Hong Kong Echo Magazine*, 8 (Summer 1996): 12–13.

Porter, Michael E., *Competitive Advantage*, New York: The Free Press, 1985

Prahalad, C. K. and Hamel, G., 'Core Competence of the Corporation', *Harvard Business Review*, 68, Reprint No. 90311 (1 May 1990).

Prystay, Cris, 'Boom in University "Twinning" Across Asia', *Asian Business* (September 1996): 60–3.

Rafferty, Kevin, *City on the Rocks*, rev. edn., London: Penguin Books, 1991.

Rayport, J. F., and Sviokla, J. J., 'Exploiting the Virtual Value Chain', *Harvard Business Review*, 73, Reprint No. 95610 (1 November 1995).

Republic of China, Government Information Office, 'Hong Kong and Macau', *Republic of China Yearbook 1996*, http://www.gio.tw/info/.

——, *Republic of China Yearbook 1996*, Taipei, 1996.

——, 'Taiwan: An Initiative into the Next Century: A Plan for Building Taiwan into an Asia–Pacific Regional Operations Center', http://www.gio.tw/info/.

——, 'The Republic of China at a Glance', Taipei http://www.gio.gov.tw/info/glance/index.html.

Republic of Singapore, Economic Development Board, 'Year in Review 1994', http://www.sedb.com.sg/annual95/review.html.

——, 'About the Singapore Economy', http://www.sedb.com.sg/annual95/brieg.html.

——, 'Singapore Has Least Corruption in Asia: PERC' Survey, http://www.sedb.com.sg/biz/other/others10.html.

——, 'Singapore Poses Least Political Risk: PERC Survey', http://www.sedb.com. sg/biz/other/others14.html.

——, 'Singapore's Business Climate', http://www.sedb.com.sg/biz/other/others.

Reynolds, Nicholas, 'End of an Era Flagged as Garment Giant Crosses the Border', *South China Morning Post: Business Post* (24 May 1994): 3.

Ridding, John, 'Allianz Expansion Puts Faith in Hong Kong', *Financial Times* (22 April 1996): 27.

——, 'Fears of "Hollow" Hong Kong Grow as China Takeover Nears', *Financial Times: Weekend* (17/18 February 1996): 5.

Roell, Sophie, 'Realism Enters Chinese Listing', *Financial Times* (9 September 1996): 31.

Rowlinson, S. M. and Walker, A., *The Construction Industry in Hong Kong*, Hong Kong: Longman Hong Kong, 1995.

Ruthven, Phillip, 'Australia's Positioning within The Asia-Pacific,' in ICTC Pty. Ltd., *Australian Enterprise Report*, http://www.icic.com.au/ae/articles/137.html.

Schive, Chi, *Taiwan's Economic Role in East Asia*, Washington, D.C.: Center for Strategic and International Studies, 1995.

Segal Quince Wicksteed Ltd., 'Strategic and Organisational Review of the Vocational Training Council: A Final Report to the Secretary for Education and Manpower', Hong Kong, 1996.

Shanghai Internet Trading and Consultancy, 'Economic Structure' and 'Living Standards', http://china-window.com/shanghai/shbf.

——, 'Investment', http://china-window.shanghai/inves/tu4.html.

Silverman, Gary and Saywell, Trish, 'Cramming Classes: Supply of College Places Doesn't Meet Demand', *Far Eastern Economic Review* (14 November 1996): 26–8.

'Singapore Poses Least Political Risk: PERC Survey', *Straits Times* (11 March 1996), http://www.sedb.com.sg/biz/other/others14.html.

Skeldon, Ronald, 'Hong Kong in an International Migration System', in Ronald Skeldon (ed.), *Reluctant Exiles? Migration from Hong Kong and the New Overseas Chinese*, Hong Kong: Hong Kong University Press, 1994, pp. 21–51.

——, 'Reluctant Exiles or Bold Pioneers: An Introduction to Migration from Hong Kong', in Ronald Skeldon (ed.), *Reluctant Exiles? Migration from Hong Kong and the New Overseas Chinese*, Hong Kong: Hong Kong University Press, 1994, pp. 3–18.

Smart, Josephine, 'Business Immigration to Canada: Deception and Exploitation', in Ronald Skeldon (ed.), *Reluctant Exiles? Migration from Hong Kong and the New Overseas Chinese*, Hong Kong: Hong Kong University Press, 1994, pp. 98–119.

Stalk, Jr., G.; Evans, P.; and Shulman, L. E., 'Competing on Capabilities: The

New Rules of Corporate Strategy', *Harvard Business Review*, 70, Reprint No. 92209 (1 March 1992).

Statistical Yearbook of Jiangsu, Beijing: China Statistical Publishing House, various years.

Statistical Yearbook of Liaoning, Beijing: China Statistical Publishing House, various years.

Statistical Yearbook of Shandong, Beijing: China Statistical Publishing House, various years.

Statistical Yearbook of Shanghai 1995, Shanghai: China Statistics Publishing Co., 1995.

Statistical Yearbook of Shanghai 1996, Beijing: China Statistical Publishing House, 1996.

Sung Yun-wing, ' "Dragon Head" of China's Economy?', in Y. M. Yeung and Sung Yun-wing (eds.), *Shanghai: Transformation and Modernization under China's Open Policy*, Hong Kong: Chinese University Press, 1996, pp. 171–98.

——, 'The Economics of the Illegal Trade between Taiwan and Mainland China', paper presented at International Pacific Rim Conference of the Western Economic Association, January 1994.

Sung, Yun-wing; Liu Pak-wai; Richard Yue-chim Wong; and Lau Pui-king, *The Fifth Dragon: The Emergence of the Pearl River Delta*, Singapore: Addison Wesley Publishing Co., 1995.

'Survey on International Telecommunications', *The Financial Times* (19 September 1996): XXII.

Survey Research Hongkong Ltd. (SRH), *AmCham Business Confidence Survey: Management Report*, Hong Kong, November 1995.

Swire Group, 'Reorganisation of Industries Division Head Office', *Swire News*, 22, 4, 1995: 17.

Tabakoff, Nick, 'Mainland Firms' Secretaries Get Training Boost', *Sunday Morning Post: Business Post* (29 September 1996): 5.

Tang, James T. H., 'Hong Kong's International Status', *The Pacific Review*, 6, 3 (1993): 205–15.

Tang Shu-hung, 'The Economy' in Joseph Y. S. Cheng and Sonny S. H. Lo (eds.), *From Colony to SAR: Hong Kong's Challenges Ahead*, Hong Kong: Chinese University Press, 1995, pp. 117–50.

Tatlow, Dermot, 'Hong Kong's Free-Market Myth for Service Industries', *Executive* (September 1996): 24.

'The *Asiaweek* 1000: Top Enterprises by Country: Hong Kong', *Asiaweek*, 22, 47 (22 November 1996): 70–169.

Thornton, Emily, 'Bitter Pill', *Far Eastern Economic Review* (31 October 1996): 58–9.

Tien, James, 'The Brains Revolution but Not Quite', *Hong Kong Echo Magazine*, 8 (Summer 1996): 54–5.

'Trading Firms with Manufacturing Related Functions', *Hong Kong Monthly Digest of Statistics* (August 1996): FA1–FA10.

Tripathi, Salil, 'Capital Cities: Singapore Swing', *Asia, Inc.* (February 1996): 38–44.

'Underpowered', *The Economist* (9 March 1996): 6.

United Nations Conference on Trade and Development (UNCTAD), *1996 UNCTAD Trade and Development Report*, New York and Geneva: United Nations, 1996.

——, *World Investment Report 1995: Transnational Corporations and Competitiveness*, New York and Geneva: United Nations, 1995.

——, *World Investment Report 1996*, Fact Sheet No. 2, 24 September 1996.

——, *World Investment Report 1996: Investment, Trade and International Policy Arrangements*, New York and Geneva: United Nations, 1996.

Ure, John, 'Telecommunications', in Joseph Y. S. Cheng and Sonny S. H. Lo (eds.), *From Colony to SAR: Hong Kong's Challenges Ahead*, Hong Kong: Chinese University Press, 1995, pp. 431–55.

Vogel, Ezra F., *One Step Ahead in China: Guangdong under Reform*, Cambridge, Mass.: Harvard University Press, 1989.

Walker, Anthony, *Hong Kong in China: Real Estate in the Economy*, Hong Kong: Brooke Hillier Parker, 1995.

Wang, J. J., 'Transport', in Stephen Y. L. Cheung and Stephen M. H. Sze (eds.), *The Other Hong Kong Report 1995*, Hong Kong: Chinese University Press, 1995, pp. 329–42.

Weidenbaum, Murray and Hughes, Samuel, *The Bamboo Network: How Expatriate Chinese Entrepreneurs Are Creating a New Economic Superpower in Asia*, New York: The Free Press, 1996.

Wong, Richard Y. C., 'Understanding Competition in Hong Kong', reprinted from *HKCER Letters*, Hong Kong Centre for Economic Research, 20 (May 1993).

Wong Siu-lun, 'The Entrepreneurial Spirit: Shanghai and Hong Kong Compared', in Y. M. Yeung and Sung Yun-wing (eds.), *Shanghai: Transformation and Modernization under China's Open Policy*, Hong Kong: Chinese University Press, 1996, pp. 25–48.

Wong, Teresa Y. C. and Kwong Kai Sun, 'The Role of Hong Kong in Asia's Regional Economic Growth and Development', in Ng Sek Hong and David G. Lethbridge (eds.), *The Business Environment in Hong Kong*, 3rd edn., Hong Kong: Oxford University Press, 1995, pp. 162–89.

World Bank, *From Plan to Market: World Development Report 1996*, New York: Oxford University Press, 1996.

——, *The East Asian Miracle: Economic Growth and Public Policy*, New York: Oxford University Press, 1993.

Wu, Friedrich and Sin Yue Duk, '(Overseas) China, Inc.', *The International Economy* (January/February 1995): 33–5.

Yahuda, Michael, *Hong Kong: China's Challenge*, London: Routledge, 1996.

Yamaguchi, Masaaki, 'The Emerging Chinese Business Sphere', *Nomura Asian Perspectives*, 11, 2 (July 1993): 3–18.

Yeh, Anthony G. O., 'Planning and Management of Hong Kong's Border', in Joseph Y. S. Cheng and Sonny S. H. Lo (eds.), *From Colony to SAR: Hong Kong's Challenges Ahead*, Hong Kong: Chinese University Press, 1995, pp. 261–91.

——, 'Pudong: Remaking Shanghai as a World City', in Y. M. Yeung and Sung Yun-wing (eds.), *Shanghai: Transformation and Modernization under China's Open Policy*, Hong Kong: Chinese University Press, 1996, pp. 273–98.

Yeung, Henry Wai-chung, 'The Historical Geography of Hong Kong Investments in the Asean Region', *Singapore Journal of Tropical Geography*, 17, 1 (1996): 66–82.

Yeung, Y. M., 'Introduction', in Y. M. Yeung and Yun-wing Sung (eds.), *Shanghai: Transformation and Modernization under China's Open Policy*, Hong Kong: Chinese University Press, 1996, pp. 1–23.

Yeung, Y. M. and Sung, Yun-wing (eds.), *Shanghai: Transformation and Modernization under China's Open Policy*, Hong Kong: Chinese University Press, 1996.

Yu, Xiao, 'Public Puts Hope in Future', *South China Morning Post*, (5 October 1996): 10.

Zhan, James Xiaoning, 'Transnationalization and Outward Investment: The Case of Chinese Firms', *Transnational Corporations*, 4, 3 (5 December 1995): 71, Figure 1.

INDEX